Miracle-Gro® Complete Guide to Orchids

Meredith® Books
Des Moines, Iowa

Miracle-Gro Complete Guide to Orchids
Editor: Marilyn Rogers
Contributing Designer: Ernie Shelton
Contributing Technical Editor: Ned Nash
Contributing Writer: Name
Copy Chief: Terri Fredrickson
Copy Editor: Kevin Cox
Publishing Operations Manager: Karen Schirm
Senior Editor, Asset and Information Management: Phillip Morgan
Edit and Design Production Coordinator: Mary Lee Gavin
Art and Editorial Sourcing Coordinator: Jackie Swartz
Editorial Assistant/Photo Researcher: Susan Ferguson
Book Production Managers: Pam Kvitne,
   Marjorie J. Schenkelberg, Mark Weaver
Imaging Center Operator: Jill Reed

Contributing Copy Editors: Fern Marshall Bradley, Fran Gardner
Contributing Technical Proofreaders: Ron McHatton
Contributing Proofreaders: Stephanie E. Boeding, Barbara Rothfus
Contributing Photographer: Doug Hetherington
Contributing Map Illustrator: Jana Fothergill
Contributing Indexer: Kathleen Poole
Other Contributors: Janet Anderson, Debra Regennitter, Margaret Smith

Meredith® Books
Editor in Chief: Gregory H. Kayko
Executive Director, Design: Matt Strelecki
Managing Editor: Amy Tincher-Durik
Executive Editor: Benjamin W. Allen
Senior Associate Design Director: Tom Wegner
Marketing Product Manager: Brent Wiersma

Executive Director, Marketing and New Business: Kevin Kacere
Director, Marketing and Publicity: Amy Nichols
Executive Director, Sales: Ken Zagor
Director, Operations: George A. Susral
Director, Production: Douglas M. Johnston
Business Director: Janice Croat

Senior Vice President: Karla Jeffries
Vice President and General Manager: Douglas J. Guendel

Meredith Publishing Group
President: Jack Griffin
Executive Vice President: Doug Olson

Meredith Corporation
Chairman of the Board: William T. Kerr
President and Chief Executive Officer: Stephen M. Lacy

In Memoriam: E.T. Meredith III (1933–2003)

Photographers
Photographers credited may retain copyright © to the listed
photographs. L=Left, R=Right, C=Center, B=Bottom, T=Top

Cover Photographer: Bill Stites
Page 3- Doug Hetherington

William D. Adams: 212L; Adam Albright: 142L; Greg Allikas:
4TL, 4BR, 5BL, 5TR, 5BR, 8C, 10TL, 18, 19BC, 24, 27R, 29R,
32L, 33T, 34T, 34B, 41, 47, 49B, 52, 53TL, 55R, 56, 60B, 61TL,
61CL, 61BL, 61BR, 62TL, 62CL, 62BL, 62TC, 62TCT, 62BC, 62R,
67BL, 72L3DOWN, BL, 73C, 74TL, 76T, 77, 78, 79R, 80L, 80BR,
81TL, 81CL, 81BL, 81TR, 82TR, 82BT, 83TL, 83TLi, 83TR,
83BR, 84BR, 84CR, 85TL, 85CL, 85BL, 85R, 86L, 86TR, 86BR,
87TL, 87BL, 87TR, 87BR, 88L, 88TR, 89R, 92L, 92TR, 94R,
96BR, 99R, 100BL, 102L, 103BR, 104BL, 106BL, 106R, 107TL,
107R, 109TR, 110R, 111L, 112TL, 112BL, 113BL, 114L, 116BR,
118T, 119TL, 119BR, 120L, 120TR, 120BR, 121TL, 121BL, 121R,
123BR, 124L, 126R, 127R, 128TL, 128BL, 129TR, 130R, 133TR,
133BR, 134L, 135TL, 136L, 136TR, 136BR, 137L, 137R, 138R,
142TR, 142BR, 143R, 144L, 144R, 145TL, 145BL, 145TR,
145BR, 146L, 147TL, 147BR, 151L, 152TL, 152R, 153TR,
153BR, 156TR, 157R, 158TL, 159TL, 159TR, 162L, 162TR,
166BR, 167L, 168R, 169L, 169BR, 170TR, 170BR, 171L, 171R,
172R, 175L, 176TL, 177R, 178R, 179R, 180TL, 180R, 181L,
183BL, 183TR, 184BL, 184R, 185TL, 185BL, 185BL, 190TL,
190R, 191TL, 191CR, 192TR, 193TL, 193BL, 194L, 195TL,
195BL, 196TL, 196BL, 19LR, 19LBR, 197R, 198R, 199TR, 200L,
200R, 203L, 205TL, 205TR, 206TL, 207R, 209L, 210TR, 211TL,
212R; Liz Ball/Positive Images: 48BL; Allen Black: 74BL, 74C,
84TR, 146TL; blickwinkel/Alamy: 84TL; Bio-Photo Services/
Kerry Dressler: 57TL, 71BR, 83BL; Derek Fell: 32R, 35T, 96BL,
153BL; Michael & Patricia Fogden/Minden Pictures/Getty
Images: 8TL; Charles Marden Fitch: 11BL, 75TR, 75CR, 75BR,
93BR, 95TR, 96TR, 98TL, 98BR, 103TR, 104TL, 105TR, 108R,
109TL, 112TR, 113TL, 113R, 115TR, 117TL, 125L, 130L, 131TR,
139L, 139BR, 148R, 149TL, 150, 151R, 152BR, 153TL, 158BL,
159BL, 159BR, 160, 161R, 166R, 173R, 174R, 178TL, 194R,
195TR, 203BR, 203BR, 205BL, 209R, 210BR; Brett Francis
(Oort)/Wikipedia Commons Images: 165L; Steven A. Frowine:
88BR, 95BR, 98TR, 109BR, 117R, 125TR, 125BR, 131BR, 149BL,
157TL, 162BR, 163, 164, 172L, 176BL, 176BL, 182T, 184TL,
185R, 186TL, 186TR, 186BR, 190BL, 192TL, 192BL, 192BR,
193TR, 193BR, 199L; John Glover: 105TL, 116TL, 118B; John
Glover/Positive Images: 114TR, 128R, 170L; Jerry Harpur: 182B;
Raymond Hui: 198L; Eric Hunt: 105BL, 113R, 199BR; Bill
Johnson: 94TL, 97TR, 135BL, 206R, 213R; Donna Kirschan:
35B, 112BR, 123TR, 143L, 180BL; Arne Larsen: 101BR, 117BL;
Chuck Morin/Paramount Orchids: 98BL; Jerry Pavia: 94BL,
96TL, 104R, 129BR, 140R, 154R, 168L; Jay Pfahl/Graeme Teague
Photography: 99L, 179BL, 187R; Richard Shiell: 116TR, 175R;
Pam Spaulding/Positive Images: 119TR; Albert Squillace/
Positive Images: 19TR; Joseph G. Strauch, Jr.: 93TL, 95L, 100R,
201BR; Taylor Precision Products: 48R; judywhite/
GardenPhotos.com: 20, 80TR, 195BR.

All of us at Meredith® Books are dedicated to providing
you with the information and ideas you need to enhance your
home and garden. We welcome your comments and suggestions
about this book. Write to us at:
   Meredith Corporation
   Meredith Gardening Books
   1716 Locust St.
   Des Moines, IA 50309–3023

If you would like more information on other Scotts products,
call 800/225-2883 or visit us at: www.scotts.com

Contents

Understanding orchids

Plants of mystery with exotic color combinations and enticing fragrances from around the world, orchids have come to epitomize everything glamorous about flowers. Even more popular today than they were during the Victorian era, orchids continue to fascinate hobbyists and casual admirers with their varied and beautiful flowers. Their breathtaking floral displays make them highly desirable plants indoors and out, and there are thousands of species and cultivars from which to choose. Most orchids are reasonably priced and many are easy to grow.

Miracle-Gro's *Complete Guide to Orchids* is a starting point to build your orchid collection. The first chapter is an overview of the plants—how their names are created, the ways in which their anatomy is unique in the plant world, and the variety of growth and blooming habits among the different species. Chapters that follow will help you decide which orchids are best suited to your home and the way you garden indoors as well as show you how to grow healthy orchids and keep them in bloom.

The last portion of this *Complete Guide* is a comprehensive encyclopedia of hundreds of today's most popular orchids. Along with descriptions, it includes information on finding and growing each one. Colorful photos and at-a-glance cultural requirements will help you identify orchids that suit you best. In no time, you'll be right at home in the exotic world of orchids.

Breadth of the orchid family

What is it about these fascinating plants that draws some people to collect them to obsession? To begin with, the orchid family, or *Orchidaceae*, is one of the three largest families of flowering plants, comprising more than twenty-five thousand naturally occurring species. (The other two big families are *Poaceae,* the grass family, and *Asteraceae,* the sunflower family).

Orchids grow nearly everywhere in the world—from Tasmania near the Antarctic Circle to sites close to the Arctic Circle. They grow in the tropics in steamy climates at sea level and at cooler elevations of 12,000 feet and higher. Native orchids thrive in streambeds and in deserts; they flourish on tree limbs and on rocks and in soil.

Orchid plants range in size from minuscule to truly enormous. For example, some bulbophyllum (fleshy leaf) orchids are less than a fifth of an inch tall, while tropical vanilla vines may trail more than 400 feet in their native habitat. Canes of recently discovered New World sobralia orchids grow higher than 20 feet tall; and individual pseudobulbs of *Grammatophyllum speciosum* can reach 12 feet or taller and weigh more than a ton.

Similarly, flowers can be tiny or large, ranging from a fraction of an inch long to longer than 36 inches for some of the largest slipper orchids, including paphiopedilum and others with large flower pouches.

Flowers may last a few hours, several days, or weeks. Some—such as a few dendrobium types of orchids—bloom for nearly nine months.

Blooms in every color and every color combination appear throughout the year, with perfumes ranging from sweet to spicy to floral to unscented to the smell of rotten flesh. As you'll find in the pages of this book, orchids are unlike any others in the plant world.

▲ With just these four orchids, you have a glimpse of the diversity in the orchid family. They include purple paphiopedilum, white phalaenopsis, oncidium with its spray of yellow dancing ladies, and the tiny white blooms of ludisia.

A brief history

From the time Europeans began exploring Asia and the New World, plant-seekers looked for exotic varieties to take home. It wasn't easy for these early horticultural explorers to obtain or successfully grow orchids and other exotics.

Imagine, if you will, the journey that faced ocean travelers during the 19th century. Transoceanic transit was perilous. By sail or steam, passengers faced weeks or months of uncertainty. Arriving at their destination, explorers hired porters to guide them to unexplored regions to scout and gather specimens for their collections and to sell.

On the return trip, the arduous process was reversed. Perishable plants were packed in cramped crates, exposed to sweltering heat or punishing cold until arrival in port.

In the new location, the first point of plant distribution was generally an auction house where sales drew not only pioneering nurserymen but also representatives of the wealthy, whose passion for the unusual drove prices to astronomical levels. Large plants—massive orchids that could have dozens to hundreds of blooms—

▲ *Brassolaeliocattleya* Waianae Leopard 'Chung Hua' is a fine example of the degree to which orchid hybridizing has developed since the discoveries of the 1920s allowing large-scale production of orchids from seed.

▲ In the early 1800s, botanical drawings such as this were the closest most people would ever come to seeing an orchid. Now you can find them even at the hardware store.

and newly discovered species realized the highest prices, often reaching the equivalent of tens of thousands of today's dollars. Often even the wealthiest bidders were only able to own new species in illustrations or on pressed herbarium sheets.

Those fortunate enough to acquire plants believed that orchids and other tropical plants required steaming hot environments to match their supposed native habitats. Growing areas were kept hot, dark, oppressively damp, and unventilated. Many plants, already stressed from the long journey, quickly died.

Not until the mid-1800s did orchid fanciers begin to understand what these plants needed to survive: light breezes, moderate humidity, and dappled sunlight.

From habitat destruction to hybrid revolution

As orchid growers learned how to keep their orchids alive and blooming, demand for the plants increased. Because no one had yet discovered how to germinate orchid seeds in large numbers, the only way to acquire new plants was to collect them from the wild. And collectors continued to strip plants from their natural habitats.

Then in the 1920s, Lewis Knudson of New York's Cornell University unlocked the secret. His technique increased seed germination, so one seedpod could produce thousands of seedlings. Soon growers began hybridizing orchids and creating plants in myriad colors and forms. Knudson's work revolutionized the orchid industry, turning it into the global market it is today, with more than 110,000 registered hybrids.

From cramped cargo containers to auction houses decades ago to beautiful bloomers for sale nearly everywhere today, orchids are readily available to everyone. And despite their beautiful mystique, only a few are hard to grow.

How orchids grow

Many people who are new to growing orchids regard them as simply another potted plant and fail to recognize how they grow in nature. That way of thinking is reinforced by large nurseries that produce the most common orchids on the market, growing plants in all-purpose potting mixes similar to those used for other houseplants.

Under mass cultivation, ordinary potting mixes encourage rapid growth and hold down production costs so orchids can be sold for less. In home environments, mass production methods are less likely to be successful.

To be successful in growing orchids at home, it's crucial to understand where and how orchids grow naturally.

In the air

By far, the majority of orchids grow in nature as epiphytes, where their roots are exposed to the elements. Loosely translated, epiphyte means "upon a tree." Epiphytic orchids absorb moisture from the air and nutrients from decaying organic matter that collects around their roots. In their natural habitats, other common houseplants—bromeliads, begonias, African violets, ferns, philodendrons, and peperomias—also live as epiphytes, in growing conditions similar to orchids.

Native inhabitants of many parts of the tropical New World consider epiphytic orchids to be parasites because they grow on trees. They are not. Orchids derive no nutrients from host plants and are not harmful to their host unless they grow so large and heavy that the tree

branches, which may already be weakened, break under the weight.

When you understand growing conditions in tropical and subtropical forests, it is easy to see why epiphytic orchids and other plants adapt to growing on trees. The forest floor provides little in the way of light or nutrients. Typically, the forest canopy consists of several layers of increasingly shade-tolerant trees. At ground level, the light is too dim to support plant growth. (The only places that lush foliage grows from the top canopy to ground level are along rivers where light can penetrate equally.)

Even the forest floor is primarily free of plant litter because organic material that reaches the lowest levels is quickly digested by microorganisms, thus providing more nutrients for the growing trees. Plants that adapt to living on trees thrive because they are closer to sunlight and fresh air, while gathering the nutrients needed to survive from organic matter such as bird droppings and decaying leaves caught in the crooks of tree limbs.

To cope with the variations in light and moisture available in the forest canopy, epiphytic orchids have evolved several characteristic features. Many plants— especially those growing in the upper canopy—have thickened succulent leaves and stems, which are called *pseudobulbs,* to store moisture. And all epiphytic orchids have a well-developed layer, a corky material that's called *velamen,* on their thick exposed roots. Velamen readily absorbs moisture and protects the root center where the transfer of water

▲ *Masdevallia amabilis* **grows on a boulder in Peru.**

▶ **Epiphytic orchids such as this cattleya thrive outdoors on trees in warm winter regions of Florida. The large white roots (inset) work their way into crags or fissures within the bark and become attached to the tree.**

to the rest of the plant occurs, protects against excessive water loss, and helps the root adhere to the tree.

● **Lessons for home growing** Some orchids live high in tree canopies where light is strong and the air dry. Others grow lower in dappled light with plentiful humidity and moisture. Knowing the origins of your plant will improve your success with orchids. Plants that thrive in higher perches are tolerant of dry home-growing conditions but need bright light. Lower dwellers grow well in low light yet require high humidity and do not tolerate dry conditions.

Air is equally critical to epiphytic orchid roots as is moisture. Roots that are constantly wet do not receive necessary oxygen and eventually rot. Orchid potting mixes used for growing orchids in homes should be both moisture retentive and fast draining so roots have access to necessary moisture and air. Some orchids will thrive best when mounted on a slab of cork or tree fern to replicate their natural habitats.

On rocks

Yet another group of epiphytic orchids grows on rocks. These lithophytes—literally meaning "upon a rock"—exist in some of the harshest habitats, thriving on rock faces and fissures that have minimal organic matter. They also withstand searing tropical heat and sun as well as periods of extended dryness and minimal nutritional resources.

As with tropical-forest orchids, water-storing pseudobulbs and water-absorbing roots contribute to survival. Lithophytes also have hard waxy leaves and bulbs, which help them resist desiccation and intense solar radiation. In many cases, plant growth has been so restricted by extreme environments that plants evolve to dwarf varieties.

● **Lessons for home growing** Because these plants have adapted to harsh environments, you may be tempted to consider lithophytes as the ideal plant for beginning orchid growers. But they are generally difficult to grow: They do not do well under nursery culture so they're not readily available to the public, and only the most experienced orchid hobbyists have much success with them. Lithophytes require constant humidity, warm sunny weather, rocks to grow on, and a daily drenching for roots and rocks. They are even intolerant of being brought indoors for the briefest of times to escape cold winter weather.

Some lovely jewels exist in this group to tempt both beginners and experienced growers. But, for the most success if you're new to growing orchids, first work with epiphytes.

In or on soil

The third major orchid group is terrestrials, ones that grow in or on humus-rich soil. Terrestrial orchids fall into two general classes: those that grow with their roots *in* the soil (true terrestrials) and those that grow with their roots *on* the soil, reaching out into the rich leafy compost covering the soil (semiterrestrials).

True terrestrial orchids, such as the North American native lady's slipper

▲ The roots of epiphytic species are covered with a dense, white, waxy coating of velamen.

(*Cypripedium* spp.), generally occur in temperate climates, but some tropical and subtropical species exist. Although it would seem as though true terrestrials would be the easiest of all orchids to grow, they are actually the most difficult to keep alive. Most have developed a complex symbiotic relationship with the microorganisms in the native soil, without which the plants cannot survive.

Keeping them alive outside of their natural habitat is usually beyond the skill of all but the most experienced growers. They require an environment that closely mimics the one in which they naturally grow. You will have more success if you live near their native environment. Be aware that the Endangered Species Act protects the plants. Never dig them from the wild.

Semiterrestrials orchids are the ones that are most often available for home growing. This group includes cymbidium and phaius orchids as well as the jewel (macodes and ludisia) and tropical lady's slipper (paphiopedilum and phragmipedilum) orchids. Many have well-developed pseudobulbs to protect against seasonal dryness, and their roots are almost always thick and succulent to store water.

Some, such as jewel orchids and lady's slippers, do not have pseudobulbs, but their fleshy roots help them survive short dry periods. The natural habitat of these orchids is often shady; thus, many tolerate the low light levels typical in homes.

Others, such as cymbidiums and phaius, come from forest clearings and are better suited to patio culture where they can receive the abundant sun they require to prosper.

● **Lessons for home growing** Most semiterrestrial orchids are similar to their tree-dwelling relatives. The roots are thick and succulent to protect against seasonal dryness, like those of epiphytes, and many have pseudobulbs. They require good drainage and aeration around roots as well as sufficient humus to maintain a consistently and slightly moist environment.

Like epiphytes, they do not do well in ordinary potting soil; however, a soilless mix that contains peat moss along with large particle materials—perlite, charcoal, or bark chips—that provide drainage and aeration is suitable for semiterrestrials.

▲ This yellow lady's slipper is native to the forested northeast United States. Other native species can be found in the West, in mountainous areas, and in Canada.

▲ Sympodial orchids, such as *Oncidium* Twinkle, spread outward from the center of the plant. They have several growing points.

Growth habits

Something that a novice may first notice and comment on about an orchid is its distinctive growth habit. Orchid habits are unusual enough that, even coming across an unfamiliar plant, you're likely to know that it's an orchid—whether it's in bloom or not.

In the orchid family there are two basic growth habits: sympodial and monopodial. Because orchids are more often in leaf than in flower, recognizing these habits helps distinguish among different orchids, and understanding growth habits helps when potting the plants.

● **Sympodial** Orchids with a sympodial growth habit produce rhizomes— horizontal stems—that creep along the top of the growing media or immediately below its surface. In nature you can see the rhizomes spreading outward and upward on tree trunks or limbs. In containers rhizomes spread across the soil. When they run out of soil, they crawl over the rim and creep down the side of the pot.

Upright growths originate from buds on a rhizome— similar to the way that iris, bamboo, and grass plants grow. In orchids, these new plants are called growths.

Growths may be leafy, as with lady's slipper orchids (paphiopedilums and phragmipediums), or succulent. Leafy growths may be thin and seemingly fragile; succulent growths may be thick, and covered with a waxy coating that prevents the plant from losing excess water through its growths.

Sympodial means "many footed," indicating that the growths can originate from more than one place on a rhizome, not just one central point as with monopodial orchids. Each new growth develops its own roots and eventually sends out new rhizomes. After a while the rhizomes appear to simply connect the growths.

Succulent growths are pseudobulbs, which store moisture to sustain the plant through dry periods. Although the term is often shortened to bulb in conversation, pseudobulbs are not true bulbs, such as tulips or daffodils.

Pseudobulbs come in different shapes: Round, oval, egg shape, conical, oblong, and pencil shape are common. Long, thin pseudobulbs, such as those of several dendrobium species, are called canes. Pseudobulbs may be as small as a pea or several feet tall. Or they may be indistinguishable from the rest of the plant.

The newest pseudobulb on a stem is the one from which flowers arise, and it is the source of the next growth to develop. You'll see a new stem, called an active eye, coming off the base of the growth. All pseudobulbs have eyes, but only the youngest one is active. As the active eye begins developing and pulling away from the pseudobulb, new green-tipped roots form at its base.

Older, bloomed-out pseudobulbs are called back bulbs. These will not bloom again and may eventually lose their leaves. Because they have eyes, though, you may be able to use them to propagate a plant.

Most orchids need to develop three to five pseudobulbs before they can bloom. For sympodial orchids, the inflorescences (flower stems carrying one or more blooms) may emerge from leaf axils at the base of the leafy growth (as in oncidiums) or from nodes along the pseudobulb (as in dendrobiums); or they may emerge from the top of the pseudobulb (as in cattleyas) or directly from the rhizome (as in bulbophyllums).

With their water-storage capabilities, sympodial orchids are often better able to withstand low humidity and periods of dryness than monopodial orchids. They also have a much broader habitat range—from the hottest climates to the coldest. These traits mean that many sympodials are better suited to average home-growing conditions.

● **Monopodial** Monopodial orchids include vandas and phalaenopsis (one of the most popular orchids because it is ideally suited as a houseplant). The term monopodial means "one footed," indicating that the growth originates from a

▲ Phalaenopsis are monopodial orchids with single, short stems.

▲ Vandas are the ones most people recognize as monopodial orchids.

▲ Phalaenopsis have long arching flower stems that dance in a breeze like moths.

single point. All have one main upright stem with leaves along its length. Some monopodials, such as ascocentrums, branch along the stem and at the base to quickly form a floriferous clump. Both branching and nonbranching types will have one main stem that remains larger and stronger than the other stems.

With few exceptions, monopodial orchids tend to be native to tropical regions where temperatures are warm and humidity is high. Although some monopodials have fleshy, succulent leaves, they lack any well-defined water storage organ and so require extra attention when grown as houseplants.

Inflorescences of monopodial orchids arise from the axils of the leaves—the joint where leaves branch

▲ The flower stems of phaius stand erect and are 2 to 3 feet tall.

from the stem. The inflorescence may be branched or unbranched.

Other differences

Some orchid species are so tiny that they fit in a thimble, while others grow 5 feet or more tall and wide, needing the space of a greenhouse or an outdoor patio to accommodate the foliage mass and blooms.

Orchids that grow up to 18 inches tall are typically the favored size for indoor cultivation. Many hobbyists specialize in growing miniature and compact orchids, which take up less space on a windowsill or under lights. Miniatures also are easy to move around, finding the best spot with the right amount of light, air movement, warmth, and

▲ Flowers of *Sophrolaeliocattleya* Tangerine Imp (small) and *Cattleya* Hawaiian Wedding Song 'Virgin' demonstrate the difference in sizes.

humidity for the best growth. Many compact species occur among the ascocentrum, cattleya, dendrobium, masdevallia, paphiopedilum, phalaenopsis, pleurothallis, and restrepia orchid groups, as well as others.

● **Shapes** In most garden plants, growth habit refers to the plant's shape. The habit may change over the course of the year, as in the case of garden perennials that have a low mounded habit in leaf and an upright habit when they bloom.

With orchids, the terms for the shape of the plants are plant appearance and flower carriage, and these traits vary greatly among species.

The plant appearance of some orchids is distinctly upright, as with zygopetalums and cane dendrobiums. Others, such as renanthera, are vinelike while a few, such as vanilla, are true vines. Still others are bushy as a garden plant. Many simply look like an upright monopodial or a spreading sympodial orchid.

The floral carriage of some orchids may appear to cascade, as with *Oncidium*

▲ Some orchids such as spathoglottis have a habit much like a daylily.

Twinkle or *Dendrobium aggregatum;* be upright, as in paphiopedilum; or arch, like phalaenopsis. Plants may carry one flower per flower stem or hundreds.

The group called jewel orchids, which includes ludisia and macodes, are grown for their attractive foliage. Others, such as

▲ Although most orchid flowers are called spikes, few are true spikes, in which the flowers attach directly to the stem without a stalk.

cattleyas, are famous for their large ruffled flowers (cattleyas have long been favored for and are well-recognized in magnificent corsages).

Some orchids, such as masdevallias and restrepias, are grown for their unusual flower shapes, while orchids such as zygopetalum or rhyncholaelia are popular for their delightful fragrances.

Parts of an orchid plant

Orchids have such an astonishing array of plant sizes, forms, and aspects that conventional horticultural terms are often inadequate. Orchid hobbyists have many terms for their plants, and these terms may be unfamiliar to newcomers.

One commonly used term is growths. A growth is an individual component of a sympodial plant, usually consisting of the pseudobulb and its leaves.

Orchids without noticeable pseudobulbs are also said to have growths. On these plants a growth consists of the developing daughter plant, or the new leaves, on the rhizome.

Orchids, especially paphiopedilums, are often sold as divisions and priced by the growth. In the case of paphiopedilums, one growth is a mature fan of leaves, and a typical division consists of one or two flowered growths and one developing growth that has not yet bloomed. A flowering size cattleya division has three to five growths, two to three older bloomed-out growths and their leaves and two to three developing growths, from which the next flowers arise.

The "front" of the plant is the newest portion, which either has not yet flowered or has just finished flowering. The "back" of the plant encompasses the older growths, which have already flowered and may or may not retain leaves.

These terms are often used in cases such as a "front division," which would be a portion of the plant containing several young growths, plus an active eye or lead growth, the latest growth to develop from a rhizome. Or you might hear about "back bulbs" or a "back division," which would refer to older growths that have no actively growing lead. These generally take a year or more to produce flowers from a newly sprouted lead growth.

Back of the plant with bloomed-out pseudobulbs

Last growths to have flowered

One growth

Pseudobulbs

Front of the plant (the next growth to bloom)

Rhizome

▲ Sympodial orchids have a front (the newest growth) and a back (the oldest growth). They may have visible pseudobulbs joined by a rhizome, which creeps along the top or just beneath the soil.

PARTS OF AN ORCHID PLANT

Actively growing roots have green tips.

Oval or egg-shape pseudobulb

Oblong pseudobulb

New or lead growth starts out small and is called an active eye.

A rhizome is a long, creeping stem from which new pseudobulbs—called growths—sprout.

Pencil-shaped pseudobulbs called canes

Orchid flowers

Many features set orchids apart from familiar plants, and it might be easy to overlook discussing blooms. Unless, of course, the plant is in bloom. Then it's the center of attention, and the highly distinct nature of an orchid flower comes into its own. Blooms may be beautiful or bizarre, bright color or dull, elegant or exotic, sweetly perfumed or pungent, ephemeral or long-lasting, simple or intricate, minuscule or huge. They are never boring.

Flower anatomy

Orchids are monocots, and their flowers have the same botanical structure as those of grasses, irises, lilies, and other monocots, with all parts occurring in threes. They have three petals (the inner whorl) and three sepals (the outer whorl, which often look just like the petals). Sepals generally are arranged in a triangle behind the petals and may be the same shape and color as the petals or they may be different.

The three petals are in a triangle. Two of the flower petals have a familiar appearance; the third petal forms a labellum, or lip, which can be nearly any size, shape, or color.

In the center of the flower are the plant's reproductive organs, joined into one part called a column. The column size and shape varies depending on the orchid and can be an identifying feature among the different types.

Pollinators influence appearance

Most orchids are pollinated by insects; yet birds, and moths are also important pollinators. In high elevations, where cool temperatures deter many insects, birds perform much of the pollination.

Members of the Angraecoid group, many of

PARTS OF THE FLOWERS

Orchid flowers are different from those of any other blooming plant. They consist of three sepals that look like petals; three petals, one of which is modified into a lip or labellum; a column that contains the reproductive parts; and a pollinium, which holds the pollen. The lip attracts pollinating insects to the flower and directs them to the column. The shape and size of each part varies greatly among species; in some they may be hard to recognize. Fragrance is produced in the sepals, petals, or the labellum, depending on the species.

Sepals

Sepals are usually the least showy part of an orchid flower and in some, such as tolumnias, they are insignificant. Generally, sepals form an equilateral triangle framing the petals from below; this is considered the ideal form for orchids. In a few orchids, such as the slipper orchids, bulbophyllum, and pleurothallis, the two lower sepals are often fused into one.

Petals

The two upper petals may be significantly larger than or the same size as the sepals, while the bottom petal is modified into a lip, the labellum. On most orchids, upper petals are either held horizontally to form a triangle with the lip or held at a slight upward to 45-degree angle. Both arrangements are considered ideal forms for an orchid. In some species, petals droop or sweep forward, a less desirable trait.

Labellum

The labellum, or lip, is formed from the third and lowermost petal of the flower. It may be smaller and less noticeable than other flower parts or large and showy with frills and ruffles. The color may be the same as the flower (called concolor) or contrast highly. To guide pollinators, the lip often has bright spots, or "eyes," as well as lines of color, which may or may not be visible to the human eye.

In slipper orchids, the labellum is cupped. In paphiopedilum and phragmipedium species, the lip forms a pouch. Other orchids, such as dracula and some dendrobium species, also have lips in cuplike shapes. All such petal modifications guide insects to the pollen.

Hybridizers have worked for more than 150 years to develop lips far showier and more bizarre than natural species.

Column

The column contains the reproductive structures of the orchid flower and is the orchid's most anatomically distinct organ. Orchid pollen is clumped in waxy masses called pollinia, which is usually held at the front of the column on the anthers, or male flower parts (see page 75). The stigma (female part) that

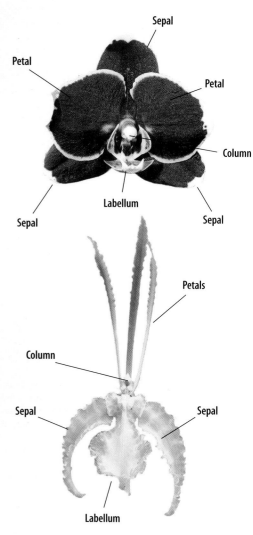

▲ Although orchid flower shapes vary greatly, as in phalaenopsis (top) and psychopsis (bottom), they all have the same flower parts.

receives the pollinium is often located behind the anther and close to the ovary. (The ovary is located in the stem at the base of the flower.)

This placement helps to avoid self-pollination, allowing the pollinator to enter the flower, leave the pollinium from another flower on the sticky surface of the stigma and pick up the pollinium from this flower on its way out.

A variety of other mechanisms within the flower also helps prevent self-pollination. In cattleyas, an insect (usually a bee) is lured beneath the column by fragrance and color. On the way out, the pollinia attach to the back of the bee. In catasetum, pollinia are spring-loaded. When a bee or fly bumps the flower, the pollinia eject from the column onto the insect's body, where they stick and are carried to the next flower on the bee's path.

which are native to subtropical Africa and include angraecum, aerangis, and jumellea orchids, are pollinated by night-flying moths. These orchids have large pale white or green blooms and haunting perfumes to lure pollinators where visibility is limited.

● **Strategies** Of course, pollinators do not visit flowers to pollinate them, but rather to seek nectar, a mate, food, or for numerous other reasons. Flowers must attract pollinators through a maze of competing stimuli. Orchids have unique ways to ensure pollination.

Some have evolved blooms that look like those of flowers that provide nectar. Blooms of others look like an insect, such as a bee, and mimic its action. Still others exude powerful pheromones to lure insects in search of a mate.

Some orchids have attractive fragrance. This strategy has the advantage of luring pollinators from farther away than visual cues. In the wild, fragrant orchids release their perfume to coincide with the time of day when their pollinators are most active. Notice that some orchids have fragrance early in the morning, others during the warmest part of the day, and still others in the evening after sunset.

Orchids have wide and varied scent palettes, with aromas ranging from sweet to musky to spicy to fetid

POLLINATORS AND FLOWERS

Pollinators and orchids have evolved cooperative arrangements. For example, fragrant *Angraecum sesquipedale* has one of the largest orchid flowers, sometimes reaching 8 inches across with an 18-inch-long nectar-bearing spur. Charles Darwin speculated that it must take a moth with a matching 18-inch-long proboscis to pollinate such a bloom. Decades passed before its discovery, but such a moth does exist, and it is the orchid's only pollinator.

and beyond. Fragrances may be delicate or overpowering; some are imperceptible to humans. Appealing scents include rose, jasmine, hyacinth, citrus, cinnamon, vanilla, coconut, and watermelon. Fetid aromas attract insects that feed on rotting matter, such as flies. Orchid flowers pollinated by moths have haunting perfumes and large white or green blooms to lure pollinators during darkness.

Flowers pollinated by birds have a much different appearance than those pollinated by insects. Typically bright red or orange, they have tubular blooms. In addition bird-pollinated blooms at high altitudes tend to be longer lasting than other orchid flowers; birds are less active pollinators than insects and longer bloom time ensures that the plants are pollinated.

● **Size** Orchid flowers can be tiny or huge. As with color and scent, flower size is influenced by an orchid's pollinators. It is easy to understand why large showy blooms attract pollinators, but, in actuality, orchids are more likely to have tiny drab blooms than huge colorful ones. Indeed, a visit to a tropical forest would reveal a wealth of small plants with equally small blooms and few large-flowered orchids. Anyone who has visited such a habitat will understand why: The clouds of tiny insects swarming through the forest are the primary pollinators in the forest.

Night-flying moths are the frequent pollinators of the largest orchid flowers, which stand out by their sheer size.

● **Flower shape** In orchids, the sepals and petals attract pollinators, while the lip directs the pollinator to the column. The lips of many orchids have become modified into wild and intricate shapes, functioning to attract and trap pollinators. For example, the bucket orchid, coryanthes, which is pollinated by bees, has a sweet liquid-filled pouch-shape lip and a hypnotic perfume. Bees are

first attracted to the scent, which seems to drug them. In the weakened state, they fall into the pouch, which has downward-facing hairs that prevent escape except by the one route that ensures pollination of the bloom.

● **Inflorescence type** Botanically, inflorescence refers to the entire group of flowers on a stem and the arrangement within the group. A flower stem may be topped with one flower— a single inflorescence— or dozens of flowers. Many terms apply to the arrangement when the inflorescence consists of more than one bloom. Orchid growers, however, forgo those terms, using inflorescence to refer to the entire flower stalk, no matter its shape or arrangement.

The number of blossoms in an inflorescence has evolved to ensure efficient pollination. Large single orchid inflorescences develop in areas where it is easy to find a pollinator, almost guaranteeing pollination. In general, the larger the flower in proportion to plant size, the more energy it demands and the fewer flowers will be produced. Such pollination strategy works only in areas where timing of blooms and pollinator presence coincide and pollinator population is large enough to find and pollinate every flower in the orchid population. A shotgun approach, with numerous small flowers in a large inflorescence, is often a better way to ensure reproduction.

Orchid inflorescences may be upright and branched, upright and unbranched, or branched and arching from the weight of the blooms. Individual blossoms may open sequentially over time or all at once. Flowers that open all at once are a larger target for pollinators, while flowers that open sequentially offer a smaller target but longer time.

Bloom times

Most orchids have a flowering season, and each species blooms at about the

same time every year. A few orchids will bloom multiple times a year if they are grown under ideal circumstances. Flowers develop in response to day length or to temperature changes, ensuring a peak blooming time that coincides with the presence of pollinators.

When you purchase a plant that is in bloom, chances are it will bloom for you again the following year at roughly the same time. Depending on your growing conditions, the exact timing may vary by as much as four weeks.

Flowering depends on plant size as well as its natural bloom season. If a plant is not in bloom when you buy it, ask the seller whether it is of flowering size. Look for signs that the plant has bloomed in the past, such as spent flower stems.

A plant that has previously bloomed will bloom again during its normal flowering season. When considering small or young orchids, ask the grower how long you should expect to wait before it flowers. Some slipper orchids and bulbophyllums take several years to produce their first flowering-size growths (once started, plants bloom regularly each year).

For phalaenopsis, these bloom season guidelines don't apply to new plants. Because phalaenopsis are the most popular orchids and among the best for home growing, blooming plants are sold year round. Commercial growers manipulate the plants so they will be in bloom when available for sale. The natural flowering season for phalaenopsis is late winter to spring for pink and white flowering plants; yellow and novelty phalaenopsis also bloom in summer. In home settings, plants will revert to their regular bloom time.

Life span of flowers

It's impossible to generalize how long orchid flowers will last. Some are open only a few hours, other blooms last for months. Flowers remain open depending on the length of time needed to attract their pollinator, and are balanced by the amount of energy that each plant uses to keep its flowers open.

Some orchids, such as coryanthes and stanhopea, have large, complex, strongly fragrant blooms that consume lots of energy. The size and pungent perfume effectively attract pollinators within a day or two, so flowers quickly fade.

Others, such as *Dendrobium crumenatum,* bloom in response to a temperature drop brought about by rain storms. During storms, which last a few hours at most, their pollinators are active with enough flowers to ensure reproduction. These flowers fade quickly as well.

Orchids at higher, cooler elevations have fewer potential pollinators in the harsh environment. There, flowers last a long time, allowing bird pollinators enough time to find and pollinate blooms. For example, the small bright-color blooms of *Dendrobium cuthbertsonii* may be open as long as nine months.

Because most orchids on the market are hybrids, breeders might be expected to aim for increased bloom periods for their plants. Doing so has not proven an easy task, and traits such as fast growth, ease of flowering, and bright bloom color have become more attainable goals.

Under home conditions, most orchid flowers last from two weeks to two months. Orchid flowers last best when plants are well watered, receive the right amount of light and fertilizer, and are grown in the right temperature, away from forced-air heat and air-conditioning.

▲ *Dendrobium* Golden Aya flower stems emerge from leaf nodes on the stem.

▲ *Dendrobium aggregatum* flower stems emerge from the pseudobulb.

▲ Flowers of phalaenopsis and similar orchids, such as this *Doritaenopsis* Shawangunk Sunset, can last for months.

In splash-petal orchids such as *Brassolaeliocattleya* Momilani Rainbow, all petals resemble the lip.

▲ Flowers of *Laeliocattleya* Secret Love Hysing emerge from the pseudobulb.

PELORIC ORCHID FLOWERS

In some orchids all three petals are modified to look like a lip. The technical term for this trait is *pelorism,* and flowers demonstrating the feature are called *peloric.* A few peloric orchids have what is called splash petals. These flowers are often more symmetrical and usually less orchidlike.

Splash-petal cattleyas are bred from a *C. intermedia aquinii* with the mutation that was found in nature. Seedlings from this plant have been crossed with cattleyas that have darker petal flaring. Resulting hybrids are among the showiest of all orchids, with elaborate petal markings, sometimes in three or more colors.

Spontaneous mutations, often during tissue culture, have resulted in peloric phalaenopsis orchids that have liplike petals with a fleur-de-lis appearance. These orchids rarely breed true in subsequent generations and may not even be faithfully reproduced by cloning. *Phal. equestris* and its hybrids seem to be prone to peloric flowers.

Some growers find splash-petal flowers pleasing; others consider them freaks. Savvy growers purchase only blooming plants to be sure the desired characteristics are displayed.

Naming orchids

Orchid names are often confusing and they sometimes are contradictory. With the huge number of species and hybrids in the family, understanding and using orchid names can be quite complex, even though their botanical naming conventions follow the same taxonomic rules that govern the naming of all plants.

Orchids were first known by descriptive names that were anything but precise. For example, the family name Orchidaceae is derived from the early Greek word *orchis*. Orchis means "testicles" and refers to the shape of the tubers of a group of terrestrial orchids.

Confucius coined the name *lan*, meaning "king of fragrance," about 2,500 years ago. The name referred to the sweet scent of a native Chinese orchid, although no one knows exactly which one. There are a number of Chinese cymbidiums to which the name could apply; and lan eventually became the Chinese name for orchids in general.

Because popular names can be inaccurate, scientists have developed a universal system for naming plants and animals.

The binomial system

Modern taxonomy, the precise descriptive naming of organisms, began in the 18th century with Carl von Linné (also called Linnaeus). He founded the binomial system, in which genus and species designations are used to denote plants and animals by Latinized names.

Since the time of Linnaeus, botanists and zoologists have worked to identify and describe all plants and animals, each one with a unique name used to identify the particular organism.

Although botanists may sometimes disagree on the classification of a plant, the binomial system is an accepted way to provide a commonly understood framework for discussing any plant. For example, if you were to chat with any orchid grower in the world about *Brassavola nodosa,* no matter what language you speak, you'll know that you would be discussing the same plant.

Knowing the correct botanical name of an orchid may also give you a clue about its cultural requirements, which may help you make successful orchid choices to acquire exactly the plants you want.

What's in a name?

Binomial or botanical names are composed of two parts: the genus and the specific epithet. Together they make the species name. If the plant is a cultivar, variety, or hybrid, that name is tacked onto the species name.

● **Genus name** Genus (plural: genera) refers to a group of plants or animals that are so similar they are hard to distinguish from one another. For plants, the

The name of an orchid tells you a lot of about the plant, although you often need a lot of background to figure it out as with this *Recchara* Frances Fox 'Sun Spots'. Recchara is the result of crossing *Brassavola, Cattleya, Laelia,* and *Schomburgkia* orchids and is named for the breeder name with -ara added to it. A further cross between *Brassolaeliacattleya* Polka Dot and *Schomburgkia tibicinis* created the hybrid Frances Fox.

▲ Because orchids have the almost unique ability to produce intergeneric hybrids—hybrids containing two or more genera—and orchid growers love to create new hybrids, it is important for beginning growers to learn how orchid names are formulated.

from others in the species, but not different enough to justify a new species name. If such a group is found in nature, it is called a variety. If created by humans—such as through hybridizing or propagating a mutation—it is called a cultivar, which is short for cultivated variety.

● **Hybrid name** A hybrid is the result of a cross between two species or hybrids, which may be in the same or a different genera.

A species or hybrid crossed with a species or hybrid in the same genus result in an interspecific hybrid, also called an interspecific grex. Related orchid species will interbreed in nature and in cultivation. Although interspecific hybrids are less common in the wild, they may form the basis for new varieties, if not new species, when populations become stable and self-replicating.

Crossing a hybrid with a species or another hybrid results in a complex hybrid.

A hybrid resulting from a cross between two species in different genera is called an intergeneric hybrid or intergeneric grex.

Hybrids complicate naming

The naming of orchids is more complicated than for other plants because of the huge number of hybrids in the family. The naming of hybrids is an art in itself and includes descriptive monikers as well as memorial titles, such as *Cattleya* Dear Old Mom. According to the rules, however, when any two species in the same genus are bred together, all resulting progeny will always have the same hybrid name.

For example, the hybrid that results when *Cattleya mossiae* is crossed with *Cattleya warscewiczii* is always *Cattleya* Enid, one form of which is white with a purple lip and another which is all lavender with a darker lip.

Even when cultivars of one or both parents are used to

classifications are usually based on similarities in the anatomy of the flowers. However, some groups are alike in their growth habits as well. Examples of well-known orchid genera include *Cattleya, Oncidium,* and *Phalaenopsis.*

● **Specific epithet** Species are the individual members of a genus. (Species is the same whether singular or plural.) These are denoted by the second part of a botanical name, the specific epithet.

Plants form species when a population is isolated from the other members of the group and begins to diverge into a distinct population that breeds true to itself. (In other words, when Species A is pollinated by another Species A, the offspring are always Species A.)

Populations can be isolated by one or more factors: geography (the plants live in different places), season (they flower at different times), pollination (they attract

different pollinators), mechanics (they have anatomical differences), or physiology (the plants are not genetically compatible).

● **Variety or cultivar name** The orchids in a species are all similar. But because they can cross-pollinate in nature, they may vary in flower size, shape, and color as well as in shape, size, or color of leaves, stems, and pseudobulbs. Sometimes certain plants in a species share a characteristic that makes them different

Sander's list

The Royal Horticultural Society (RHS) is the official keeper of orchid taxonomy and hybrid names. To be officially recognized, orchid hybrids must be registered with the RHS, which publishes the names of all registered hybrids in *Sander's List of Orchid Hybrids*. This reference is published every five years with monthly updates in the *Orchid Review*, the official publication of the RHS. Today, find updates at www.rhs.org.uk/plants/registration_orchids.asp

make the cross, the name of the resulting hybrid is still *Cattleya* Enid. The hybrids may look quite different from the typical *Cattleya* Enid. For example, *Cattleya* Enid bred from cultivars may have lavender flowers with a purple lip or rose-and-coral

blooms with a darker rose lip. These variations are distinct cultivars of the original hybrid and are given cultivar names, such as *Cattleya* Enid 'Fairy Queen' or *Cattleya* Enid 'United Nations'.

Intergeneric and complex mixes

Intergeneric hybrids are even more complicated when it comes to naming. These hybrids—always created by crossing two or more genera—can occur between species, between hybrids, or between hybrids and species.

The genus name of the resulting progeny is itself a hybrid between the names of the two parents. For example, a cross between laelia and cattleya orchids is given the genus name of *Laeliocattleya* (*Laelia × Cattleya*). A cross between odontoglossum and oncidium is called *Odontocidium*.

AN ORCHID FAMILY TREE

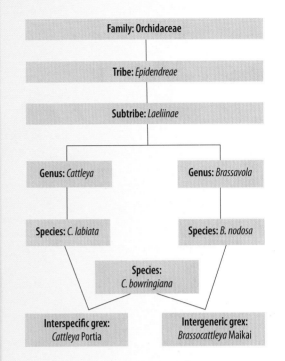

Family: Orchidaceae

Tribe: *Epidendreae*

Subtribe: *Laeliinae*

Genus: *Cattleya* — Genus: *Brassavola*

Species: C. labiata — Species: B. nodosa

Species: C. bowringiana

Interspecific grex: Cattleya Portia — Intergeneric grex: Brassocattleya Maikai

---

DEMONSTRATING HYBRIDIZATIONS AND NAME CHANGES

Cattleya skinneri (left) and *Cattleya aurantica* (right) are different species in the same genus.

Laelia purpurata is also a species orchid, unrelated to the cattleyas.

A cross between *C. skinneri* and *C. aurantica* results in a hybrid with a new hybrid name: *Cattleya* Guatemalensis.

Crossing *L. purpurata* with *C. aurantica* results in the intergeneric hybrid *Laeliocattleya* Canhamiana.

Crossing *L. purpurata* with a third hybrid species, *Brassolaelia* Morning Glory results in a new as yet unnamed complex hybrid. You can see how each species brings new shapes and colors to the crosses.

▲ Miltonia, odontoglossum, and odontocidium are all members of the odontoglossum alliance.

Hybrid names are neither italicized nor enclosed in single quotes. They are merely capitalized, as in the name *Brassolaeliocattleya* Bryce Canyon.

Cultivar names are not italicized; they are capitalized and enclosed in single quotes, as in *Brassolaeliocattleya* Pamela Hetherington 'Coronation'.

In orchids—and in other plants—the genus name is sometimes used informally as the plant's common name. In that case, the name is written lowercase without italics.

As a beginner, you may feel the names are too much of a mouthful. As you become more familiar with orchids, though, their names will soon roll off your tongue.

ORCHID ALLIANCES

Among orchid hobbyists, species and hybrids are often grouped into alliances, for example the cattleya alliance, as a shorthand way to refer to similar plants. An alliance is a group of closely related genera, often the ones that can be bred with one another. (Not all genera will cross with other genera.)

COMMON ALLIANCES

Beginning orchidists will want to know about several important alliances that are used often as generic names for certain types of orchid plants.

The cattleya alliance (most commonly referred to as cattleyas, or "catts") consists of the *Laelinae,* a subtribe within the orchid family. There are dozens of members to this alliance. The major ones commonly used to create complex hybrids are:

Brassavola	Rhyncholaelia
Cattleya	Sophronitis
Laelia	

Minor members include:

Barkeria	Encyclia
Broughtonia	Epidendrum
Diacrium	Laeliopsis
(now known as	Tetramicra
Caularthron)	

The odontoglossum alliance, or "odonts," consists of members of the subtribe *Oncidinae.* This group is also called the oncidium alliance.

Ada	Comparettia	Odontoglossum
Aspasia	Miltoniopsis	Rodriguezia
Brassia	Miltonia	Tolumnia
Cochlioda	Oncidium	

The vanda alliance, sometimes called vandaceous orchids, includes:

Aerides	Doritis	Renanthera
Arachnis	Neofinetia	Rhynchostylis
Ascocentrum	Phalaenopsis	Vanda

The pleurothallid alliance, or pleurothallids, includes:

Dracula	Masdevallia	Porroglossum
Lepanthes	Pleurothallis	Restrepia

These are the major alliances, and other important alliances exist within the orchid family, including the zygopetalum alliance, or the "soft leaf" group; the maxillaria alliance, which includes *Lycaste, Anguloa,* and *Maxillaria;* the cycnoches alliance; and the stanhopea alliance. Because these are colloquialisms, there are no technical rules for use or inclusion of species and hybrids; rather, they are popularly coined and used.

When three genera are involved, the resulting hybrid genus can be a combination of the three names, as in *Brassolaeliocattleya (Brassavola × Laelia × Cattleya).* Or it may be given the last name of someone the breeder wants to honor, latinized and ended with –ara, as in *Potinara* *(Brassavola × Laelia × Cattleya × Sophronitis)* or *Lowara (Brassavola × Laelia × Sophronitis).*

Orchid breeders enjoy experimenting and often stretch the boundaries of hybridizing with crosses that might seem impossible. Today there are complex hybrids made from nine different genera. Even orchid enthusiasts can find it challenging to keep the names straight.

Writing orchid botanical names

Botanical names are always written with genus name first and specific epithet second, such as *Cymbidium ensifolium.* The name is italicized; the first letter of the genus name is capitalized, and the specific epithet is lowercase.

Variety names are written alongside the specific epithet in lowercase and italicized, as in *Cattleya intermedia aquinii.*

HERE'S A TIP...

New names
Historically, plants have been organized into genera according to arrangement of flowers. However, since scientists have developed the ability to read the genetics of organisms, they've discovered relationships noticeable only at the genetic level. Taxonomists have begun renaming plants according to these discoveries. Whether these relationships are eventually validated remains to be seen; traditional naming conventions may break down over time.

ORCHID NAME ABBREVIATIONS

In a group as large and diverse as the orchid family, abbreviations are a necessity. Imagine having to write brassolaeliocattleya every time you refer to the genus. Because orchids go by botanical names rather than common names, it's especially important to differentiate among the plants. (Other botanical plant names are abbreviated as well; however, the convention is to use only the first letter of the genus name. This would not work for orchids.)

Naturally occurring genera have simple abbreviations that are easy to recognize, such as *C.* for *Cattleya*, *L.* for *Laelia*, *Onc.* for *Oncidium*, and *Den.* for *Dendrobium*. Abbreviations for hybrid genera reflect their complex makeup, such as *Blc.* for *Brassolaeliocattleya* and *Pot.* for *Potinara*. A few genus names are used in their entirety, such as *Disa* and *Phaius*.

The following are abbreviations for orchids listed in this book:

Abbreviation	Genus name
Aergs.	*Aerangis*
Angcm.	*Angraecum*
Angth.	*Angranthes*
Ang.	*Anguloa*
Anct.	*Anoectochilus*
Aslla.	*Ansellia*
Ascda.	*Ascocenda*
Asctm.	*Ascocentrum*
Ascps.	*Asconopsis*
Bark.	*Barkeria*
Bllra.	*Beallara*
Bif.	*Bifrenaria*
Ble.	*Bletilla*
B.	*Brassavola*
Brs.	*Brassia*
Brsdm.	*Brassidium*
Bc.	*Brassocattleya*
Bl.	*Brassolaelia*
Blc.	*Brassolaeliocattleya*
Bro.	*Broughtonia*
Bulb.	*Bulbophyllum*
Burr.	*Burrageara*
none	*Cadetia*
Cal.	*Calanthe*
Ctsm.	*Catasetum*
C.	*Cattleya*
Ctna.	*Cattleytonia*
Chdrh.	*Chondrorhyncha*
Cnths.	*Cochleanthes*
Cda	*Cochlioda*
Coel.	*Coelogyne*
Colm.	*Colmanara*
Cyc.	*Cycnoches*
Cym.	*Cymbidium*
Cyrt.	*Cyrtopodium*
Dar.	*Darwinara*
Dgmra.	*Degarmoara*

Abbreviation	Genus name
Den.	*Dendrobium*
Ddc.	*Dendrochilum*
Diacm.	*Diacrium*
Dial.	*Dialaelia*
none	*Disa*
Dtps.	*Doritaenopsis*
Dor.	*Doritis*
Drac.	*Dracula*
none	*Dyakia*
E.	*Encyclia*
Epc.	*Epicattleya*
Epi.	*Epidendrum*
Gga.	*Gongora*
Gram.	*Grammatophyllum*
Hknsa.	*Hawkinsara*
Hwra.	*Howeara*
Hya.	*Huntleya*
Jum.	*Jumellea*
L.	*Laelia*
Lc.	*Laeliocattleya*
Lpt.	*Leptotes*
Lus.	*Ludisia*
Lyc.	*Lycaste*
Mclna.	*Maclellanara*
Mac.	*Macodes*
Masd.	*Masdevallia*
Max.	*Maxillaria*
Mxc.	*Mexicoa*
Mtssa.	*Miltassia*
Milt.	*Miltonia*
Mtdm.	*Miltonidium*
Mltnps.	*Miltoniopsis*
Neof.	*Neofinetia*
Neost.	*Neostylis*
Oda.	*Odontioda*
Odbrs.	*Odontobrassia*
Odcdm.	*Odontocidium*

Abbreviation	Genus name
Odm.	*Odontoglossum*
Odtna.	*Odontonia*
Onc.	*Oncidium*
Paph.	*Paphiopedilum*
Pes.	*Pescatorea*
none	*Phaius*
Phal.	*Phalaenopsis*
Phrag.	*Phragmipedium*
Pln.	*Pleione*
Pths.	*Pleurothallis*
Pot.	*Potinara*
Prom.	*Promenaea*
Pyp.	*Psychopsis*
Psgmrc.	*Psygmorchis*
Ren.	*Renanthera*
Rstp.	*Restrepia*
Rhynch.	*Rhyncholaelia*
Rhy.	*Rhynchostylis*
Rdza.	*Rodriguezia*
Sarco.	*Sarcochilus*
Schom.	*Schomburgkia*
Sdr.	*Sedirea*
Sob.	*Sobralia*
Sl.	*Sophrolaelia*
Slc.	*Sophrolaeliocattleya*
Soph.	*Sophronitis*
Spa.	*Spathoglottis*
Stan.	*Stanhopea*
Tolu.	*Tolumnia*
Trctm.	*Trichocentrum*
Trgl.	*Trichoglottis*
Trpla.	*Trichopilia*
V.	*Vanda*
Vl.	*Vanilla*
Vasco.	*Vascostylis*
Wils.	*Wilsonara*
Z.	*Zygopetalum*

Selecting orchids

When confronted with the dazzling array of beautiful orchids at your local garden center, orchid show, or nursery, how do you select just the *right* one? There are two parts to the answer: First, find a species that will survive the growing conditions you have to offer. Otherwise, you might spend a lot of time inspecting plants that you really shouldn't buy, even if healthy. Second, take care to ensure the plant is healthy before buying it.

● **Health** Even when you buy an orchid as a floral arrangement or centerpiece, the health of the plant matters. Buying a healthy plant ensures that you get the best value for your money. An advantage of using orchids as decoration is the long-lasting nature of the flowers. For the price of a bouquet that may last a few days, you can have a lovely plant with flowers that last weeks or months. If you purchase an unhealthy or damaged specimen, the flowers will not have a chance to live up to their potential.

Often, beginning growers are distracted by the blooms, paying little attention to the condition of the plant, which is what experienced buyers look at first.

To determine a plant's health, first check the leaves, which should be firm and unbroken (a little damage is OK). Also look for signs of insect activity and disease, such as leaf spots, sunken lesions, spots on the flowers, or mushy tissues.

Next check the roots. Notice whether the orchid is firm in its pot, meaning it has been in its pot long enough to develop a good root system that holds the plant securely. Inspect any visible roots; they should be succulent, white with greenish tips. Avoid orchids with shriveled or brown, unhealthy-looking roots. Peek in the drainage holes in the bottom of the pot to check whether the potting medium has decomposed. You should be able to make out individual pieces of bark or other media. Roots that have grown out of the drainage hole may be dark, but they should not be slimy or rotten.

For plants in bloom, check whether the inflorescence is fading—few buds with the oldest flowers browning or wilting—or has many buds yet to open. Ideally, only a few at the base of the flower stem will have started blooming. Avoid touching the flowers; oils on skin may cause flower edges to turn brown.

● **Will it live?** Many orchids are picky about their growing conditions. Buying one that won't grow in the only spot you have available is a sure path to failure.

Before choosing an orchid, talk with a vendor who can help you assess your needs and conditions. For example, do you want to grow orchids in an outdoor garden area? Or are you contemplating building a greenhouse or sunroom? Do you want to grow orchids in a sunny window where flowering plants already thrive? Or do you intend to set up a small indoor light garden where you can grow a variety of

▲ When buying orchids at a show, chat with the grower to get advice on caring for the plants as well as for help in selecting the best type of orchid for your situation. Avoid letting the overwhelming beauty of the flowers be the sole guide to your purchase.

▲ When shopping look for a healthy plant with unspotted leaves, firm pseudobulbs, white roots, and if in bloom, buds remaining to open.

Buying orchids

Good-quality orchids, large flowering plants as well as small young ones, are available in a broader range of venues than ever before. Florists and supermarkets typically stock a few orchids as gift plants for holidays such as Mother's Day and Easter. In addition, plants and orchid-growing supplies can be found as close as your local home improvement center, while many communities are home to dedicated orchid nurseries.

With so many options, how do you know which is best? Each venue has its pros and cons.

Nontraditional stores

The primary increase in availability of orchid plants over the past decade has occurred in nontraditional venues, such as home improvement centers and supermarkets, places that were once unfamiliar places to find flowering orchids. In most cases, nurseries supplying the mass market began as growers of exotic houseplants, such as bromeliads. As consumer demand for colorful potted plants grew, growers took the opportunity to shift to new plants, such as orchids.

Widespread availability of orchids has its drawbacks. People who never before considered buying an orchid are doing so. However, retail staff are seldom trained in orchid growing and the supplier may know more about producing orchids as crops than growing them in typical home conditions. Neither can advise you on keeping the plants alive. Anyone new to orchids, then, is likely to be frustrated with the plants.

The pros of nontraditional orchid sources are that most offer common, easy-to-grow species at fairly low prices. These orchids easily adapt to home culture if given a bright east, west, or south (but not north) window and regular watering and feeding.

Exercise caution, however, with selections because few stores employ orchid experts who know how to handle the plants. Examine the offerings thoroughly before buying and select only those that are perfectly healthy.

Ask staff about arrival schedules for their orchid shipments. Buying plants soon after the shipment arrives ensures the orchids will not be stressed from neglect at the store.

Nurseries

Dedicated orchid nurseries are the first choice of many hobbyists who are looking for specific plants. And even if you're not on a quest for a particular orchid, it's thrilling to visit a large nursery where orchids are the primary crop.

Two types of nurseries grow orchids: traditional orchid nurseries where orchids are the primary or only crop, and general landscape nurseries that offer selections of popular flowering orchids along with many other plants. Both have their advantages.

Traditional orchid nurseries usually have the best selection and provide an opportunity to chat with people who know the plants best. Unfortunately, with the proliferation of mass-market orchids, the number of traditional orchid nurseries has declined. Visiting the remaining ones is a privilege—and a must for anyone seriously interested in orchids. Check the phone book and search online to find one in your area.

General nurseries often carry blooming orchid plants,

houseplants under artificial light? Each circumstance calls for a different type of orchid.

An experienced professional can help you determine which orchids are best for your conditions. A grower can tell you whether the plant is a periodic bloomer or one that performs only with special treatment and whether the flowers last in the home or only in greenhouse conditions.

When you can't easily find a professional for orchid advice, carry this book with you to the store and use the encyclopedia section as your guide. Each entry outlines required growing conditions and identifies whether plants are easy or difficult to grow.

At the store, check plant labels, which often provide growing information. Look for a description of the plant's mature size and whether it is compact. Then consider the size of your growing area. Not all orchids offered for sale are good candidates for growing in a home. Some are too large to be managed indoors. Large

▲ Check roots before buying and avoid plants that have desiccated or rotted roots like these.

size is more than just an inconvenience. Supplying adequate light to a large plant can be difficult.

Consider how you will provide light to the orchid. Some require more light than provided on a windowsill, others thrive in dim light, some grow only outdoors.

Finally, once determining the plant's health, you can consider its blooms. In addition to their color and form, check the number of new growths and the number of eyes on each one. The more growths and eyes, the more likely the plant will be free-flowering.

Buying orchids *(continued)*

especially if one of the owners or growers has an interest in orchids. In this environment you can at least be assured that folks who care about plants have cared for the orchids. Because nursery staff deal with the public daily, their advice is likely to be offered in terms that are familiar to beginners. And because their experience is based on growing orchids in a general gardening environment, they may be able to provide the confidence you need to successfully grow the plants.

As you begin your search for orchids, visit nurseries regularly to get to know the staff and see different plants as they come into bloom. Some nurseries offer classes, advice, and informational websites.

Many specialty growers are located in areas where plants are raised outdoors year-round or where the climate is mild enough that greenhouse cultivation is affordable. If a nursery is not close by, visit botanical gardens and orchid shows, or shop by mail order via print or online catalogs.

Mail order and online sources

Hundreds of mail order and online sources exist, ranging from large corporate specialty orchid growers to mom-and-pop operations to hobbyists who are trying to support their orchid-buying habits.

Big nurseries publish glossy color catalogs; small firms may send out photocopied pages listing only the orchids' names and prices. The size of the business does not necessarily have any relationship to the

AVAILABILITY

The ease with which you can find the orchids in the encyclopedia is identified as:
Common Readily available; sold at garden centers and home improvement stores.
Specialty growers Less easy to find; sold by specialty nurseries, which may be local or on the Internet.
Rare Hard to find; may be available from a few specialty growers. Use orchid society connections to find these.

▲ Commercial suppliers grow hundreds, even thousands of orchid plants at a time in a greenhouse.

quality of the product.

Until you become an expert, use photos and descriptions to help you make decisions about which orchids to buy. As a beginner, you may want to buy blooming-size plants, which are larger and perhaps easier to keep alive.

● **Catalogs** The best catalogs spell out the information needed—the plant's entire name, parentage if it's a hybrid, cultural requirements, stage of growth, size, pot size, and price.

Catalog writers use several methods to describe plant size; most list pot size. Additional information will help you sort out exactly what is offered. For example, "blooming size" means that with proper care the orchid should bloom within a year of purchase.

The number of pseudobulbs is often listed for sympodial orchids such as cattleyas. This is helpful because many species begin blooming when they have developed a certain number of pseudobulbs.

Monopodial orchids are often sold by the inch. For example, phalaenopsis orchids are measured from the tip of one leaf to the tip of the opposite leaf. A leaf span of 8 to 12 inches is generally considered blooming size for phalaenopsis.

● **Online** Many online sites are connected to the same companies that publish catalogs. Online catalogs are regularly updated to reflect plant availability, making it convenient for hobbyists to locate specific plants, share information with growers, and comparison shop. Online sales are also held.

Reputable orchid nurseries provide healthy plants that are as represented in the description. Still, as with any resource, be alert to possible discrepancies. For example, the quality of photos and descriptive information is not always a reliable indicator of plant health.

Make sure you know your source. Anyone can set up a website or offer plants at online auctions, and it can be difficult to find out who is running a site. Be wary of extremely inexpensive plants, which may be damaged or illegally harvested. If a price seems too good to be true, it probably is. Similarly, a much higher price does not guarantee a better orchid. Most U.S.-grown orchids are priced the same no matter the seller because producing orchids generally costs about the same throughout the country. Buying bare-root plants is often a gamble. If you buy from an unknown grower, assume that the plants may be different from what you expect them to be.

The best advice is to buy only from vendors with which you or a trusted associate has had first-hand experience. Ask hobbyists in your area whether they have purchased plants or supplies from specific vendors, and ask whether they were satisfied with what they received. Also join online orchid forums to ask members to rate a nursery's performance and reliability.

Botanical gardens

Botanical gardens play a small but important role in the sale of orchid plants. Some gardens propagate, on a limited scale, their rare or unusual plants that might not otherwise be available to the public. Others supplement their income by offering flowering orchids from specialty growers. In either case, your purchase supports the overall conservation and educational mission of the garden.

Orchid shows

No better place exists to get a quick education in all aspects of orchid culture and folklore, and no other venue offers such a broad selection of supplies, reliable information, and plants to see and touch as you choose them. Orchid shows are the equivalent of visiting an orchid nursery, and orchidists often plan months ahead to attend shows to

READING AN ORCHID LABEL

Labels from traditional orchid nurseries generally list the orchid's parentage, for example, *Blc.* Ranger Six × *C.* Old Whitey, on one side of the label. The pod, or female parent, is always listed first, while the pollen, or male parent, is second. The genus is almost always abbreviated. If the plant is a species orchid, the label will simply state the name of the species, for example, *Onc. ornithorhynchum.*

The reverse of the label lists nursery name, address, phone number, and other contact information. Rarely do such labels provide care information.

Labels of mass-market orchids generally provide only the hybrid or species name, for example, *Colm.* Wildcat. They rarely list hybrid parentage. Sometimes only a genus name, such as *Phalaenopsis,* is given. Occasionally, a common name, such as moth orchid, is provided on the label. As retailers demand more precise information, new labels are showing detailed names similar to traditional orchid nursery labels. Most mass-market labels provide simple care instructions, such as "grow shady, warm, and keep evenly moist."

When growers have special trademarks or a logo, it will appear on the reverse side; but rarely is direct contact information printed. Mass-market growers do not want to talk with individuals. Instead they want you to contact the retailer that sold the plant.

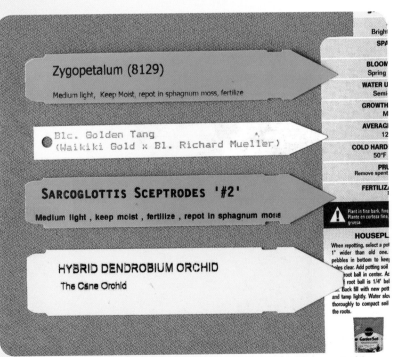

Plant tag information can range from good to minimal. Some provide only the common name of the orchid; others go so far as to provide its parentage. Mass market labels may treat an orchid like a garden plant. The best tags state the plant's name and heritage and provide growing information along with name of the grower.

Buying orchids *(continued)*

purchase from the generous selection shown by national and international vendors.

Often plants are found at shows that are not otherwise available, at prices that are hard to beat. The great variety of plants at shows creates competition and can make prices reasonable. Even so, the prices charged for the plants could be high.

Domestic orchid nurseries often charge more for plants than some international vendors because domestic vendors have potted and nurtured the plants until established and they have paid U.S. wages.

The main caveat about orchid shows as a source of plants is to be leery of plants that are offered by nurseries

NEW ARRIVALS

Mail order orchids may be shipped in pots or bare root. Sending the plants bare root lowers shipping costs and allows you to easily plant the orchids in your preferred medium.

Knowledgeable orchid growers know how to pack and ship perishable flowering plants to arrive in top condition. Even so, inspect the package when it arrives, looking for damage that may have injured the plants. As you slice the taped openings with a box cutter or knife, take care to make shallow cuts and prevent injuring the plants. Carefully remove packing materials.

● **Bare root** Inspect bare root plants for damage or excessive moisture. Experienced growers dry out plants before shipping to reduce chances of moisture-related damage in transit. Check for insects that may have hitched a ride.

Immediately unpack new arrivals and check their condition. Water and trim damage as necessary.

Cut off damaged portions with a sharp sterilized knife or razor blade. Use a new blade for each plant or sterilize the knife between plants to avoid spreading viruses or other diseases. Pot the plants in an appropriate container and medium. Treat the plants as needed for diseases and insects, then keep treated plants separate from other orchids until the problem is controlled.

● **Potted** Packed and potted orchids usually have the medium secured with tape. Carefully remove the tape, then inspect plant root conditions, leaves, and flowers. You may need to re-secure the medium in the pot before checking the roots to avoid spilling the medium. In an upright position, tap the pot firmly on a hard surface to settle and firm the medium.

As with bare-root orchids, plants should have been allowed to dry before shipping to prevent rot. Cut off any damaged plant portions following directions given above for bare root plants; then water the plants. If the pot is broken, slip the orchid into a new pot, taking care not to disturb the roots unless they are damaged. Treat plants as needed for diseases and insects.

Move new plants into your growing area. If plants have been shipped a great distance from a different climate, acclimatize them by placing them where the growing conditions are most similar to their previous environment. Gradually move them into their permanent location.

LOCAL PURCHASES

When you bring new plants home, check for diseases and insects, then treat appropriately when needed. Isolate plants from other orchids until you are sure that any problems have been corrected.

Water new plants carefully. Mass-market orchids, often grown in small nursery pots, have been watered and fertilized to speed growth to flowering size. When ready for sale, they may be moved to bigger pots with a different medium, such as long-strand sphagnum moss to fill spaces. Take care to avoid over- or underwatering new plants.

After the plant finishes blooming, carefully knock it out of the pot and check the roots and soil condition. If the medium has broken down or you find two kinds of media in the pot, repot it (see page 63).

from the Southern Hemisphere. These may fail because the plants have difficulty adapting to seasons that are the reverse of their natural environment.

▲ Many botanical gardens offer the opportunity to see and compare a large variety of orchids as well as to purchase healthy plants often grown at the garden.

More about shows

Joining a local orchid society is a great way to meet other orchid lovers, learn about new plants, and exchange cultural tips and other information as well as be among the first to learn about scheduled orchid shows, both locally and across the country.

Members of the local society, experienced growers and orchid nurseries enter their finest plants in regional, national, and international shows to be judged by experts in the field. Even if you aren't ready to put your own plants into competition, you'll want to attend one of the major orchid shows. Doing so is one of the best ways to quickly learn about a vast array of orchids. At the show you can get an idea of the great variety of orchids that are available on the market, learn how to grow new types in your own home, and see what characteristics make an orchid an award-winner.

Take a day to walk around the show, closely observing the flowers and the size and condition of the plants. The growers at the show will be experienced and familiar with most types of orchids. By seeing their plants, you will learn exactly how your orchids should look when grown well.

The sales area will be nearly as helpful as the show. Peruse the wide variety of plants for sale to widen your knowledge much more than by visiting nurseries or working with your own collection.

Your goal as you study plants at an orchid show is to start to learn the general signs that indicate good health and regular flowering. Look for plants that are healthy and prolific and that show evidence of regular flowering by the presence of old flower stems. Plants that have won cultural awards at local shows may be good candidates for your collection as they have proven to produce freely and easily.

HERE'S A TIP...

Preview parties
Attend the preview party or the opening day of an orchid show to find the freshest flowers and the greatest variety of plant choices.

MAJOR ORCHID SHOWS

- American Orchid Society Members' Meetings (held twice yearly in conjunction with regional orchid shows, www.aos.org)
- Greater New York International Orchid Show (Greater New York Orchid Society, www.gnyos.org)
- Miami International Orchid Show (South Florida Orchid Society, www.southfloridaorchidsociety.org)
- Pacific Orchid Expo (San Francisco Orchid Society, www.orchidsanfrancisco.org)
- Santa Barbara International Orchid Show (www.sborchidshow.com)
- World Orchid Conference (held every three years at a different venue, www.19woc.com)

Judging standards

You may someday want to enter a favorite orchid in a show to find out how it compares to others like it. Orchids are judged in two ways. The first, known as ribbon or show judging, recognizes the best orchid of its type on display at that show. This method is typically used at regional orchid society meetings and seasonal orchid shows.

The second way, quality judging, is based on absolute standards of beauty and excellence for a given type of orchid. Judges use their collective experience and knowledge to evaluate an orchid against all others of that particular type in the world.

Judging scores are based on a point system. Quality judging may be used at local or regional shows and is always used at the dozens of regularly sanctioned monthly competitions scheduled throughout the world.

The American Orchid Society (AOS) has the best-known judging system, and its judges must train for six years or longer to become fully accredited; AOS awards are highly coveted. International societies, such as the Royal Horticultural Society (England), Deutsche Orchideen-Gesellschaft (Germany), and the Japanese Orchid Growers Association (Japan), have their own judging systems.

The AOS gives out more than 2,000 awards at more

▲ Two types of awards are given at most shows: ones for the orchids best representing their type at the show (show or ribbon awards) and ones for orchids meeting national or international standards of excellence for their type (quality awards).

AWARD-WINNING ORCHIDS

Thanks to widespread tissue-culture propagation methods, awarded orchids are increasingly available in the trade. Here are a few of the easiest to find:

- *Ctna.* Whynot 'Roundabout' AM/AOS
- *Lc.* Angel Heart 'Hihimanu' AM/AOS
- *Paph.* Maudiae 'Magnificum' FCC/RHS
- *Phal.* Baldan's Kaleidoscope 'Golden Treasure' AM/AOS
- *Dgmra.* Flying High 'Star 'n Bars' HCC/AOS
- *Bllra.* Marfitch 'Howard's Dream' AM/AOS
- *Brs.* Rex 'Sakata' AM/AOS)
- *Colm.* Wildcat (many awarded cultivars in circulation)
- *Slc.* Jewel Box 'Dark Waters' AM/AOS

All of these winners would make great beginner's plants, unlike many awarded plants, and all have been widely propagated and so are readily available.

MAJOR ORCHID AOS AWARDS

Flower quality awards are given on a scale of 100 points:

- 89.5+ First Class Certificate (FCC/AOS)

Between 10 and 20 of these highly prized awards are given each year.

- 79.5–89.4 Award of Merit (AM/AOS)

Given more often, this prize is indicative of very high quality.

- 74.5–79.4 Highly Commended Certificate (HCC/AOS)

Good quality, the most frequently given award.

American Orchid Society

AWARD OF MERIT

Awarded to Ascocenda Haad Ravai
'KG's Burnt Orange', 82 points

Exhibited by Greg Allikas and Kathy Figiel
at West Palm Beach, Florida on August 25, 2001

CHAIR, JUDGING COMMITTEE   PRESIDENT

than 100 orchid shows and 50 monthly competitions each year. The AOS also recognizes botanical rarities (Certificate of Botanical Recognition CBR/AOS), horticulturally interesting species (Certificate of Horticultural Merit CHM/AOS), and cultural excellence (Certificate of Cultural Merit CCM/AOS).

The relevance of flower awards to the commercial market is a subject of debate because a flower-quality award does not predict the overall performance of a given cultivar. When you buy at a show, beware the trap of thinking that just because a flower has won an award it would be a good addition to your collection.

In the same way that highly bred show-winning dogs don't always make the best pets, prize-winning orchids are not always the easiest or most satisfactory for home growers. They may be temperamental or flower only rarely. Indeed, it seems that some orchids win awards only because they are known to be difficult to bloom.

ORCHID CONSERVATION

For many years wild-collected orchids—those gathered from their native environs—were the main, if not the only, plants available to growers. As seed and tissue culture has become more common and cost-effective, the market for plants collected from the wild is less important.

Wild-collected orchids are still needed as a source of new plant material. However, that job is better left to commercial growers who have the knowledge and facilities to establish and propagate the plants for a wider distribution.

Unrestricted wild collecting of orchids decimates native populations. The journey from their natural habitat to your home is perilous for orchids. Plants arrive desiccated and may be difficult to reestablish, especially ones from environments quite different from a home. It's likely that they will not survive, in which case everyone loses.

Even as wild orchids were brought into cultivation by nurseries in their native regions or by domestic nurseries, sustainable wild populations have been diminished.

RULES GOVERN ORCHID COLLECTION

All orchids are subject to the Convention on International Trade in Endangered Species (CITES), an international trade agreement established by United Nations Environment Programme (UNEP). Orchids traded (sold or carried) across international borders must be accompanied by appropriate documentation.

While nursery-propagated wild-collected plants are often available, not all of the parent plants have been harvested in a sustainable manner—at a rate less than the orchid population's ability to replenish itself. And it is not always easy to discern the reputable dealer from the disreputable.

For example, you may see orchids for sale that are represented as nursery-raised but look rough, with damaged leaves, chewed stems, and moss and lichens on the roots as though they may have been collected from the wild. Plants raised in offshore nurseries often have the appearance of wild-collected plants, however, because they are grown in areas where the conditions are fairly primitive.

Sort out the reputable from the disreputable by asking friends in the orchid society about their experiences with dealers. Be observant and quiz growers about the plants and their source. When you are satisfied with the answers, you've done the best you can.

When using the Internet, it is nearly impossible to tell whether dealers are reputable. Buy only from vendors with whom either you or a trusted associate have had positive first-hand experience.

Rather than be tempted to purchase exotic wild-collected orchids, purchase reliable plants that have been propagated from seed or long-established nursery stocks. You'll be taking part in good long-term conservation practices while acquiring better-looking and easier-to-grow plants.

Orchids for indoors

The key to success with orchids: Grow them where they grow best. Unfortunately, home conditions are not where most orchids grow best. Indoor growing conditions are often limited in light quality and intensity and are relatively dry. Light is the most limiting factor.

The natural light shining into the windows of a house is "low-energy" or angled light. Consider sunlight that shines through your windows in winter, when the sun is farthest away and angled low. Then compare that light with light entering your home in summer.

For plants, light in a home, even in summer, is akin to winter sunlight. Although rooms receive more light during summer, it's still not enough for some orchids. High-light orchids must be grown in sunrooms, greenhouses, or gardens where they will receive high-energy light all year.

Look for these traits

If your home has an area where typical houseplants grow well, light conditions and humidity levels are enough to keep low-light orchids alive. The orchids that succeed best in these conditions are those that have adapted to low-light conditions in their native habitats. These are the orchids from the forest floor and the bottom tiers of the forest canopy. Among low-light orchids are jewel orchids, phalaenopsis, paphiopedilums, and phragmipediums. Where light is a little brighter, miniature cattleya hybrids and some oncidium orchids do well.

When buying orchids to grow as houseplants, pay special attention to the mature size of the plant. Some orchids grow too large and occupy so much space that it's not possible to use the room for people to live in.

Select plants that are known as good indoor subjects. To learn which orchids do well indoors, take advantage of local expertise by joining a regional orchid society, an excellent resource for obtaining plants. And members will know what succeeds in your area and offer assistance and advice. Usually members have plants to share from their collections. An orchid that has proven to do well enough to produce extras is apt to succeed in another grower's home.

Many orchids have lovely perfumes that add an extra dimension to the home atmosphere. Some, such as *B. nodosa* and *B.* Little Stars, do well indoors. Choose orchids that release scent when you are home to enjoy it. Night-fragrant species and hybrids are

especially appropriate. For example, *Rhyncolaelia digbyana*, which requires a south window, has a potent, enchanting citrus fragrance at night. If you're home during the day, look for ones that release fragrance during the middle of the day. Some orchids require particular lighting conditions that

▲ A situation like this with sunlight coming in from several directions will allow you to grow a greater variety of orchids indoors than where the light hits the plants from only one direction.

EASY ORCHIDS

The best orchids for beginners
- are readily available from a variety of sources
- flower easily and profusely in less than ideal conditions
- have bright, long-lasting flowers displayed well above the foliage
- are relatively inexpensive
- require no special attention to grow and flower
- are compact enough to grow in a home (or on a frost-free patio)
- are tolerant of over- and underwatering

The easiest orchids to grow
Ascocentrum miniatum
Cattleya aurantiaca
Cattleytonia Why Not
Colmanara Wildcat
Doritaenopsis Pixie Star
Doritaenopsis Purple Gem
Iwanagara Appleblossom
Laeliocattleya Mini Purple
Masdevallia Copper Angel
Paphiopedilum Maudiae
Phalaenopsis equestris
Sophrolaeliocattleya Jewel Box

HERE'S A TIP...

Best orchids for windowsills or lights
Angraecum leonis
Ascocentrum ampullaceum
Cattleya luteola
Cirrhopetalum Daisy Chain
Dendrobium lawesii
Encyclia cochleata
Laelia pumila
Leptotes bicolor
Lycaste campbellii
Oncidium cheirophorum
Paphiopedilum callosum
Phalaenopsis Mini Mark

UNUSUAL ORCHIDS

Name	Unusual features
Brassavola flagellaris	Heart-shape lip
Brassia longissima	Large spidery flowers
Bulbophyllum echinolabium	Long sepals, fetid odor
Ctsm. Orchidglade	Dark red blotching
Doritis pulcherrima champornensis	Clown-type markings
Dracula soderoi	Bizarre form and color
Masdevallia spp.	Kitelike flowers
Paphiopedilum malipoense	Striking color and form
Stanhopea tigrina	Bold markings, heavy perfume

FRAGRANT ORCHIDS

Name	Scent	When released
Brassia nodosa	Spicy clove	Night
Brassocattleya Cynthia	Lemony-sweet	Day
Bulbophyllum rothschildianum	Peach	Day
Coelogyne ochracea	Spicy	Day
Cymbidium Golden Elf	Roselike	Day
Degarmoara White Wonderland	Banana	Day
Encyclia citrina	Citrus	Day
Jumellea spp.	Spicy	Night
Lycaste aromatica	Cinnamon	Day
Maxillaria tenuifolia	Coconut	Day
Neofinetia falcata	Jasmine-like	Day
Neostylis Lou Sneary	Vanilla	Night
Oncidium ornithorhynchum	Musky-sweet	Day
Phalaenopsis mannii	Orange	Day
Zygopetalum mackayi	Strong spicy	Day

▲ Even orchids requiring the lowest level of light will have trouble surviving indoors when they are this far away from a window. Plan to leave them in dim light for only a few days at a time.

may be difficult to provide; ask before you buy.

Avoid these orchids

Even when you have enough light and room for a particular orchid, if it is difficult to grow and requires special care, chances are that it may not succeed in your home. Avoid orchids that are native to regions with high humidity, those from high elevations where cool conditions are typical, and those that grow best on a mount (mounted orchids are difficult to manage indoors, especially for watering).

If you begin with challenging orchids, you may become frustrated, then never experience orchids that do make good houseplants. After you've gained experience, then extend your collection with some of the more challenging species.

At first at least, avoid orchids that look attractive only when in bloom. Some orchids are just too ugly to be year-round home decor. If you have your heart set on an unusually odd-looking orchid, find an out-of-the-way spot to grow it until it blooms, then move it to a display area.

CHALLENGING ORCHIDS

Unless you are experienced at growing orchids, avoid those that
- are not widely available and often require a search through obscure sources
- are difficult to grow, slow growing, or unlikely to flower without specialized care or conditions
- have flowers that are not necessarily beautiful by traditional standards but may have a special fragrance or bizarre shape
- require magnification to see the flowers or may need special facilities to accommodate the size
- are intolerant of poor-quality water, temperature extremes, or overfertilization
- may be costly

These challenging orchids are worth the extra effort but require a greenhouse to grow
Aerangis luteo-alba rhodosticta
Bulbophyllum rothschildianum
Cattleya walkeriana
Dendrobium cuthbertsonii
Epidendrum vitellinum
Lycaste Aquila
Miltoniopsis vexillaria
Paphiopedilum bellatulum

Orchids as outdoor plants

Two of the best places to grow orchids are outdoors under a tree and on a patio. Outdoors, plants flourish and flower with profusion. Because they receive good light, freely circulating fresh air, and moderate humidity—conditions that are similar to their natural habitats—the plants thrive.

The West Coast, Florida, Hawaii, and anywhere that frost does not occur are

Monitor plant health closely. You may notice a slight yellowing of foliage. This may be due to high light levels, but excessive yellowing may also indicate that the plants need more fertilizer more often. Careful observation of the particular circumstances will help you evaluate whether the yellowing is a symptom of high light, inadequate fertilizer or a combination of factors.

cover the top for a controlled amount of light to enter the house. Many growers tack screening or shade cloth to the sides to keep out insects. Keeping plants off the ground on benches or tables protects them from soilborne pests and diseases.

In frost-free areas where you have the space, make a shade house large enough to grow many types of orchids, including ones that are too large to grow in your home. Locate a shade house in the landscape following the guidelines for locating a greenhouse.

Outdoors year-round

Your choice for outdoor orchids depends on where you live. In California, orchids are planted in the ground as landscape plants. In fact, cymbidium orchids have long been popular for perennial gardens and landscapes on the West Coast. California specialist orchid nurseries offer an entire line of plants known as cymbidium companions, such as the Mexican *Laelia anceps* and its hybrids and some high-elevation Central American and Himalayan orchid species and hybrids.

Cymbidium orchids require cool summer nights to bloom, nights typical of the Pacific Coast. But unless the orchids have been specifically bred to grow in warm climates, they do not bloom in Florida or other southeast states with warm summer nights.

Floridians can choose from a wealth of orchid species and hybrids because the state's climate has uniformly high humidity and heat. Vandas and their relatives do well in Florida and other southeastern states, as do most cattleyas. Hybrids involving encyclia are particularly popular for their long-lasting summer blooms.

In the Pacific Northwest gardeners can plant orchids outdoors that thrive in cool

▲ Protect orchids that are sensitive to excess sunlight with a shade house made from lath or shade cloth.

conditions. Such orchids include *Odontoglossum crispum,* masdevallias from high elevations, and Himalayan species such as *Coelogyne ochracea.*

One caveat about growing orchids outdoors year-round: Be prepared to protect the plants whenever such weather extremes as hurricanes or occasional frosts threaten.

▲ In frost-free regions, epiphytic orchids can be grown outdoors on trees as they would grow in their native environment.

outdoor orchid-growing paradises. But almost every garden has a spot where houseplants thrive during frost-free months, such as an open patio, backyard deck, or balcony.

Growing outdoors

Orchids grown outdoors need significantly more water and fertilizer than orchids that are grown indoors. Water as often as the plants require, keeping track of rainfall to avoid over- or underwatering them.

If orchids yellow because of the light, create a shaded area for them, such as under a slatted bench. Or grow them in a hanging basket in the dappled shade of a tree, suspending them from low-hanging limbs, which allows maximum use of space while nourishing the plants with large volumes of fresh, moving air.

Orchids also thrive in a shade house or a screen house, greenhouse-like structures that are open to the elements on each side. Often shade cloth or slats

ORCHIDS FOR FROST-FREE YARDS

Cattleya citrina (also known as *Encyclia citrina*)
Cymbidium hybrids
Dendrobium aggregatum
Dendrobium anosmum
Dendrobium pierdii
Encyclia adenocaule
Encyclia tampensis
Epidendrum ibaguense (and related hybrids)
Laelia albida
Laelia anceps
Laelia autumnalis
Odontoglossum grande (also called *Rossioglossum grande*)
Oncidium leucochilum
Oncidium maculatum
Schomburgkia superbiens
Sobralia macrantha
Sobralia virginalis
Zygopetalum mackayi

▲ *Epidendrum radicans* (orange) and cymbidiums are landscape plants in Florida, California, and other warm-winter regions.

HERE'S A TIP...

Always indoors
The most popular orchid, phalaenopsis, is too soft and tropical to survive the extremes of outdoor weather. High winds, heavy rain, hail, sudden cold—all these and more take their toll on the health and appearance of phalaenopsis. Only in South Florida will they grow well outdoors. Unless you have a protected patio in an area where summer temperatures never drop below 60°F, keep phals indoors year-round.

Indoor orchids outdoors

If you live in an area where at least part of the year is frost-free, moving orchids outdoors during the mild months can increase the chances of success with them in winter. When they grow outside in summer, they receive an extra energy boost from the natural growing conditions.

An almost unlimited number of orchid species and hybrids can be managed this way, with two limiting factors. One is size. Some orchids may thrive so well outside that they eventually become too large to take indoors in fall.

The second consideration is the daily range of temperatures in your climate during frost-free months. For example, in the Gulf states, orchids must be able to survive hot nights and days, similar to conditions in Florida. In northern states, the East, and the West, orchids requiring cooler conditions do better. In the Midwest, choose orchids that do best in warm nights and hot days.

The transition between indoors and out is the most crucial period when growing indoor orchids outside. In spring, ease the plants outdoors, keeping them in a protected, shaded outdoor area for a few days until they adjust to the brighter light. Before bringing them indoors for winter, thoroughly inspect and clean the plants to avoid bringing in pests.

▲ When bringing your orchids outdoors for the summer, place them where they are shaded by a tree or the overhang of your house or other structure to prevent them from sunburning.

Planning a greenhouse

▲ Growing in a greenhouse allows you to provide the greatest amount of light to the largest number of orchids all year long. You can grow low-light orchids in greenhouses by placing them where they are shaded by the other plants.

Serious orchid aficionados almost always grow their plants in a greenhouse because it is the only place with nearly as much high-energy light as outdoors. With a greenhouse, you can grow a wider variety of orchids than you could grow either indoors alone or outdoors alone.

You can also control the amount and quality of light as well as carefully regulate temperature and humidity, tailoring greenhouse conditions to grow favorite orchids to the highest possible standards.

Styles

A well-designed greenhouse can be an attractive addition to the yard. Greenhouses have two basic styles: stand-alone and lean-to.
● **Stand-alone** Exposed on all four sides, this style of greenhouse ranges in design from simple do-it-yourself buildings to elaborate structures by architects or engineers. Glazing materials may be glass, fiberglass, or polycarbonate compounds, which are formulated to transmit maximum light while providing insulation against heat loss.

Because it has four sides, a stand-alone greenhouse can receive solar radiation all day when properly situated in the landscape. It also radiates heat from all four sides at night, however. During cold spells, keeping it heated can be a significant cost.
● **Lean-to** Exposed on just three sides, lean-tos abut an adjacent structure—house, garage, or other building—on one side. Designs as simple or as complex as those of stand-alone greenhouses, lean-tos may also be constructed of the same materials.

Lean-tos are a solution for space-limited situations that have insufficient room for a stand-alone greenhouse. Because only three sides are exposed to light, they receive solar radiation for only part of the day, a disadvantage. But then, they lose heat from only three sides at night, which saves on heating costs.

Some people prefer having a lean-to attached to their home, where they can gaze into the growing area to enjoy their plants any time. Although the side of the lean-to attached to the house blocks light from reaching the interior of the house at least part of the day, passive heat from a lean-to can help warm living spaces. Lean-tos can be heated with a home heating system, heated alone or in tandem with a greenhouse system, and may reduce overall greenhouse heating costs.

ORCHIDS FOR GREENHOUSES

These orchids do best in greenhouses:
● Very large or small orchids
● Orchids that require high humidity
● Orchids that require frequent watering
● Orchids that do best in very high light
● Orchids that are intolerant of dry conditions
● Orchids needing brisk air movement
● Orchids from high elevations
● Orchids from hot climates

Three-season porches

Three-season porches, or garden rooms, are similar to lean-to greenhouses. Although frequently built to take advantage of passive solar heating, these structures are excellent for growing orchids, if the light is properly managed.

Many three-season rooms are open to fresh air during mild months, giving orchids the advantage of moving air. In cold months, leaving doors between the living area and three-season room open may help heat the home. At night

▲ A stand-alone greenhouse lets you grow orchids all year and provides light that is equal to natural sunlight. It also allows you to grow numerous orchid species with specialized needs that are difficult to accommodate in typical home conditions.

▲ An attached lean-to greenhouse is an excellent choice for a limited space or when you need to save heating costs. Nearby trees can be a liability, but deciduous trees over an attached lean-to prevent the house from overheating in summer.

a home heating system can warm the orchids. To trap warm air at night, there are mechanized insulation systems for three-season porches that draw curtains across the ceiling.

Location

If you plan to build a greenhouse—stand-alone, lean-to, or three-season porch—choose a location carefully to ensure capturing optimum light and accessing adequate air circulation. It will be easier to artificially shade the structure from intense sun than to increase the sun shining through.

Ideally, the greenhouse should be oriented with its longest side running north and south, which provides the longest daily access to the most sun. No trees or other objects should shade the structure. In some areas, make sure it is protected from wind yet has natural air circulation.

Ensure that it has close access to electric or gas power and water. A stand-alone greenhouse should be erected reasonably close to your home. A lean-to should be sited on the south side of your home.

Finding a site that meets all these criteria may be impossible. Size of the yard, zoning laws, and neighborhood association rules may limit site choices. Therefore, it is important that you think carefully about how best to achieve the maximum exposure within the constraints of your space. Be prepared to adapt to the situation. Some trade-offs may mean cutting back on other plans, such as high-light vandas. A greenhouse built in the most limited location still allows for better growing conditions than a home can provide.

Planning and construction

Above all, your greenhouse should be designed to provide optimal growing conditions for orchids that require bright light and high humidity. It should also make efficient use of space to maximize the number of plants you can grow.

Design of the interior should take into account arrangement of benches and location of water supply and electrical outlets. Ensure access to plants as well as working and potting areas. Investigate how to heat, cool, and ventilate the structure, and equipment locations.

Build the greenhouse big enough to accommodate large or vining specimens. Perhaps, plan to build twice as big as you think you'll need. Your orchid collection will quickly fill the big empty space, and building big to begin with is less expensive than adding on later.

Finally, consider construction materials. Greenhouses used to be built with redwood framing and glass glazing (light-transmitting covering of the greenhouse). Today, most are constructed of steel or other metal and have plastic glazing materials (new plastics are sturdier and often better insulators than glass).

A greenhouse can be as simple in construction as polyethelyne plastic stretched over a wooden frame or as elaborate as a brick, wood, and glass structure. Greenhouses are also available as kits.

Most likely you will need a permit to build a greenhouse.

HERE'S A TIP...
How greenhouses work
Sunlight enters the greenhouse through the transparent glazing (covering material). As it enters, the light has high energy. The light bounces off plants and objects in the greenhouse, which absorb some of the energy from the light and become warm.

As the light's energy is transformed into heat, it is losing energy. This makes it less able to pass back out through the glazing and into the atmosphere. Thus, the greenhouse stays substantially warmer than the outside on a clear cool day.

At night, because no sunlight is entering the greenhouse, the heat eventually radiates out to the atmosphere and the greenhouse cools.

If you hire the work done, first visit with locals to find out which contractors and builders they recommend for this type of project.

▲ Huge orchids, such as *Grammatophyllum speciosum,* belong in a greenhouse where you can provide adequate light and don't need to worry about water damaging your home.

Environment for growth

▲ It can be difficult to have many types of orchids in a living area and provide the conditions they require: 1,000 to 4,000 footcandles of light, good air circulation, temperatures in the range of 40° to 90°F, and 50 percent or higher humidity.

Successful gardeners know that every potential growing area—both indoors and out—offers many microclimates. Within each location are spots that are warmer or cooler, brighter or shadier, drier or wetter, or more or less humid than the rest of the space; these are microclimates. A plant may thrive in one corner of a room but not in the others,

or it may grow only on one side of a patio.

This phenomenon applies to orchids as well: Within your available growing areas are niches where certain types of orchids will grow successfully but not others. Even if you don't have a greenhouse or sunroom, a naturally favorable outdoor climate, or a bright room in your home, you will find

places for many types of orchids to thrive and bloom.

You may have to experience some trial and error to discover which orchids thrive in which area. You may also need to make some alterations to the growing area to broaden the variety of orchids you can cultivate. Observing your plants, keeping daily records of the area's light, temperature, and

humidity, and experimenting by moving your orchids to different locations will help you find the best spots for orchids to prosper.

Many people who grow orchids at home have taken these steps and can share their experiences with you online, at local orchid society meetings, or at orchid shows. However, the most effective way to learn successful orchid culture is to observe the plants in your own growing space. Understanding what to look for as well as what you are seeing in your plants is the single biggest step to success with orchids.

Pay as much attention to your orchids when they are not in bloom as when they are to develop a full understanding of what they need to grow well. Note reactions to cultural practices, light exposures, and seasonal sun changes. Record air temperature and humidity levels at different times of day.

Because orchids are generally slower than most other plants to respond to changes in environmental factors, your close observations can help you anticipate problems and take advantage of beneficial conditions. You will quickly learn to see and encourage subtle day-to-day changes in healthy plants.

Also, to fully enjoy the hobby of growing orchids, cultivate a year-round interest in their growth and reaction to growing conditions. Checking on your plants daily allows you to recognize and correct any potential or arising problems, to keep plants clean and free of debris and to thoroughly enjoy the experience.

Time spent with plants is time that is serene and relaxing. It is good for your well-being and for that of your plants.

Light

Like most flowering plants, orchids grow and bloom best in as much light as they can tolerate without developing sunscald. The single most important factor in successfully growing orchids is light.

Orchids that receive the right amount of light are more attractive, more disease-resistant, and more floriferous. They are strong and healthy, with medium green foliage that may seem faded, and they have pseudobulbs that stand upright without staking or other support. Their flower stems are thick and may also be self-supporting.

When light is inadequate, leaves are unable to manufacture enough food for the plant to grow and flower well. If a plant is not getting the light it needs, all plant parts—leaves, pseudobulbs, rhizomes, roots, and flowers—decline in size and vigor. Pseudobulbs and roots may become shriveled. Leaves are generally limp, soft, and dark green. If a plant is leggy, floppy, or otherwise unable to support itself, chances are that it is not receiving enough light.

Orchids can also receive too much light. Then the foliage becomes scorched or develops a reddish or yellowish tinge. Excess light also dries out plants. The plant may bloom but its flower buds and inflorescences become deformed and the edges of the petals turn brown from the lack of water.

What's right?

No general light recommendations apply to all orchids. Many popular orchids are species that have adapted to an epiphytic lifestyle near the tops of trees where high-quality light shines. Others come from deep within the forest canopy where the trees' leaves provide dappled or total shade.

The right amount of light thus depends on plant origins. For some orchids, you may never be able to provide the proper amount of light because it doesn't exist in your environment or climate.

Three characteristics of light will determine whether you can grow a particular orchid: its intensity (the amount or brightness of the light), its duration, and its color or quality.

● **Intensity** Light is measured in foot-candles—the amount of light falling on a surface that is 1 foot away from a candle. At noon on a bright summer day, outdoor light levels can be 10,000 foot-candles or more; on an overcast day they may be as low as 500 foot-candles. The brightest window in a house may receive 4,000 to 5,000 foot-candles of light, while a foot away from the window, light levels measure as low as 500 foot-candles.

Most orchids require 1,500 to 3,000 foot-candles of light. But some do well in 500 foot-candles and others can tolerate as much as 4,000 foot-candles. Hybrids, especially intergeneric hybrids, often can tolerate a broader range of intensities.

The amount of light that an orchid needs and can withstand, however, is dependent on where it grows. For example, orchids plants that grow well outdoors in 5,000 or more foot-candles in Florida will turn brown when they receive that much light in the California desert. There, 3,000 foot-candles is enough for plants that require bright light. In the desert high light means that moisture dries quickly; plants turn brown from desiccation.

HERE'S A TIP...
Day length
Lengthening days spur some orchids to bloom; others only bloom when days grow shorter. Any orchid that receives light for a longer or shorter period each day than is optimal may not bloom. Short-day orchids may not bloom if exposed to even a few minutes of extra light.

● **Duration** This is the length of the day or how long light shines on the plant. Length of time that plants receive light is important because light and dark periods need to occur in a certain ratio in order to bloom. Most plants require 8 to 16 hours of light every day.

Plants have a limit on how much light energy they need; receiving extra light stresses them. Intensity and duration do not compensate for each other. Ideal light ranges are for an entire day, not just a portion of it, and 2 hours of bright light will not make up the difference when a plant needs 6 hours of diffused or medium light.

The cycle between light and dark and the length of each period is crucial to blooming plants because it triggers flowering. Some orchids bloom as the days grow longer toward summer. Others bloom as the days shorten from summer to fall.

● **Quality** Understanding light quality is most crucial when growing orchids under artificial light, which may not provide light in the whole spectrum as sunlight does.

Quality refers to the light's color. Light is composed of waves of energy. These waves may be long, medium, or short; length determines the color. People don't see the color within the light; they see the color of the light that is not absorbed by an object or when it is separated as it passes through a prism.

Most plants, including orchids, require light in the red and blue ranges. Blues ensure healthy, well-formed foliage growth; reds are critical for flowering.

▲ Most hobby greenhouses provide orchids with good quality light and a natural day length. In some circumstances, especially in shady situations, you may need to provide supplemental light for best performance.

Light *(continued)*

Evaluating light intensity

Light is either natural or artificial. Natural light from the sun has no substitute. If you can grow orchids solely with natural light, you will be rewarded with healthy, robust plants that bloom to perfection. Consider several aspects of natural light before deciding where to locate your plants.

Does light come from overhead, as in a greenhouse or outdoors? Is it angled, such as sun shining through a west window late in the afternoon? Light from overhead is the highest quality because it has the most complete spectrum of necessary wavelengths. Overhead light that is too

intense can be diffused in various ways.

Angled light, which loses energy as it passes through the atmosphere, has a significantly lower light value and tends to be hotter. When angled light is too low, as it often is, supplement natural light with artificial light.

Light levels vary by region and change during the year, depending on location. In summer, the sun is high in the sky, more easily blocked from shining indoors by overhanging roofs or eaves. Winter sun is lower in the sky and less likely to be blocked by tree canopies and overhangs but may be blocked by nearby structures.

The direction a window faces provides an idea of how much light is available to orchids indoors. An unobstructed south-facing

window receives bright light for most of the day and usually captures enough light to carry plants through winter. In summer, however, sun is often too intense for orchids, sometimes burning even ones that prefer high light. East- and west-facing windows strike a better balance in summer. North windows receive minimal light no matter the season.

Indoors, morning light shining through an east-facing window gives the best results for many orchids. A lightly shaded south-facing window is good and a west window is satisfactory, although the heat level will be higher. North windows almost never receive enough light to grow flowering orchid plants but may be suitable for jewel orchids, which are grown for foliage.

The direction the window faces, however, is only part of the story and you will need to pay attention to all factors. For example, many windows are shaded by outdoor plants, eaves, porch roofs, or nearby structures. A white building next door can reflect light through windows and increase light levels. Color and texture of interior walls and other surfaces also in-fluence light intensity. White and bright colors reflect light; dark colors soak it up.

If you intend to grow orchids indoors year-round, carefully measure light

▲ The closer to a window, the more light the plant will receive. However, not all windows receive the same amount of light, sometimes not even windows on the same side of the house in the same room. The only way to determine the light intensity in a window is to measure it with a light meter.

exposure at each window where you intend to place the plants.

Look through each window and make a note of any trees shading the window, nearby buildings, outdoor awnings or other objects that block sun rays.

In areas where you can move plants outdoors during summer, you can succeed with lower light indoors the rest of the year. Most growth will occur while the plants are outdoors, then they can rest during cooler indoor months. Remember to reduce watering and fertilizing indoors to restrain growth during lower-light months.

Measuring light

Perception of light is subjective; the iris of the eye changes in response to lighting. A room may seem bright only because eyes have adjusted to light levels.

To evaluate light in your home, use a light meter that can measure between 500 and 5,000 foot-candles. Read instructions carefully to learn how a particular meter works and to properly interpret readings. Meters vary; some have two or three ranges in which light is measured to enable the meter to take in all conditions, from tens of foot-candles to thousands. These may be bands around the dial in an analog meter or a digital readout.

Use a light meter as you set up your orchid growing area to see how much light the area receives and will help select orchids that will thrive in that light. A light meter can also help determine the best location for new orchids. Avoid using a meter, however, to track whether plants receive enough light; instead, rely on your observations of their reactions to varying light levels.

When evaluating light, remember that it is much easier to reduce light intensity than to increase it. If an area is too bright, you can apply shading compound (a type of white paint) to the greenhouse roof or stretch shade cloth

HERE'S A TIP...
Light meter
You can use your camera's built-in light meter to measure light levels around your plants. Set the shutter speed at 1/60th of a second and the film speed at ASA 25. Place a flat sheet of matte white paper at the same level where the plants will sit and aim the camera at it closely, being careful not to block the light. Adjust the f-stop to give the proper exposure for the ambient lighting. Use the accompanying table to convert to foot-candles. You may want to take several readings at different times of day and on cloudy and sunny days to get a reliable average.

f-stop	Foot-candles
2.8	200
4	370
5.6	750
8	1,500
11	2,800
16	5,000

over it (woven material that allows specific amounts of light to pass through). You can reduce light at a window by hanging sheer curtains or vertical blinds. Horizontal blinds are less effective because light tends to strike the plants in bands so some parts are overexposed while others receive too little light.) Another method is to move the plants a few feet away from the window to reduce the intensity of light that shines on them.

Evaluating light quality

Unlike light intensity, which can be objectively

MONITORING LIGHT LEVELS

Light can be measured subjectively by observing your orchids or objectively with a light meter. The best growers compare their subjective observations against light-meter readings often enough to learn the pattern of light and conditions. Numbers on a gauge mean little if they are used in a vacuum. It is more practical to learn light levels by close observation, backed by light-meter readings.

MONITOR LIGHT CONDITIONS THROUGHOUT THE DAY
● Are there situations that lead to more or less light during certain times of the day? Trees that block afternoon sun? An opening in the tree canopy that allows full sun for an hour or so?
● Does sun shine through the window late in the afternoon, when it might be particularly prone to producing heat?

MONITOR LIGHT CONDITIONS THROUGHOUT THE YEAR
● Does the sun dip below the tops of trees or houses during some months of the year?
● Does a tree drop its leaves during the winter months, opening up an exposure to more direct sun?
● Are days overcast for long periods of time during winter months?
● Are summers hot and bright, or overcast?

NO FLOWERS

When your favorite orchid won't bloom, the most likely reason is that the light is insufficient—*not* that you are under- or overwatering, fertilizing too much or too little, keeping the area too warm or cold, or that viruses or other diseases are attacking the plant. This is especially true when the plant has flowered before or is mature enough that it should be able to flower.

How can you tell if your plant is capable of blooming? By knowing whether it has bloomed in the past. For example, was it in bloom when you bought it? If so, you have a pretty good idea when your orchid should flower again because orchid plants typically bloom at about the same time each year. If the season is right but your orchid is not blooming, suspect that it is getting too little light.

If you don't know about the orchid's past or aren't sure when it should bloom, look at the plant. Are its growths increasing in size? In a sympodial orchid, each successive new growth should be larger than the last. In a monopodial orchid, each new leaf should be larger than previous leaves, which indicates that the plant is growing and approaching flowering size.

Also check the plant's overall condition. Is it healthy? Are the leaves or pseudobulbs generally upright and medium green? Are they turgid (tissues contain sufficient moisture) rather than wilted? Are roots supple and strong? Answers to these questions tell you whether the plant is mature enough to bloom and whether it is receiving enough light.

measured, light quality is not quantifiable. The more natural light available to your plants, the higher the quality or the broader the spectrum of the light. Like intensity, light quality can be affected by anything that filters out light, such as general air quality, fog, or clouds.

Generally, the spectrum of natural light entering through windows is fine.

Where artificial sources make up a large portion of the light a plant receives, quality may be a problem. Compensate by using a variety of light sources to ensure that plants receive the full spectrum of light energy they require.

Increasing the light

Artificial light is provided from lamps and other light

MEASURE LIGHT WITH YOUR HAND

The shadow cast by placing a hand between a light source and a surface offers an estimate of the light a particular spot in your home offers.

When the hand casts a strong sharp shadow (top photo), the light is bright. The light will be satisfactory for growing all but the highest-light orchids.

With a definite yet subdued shadow with blurred edges (bottom photo), light is medium, sufficient for low- and moderate-light orchids.

In low light, no shadow is cast and there is little contrast. Only orchids that thrive in the lowest light (lady's slippers, phals, or jewel orchids) will survive in low light.

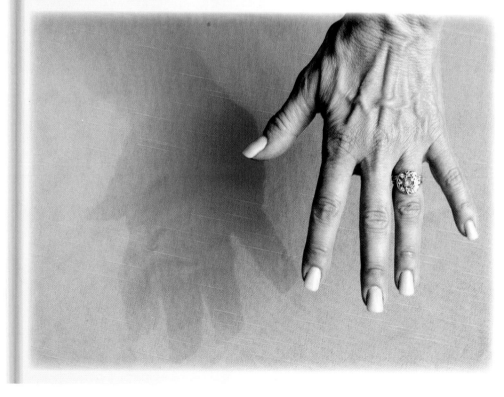

fixtures. When a growing area receives too little light, as may be the case inside a home, you must relocate plants or supplement natural light with artificial lighting. Standard vanda orchids, for example, may not get enough high-quality light in northern climates—even in a greenhouse—without supplemental lighting.

Some orchid fanciers go so far as to create elaborate indoor gardens for their plants, devoting an entire room to the plants. If you choose to take this route, you can expect fairly high start-up costs, as well as continuing energy costs, but whether the costs are more than you would pay to build a greenhouse is debatable.

When selecting a lighting system, the two most important features to consider are the heat emitted by the lamps and the color of the light. Heat dries both potting media and plants. It disfigures plants; long-term exposure stresses them. If the color spectrum is not balanced, orchids will grow poorly and fail to bloom. The light must provide a balanced spectrum that includes all colors from blue to red.

Types of lighting

• **Incandescent bulbs** are the sort used in most lamps. They produce lots of heat and provide light mainly in the red spectrum, which spurs plants to initiate flowering. Halogens are a type of incandescent bulb that have a longer life but produce even more heat. Position incandescent bulbs away from the tops of plants and combine them with other types of bulbs, such as fluorescents, that provide the blue spectrum. If combining them with fluorescent, use 25- to 40-watt bulbs and place them at least 12 to 18 inches away from the plants.

• **Fluorescent lighting** is convenient and economical in most situations because this type of lighting produces

▲ Light gardens can be set up to supplement the amount of natural light plants receive, to extend the number of hours plants are lit, or to provide all the light they receive. You'll need to pay attention to the color of the light, the amount of heat it emits, and how far away from plants to place the fixture to ensure plants get enough light without burning.

little heat and can be placed closer to the plants.

Although lighting does not add a great deal of heat to the growing area, the ballast does produce some heat. The ballast is a magnetic coil that governs the flow of current into the bulb's filament and ensures that the fluorescent tube glows.

Because the ballast is usually part of a fixture, experienced growers often rewire fixtures so that they can move the ballast away from the plants. Compact fluorescent bulbs have the ballast built into the bulb and produce more heat.

Depending on the type of bulb, light color may be cool-white, which is bluish; warm-white, with more yellow and red; or full-spectrum, most similar to sunlight.

Grow-light bulbs, another option, emit both red and blue. Both full-spectrum and grow-lights are more expensive than standard tubes. A 50-50 mix of cool- and warm-white bulbs will provide the right colors for plants at less cost.

The most common fluorescent fixtures are 4 feet long and hold four 40- or 75-watt bulbs. Such fixtures adequately light a 2-by-4-foot growing area. Most are made of aluminum, which is lightweight and corrosion resistant and helps conduct heat away from plants. Painted white, light bounces off the fixture toward the plants, increasing brightness.

Place fluorescent lights 4 to 12 inches away from plants. Because bulbs lose intensity over time, locate new bulbs farther away from the plants, and gradually lower them as they age. When replacing light bulbs, reposition the fixture 4 to 6 inches higher than it was.

● **High-intensity discharge (HID)** bulbs offer maximum brightness and are suitable for orchids needing more light than fluorescent bulbs can provide. Also use them to grow tall orchids, such as cane dendrobiums, that don't fit under fluorescent fixtures.

On the negative side, HID requires a big investment in growing space and in start-up and monthly energy costs. Also the color of the light distorts the color of the foliage and flowers, as well as everything else around the light garden. HID lights are best where you can devote an entire room to plants.

Two types of HID lights are used for growing plants: metal halide and high-pressure sodium. Both types are efficient in energy consumption. Metal halide bulbs produce light in the blue spectrum, crucial to foliage growth. High-pressure sodium bulbs give off orange and red light, which is important for flower development. Color-corrected sodium lights are available.

HID bulbs range from 400 watts to 1,000 watts. One 1,000-watt high-pressure sodium bulb generates as much light as one hundred eleven 100-watt incandescent bulbs. A 400-watt metal-halide bulb is equal to twenty 40-watt fluorescent tubes. HID bulbs must be replaced every 18 to 24 months because they weaken over time. Mount HID fixtures at least 1 foot from the ceiling and 2 to 3 feet away from plants to prevent overheating.

Other considerations

As with any advanced growing methods, research before installing lighting.

Whether you set up a small light garden in one corner of a room using only a couple of four-tube fluorescent fixtures or decide on a dedicated HID room, ascertain which plants you are most interested in growing (because it affects the sort of light you need to provide) and any limitations in household current and electrical capacity for your home. HID lights draw lots of current and may require special wiring.

Managing plants under lights

Orchids and other plants generally require a certain number of hours of light each day to grow well and bloom. If the growing area receives plenty of natural light but the daylength is short, supplement the light for a few hours a day. For example, light plants for a few hours in early morning or late afternoon in winter to extend daylight hours.

Under lights alone, orchids require 12 to 18 hours of light (see Seasonal Lighting Schedule, page 41). Set the lights up with a timer to automatically adjust day length. Some orchids require seasonal variations in day length to bloom; for these, you will need to adjust the timer every few months.

If you plan to grow orchids in living areas, be aware that some short-day orchids require an uninterrupted period of darkness. Even leaving on a reading lamp will prevent short-day orchids from blooming. Among the short-day orchids are single-leaved (unifoliate) cattleyas, *Bulbophyllum falcatum,*

LIGHT LEVELS

● **Bright** (3,000 foot-candles or more) Plants from the fringes of the forest, whether terrestrial or high in the trees at the edges of the canopy, need high or bright light. Vandas and cymbidiums are examples of high light plants.
● **Medium** (1,500 to 2,500 foot-candles) Orchids from deeper in the canopy need dappled, medium light. Many types of oncidium and cattleya orchids grow best in medium light.
● **Low** (500 to 1,500 foot-candles) Shade-loving orchids that come from the deepest parts of the tree canopy or deeply shady terrestrial situations make the best houseplants. Phalaenopsis and paphiopedilum orchids are the best-known examples. All orchids need some light to bloom, but those grown for foliage alone, such as jewel orchids, can be successfully grown in shadier locations, where there is too little light to allow flowering.

▲ Vandas are high-light and high-temperature orchids, requiring so much light and warmth that it is difficult to grow them well anywhere north of the southern portion of the United States without supplemental lighting.

Dendrobium phalaenopsis, Oncidium splendidum, and *Phalaenopsis amabilis.*

Match plants and lighting

Select plants according to the amount of light you can provide. If you decide not to use lights and do not have a greenhouse, you will more likely be successful growing orchids that prefer low light.

The most popular orchid, phalaenopsis, easily adapts to the low-light conditions found in homes. It grows well in east and west windows as well as in lightly shaded south windows.

Paphiopedilums are also good choices for low-light situations. If you have limited space as well as low light, consider growing members of the pleurothallid

group, which includes pleurothallis, masdevallia, and dracula orchids.

For higher-light situations, look for new hybrids in the oncidium group, such as wilsonara, colmanara, beallara, and odontocidiums. These do well in unshaded south windows and bright east or west windows.

In the brightest settings, cattleyas and some smaller

vandaceous orchids (ascocendas, ascofinetias, darwinaras) are excellent. In such bright areas, you are limited only by how actively you experiment.

Overhead light is provided in sunrooms, greenhouses, and outdoors, which is conducive to growing a broad range of orchids. Unless the growing area is shaded by trees or buildings or its exposure is strictly north, you will most likely need to reduce the amount of light that enters the area for at least part of the year.

Climatic considerations somewhat affect your choices. For example, standard vanda hybrids—especially yellow-flowered varieties—may not get enough high-quality light in northern climates even with supplemental lighting. In southern areas, the light may be too bright and hot for orchids from high elevations, such as odontoglossums and masdevallias.

When growing orchids outdoors year-round, select plants from areas with a temperature regime that closely matches your climate. For example, tropical orchids are successful in Florida gardens while high-elevation plants thrive in cooler Southern California.

Many orchids are native to areas in which the days are short and cool in winter, and they stop growing during the cool period. Himalayan dendrobium orchids, for example, grow in the wet monsoonal weather during summer, stop growing in cooling fall weather, then resume growth and bloom in late winter.

Giving water or fertilizer during the rest period can prevent flowering. Orchids that require a rest period are do well being grown outdoors in summer, then brought inside for winter. The lower light levels in the house brings on the rest period and lasts long enough for the orchid's summer growth matures and prepares to bloom.

IDEAL LIGHT RANGES FOR A SAMPLE OF ORCHIDS

Plant name	Light range in foot-candles							
	Low			Medium			High	
	500	1,000	1,500	2,000	2,500	3,000	3,500	4,000
Brassavola				■■■■■■■■■■■■				
Brassia				■■■■■■■■■				
Cattleya				■■■■■■■■■				
Cymbidium								
Standard				■■■■■■■■■■■■				
Miniature			■■■■■■■■■■■■■■					
Dendrobium			■■■■■■■■■■■■■■					
Epidendrum			■■■■■■■■■					
Laelia				■■■■■■■■■				
Ludisia	■■■■■■■							
Masdevallia	■■■■■■■■■							
Miltonia	■■■■■■■■■■■■							
Odontoglossum		■■■■■■■■■						
Oncidium				■■■■■■■■■				
Paphiopedilum				■■■■■				
Phalaenopsis		■■■■■						
Phragmipedium						■■■■■		
Sophronitis			■■■■■■■■■					
Vanda					■■■■■			

▲ Ludisia, one of the jewel orchids, is among the few orchids that do best in very low light.

Temperature

Orchids live in the widest environmental range of any plant family. They can be found at sea level in the hottest tropical areas and in frigid, near-permafrost conditions at high elevations and far north and south latitudes.

The majority of cultivated orchids come from areas of the world with temperatures that are comfortable for humans—generally high elevations of the tropics and subtropics. Like their native companions grown as houseplants, most orchids tolerate and even thrive in average home temperatures.

Fluctuating home temperatures—cooler at night than in the day—meet their requirements perfectly.

That said, orchids still have individual temperature needs

HERE'S A TIP...

A difference of 10° to 20°F between day and night temperatures is crucial to plant health and growth.

that reflect their native habitats. Traditionally, they are divided into four groups: cold, cool, intermediate, and warm. Cold-loving orchids are hard to grow and not suited to growing in a home, especially by beginners.

● **Cool** This group of orchids, which includes masdevallias and odontoglossums, usually comes from high elevations and requires constant temperatures in the low to mid 50s at night and below 70°F during the day. Unless indoor gardeners have a special isolated growing area or can tolerate such low temperatures in living areas, these orchids are difficult. Growers in naturally cool areas, such as the Pacific Northwest, may have success with these orchids outdoors.

● **Intermediate** The best orchids for home growing fall in this group, which includes

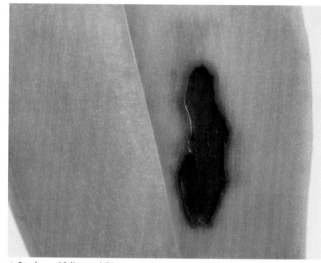

▲ Overheated foliage exhibits spots where the internal temperature of the leaf became so hot that the tissue died. Overheating often results when the orchid is getting too much sun or the light bulbs in a fixture are too close to the plant.

cattleya and oncidium orchids. They like cool to mild nights of 55° to 65°F and mild to warm days of 70° to 80°F. Temperatures that feel comfortable to you will be fine for these orchids. Although their light needs vary greatly, most will thrive in typical home temperatures.

● **Warm** These orchids originate from the lower elevations of tropical areas, where nights seldom drop below 70°F and days regularly warm to the 90s, often accompanied by very bright light.

Like cold-loving orchids, these are poor choices for home growing because it is difficult to provide such warm temperatures and high light. They do well in greenhouses in warm climates and make good garden plants in South Florida, Hawaii, and other tropical regions that have ample warmth, humidity, and sunlight. Renantheras and vandas are in this group.

One exception in this group is phalaenopsis. Although it originated in tropical areas of the South Pacific, its lower light requirements and exceptionally fast growth make it a good choice for growing indoors.

When heat-loving orchids fail, it's easy to assume that cold nights did them in. While it's true that warm-group orchids suffer during cold, wet nights, failure is more closely linked to the lack of hot days.

Some orchids, such as the Himalayan dendrobiums and Caribbean encyclias, need daytime warmth to achieve sufficient growth to flower. They can tolerate cool nights but must have hot days. In regions such as the Pacific Northwest, where overcast days may be too cool to allow proper growth, you may never succeed with these orchids.

Daily fluctuations

All orchids require cooler nights than days. Without a day-night fluctuation of 10° to 15°F, plants grow healthy foliage but will not bloom. Cool nighttime temperatures allow the plants to store the carbohydrates they manufacture during the day and will eventually use for flowering.

It's usually preferred to select orchids to match the temperature regime you can provide than to adjust temperatures to match their needs. However, as long as the plants have adequate

▲ If the surface of an orchid leaf feels hot, it is overheated. Move it to a shady spot and spray the foliage with water to cool it down.

TEMPERATURE RANGES

Plants native to high-elevation climates farther from the equator generally require cool to mild conditions—sometimes cold. (Cold-loving orchids are generally very difficult to grow.)

Plants that come from middle elevations of the tropics and subtropics grow best where temperatures are mild: Daytime highs may climb to 80°F and nights are cool but not cold, rarely below 50°F. Most orchids that do well in average home conditions will come from high- or middle-elevation areas. Orchids native to lower elevations, closest to the equator, require uniformly warm to hot and humid conditions and do best in greenhouses or outdoors in frost-free zones.

The temperature ranges below are suggestions to grow orchids successfully. Although a plant may tolerate higher or lower temperatures than shown in its range, prolonged exposure to extremes will stress plants and may interfere with flowering. Orchids, like most plants, require cooler temperatures at night. Grow plants where there is a difference of at least 10°F between day and night temperatures but no more than 30°F.

Temperature	Night	Day
Cold	40 to 50°F	50 to 70°F
Cool	50 to 55°F	60 to 70°F
Intermediate	55 to 65°F	70 to 80°F
Warm	65 to 70°F	80 to 90°F

▲ Orchids near windows can suffer cold damage during winter, especially if windows are leaky, you are growing ones such as vandas that require warm temperatures, or your region is not frost free.

TEMPERATURE TIPS

● Temperatures vary within any growing space, even indoors. At night, temperatures are cooler near windows and doors and at the floor. On clear days, air near windows is the warmest in a room, often hot enough to burn tender foliage. On those days, use a small oscillating fan to increase air circulation and moderate temperature.
● Because heat rises, areas close to the floor are cooler. Take advantage of this by growing orchids with lower temperature requirements on or near the floor. Grow warmth-loving orchids on tables, shelves, windowsills or in baskets.
● Enclose a window growing area with a plastic curtain or wooden frame covered with plastic. The covering will hold in warmth and humidity.
● Prevent plants from touching window glass in cold climates.
● Move plants away from any drafts that may affect temperature—whether warm, such as from a heater vent, or cold, such as from air-conditioning. Air-conditioning can desiccate plants as well as damage them with the cold air.

▲ Minimum-maximum thermometers may be combined with hygrometers, providing humidity readings as well as high and low temperatures.

ventilation and humidity, and they cool off at night, most orchids will tolerate higher daytime temperatures than those listed in the table, Temperature Ranges (above). Thus, the nighttime temperature you can provide is most important to consider when selecting orchids.

Keeping track

Several factors influence temperature—for example, light. As you know, temperatures outdoors are generally warmer when the sun shines than on a cloudy day. Other factors, such as air movement, humidity, and the composition of the material through which light passes—for example, glass or fiberglass in a greenhouse, a tree canopy over plants outdoors or near a window—also affect temperature.

For example, it will be hotter indoors on the sill of a closed window made of glass than it is outside the window for several reasons. For one, the glass creates a greenhouse effect by allowing high-energy light waves to pass through but blocking lower energy heat waves from escaping, so the inside temperature rises (see page 35). For another,

▲ A courtyard under a tree often provides ideal conditions for growing orchids for the summer. The shade keeps temperatures lower. Humidity is higher as is air circulation, both of which also help to moderate temperatures.

humidity is higher and air circulation greater outdoors, and this keeps temperatures lower. (Although weather reports often mention the heat index, a rating that shows how much hotter it feels when the humidity is at a certain level, heat indexes do not apply to plants. Humidity does not make plants feel uncomfortable like it does humans.)

Temperatures are cooler in a fiberglass greenhouse than in a glass one. Fiberglass allows less light to pass through, and lets in even less as it ages.

Temperatures are also cooler under a tree canopy.

Because leaves block sunlight, temperatures rise less than they would in open air.

To track the daily temperature range in a growing area and pay attention to climatic changes that could affect the temperature, use a maximum-minimum thermometer. Such thermometers provide readings of high and low temperatures so you can see at a glance how hot and cold it has been in the growing area over a 24-hour period. If you find that temperatures reach an undesirable level, take steps to raise or lower it as needed.

Managing temperature

Depending on the growing area, managing the temperature for plants can be a challenge or a snap. Indoors, options for meeting their needs will be limited. Obviously, you set the thermostat at a temperature that feels comfortable. If the comfortable setting is on the warm side, set your orchids on the floor where the air temperature is cooler. If the home is consistently cool, place plants on tables or shelves to take advantage of rising warmth.

Although orchids do best where air circulates freely, hot

or cold drafts can damage plants. Keep them away from heating and air-conditioning vents as well as from open doors and windows in winter. If you grow orchids in a window to take advantage of natural light, keep them from the glass during cold weather to avoid damage. In summer, lower shades to reduce heat from the sun.

Controlling temperatures outdoors is also challenging. Providing shade will cool them slightly, while moving them into sunlight will warm them. If you have no trees, build a simple shade structure to place over plants to reduce light and consequent heat. Water evaporation is the best natural cooler. As long as water is high quality— neutral pH and free of dissolved solids and salts—you can frequently spray orchids to cool them when temperatures rise. To avoid disease problems, spray them early enough in the day to let the foliage dry by nightfall.

In cold-winter regions, bring plants indoors before temperatures drop in fall. In frost-free areas, protect plants with blankets, tarps, or row cover during cold snaps. Temperatures will stay 2° to 3°F warmer under covers. Use a windbreak to prevent cool, drying winds from damaging plants. (Such damage is from desiccation, not cold.) Plant orchids close to a fence, hedge, or other plants to block the wind.

You have many more options for controlling temperature in a greenhouse. For example, you can raise the vents to admit more air and cool the growing area or lower the vents to shut off air flow and warm the greenhouse. Ridge vents are particularly effective when combined with bottom vents; warm air rising draws cooler air in through the open bottom vents, creating convective cooling.

Swamp, or evaporative, coolers work well in dry climates. They pull fresh air in across wet fibrous pads, which cool the air by evaporation as they blow cooled air into the greenhouse. (In humid areas where the air is already moist, this method is less effective.)

Greenhouse heating methods range from simple passive gas heaters to forced-air gas heaters to circulating warm water or steam. The best method depends on your geographical area and the type of plants you grow. In general, bottom heat provided by circulating steam is most effective because the plants are warmed by rising moist heat rather than by heated dry air.

Avoid any gas-fired heat source as well as kerosene heaters that are not vented to the outside. Both can give off fumes that harm plants and reduce the life of flowers. Electric heaters generally provide too little heat for a greenhouse and are costly to operate for the amount of heat they provide. However, for emergency use in areas that don't require winter heating, put a few small electric space heaters to use.

Temperature conditions can also be managed by placing cool-growing plants in the coolest part of the structure. For heat-loving orchids, hang them near a greenhouse roof where heat builds up or place them closer to the heat source.

IDEAL NIGHT TEMPERATURE RANGES FOR A SAMPLE OF ORCHIDS

Plant name	Cool 50–55°F	Intermediate 55–65°F	Warm 65–70°F
Brassavola		■■■■■■	■■■■
Brassia		■■■■■■	
Cattleya		■■	
Cymbidium			
Standard	■■		
Miniature	■■■■■		
Dendrobium	■■■■■	■■■■■	■■■■
Epidendrum	■■■■■	■■■■■	■■■■
Laelia		■■■■■	■■■■
Ludisia	■■■■■	■■■■■	■■■■
Masdevallia	■■■■■	■■■	
Miltonia	■■■■■	■■■	
Odontoglossum	■■		
Oncidium	■■■	■■■■	
Paphiopedilum	■■■■■	■■	
Phalaenopsis		■■■■■	■■■■
Phragmipedium	■■■	■■■■	
Sophronitis	■■■	■■■■	
Vanda	■■■	■■■■	■■■

▲ Kerosene and other gas-fired heaters can emit fumes that damage flowers and prevent blooming unless vented to the outside. A collection as large as this one represents a considerable investment of time and money. You don't want to do anything to lose it.

Humidity and air circulation

Orchids require humid conditions to grow well; moisture in humid air supplies roots with water. Unless humidity is in the 50 to 60 percent range, plants suffer stress and perform at less than their full potential. You can keep track of the moisture in air by measuring relative humidity.

How humidity works

Relative humidity is a measure of the amount of water vapor in a volume of air compared with the amount of water vapor the air has the potential to hold. As temperatures rise, the atmosphere's capacity for water increases because warmth increases the air's volume. If the amount of moisture in the air remains at the same level, relative humidity drops. The opposite occurs when temperatures go down. The air's volume decreases. If the amount of water remains the same, relative humidity goes up.

In practical terms, this means you need to keep an eye on the humidity in your growing area and add moisture to the air when the temperature increases. If you fail to do so, the plant's physiological processes suffer and it will become stressed. In areas such as the East Coast and Midwest where moisture levels in the air rise as the temperatures increase, maintaining a healthy humidity will be easier. On the West Coast where ocean currents stay cool, drier air accompanies warm temperatures and orchid growers need to watch humidity closely.

Measuring humidity

Although you can eventually learn to sense whether a growing area is humid enough, being right about how humid a spot is can be difficult. Confirmation from a calibrated instrument, a hygrometer, provides precise humidity measurements.

The simplest and least expensive hygrometers have dials that show relative humidity as a percentage.

These tools contain a fibrous material connected to the needle that shrinks and swells depending on humidity. Digital models are available and may be found combined with minimum-maximum thermometers.

More accurate and more expensive hygrometers combine two thermometers. One of the thermometers is moistened. As it dries, it measures the temperature of the evaporating water, or the "wet bulb" temperature.

The other thermometer is kept dry so that it measures air temperature. After taking both readings, you consult a table to convert the readings to relative humidity. These hygrometers are also called wet-dry thermometers.

To use a hygrometer, place it about midway between the floor and the ceiling, preferably among the plants, where the humidity reading is most likely to be represented. Leave it in place for about two hours (or the time period recommended by the manufacturer) before checking the humidity level. It takes some time for the reading to register accurately on the hygrometer.

What to expect

Unless you live in an arid climate or at a high elevation, the outdoors will almost always be more humid than a home, especially in summer. Air-conditioners and furnaces dry out indoor air as they operate, and furnishings absorb moisture from the air.

Greenhouses offer the ability to harness and control humidity, which is one of their best advantages. The structure holds and keeps the moisture that the plants inside transpire, keeping the atmosphere naturally moist.

In regions where humidity is naturally high, and in enclosed growing areas such as greenhouses, humidity can rise to unhealthy levels if not monitored. At humidity levels of 80 to 90 percent,

▲ For the most accurate humidity reading, use a wet-dry thermometer. Check the temperature difference between the dry and wet thermometer, then consult a chart to determine relative humidity.

moisture will condense out of the air whenever the temperature drops, even just slightly. This condensation leaves a layer of moisture on plants in which fungal and bacterial diseases thrive.

Managing humidity

Maintaining humidity at proper levels is one of the most difficult tasks for growing orchids. In some cases, you have no options. For example, raising the humidity in a home could damage your house, clothes, and furnishings. Home humidifying systems help somewhat, but you are limited to providing a humidity level that meets comfort levels for those who live with you. Portable humidifiers, even though they can raise the humidity in a smaller area than a whole-house system, are impractical. Excessive humidity can damage homes.

The best way to provide extra humidity for your indoor orchids is to grow them in groups. In groups their collective transpiration and the moisture evaporating from the growing media combine to create a moist microclimate.

You might also drape the growing area with plastic sheeting to trap plant transpiration and evaporation so the humidity rises quickly.

If the light in a bathroom or kitchen is adequate for growing orchids, move plants

▲ Humidity is higher in a group of plants. The close quarters hold in water evaporating from the soil and moisture given off through transpiration.

▲ Bathrooms are often the most humid room in a home. If light is adequate, the bath may be the best place to grow some types of orchids indoors.

to those areas, which typically have higher humidity than other rooms.

You may have heard that misting foliage or placing orchids on trays filled with gravel and water are good ways to raise humidity. Misting is a short-lived temporary fix. It raises humidity for only as long as it takes the foliage to dry. Gravel trays make watering orchids easier by catching the overflow but they have little effect on humidity.

● **Outdoors** It is usually easier to raise humidity outdoors. Except in dry climates, humidity is almost always higher outdoors than inside. When temperatures rise, spray plants and the ground beneath them with water to raise humidity quickly (this technique also works for orchids growing in a terrarium).

In areas with extremely high humidity, ensure that the plants have adequate air circulation around them to prevent diseases from developing. Also water potted orchids less often.

● **Greenhouse** In such a structure you can closely monitor humidity and keep it at the most favorable level for your plants. "Damping down"—hosing the walkways and area under the benches—is an easy way to raise humidity, especially in dry climates. Evaporation cools the greenhouse as it adds moisture to the air. In extremely dry conditions, you may also want to hose off, or mist, the plants in a greenhouse. In more humid areas, doing this can increase prevalence of waterborne diseases and leave mineral deposits on the foliage. If humidity becomes too high, open the top vents to release the stale air and bring in fresh air.

Bacterial and fungal diseases and other problems thrive in high humidity and can take hold when a greenhouse is overly humid. Rising temperatures and moisture levels exacerbate the situation, making the greenhouse even more humid and spurring disease growth.

Adding exhaust fans to draw humid air out of the greenhouse will help. Also, water early enough in the day that the plant foliage has time to dry before nightfall. If problems develop, identify the disease and apply the appropriate remedy.

▲ Humidity trays actually have little effect on humidity; however, they are an aesthetic way to support plants and make it easy to water them.

Air circulation

The native habitats of most cultivated orchids are known to have almost constant movement of fresh air. Air circulation and humidity are closely allied. As air moves, it takes moisture away from plants, which dries foliage. When air is still, that's when problems appear.

Crowding plants in groups creates dead spaces where air fails to circulate. Crowding also makes it easy for pests and diseases to move from plant to plant. Place orchids with enough space between that air reaches all sides of the plants and leaf temperatures stay cool. If necessary, reduce the number of plants, discarding any that

don't bloom reliably or well, leaving the remaining plants enough room to thrive.

If possible, and when weather permits, keep a window open in the growing area—even just a crack. In cold weather, use a fan to circulate air. Place the fan and aim its air flow where it won't make the room too uncomfortable for the people in it. You may also use a ceiling fan to increase air circulation and mimic the gentle breezes in the leafy canopy of a tropical cloud forest; it also helps raise or lower temperature as needed. In warm months move plants outdoors, if you can, for the best possible air circulation.

After a while, as you hone your observation powers, you'll walk into your growing area—indoors, outdoors, or greenhouse—and know immediately whether conditions are right. That's when you will have graduated from being an orchid keeper to an orchid grower.

◀ Ceiling fans in a room or other enclosed space, such as this lean-to greenhouse, are often enough to keep air moving. The larger the area, the more fans that will be needed.

Caring for orchids

▲ Once you have set up a growing area that provides all the necessary conditions for healthy orchids, it's time for the fun stuff: watering, fertilizing, and just generally nurturing and interacting with your plants.

Once you decide on the best place to grow orchids, begin to focus on the factors that you can control: watering, fertilizing, and potting the plants. These three tasks are crucial to the success of orchids.

Orchids need to be watered with good-quality water at the time they need it. They require regular feeding with a fertilizer appropriate to their growing medium. Plants that outgrow their containers must be repotted in the correct mix, in the right-size pot, at the proper time of year. How well these tasks are managed separates average orchids from fabulous ones.

An important concept to grasp about orchids: They can't be forced to grow any faster than they normally grow or bloom before they're ready. Rather, you allow their success by providing conditions and ingredients necessary for growth.

Experienced growers have no tricks or secret methods that give them an edge over beginning orchid growers. Experienced growers succeed because they have learned that long-term observation provides important information. Learning what to look for, correctly interpreting what is seen, and putting this information to work allows growers to have orchids that perform to their potential.

Watering

A key to growing healthy orchids is paying attention while you water. After all, when you're completely focused on your plants, that's when you're most likely to discover that they need something. For example, they may have a pest or other issue that affects their health, or they may need more sun or fertilizer. So cultivate the habit of inspecting your orchids every time you water them.

Watering orchids begins with being aware of the plant's anatomy. Unlike most plants, epiphytic orchids have thick roots coated with a layer of velamen. In nature, the roots are exposed to air or may be covered with a thin layer of moss. The corky coating of velamen protects the roots from losing too much moisture in exposed conditions and it quickly absorbs available moisture and dissolved nutrients.

Potted orchids require air as well as moisture around the roots. Watering, then, is closely linked to the potting medium in which the plant grows because the medium influences the mix of air and moisture around roots—it also affects frequency and amount of water needed.

Trying to grow orchids in typical houseplant potting soil composed of peat moss and other water-retentive materials would kill the plants. Such soil contains less air than orchids require; the roots would suffocate and rot. Ideal potting media for orchids are composed of large-particle materials that let water flow rapidly through, creating an environment of humid air around roots. (Thin, fibrous houseplant roots would shrivel and die planted in such media.)

Knowing the condition in the native habitat is also important to understanding how much water it requires. Wherever it originated, the orchid developed strategies for dealing with the amount of water available. For example, orchids such as encyclias and cattleyas that grow high in the tropical canopy where light is bright and air movement vigorous—both drying conditions—have well-developed pseudobulbs for water storage and large, extensive root systems to trap moisture. Most have thick, leathery leaves that stand up to bright light and conserve water, and most are adapted to seasonal dryness.

Planting such orchids in a water-holding mix and watering frequently can suffocate roots and kill the plants. These orchids need a coarse, fast-draining medium, and the mix should be nearly dry before you water again.

Pay attention to whether the plant is drying quickly, which signals that it needs more frequent watering, or whether the plant is drying slowly, which indicates less frequent watering is called for. Also be sure to provide a seasonal dry period if the plant's native habitat provided one.

Conditions deep in a forest canopy are less drying; light is dim, and air movement is less vigorous. Roots may be protected by a layer of water-retentive moss. Orchids from within the forest canopy, such as pleurothallis and pescatorea, have no need for, so have not developed, water storage organs. Nor have they adapted to seasonal dry periods, because consistent moisture is available throughout the year. Leaves of these orchids are usually thinner and softer. Such orchids do best in fine-grade water-retentive mixes kept evenly moist.

"Evenly moist" is a difficult concept to explain in precise terms. Essentially, never let potting medium dry, but don't keep it sopping wet. Instead, water, then watch to see how fast the medium is drying, and water again before it is dry. If you think the soil will be dry tomorrow, water today.

When to water

Many beginning orchid growers wonder whether there is a quick and easy method to know when to water, especially because orchids don't wilt like some houseplants. Unfortunately, no. However, some easy-to-observe clues can guide you. Clues work best when the plant comes from an orchid grower, less well from a mass merchant. One clue is the potting medium. Orchids that prefer even moisture are usually grown in fine-textured medium. Ones that prefer to dry between watering are usually grown in a coarse mix.

Foliage texture and pseudobulbs are also clues. Orchids with thin foliage and small or insignificant pseudobulbs need more water more frequently. Ones with thick, succulent leaves and strong pseudobulbs can stand drier conditions.

Pots and roots also may be clues. Savvy growers plant orchids that need to dry between watering in clay pots, and they grow orchids that prefer evenly moist soil in plastic pots. Because plastic is lightweight and easy to handle, many orchids are sold in plastic pots.

Orchids with thick or coarse roots prefer to dry between watering; fine-rooted orchids prefer to be evenly moist—both of which are generalizations. For example, moisture-loving orchids—such as vandas and phalaenopsis—have thick roots. Fine-rooted oncidiums, tolumnias, and others do not tolerate wet conditions; they must dry completely between waterings.

Mounted orchids

Mounted plants require slightly higher humidity—in the 60- to 70-percent range—than potted orchids to ensure that roots don't dry. Also, mounted orchids require more frequent watering than do potted ones. During warm months, daily watering may be needed.

During frost-free periods, grow mounted orchids outdoors where you won't be concerned about damaging furnishings as you water. In rainy areas, the plants may not require supplemental watering. In dry areas, however, daily watering is a must.

Be sure to provide a winter rest for mounted orchids that need one. Hold off watering and take them indoors if necessary to keep them out of the rain.

WATERING TERMINOLOGY

Watering is the most challenging orchid cultivation skill to master. The following recommendations are used to describe watering needs for orchids discussed in this book:

Term	Definition	Action
Keep continuously moist	Roots should never dry. These orchids come from high rainfall areas and lack the water storage capability to endure even brief dryness.	Keep roots wet but not soggy. Water as frequently as needed, as often as every other day if that is what it takes.
Keep evenly moist	Plants tolerate some drying; keep roots from drying completely between waterings.	Water once or twice a week.
Let dry between waterings	Let the growing media or mount become almost dry before watering. However, avoid letting either one become completely dry except when plants are dormant.	Water once a week or less.

▲ Inserting a skewer, chopstick, sharpened pencil, or your finger will help you determine whether the medium is dry enough to water. When many grains of organic matter stick to the skewer, as here, moisture is adequate for an orchid that does well when kept evenly moist. For orchids that require continuous moisture, it's time to water.

Testing for dryness

Insert your finger, a sharp pencil, or a skewer into the growing medium, taking care not to damage roots. If using a pencil, sharpen it beforehand; twist it a few times in the potting mix, then pull it out.

If the medium feels moist to the touch or the tip of the pencil feels damp or is dark in color, wait to water.

For orchids that need continuous moisture, water while the soil feels slightly moist or the pencil is not wet but many grains of organic matter stick to it.

For orchids that do best when their medium is kept evenly moist, water when the medium feels nearly dry or the pencil comes out dry with just a few grains of organic matter sticking to it.

HERE'S A TIP...
Orchid roots turn bright green whenever you wet them with water.

For orchids that should stay on the dry side, water when the medium feels dry or nothing sticks to the pencil.

Some media are difficult to work your finger or pencil into. Several other techniques will help you tell whether plants really need water.

● **Weight** Pick up the plant in its container. Wet plants will be heavier than dry plants. Pick up several plants of various sizes right after they have been watered; feel how heavy they are. Pick them up again at one- and two-day intervals after watering to get an idea how much weight they lose as they dry. With a little practice, you'll be able to tell how much water is left in a pot just by picking it up.

Water plants that prefer to be evenly moist when they are still a little heavy with moisture. Allow plants that prefer to dry between waterings to remain light for a day or so before watering them again.

● **Visible moisture** Look at the bottom of a pot to see whether any moisture shows through the drainage holes. Generally, if you can see moisture, the plant does not need water.

● **Root ball** Because a well-rooted orchid forms a tight root ball, you can remove the pot to examine the roots. Give the pot a couple of taps and the plant will slip right out. You'll be able to see the state of the mix and get a good idea of the health of the root system. Obviously, this isn't a technique to use with a freshly potted or poorly rooted plant.

● **Moisture meter** These instruments have several drawbacks. For example,

HERE'S A TIP...
Avoid extremes
Meeting orchid water needs is a matter of thoroughly wetting the potting medium with copious amounts of water and avoiding moisture extremes. Avoid swinging from watering too often to not often enough. Orchids react slowly to cultural changes and often do poorly with frequent changes. Remember that most cultivated orchids come from areas where temperatures and moisture are relatively constant all year. If you can emulate those conditions in your growing area, the plants will be much better for it.

because orchid mixes are coarse textured with large open pores, readings will be variable. If you research and work with a meter so it works reliably for you, then it can be useful; however, don't rely on it so much that observation skills become stale.

WATERING CLUES AND TIPS

When does an orchid need water? When doesn't it? Try these techniques to figure out when and how to water:

● Lift the pot to get an idea of how much moisture remains in the potting mix. If the pot seems heavy, it's probably plenty moist. If it feels light, it's time to water.

● Insert a sharpened pencil or a toothpick, skewer or chopstick 2 inches into the potting mix to check moisture. If the pencil or toothpick is damp or has bits of potting mix stuck to it when you pull it out, the plant is moist enough. If it is dry, water.

● If a plant is dry too long the potting mix may be difficult to rewet and water may run through the pot without soaking the mix. To rewet the medium, water once, wait 10 to 20 minutes, then water again. Repeat as needed until the pot gains noticeable weight, indicating the medium is moist.

● If actively growing plants are allowed to dry completely mineral salts will build up and injure the roots.

● Orchids with shriveled pseudobulbs or accordion-pleated leaves have root problems which may be caused by under- or overwatering.

● Older potting mix holds water longer than fresh mix. Water newly potted orchids more often than orchids that have been potted for some time.

● Frequent watering does not compensate for low humidity or lack of roots.

● Avoid splashing water from plant to plant—many diseases are waterborne and are easily transmitted this way.

● After potting, mounting, or staking an orchid, move the plant to a slightly shaded location and reduce or withhold water for a week or so until the roots have had time to heal.

▲ Damage from using softened water looks the same as salt damage and foliage damaged from overfertilization. Leaf tips and edges become dry and crispy because the salts in the water are pulling moisture from plant tissue.

How to water

Water orchids thoroughly, liberally pouring water through the potting medium. Make sure to moisten the entire root system; the coarse media used for orchids will not distribute water around the mix in the way that houseplant potting soil does.

Use room temperature water. Cold water shocks the roots and can damage the leaves of sensitive orchids such as phalaenopsis.

Continue watering even after water begins to exit the drainage holes. This thorough soaking flushes any accumulated salts out of the pot and provides the even moisture that encourages a large, healthy root system.

Indoors, the easiest way to thoroughly flush water through the medium is to take the plants to a sink or a tub. If you don't want to move the plants around, consider growing them on a large humidity tray, which will catch more overflow than a small houseplant saucer can. Never leave plants sitting in water for more than half an hour.

When grouping plants, organize them by pot size, kind of orchid, and type of container (terra-cotta, wood slat, or plastic) to ensure that all your orchids are watered on the appropriate schedule.

▲ Because orchids are potted in fast-draining growing mix, watering can be messy. If you have only a few orchids, put them in a sink and let water run through the planting mix.

Watering *(continued)*

Check water quality

Using good-quality water makes all the difference in the world to orchids. Species that originate in consistently moist environments are especially sensitive to poor-quality water and may show poor root growth when such water is used. Good-quality water enables plants to produce and maintain a healthy root system, one of the hallmarks of a well-grown orchid. Plants with a healthy root system better tolerate occasional drought when the medium dries out. There are two aspects to water quality: pH and dissolved solids.

● **pH** Orchids grow best in water that is neutral (pH 7) to slightly acid (pH 6) rather than alkaline (above pH 7). Good-quality water, then, has a neutral or near-neutral pH.

As a generalization, the best water quality is found in areas where rainfall is plentiful; the most problematic water exists in arid regions. Dry regions tend to have alkaline water; pH in moist ones is usually neutral to acid. In areas where acid rain is common, the pH may be too low for orchids.

● **Dissolved solids** Mineral salts, nutrients, and other elements in the water raise the pH, making it more alkaline, and many of these materials can damage plants.

Plants take up water from soil more quickly than they can absorb dissolved solids in the soil. In water with high concentrations of dissolved solids, the concentration of dissolved solids in the soil continually rises as soil dries. As concentrations rise, plants grow poorly, begin to lose roots, and display the same symptoms as orchids not getting enough water. They may have shriveled pseudobulbs and burned leaf tips, especially on soft-leafed plants such as zygopetalums, oncidiums, and sobralias.

Water in some regions naturally contains dissolved salts. For example, alkaline water contains about 200

▲ Although the outdoors often provides the ideal growing environment for orchids, you must pay greater attention to watering. The higher light levels, summer warmth, and breezes dry them quickly, especially in regions where humidity is low.

parts per million (ppm) of solids, often in the form of mineral salts. Most water treatment facilities remove many of the salts; untreated well water, however, will contain all that's common in the area.

Local water treatment facilities can provide information about pH and dissolved solids in the water. If you use well water, consider having the water tested before using it on your orchids. Ideally, dissolved solids content should be below 200 ppm and the pH should be neutral to slightly acid (pH 6 to 7).

Never use softened water on plants—orchids or other houseplants. The process for softening water generally uses sodium chloride (table salt) to displace the other ions in the water that make it hard. Using it on plants is like watering with sea water.

● **Bottom line** Watering is much easier when you have good-quality water. The healthy root system that it promotes will more efficiently take up water and fertilizer and serve as a water reservoir. Poor-quality water discourages vigorous root growth, hinders nutrient uptake, and forces you to

tread a fine line between overwatering and under-watering. If you water too often in an effort to avoid salt buildup in the soil, the mix becomes waterlogged, breaks down quickly, and kills the roots. If you water at the normal interval for your plants, salt concentrations rise, exacerbating root-growth and fertilizer problems.

Fixing poor quality

If the water is alkaline and high in dissolved solids, installing a reverse osmosis (RO) water system can be a welcome improvement. RO works by passing water through a differentially permeable membrane that prevents salts from passing through. Highly concentrated wastewater (discarded or used to water landscaping) stays on one side of the membrane and good-quality water comes out of the faucet.

Treating water by passing it through a reverse osmosis system can waste water. However, you may find that you can water less often because the RO water does not build up harmful salt deposits in the soil. And RO water is preferable to distilled water, which has some of the minerals that orchids—and people—require. RO water contains a low level of these minerals, and with RO water, you may not need to use as much fertilizer. Because

fertilizer is more easily used by plants when water is clean, a lower concentration of fertilizer can be applied with RO water than when using tap water.

Overwatering

Rather than the quantity of water given orchids at any one time, overwatering refers to how often you water them. At each watering it is important that your plants receive enough water to thoroughly soak the roots and flush accumulated salts from the potting media. However, if you water too often, the potting mix never dries, the velamen remains soaked so no air exchange occurs, and roots die. Instead of their normal plump, white appearance, roots become dark and mushy.

Overwatering also causes the medium to decompose prematurely. It will look more like potting soil than open, porous material. Without roots to take up water and no air spaces remaining, the mix becomes a soggy mess with poor growing qualities.

The most reliable early warning of overwatering is darkening and deterioration of surface roots. Other symptoms include shriveled pseudobulbs, wrinkled foliage, and a generally limp appearance. If you continue to overwater, the plant becomes unstable in its pot as its root system shrinks.

You can give new life to an overwatered orchid when you catch it early enough. Repot the plant in fresh orchid mix. First, cut away all dead roots, trimming them as close to the pseudobulb or plant crown as

▲ Underwatered orchids develop shriveled pseudobulbs. The leaves of thin-leafed species become pleated. Unlike overwatered plants, the roots stay plump and white.

▲ An overwatered orchid has a poor root system and shriveled pseudobulbs. The potting mix is dark and broken down from being kept too wet. The short brown roots are characteristic of root death. To save the plant, repot it in fresh mix in the smallest possible pot, reduce watering, and keep the plant in a humid, shady location.

possible. Take care to remove all old medium meshed into the roots. Spray the roots with a broad-spectrum fungicide. Place the plant in a clay pot that has a few pieces of plastic foam at the bottom but no potting medium, then water the plant as you normally would.

Evaporation from the pot will create a humid environment around the roots. When new root tips grow ½ inch long, repot the orchid in fresh potting medium.

Underwatering

Underwatering can be as problematic as overwatering, but it is a less common problem. It occurs most often when orchids grow outdoors—drying winds and inattentiveness add up.

Underwatering concentrates dissolved solids around the roots, which raises the pH and hinders root growth and nutrient absorption. Symptoms such as leaf tip burn develop.

The good news is that underwatered orchids bounce back more quickly than overwatered ones. Underwatering is much less

FACTORS AFFECTING WATERING

MORE WATER
Environment:
   Bright light
   High temperatures
   Low humidity
   Windy days, if outdoors
Plant:
   Thin leaves
   Small or no pseudobulb
   In small pot
   On a mount or in a basket

LESS WATER
Environment:
   Low light
   Low temperatures
   High humidity
   Little air movement
Plant:
   Thick leaves
   Good size pseudobulbs
   In plastic pot

likely to kill roots or plants than overwatering. In fact, roots stay plump and white.

The danger of underwatering is that once the potting medium becomes thoroughly dry, it is difficult to rewet. Once dry, you must make a special effort to get it to hold water again.

Thoroughly water a completely dry plant once, then let it rest for half an hour or so and water again. Pick up the pot; if it is still light, repeat the process as many times as necessary until you feel a difference in the weight of the pot. Each time the medium will retain a little more moisture during the rest break. Eventually, it will regain its normal water-retentive capacity.

Another rewetting method is to submerge the pot in a sink or bucket of water and let it stand in the water until the potting mix retains moisture. Use the water in the sink or bucket only once, discarding it between plants and cleaning the sink or bucket to prevent the spread of waterborne diseases among plants.

Fertilizing

As you do when watering orchids, you want to mimic the fertility regime that your orchids adapted to in their native habitats as closely as possible. In nature, the most common orchids, epiphytes, receive a constant supply of nutrients in the form of a mild nutrient soup that washes over their exposed roots. This soup contains elements, such as bird droppings and materials deposited by the wind, picked up by water as it washes through the tree canopy. Terrestrial orchids, however, obtain nutrients from organic matter in soil.

The potting media that orchids grow in do not hold nutrients in the way that potting soil for houseplants does. Water flows through the coarse-textured orchid media, which lack small pores to hold onto applied fertilizer. For that reason, it's important to fertilize regularly with a high-quality balanced fertilizer. Regularly, however, is up for debate.

Several schools of thought

There has been little university research into nutrient needs of orchids, and many recommendations for fertilizing orchids are based on advice passed down over the years rather than solid evidence. How often you should feed your plants and which strength to use are where recommendations vary the most.

Some growers advise using the constant-feed method—fertilizing "weakly weekly." With this method, apply one-fourth to one-half the labeled rate of fertilizer once a week for three weeks. The fourth week, flush the medium with plain water to rinse out any built-up soluble salts (dissolved solids). Arguments for this regimen hold that orchids require a constant mild fertilizer solution to mimic the dilute nutrient solution washing over the roots in nature.

Some orchid growers recommend fertilizing once a week with a full-strength solution. With this strategy, plants need to have soluble salts flushed from the growing medium more often. Yet others say to fertilize once a month with a full-strength solution.

Which is right? Recent studies have found that under ideal conditions, some orchids grow best with weekly full-strength feedings. Ideal conditions, however, are key to this recommendation. What actually works depends on the orchid, the growing conditions, and how you like to do things. In typical home conditions or during the winter, feeding once a week may be too much because the plants grow more slowly in the lower light, dry air, and cooler temperatures.

What to use

The best fertilizer for orchids contains nitrogen, phosphorus, and potassium in a 1:1:1 or a 3:1:1 ratio. Which one you use depends on the potting medium in which the orchids grow. Use the 1:1:1 ratio for orchids that are growing in any medium except bark. Use the 3:1:1 ratio for orchids growing in bark, which requires higher amounts of nitrogen because naturally occurring microorganisms break down the bark and compete with plants for the nitrogen. Extra nitrogen ensures that the orchids aren't short-changed.

Check the fertilizer label to find the ratio of the nutrients. The amounts of nitrogen, phosphorus, and potassium are prominently listed as three large numbers, which represent the ratio of those nutrients in the fertilizer. For nutrients in a 1:1:1 ratio, buy a 20-20-20, 10-10-10, or 5-5-5 fertilizer; for a 3:1:1 ratio, choose 30-10-10 or 15-5-5.

As you read the label, look for other nutrients in the fertilizer. Orchids require several minor nutrients, including calcium, magnesium, and iron. Also check the source of the nitrogen in the fertilizer. Ammoniacal or nitrate sources are more expensive than urea, but urea releases its nutrients slowly unless temperatures are warmer than 60°F when it may be washed from the pot before the plant can use it.

Liquid fertilizers or soluble fertilizers mixed with water are easy to use. Granular slow-release fertilizers feed plants for three to four months with one application. The amount of nutrients they release, however, may be too much for some orchids. Use these with heavy feeders, such as cymbidiums.

Always use a fertilizer from reputable, well-known suppliers for the most reliable quality of ingredients. As with other growing supplies, the extra cost of a name-brand, high-quality fertilizer is quickly repaid by quality of plant growth.

Although it is not necessary to buy a product specifically formulated for orchids, select a product that provides specific directions and a feeding rate for orchids.

Overfertilization

It is better to underfertilize than to overfeed orchids.

▲ Liquid and soluble plant foods are easy and convient to use. Feed orchids once a week, mixing the fertilizer at one-quarter, one-half or the full label rate. If using the full-strength rate, be sure to water well so as to flush mineral salts from the media. Cut back on feeding during dormant periods.

▲ Well-fertilized orchids have good foliage color, strong stems, and grow at a consistent rate (right). Orchids in need of nutrients grow slowly and bloom poorly (left). Overfertilized orchids turn brown at their leaf tips and along their edges.

▲ Crusty white deposits on pots are a sign that you are overfertilizing, the water contains excess minerals, or that you are not watering thoroughly enough to wash the salts out of the medium.

HERE'S A TIP...

Watering & fertilizing
If an orchid is showing a reduced need for water, it probably needs less fertilizer as well.

accumulating in the potting mix. Deposits often result from using water that contains high concentrations of dissolved solids.

Overfertilizing can exacerbate the problem, especially if the amount of water poured over the roots is too little to flow from drainage holes.

When mineral deposits are apparent, scrub them off the pot, then thoroughly flush the soil with water. Take care to thoroughly water according to the regular schedule, allowing excess water to flow out of the pot.

If your water is alkaline or contains dissolved solids, use water that has been run through a reverse osmosis system (see page 54). Applying a fertilizer with an acidic reaction, such as Miracid, can also help prevent fertilizer salt buildup.

HERE'S A TIP...

Read the label!
Always follow label directions that accompany any fertilizer product. If you follow the "weakly weekly" path, cut the application rate printed on the label. Remember that 20-20-20 is more concentrated than 10-10-10, which is more concentrated than 5-5-5. Whenever switching to a different fertilizer product, always follow the new application recommendations rather than going by memory of what you used with the previous product.

Underfertilizing simply slows them down. Overfertilizing can damage plants, causing leaves to become dark green and soft, and making plants more susceptible to disease and less likely to bloom.

Overfertilization often occurs when growers are sloppy in measuring or believe that a little more will help their plants. More is not better. When labels list one tablespoon or one teaspoon, use a level measure, not a heaping one.

Overfertilization is a problem when plants are fertilized more frequently than they require—such as orchids grown in cooler temperatures or less light than ideal. In such conditions, plants grow more slowly and therefore require a lower level of nutrients. When fertilized as if growing in optimal conditions, orchids may have weak growth.

When growing plants in less than ideal conditions, always reduce the fertilizer, either the concentration (from full to half strength) or the frequency of feeding (from every week to every other week or once a month or less). Many orchids need little or no fertilizer during winter when light is reduced and temperatures low.

Some orchids will not bloom if given too much nitrogen at the wrong time of year. Cymbidiums, for example, bloom poorly or not at all if given high-nitrogen fertilizer once their growths are mature enough for flower initiation (usually around August and September).

Many types of seasonally growing dendrobiums are also particular about nitrogen once their growths are mature. For example, *Den. nobile* and others from monsoonal regions where moisture, and thus growth, are restricted to a defined season will not bloom if fed while they are resting.

Water and fertilize these types of orchids heavily, beginning as soon as you see new growth. Begin to taper off feeding as the growth reaches maturity in late summer. Stop fertilizing before the orchid is fully mature so any residual nitrogen is flushed out of the soil by thorough watering before blooming begins.

Mineral deposits

Mineral deposits—crusty white areas on pots and plants—are symptoms of salts

▲ Look for a fertilizer in which the nitrogen, phosphorus, and potassium content is in a 3:1:1 ratio if your orchids are planted in fir bark. You can find the ratio on the product's label under guaranteed analysis, along with information about the other nutrients provided.

Growing orchids in containers

Choosing what to use for pots and potting media once you get the plants home may be confusing, especially considering the types of media and pots that commercial growers use as well as the variety of media and styles of pots that are on the market.

Commercial growers choose potting media and container materials and sizes based on how well they work in mass plant production. Mass growers use small pots to avoid stagnant conditions around roots and to pack more plants onto a bench. They choose a particular potting medium to reduce watering and, in turn, labor costs. And they select plastic pots over terra-cotta, slatted baskets, and mounts for easier shipping at less cost.

Florists often dress up mass-produced orchids before selling them, taking them out of the utilitarian pots, wrapping the roots with sphagnum moss, and putting plants in decorative pots.

The pots and potting media used by commercial growers and florists are fine for growing orchids, but they're not necessarily the best examples to follow for home growing. As with all aspects of orchid culture, understanding how the plants grow in nature will help you make good choices in pots and potting media for your orchids.

In their native habitats, few orchids grow in or on the ground or have their roots covered with soil. Instead, they grow on trees in open conditions where roots are subject to alternate drying and wetting cycles. The more closely their growing conditions are duplicated, the better your orchids will do.

Certain types of containers, such as mounts and baskets, mimic these natural conditions better than others. However, it's your choice of potting medium that ensures the airy conditions that most orchids prefer.

▲ Container choices range from utilitarian plastic and terra-cotta, to decorative containers with cutouts on the sides to allow air circulation, to open, slatted or wire baskets, and tree fern fiber pots, as well as mounts of any size, shape, and material.

Choosing containers

The type of pot that is best for duplicating native growing conditions depends on growing space and habits, available resources, and, to a certain extent, the orchid's preferences.

● **Clay vs. plastic** Clay pots are decorative, relatively inexpensive, porous, heavy, and difficult to sanitize for reuse. Plastic is lightweight, utilitarian, inexpensive, nonporous, and easy to clean. Some orchids grow better in clay, others in plastic. Experiment to find the best choice for your orchids. However, the following guidelines can help.

Your practices If you have a tendency to overwater, clay pots are a good choice because their porous nature allows the potting mix to dry quickly. And as long as the water quality is good, you won't have to worry about mineral deposits building up on the sides of the pot.

If you tend not to water on a regular schedule or have poor-quality water, choose plastic pots. In nonporous pots, the potting mix stays moister longer and dissolved salts won't build up on the outside.

Native habitat Orchids native to high-rainfall areas may do better in plastic; the soil stays moist in plastic because water doesn't evaporate through it. Plastic pots are also light and easy to move to the sink for watering.

Even though plastic holds moisture, if your home is unusually dry you may still need to water nearly as often as plants in clay pots.

Outside vs. inside Outdoors in a high-rainfall climate, clay pots work well. They dry quickly after rains and are heavy enough to remain upright in strong winds. Orchids that originate in seasonally dry areas and require a yearly dormant period may grow better in clay, indoors or out.

Drainage Look for plastic and clay pots with multiple drainage holes, which means the bottom of the pot can dry quickly and increase aeration through the container.

Size and shape Both clay and plastic pots are available

Fit the pot to the roots
Resist the urge to put a plant in a larger pot than necessary in the hope that it will grow into the pot—it won't. It will be detrimental to the orchid. Choose pot size based on root size, not foliage size.

in traditional shapes and sizes: styles in which the pot is taller than it is wide, and in shallow pan or "azalea" styles that are wider than tall. Many growers prefer pan-style pots because orchid roots generally grow out horizontally instead of downward. Broad shallow pots create more stability even when filled with top-heavy orchids.

Some terrestrial and hemiepiphytic orchids, including cymbidiums (especially oriental types related to *Cym. ensifolium*), phaius, and paphiopedilums, grow better in traditional-style containers because their roots grow deeper. The pots also help to retain moisture.
● **Open baskets** Wire or wood-slat baskets are excellent for orchids that grow large. The center of a large plant can rot because it is not actively rooting and the medium under the center becomes stagnant. Baskets provide excellent drainage and root aeration, which help mitigate the problem.

Baskets are also a good choice for orchids with cascading or pendulous foliage or flowers. Elevating them maximizes growing space and shows off the flowers at eye level.

Slatted wood baskets, often imported from Southeast Asia or the Philippines, are generally reasonably priced. If you live where humidity is naturally high, you can grow vandaceous orchids in slatted baskets without potting mix, relying on the limited water retention of the basket along with the substantial root mass to sustain the plant. Some growers hang vandaceous orchids from wires in a greenhouse with nothing around the roots. With high humidity (above

POT, MOUNT, OR BASKET?

Best for mounting
● Orchids that climb with each growth on the rhizome higher than the preceding growth
● Orchids in which the growths are widely spaced on a rhizome, so they are hard to pot
● Orchids adapted to dry habitats
● Orchids that have pronounced pseudobulbs; thick, heavy leaves; and large, heavy roots that do not branch
● Deciduous orchids that require a dormant period

Best for growing in pots
● Orchids with soft foliage and small or no pseudobulbs
● Orchids with fine roots that branch freely
● Orchids with a horizontal growth habit and closely spaced growths
● Orchids with a clumping, freely branching habit
● Orchids that need constant moisture

Best for clay pots
● Orchids with pronounced pseudobulbs; thick, heavy leaves; and roots that tolerate periodic drying
● Tall or top-heavy orchids with small root systems
● Large orchids

Best for plastic pots
● Orchids with soft foliage and small or no pseudobulbs
● Orchids that have a fine, heavily branching root system
● Small orchids that need moisture

Best for growing in slatted baskets
● Heavy-rooted monopodials that require fast drainage and excellent air circulation

70 percent), frequent irrigation, and close attention, some orchids thrive in those conditions.

Wire baskets lined with sphagnum moss or a similar material are a good choice for orchids such as stanhopea (whose flowering stems hang straight down from the pseudobulbs) and for ones such as gongora (with flower spikes that grow straight out from the base of the pseudobulbs then turn down).
● **Decorative containers** As with houseplants, orchids can grow in nearly any container: glazed or unglazed ceramic pots, wood tubs, pots with built-in saucers, or any other material that will hold soil and not fall apart when it is wet. Consider several factors when selecting nontraditional containers. Most important, look for drainage holes. If necessary, drill holes in the container. Use the appropriate bit for the material, for example, a masonry bit for ceramic pots. Or find a way to raise the plant off the bottom of the container to prevent roots from standing in water. A decorative container can be used as a cachepot, removing the plant from the cachepot for watering. Don't allow orchids to stand in water in cachepots or drainage saucers; empty the water when the water has drained.

Sizing pot to plant

Choosing the proper size pot for a plant, whether sympodial or monopodial, is one of the finer points of orchid growing. The plant will quickly outgrow a too-small pot and will probably need watering more frequently than is practical. In a too-large container, the medium will remain wet, becoming sodden and breaking down more rapidly than it ordinarily would.

Size the pot for the root mass, not the foliage. For a sympodial orchid, take into account the amount of growth the plant will make

▲ Size the pot to the size of the root ball, not the plant top. In sizing the container, it is important to allow room for two years of growth, which depends on the size of the orchid and the distance between pseudobulbs on the rhizome.

▲ Mounting materials should have numerous crevices in which the roots can grow under and through to make a tight attachment to the mount.

but some originate in such humid areas that managing their moisture is difficult. The best choices for growing on mounts are orchids with well-developed pseudobulbs and strong roots.

Some orchids take to mounting better than others, for example, ones that have a pendulous habit, such as stanhopeas and gongoras. Species that require a dry period do well mounted. Mounts allow for rapid drying and make it easy to completely withdraw water.

Good orchid mounts resist rot, have nooks and crannies for roots to follow and attach to, and can hold some water. Commonly used materials are cork, oak bark, tree-fern slabs, manzanita branches,

and other hard, rot-resistant woods. Driftwood is another possibility, but if you collect it from the seashore, be sure to rinse off any salt. Leave the pieces outdoors for a couple of years to let the rain leach salt from within the wood.

You can also mount orchids on trees in frost-free areas. Avoid trees with shedding bark that could slough off the orchid.

during the time it will be in the pot, typically two years. Look at the size of the bulbs. When the oldest bulb is placed against one side of the pot, there should be room for the orchid to grow two new bulbs between the existing lead bulb and the other side of the pot.

Some orchids, such as phaius, should be slightly overpotted—in a larger pot than their roots seem to require—to allow for rapid growth. Others, such as miltoniopsis and dendrobium, do best when slightly underpotted in proportionately small pots.

Pot a monopodial orchid in the smallest pot that will hold its root mass easily. If you have trouble deciding between two sizes of pots, pick the smaller one.

Terrestrial orchids

In general, terrestrial orchids can be grown in the same types of soil and potting media as epiphytes because most are hemiepiphytes. In other words, they live on the ground rather than in it. They are accustomed to living in the light and airy forest duff composed of leaf litter and other organic matter in

varying degrees of decomposition. The roots of terrestrial hemiepiphytes spread out through the top layer of humus and are often thick and succulent to serve as water storage organs.

Semiterrestrials generally require larger pots than epiphytic orchids the same size because they have robust root systems. Finely textured potting medium provides growing conditions similar to the forest duff, but avoid houseplant potting soil.

You can grow them in clay pots, however, plastic is more practical for its lighter weight and better water retention, which allows the plants their preferred even moisture.

Mounts

Mounting is an excellent way to stretch your growing area, because the orchids don't occupy bench space but are hung from the ceiling or from vertical supports such as fences. Like baskets, mounts provide growing conditions that nearly match native environments. Mounted orchids are especially natural looking and effective in display.

Nearly any epiphytic orchid will grow on a mount,

▲ Slatted baskets are excellent for growing orchids needing very good drainage, such as large plants like this *Gongora unicolor,* and orchids with cascading flowers.

Choosing the best potting medium

Selecting the best medium depends on your watering preferences, local growing conditions, and what is available in your community. If you like to water (maybe more than orchids prefer) or if you live in a naturally humid area, choose a fast-draining medium such as tree-fern fiber or aggregates and other inert materials. Because water moves through them so quickly, they protect plants from overwatering and last well under moist conditions, so you don't need to repot often.

If you live in a dry area or water less often than your orchids desire, you may have better success with fir bark-based media. These are the most widely available potting media for orchids, and nearly all growers have success with them. In addition, most orchid-growing advice is based on the use of fir bark.

One of the best sources for discovering what works well in your area is a local orchid society, where you can find a wealth of information from people who are happy to share their experiences.

About growing media

The main function of a growing, or potting, medium is to support the plant and to supply water and nutrients. All widely used orchid media do this as well as share certain characteristics: They are inexpensive, readily available, and easy to use, and they provide the right root conditions for the plants and last for at least 18 months.

Orchid media should be both moisture retentive and well drained and airy. Otherwise, plant roots may rot. (Many orchids should be grown on mounts of cork, tree fern, or similar material, to more closely replicate their natural habit and to allow their roots the air they need.)

Although all orchid growing media share these characteristics, not every medium is appropriate for every situation. Commercial growers especially have different requirements for the media they use than do home growers. When you take home a new orchid, you may have trouble simply because of the potting medium in which it is grown.

Fir bark

Fir bark is the most widely used medium. It lasts 12 to 18 months before breaking down and is available in three grades to meet the needs of different orchid species.

Fine-grade fir bark (⅛ to ¼ inch) is suitable for terrestrial and fine-rooted orchids such as some oncidiums. Medium-grade fir bark (⅜ to ⅝ inch) is good for

Coarse fir bark

Medium fir bark

Fine fir bark

most epiphytic orchids, including cattleyas and phalaenopsis. The coarse grade (¾ to 1 inch) is best for vandas and other orchids requiring quick drainage.

Fresh fir bark is similar to peat moss in that it is difficult to wet. Some growers soak the bark for a day or two before using it. This ensures that the bark is thoroughly wet, and it eliminates dust.

The original source for fir bark was lumber mills that processed old-growth douglas fir. Today, it comes from farmed trees. The bark of farmed trees is not as high in quality as that of the old-growth trees.

Because fir bark is less readily available now than in the past, it is often used as a major component of potting mixes rather than on its own.

Soilless mixes

Miracle-Gro Orchid Potting Mix

All potting mixes on the market are soilless. Originally developed for the greenhouse industry, the mixes make it easy to manage watering and fertilizing while ensuring adequate air circulation around the roots. Their light weight also reduces shipping costs for growers as well as makes it easier for gardeners to move their plants around their gardens and homes.

Soilless mixes are usually made from peat moss or coconut husk fiber, which hold water and nutrients, mixed with materials such as perlite to lighten the mix and ensure that water drains through the medium. Avoid planting orchids in soilless mixes intended for houseplants; they hold too much water for orchids and too little air. Instead, look for one labeled specifically for orchids; it will contain larger chunks of bark or other materials.

You may find that watering is more difficult to gauge in soilless mixes, since they hold more moisture than other media. If you have a tendency to underwater, that may be a good point. But if you tend to overwater and happen to buy plants growing in a soilless medium, repot them into a faster-draining medium.

Sphagnum moss

Also sold as long-fiber sphagnum, this material is a good medium for small orchids such as pleurothallis, orchids in small pots, and seedling orchids. Many commercial growers in Hawaii and elsewhere pot in sphagnum.

Sphagnum moss is sold dry or as living moss. It holds lots of water and dries slowly. When it dries completely, it is difficult to rewet without thoroughly soaking it. Alkaline water kills living moss and makes it toxic to the plant.

A lightweight medium, sphagnum does not have the substance to support heavy plants. Learning to pot with sphagnum moss can take some time. It is, however, ideal for rescuing orchids that have lost their roots. Its natural antibiotic properties and outstanding water

Sphagnum moss

retention will help the plant survive while new roots grow.

Aggregates and other inert materials

Increasingly, fir bark is being replaced with aggregates and other inert manufactured materials, such as rock wool, perlite, and expanded clay pellets (also called aliflor) and by mined substances, including pumice, volcanic rock, and diatomaceous earth. Commercial growers rarely use these materials, because of their weight.

These materials are fast draining, long lasting and well suited to areas with high humidity and tropical rains. Most are heavy, except perlite and volcanic rock.

Perlite is commonly added to soilless media, where its

Perlite

Rock wool

Expanded clay pellets

size aids drainage and aeration; it is rarely used alone. Expanded clay comes in several sizes; it is usually added to mixes rather than used alone, but it is a favorite with Florida growers for their outdoor orchids. Rock wool is common in Europe but rarely used in North America.

Pumice is sometimes substituted for perlite. In Hawaii, easily obtained volcanic rock is a favorite choice. Diatomaceous earth, or diatomite, is used often on the West Coast in mixes.

Because all of these materials provide excellent drainage, you must increase your watering frequency when using them. All are relatively heavy so they are good for orchids growing outdoors. Keep an eye on the medium's pH if the orchid is growing in any of these materials alone.

Tree-fern fiber

This fiber is harvested from the processed trunks (and sometimes roots) of giant tropical tree ferns. It is one of the best and longest-lasting orchid media. It provides excellent drainage—a plus in humid rainy regions—and ideal growing conditions for many orchids.

It is sold in various forms: short wiry pieces, finely ground and coarse particles, plaques for mounting, and baskets. Tree-fern fiber is also used as a component of orchid potting mixes.

Considered an endangered species, it is becoming increasingly expensive because supplies are dwindling (it is allowed to be exported with proper documentation). For that reason, few commercial growers use tree-fern fiber.

A major disadvantage of tree-fern fiber is that it becomes toxic as it ages, even though aged fiber looks no different from new fiber. Plants suddenly decline for no apparent reason. The fiber is also difficult to separate from roots when repotting.

Loose tree-fern fiber

Tree-fern fiber mounts and pots

Adjust your watering practices to match the fast drainage of tree-fern fiber. Wear gloves when working with it to avoid cutting your hands.

Coconut husk fiber and chips

Coconut husk fiber

Coconut husk chips

The byproducts of the coconut processing industry are excellent for orchid

growing. In addition, the plants from which they come renew themselves quickly. Be sure of your source, however. Fiber and chips must be processed properly because contamination from ocean salt spray makes coconut byproducts useless for growing any kind of plant.

Coconut fiber, which is also called coir, is substituted for peat moss in orchid-growing mixes. Except for a few large fibers, it is nearly indistinguishable from peat. Commercial growers prefer coconut fiber for its cost. Home growers often find it hard to manage because its properties are similar to those of potting soil.

Coconut husk chips offer many of the same properties as fir bark and are a fine substitute. The chips are long-lasting in humid areas.

Osmunda fiber

Osmunda fiber

For much of the history of American orchid growing, osmunda fiber was the only medium available. Derived from the roots of ferns in the *Osmunda* genus, it is a long-lasting medium.

Supplies of osmunda fiber declined in the late 1940s, and growers switched to fir bark. However many orchid specialists still prefer it. It is a good choice in situations where its long life is an advantage, such as in baskets.

The fiber is sold in bales or bags containing clumps of fern roots. These you cut to size for potting. When only small amounts are needed, shred it by hand. Both tasks require skill and strength.

Potting and repotting

As a general rule, orchids need to be repotted every two years when the medium breaks down or plants outgrow their container. It's important to repot them at the right time of year when their roots are actively growing.

Repotting at the wrong time of year has caused many orchids to fail. Because no matter how carefully you work as you repot, turning the plant out of its pot and removing old medium damages roots. Most of the existing roots die. If you are doing this when roots are not already growing, no new roots will form. Without new roots to replace the damaged ones, the plant uses up its nutrient reserves and begins to wither.

An orchid potted at the right time—when you see green ends forming on the tips of roots—will continue growing as if nothing had happened. Some orchids, such as many phalaenopsis, form new roots at any time of year. Most orchids, however, have a rooting season and do not begin to develop new roots until new growth is at least partially developed. For example, cattleyas that bloom from winter into spring develop roots in spring and early summer, just after flowering finishes. Although phalaenopsis form new roots all year, new root growth slows when flowers initiate.

Avoid repotting when new growth is first emerging. New roots emerge some time after the new growth and handling the plants at this time can damage the new growth.

Plan to repot most orchids in spring after new growth is partially developed. At this time, expect new roots to form on most orchids. If you can't repot in spring, the next best time is June, when days are longest. The sooner you repot after plants begin growing new roots, the longer they have to settle in before the active growing season is over and the more successful you will be.

As you become familiar with your orchids, you will learn at which point they initiate roots and the plants' stage of growth when they do so. Then you can schedule repotting with accuracy. Experienced growers date the plant tag so they know when to repot again.

There are times you should repot even though the orchid is not growing new roots; for example, if the plant is knocked out of its pot, if the plant's roots have died, or in any other emergency situation. When you repot at a less than optimal time, keep the plant in a shady location; provide a humid atmosphere around the roots, but also keep the plant on the dry side until new roots begin to form. The combination of dry roots, humid atmosphere, and shade will often spur new root growth.

Reasons to repot

Many orchid hobbyists like to repot their orchid as soon as they take it home so the plant is growing in a potting medium with which they are familiar. Several other factors can influence whether you repot before the two-year general guideline is up.

● **Decomposed media**
All potting media eventually break down. Broken-down medium loses its drainage capabilities and becomes sour, often with a drastically changed pH. This occurs every 18 to 24 months with fir bark-based media. If you have sized your plant appropriately, it will have outgrown the pot by that time anyway.

Even long-lasting potting media, such as osmunda and sphagnum, will show signs of decay over time.

The first time you successfully shift an orchid from spent medium to fresh, you will be astounded at the difference. Not only will the plant look better when it is clean, but also it will seem to have new energy for a fresh growth spurt.

● **Type of orchid**
Paphiopedilums in particular benefit from fresh media and often benefit when repotted yearly. Others require frequent potting because their special needs speed the breakdown of the medium. For example, miltoniopsis grow best when planted in small pots and watered frequently. The frequent watering quickly breaks down the media.

● **Plant too large for pot**
Orchids eventually outgrow their pots, whether they are upright monopodials, such as vandas, or spreading sympodials like cattleyas. Even if the medium is intact, when plant roots show, it needs a bigger pot.

HERE'S A TIP...
If you have to repot at other than an optimal time, keep the plant slightly dry and in a shady, humid location until new root growth appears.

BUYER BEWARE

Commercial orchid growers tend to pot their orchids in mixes that produce very fast growth in the near-optimal conditions they can provide. Often these mixes are not suitable for long-term use. Some growers repot plants before selling them to improve aesthetics; others ship as is. In some cases, the plant may have been in the pot long enough for the mix to break down. Because of this, it's important to investigate the condition of the potting mix thoroughly before buying to determine which potting material was used and its condition.

Check to see whether a plant is established or loose in its pot. If loose, it most likely has been recently repotted, and the roots haven't filled the container. If it is well established, slip the plant out of its pot to look at the mix. If the mix is composed of fine particles, it has begun to break down and you will want to repot the plant soon after taking it home. In most cases, if a plant is in bloom when you buy it, you can wait until it finishes blooming to repot. Only rarely must flowers be sacrificed to save a plant.

You may find that the mix is waterlogged or dried out because of improper watering by store employees. Again, you may need to repot, or you may just need to ease the plant back into a regular watering routine.

If you are fortunate to have an orchid nursery in your community, you will probably not have to worry about these problems. The grower will have tended the plants for some time and be familiar with their requirements. You can ask about the status of any particular plant and what sort of care it will need in your growing area.

Tips for each type of orchid

Monopodial A monopodial orchid may simply need more room for its roots or it may have grown too tall, becoming top heavy and leafless on lower stems. If the main problem is with the root ball, shift the plant to a container a size or two larger and fill in with fresh mix.

Seldom do you need to repot a monopodial orchid because it is too tall; it's not uncommon for a vanda or dendrobium to grow 6 feet tall while in a 6-inch pot.

Only when the plant becomes leggy, losing its lower leaves, is repotting indicated. Generally, leggy monopodial orchids will benefit from being set lower in the pot. To do this, you must remove enough of the old mix to get to the bottom of the stem. Usually but not always, there is a section of rootless stem that can be removed, allowing you to set the plant lower in the pot.

Ideally, place the plant low enough in the container that

Potting and repotting *(continued)*

▲ Cramped conditions in which the orchid has no room to expand any further in the pot means the plant is ready to be repotted into a larger container.

▲ When the individual bark chunks in a potting medium break down into small chips and fine particles, it is no longer providing the best conditions for orchid growth. This is a good indication that you need to repot.

▲ A pot-bound orchid obviously needs to be moved to a new container, as do ones that are cramped in their pots. Less obvious is the situation in which roots are growing out of the pot. You will have difficulty removing the roots from the side of the container without ripping them off. Soaking the pot first can help.

POTTING TIPS

Always use the highest-quality ingredients available, even if they are more costly, because their better growing characteristics and longer life mean healthier plants and less need for repotting.

● Even the best medium will require some cleaning. Soak fir bark in water before using it to wet the material thoroughly and remove any fine particles or dust, which will settle to the bottom of the sink or bucket.

● Always sterilize your cutting tools between each plant. Holding a tool over an open flame is the most reliable method. Use a self-igniting, push-button propane torch.

● Do not use plastic "peanuts" (packing material) in the bottom of pots for drainage. Many of these materials are made of a starchy substance that dissolves in water.

● Label your plants with the date you potted them, to help you remember when to repot.

● Houseplant potting soil is not suitable for most orchids (jewel orchids and some terrestrials are the only exceptions).

● Most orchids that need to be divided will almost do it themselves, breaking apart at natural separations.

● Remove older, leafless bulbs with a simple twisting motion. Avoid cutting if you can.

● Newly repotted plants, especially those with poor roots, need a humid atmosphere while they are reestablishing. A simple trick is to bend a wire coat hanger into a loop large enough to form a frame over the plant, then place a clear lightweight plastic bag over the makeshift frame. Leave the bag open at the bottom for air circulation and keep the plant out of direct sun.

HERE'S A TIP...

Check orientation

After cleaning the roots, hold the orchid so its growths are straight up and down. If growths appear to stair-step up the rhizome, with each subsequent growth a little higher than the previous one, the orchid has a natural desire to climb a tree. Pot the plant so its growths are at an angle in the pot to ensure that the rhizome is level on the potting media. Otherwise, some of the rhizome and pseudobulbs will be buried while others will be above the medium.

TOOLS & MATERIALS

You'll need these materials whenever potting, repotting, or mounting orchids.

● **Sterilizing tools:** butane or propane torch or single-edge razor blades (use one for each plant)

● **Cutting tools:** scissors for thin plant material, bypass pruning shears for thicker plant material; pliers for cutting and bending wire

● **Cleaning tools:** toothbrush for scrubbing plant parts

● **Stakes:** bamboo, wire, or other material, or braided bell wire to make your own; rhizome clips

● **Ties:** twist-ties, hook-and-loop garden tape, raffia, or waxed florist's tape

● **Plant labels and marker**

when the pot is filled, the level of the medium just touches the bottom leaves. This allows roots that are emerging from the stem to immediately touch the medium and grow into it.

You may be tempted to put the orchid in a larger pot that allows you to set the plant lower so that the new roots will be close enough to the medium. However, you still must size the pot to the root ball. The pot should be only a little larger than the roots. Give roots enough room that they fit comfortably with no more than 1 inch of space between them and the pot on all sides.

Sympodial Some sympodial orchids, such as the soft-leaved members of the zygopetalum group, have such short rhizomes that there is no room between individual growths. Handle these as you would a monopodial. Once the plants have filled their pots, shift them into a larger container or divide the plants into sections of three to five growths each. Usually each division will be about the same size and require the same size container as the original plant occupied.

Sympodials with longer rhizomes, such as cattleyas, laelias, and brassias, may have an inch or more between bulbs. These seem to march across the pot and grow right over the edge. You can repot the entire plant into a container that works with the size of the root ball and provides room for two years' growth. Or you can divide the plant into sections containing at least three pseudobulbs; this size ensures a flowering plant. Choose a container size that will fit the roots of the divisions and allow for two years' growth.

You may consider using a shallow pan-type pot that is wider than it is tall to accommodate the plant without having too much potting mix underneath the roots. The size of the roots and the top growth will match the container.

Fill the container with potting mix to the level of the rhizome, which should always be set level, even if growths lean. If you instead orient the growths so that they are upright, the rhizomes may climb out of the pot rather than grow into the soil.

After repotting, you may need to secure the rhizome or pseudobulb of sympodial orchids. Use a rhizome clip, which fits over the rim of a pot and stretches from one side of the pot to the next. Or insert a couple of stakes on each side of the plant to hold it steady.

Potting step-by-step

1. Soak the medium up to 24 hours before potting so that it packs uniformly and doesn't wick moisture from plant roots when they are potted. Longer soaking may speed decomposition of the media. Soak the orchid in a separate container of water so roots become more pliable.

2. Remove the orchid from its pot and clean as much of the old mix from the roots as possible. Massaging the roots may help loosen their hold on the old medium; however, some roots will have grown through the pieces.

3. Cut off dead, damaged, and rotted roots and growths as needed. Sterilize tools between each cut.

4. Select a pot for the plant by checking the root size of the orchid against the size of the new container. Roots should fit comfortably without being jammed in or swimming in the space.

Ensure 1 inch on all sides around the roots of monopodial orchid. Set a sympodial orchid at the edge of the container; there should be room across the pot for two years of growth—based on the size of pseudobulbs and the distance between them. For a medium-size orchid that's about 2 to 3 inches of space.

5. Put enough bark in the bottom of the container to raise the plant to the proper level. For a sympodial orchid, the rhizome will be about 1 inch below the rim of the pot; a monopodial orchid is at the right level when the bottom set of leaves touches the potting media.

6. For a sympodial orchid, place the back bulb or oldest portion of the plant against the edge of the container.

For a monopodial, set the plant in the center of the pot.

7. Add potting medium around roots, holding the plant with one hand while

Potting and repotting *(continued)*

adding mix with the other. Occasionally tap the plant on a counter to work medium down into the roots and firm mix in the pot.

8. Continue filling until the potting medium is ½ to ¾ inch below the rim of the container to allow room for water to drain through the mix without spilling over the top of the pot. Tap the pot once again, then fill any holes that may have resulted.

9. The roots left after a good cleaning are not always enough to anchor the plant. If the roots are not secure and the plant jiggles in the pot, the emerging root tips may be damaged and fail to grow.

Slip a rhizome clip over the rim of the pot, bending it tightly over the rhizome so it holds the rhizome in place. You can purchase clips or make your own.

10. If the orchids are tall or the rhizome needs to be held at an angle to grow horizontally, secure each pseudobulb with a stake.

Insert a stake beside the growths and tie them to the stake (see Tools & Materials, page 65). With experience, you will learn to stake the plant so that it looks natural.

11. Label the plant with its name, color, season of bloom, and potting date.

12. Water immediately after potting to further settle the mix, then move the orchid to a spot that has a moist or humid atmosphere. Keep the medium nearly dry as it develops roots to discourage root rot and to encourage root growth.

Wait to begin watering and fertilizing regularly when you see renewed root growth on the repotted orchid.

POTTING ORCHIDS

1 Remove as much potting media as you can. Soaking the roots for an hour or so before starting makes them more pliable and less susceptible to damage. You won't be able to remove all media because roots grow into pieces of bark. Cut off damaged roots.

2 Set sympodial orchids at the side of the pot with the oldest growth against it. Recheck that roots have enough room for two years of growth, then add soil to within ½ to ¾ inch of the pot rim.

3 Set a monopodial orchid in the center of the container low enough that when the pot is filled to within ½ to ¾ of the rim, the medium touches the lowest leaves.

4 Rap the potted orchid against a hard surface to help settle and firm the medium. Fill any holes that open up with the rapping.

5 If the plant is loose in the pot, hold it in place with a rhizome clip, which slips over the pot rim and stretches across the container to pin down the rhizome. Letting the orchid move around in the pot slows reestablishment because it damages new roots.

Orchids on mounts

Orchids are mounted in a way that most closely approximates their natural style of growth, which may have them oriented on the mount vertically or horizontally.

Climbing orchids grow on tree trunks; each new growth on the rhizome emerges a little higher than the previous growth. Climbers do best on vertical mounts. Orchids that grow in a straight line, as they might along a branch, with all new growths emerging from the rhizome at about the same level, adapt well to horizontal mounts, which are also called rafts or slabs.

Almost any orchid can be trained to a vertical mount but not all will adapt to a horizontal raft. Climbers will try to climb off the raft, appearing as though they are on stilts because the roots grow down to reach the substrate as the rhizome climbs higher and higher.

The mounting process is easy and starts with determining your orchid's style of growth.

Mounting step by step

1. Select a mount in the proper orientation for your orchid. If it has a grain to it, make sure the grain runs in the same direction as you plan to mount the orchid so

▲ Mounting materials provide many opportunities to allow your creativity to flow. Besides commercial mounts, consider driftwood, tree burls, split bamboo, or nearly any other material that provides a surface in which the orchid can root.

BEST ORCHIDS FOR MOUNTING

Aerangis luteo-alba rhodosticta
Angraecum didieri and *leonis*
Barkeria spp.
Brassavola nodosa
Cattleya luteola and *walkeriana*
Dendrobium aggregatum and *jenkensii*
Laelia anceps, autumnalis, and *gouldiana*
Maxillaria tenuifolia
Miltonia spectabilis
Oncidium onustum
Sophronitis cernua

▲ Spread the plant out in order to see whether it has vertical or horizontal growth. It sometimes helps to look at the rhizome from the top down. This orchid grows horizontally.

▲ Mounting comes close to replicating the natural situation of many orchids. If you live in a frost-free region, mount the orchid, then hang it on a tree trunk or branch. It will eventually move off the mount and onto the tree.

the orchid will look natural and grow better. Make a hanger from wire and attach it to the mount.

2. Make a pad of sphagnum moss, about the same diameter as the plant's base, to cushion the plant against the mount.

3. Position the pad near the bottom of a vertical mount and to the appropriate side of a horizontal raft. Try several placements to obtain the most secure and natural positioning. Staple the pad to the mount, set the plant's base on the pad, and arrange the roots to extend outward.

4. Check that the rhizome is level against the surface of the mount and that new growth is aligned to continue along the mount rather than pull away from it.

5. Until roots establish, secure the plant to the mount with fishing line, twine, wire, staples, or other water-resistant materials. Electrician's staples work well—their flat edges are easily pressed into wood or cork. As a layer of rust forms, they'll blend into the mount.

Attach the plant securely but not so tight as to cut into rhizome or roots. After the plant is established on the mount, you can remove the tying material.

▲ Determine the best position for the orchid on the mount, then moisten a wad of sphagnum moss and place it in that spot. Staple the moss to the mount or hold it in place with fishing line.

situation so that it continues to grow healthily.

If several pseudobulbs have grown off the edge of the mount, cut off these growths when they are about to start rooting and attach them to another mount.

If the mounting material has begun to break down or the orchid has outgrown the mount, remount it. To do this you simply wire the old mount to a larger fresh piece of mounting material. The orchid continues to grow without interruption.

In frost-free areas, you can hang a mount on a tree trunk. Eventually, the orchid outgrows the mount and attaches to the tree.

WHY WITHHOLD WATER?

Withholding water from newly potted or mounted orchids may seem counter-intuitive. It is a common practice, however, known as keeping plants dry at the roots. Orchid growers do this because the roots remaining after potting are not always able to take up moisture. Adding water is akin to drowning the plant. Allowing increased air at the roots helps the plants heal and encourages new root growth.

6. Make a hanger out of heavy-duty wire, if the mount doesn't come equipped. Make a plant label with a hole in it, and attach to the hanger. Move the orchid to a shady, moist or humid spot until roots attach to the mount. Water infrequently until the plant becomes established, usually in six to eight weeks.

Remounting

Mounted orchids require remounting less frequently than potted plants need repotting. Eventually, however, you will need to either transfer the orchid to another mount or otherwise change the plant's growing

▲ After placing the pad, set the plant on top then securely attach the orchid to the mount. Monofilament fishing line is nearly invisible. You can also use staples, twine, or wire. Take care to not cut into the roots or rhizome with the tie.

Staking

A well-grown orchid plant is self-supporting and does not need to be staked; however, many orchids do better with some help. For example, you may need to stake after potting to help secure the plant in the pot while it reestablishes roots. It also helps to stake a rootless plant that you are rescuing. New roots that are just starting to grow, whether right after potting or when a plant is rescued, are easily damaged if the plant is loose in the pot. Staking is also a useful way to protect a developing flower spike.

Proper staking is an art that is essential to the showy display of orchids. It is a technique you learn by experience and by observing the techniques of others.

Basic staking

When additional support is needed, do it as gently as possible and in the most unobtrusive way. Place a stake next to the emerging inflorescence. Where to tie the stem to the stake depends on the type of orchid.

The goal is to stake the flower stem in a way that allows for the best view of the flower while enhancing the orchid's natural presentation. For example, paphiopedilum have strong flower stems that can support the weight of the flower but the flower nods. To best exhibit the flower, place a stake next to the stem as it begins to open. Tie the stem to the stake just below the bottom flower. If you wait until the flower opens then stake, it will face the viewer, which is unnatural.

For single-flowered orchids place a short stake near the pseudobulb or near the fan of leaves of orchids without pseudobulbs. Tie the plant to it at the junction of the pseudobulb and leaf.

Lycastes tend to have multiple individual flowers that emerge from the base of the lead pseudobulb. For such orchids, you may need to stake each flower individually so that all are viewed properly. On the other hand *Lyc. aromatica*, which may have 15 or more flowers from each lead growth, often needs no staking.

Materials

Green bamboo and wire are the only types of stakes

▲ Among the supplies you'll need for staking are bamboo, flexible wire, or pre-fab metal stakes and twist ties, clips, or a roll of hook-and-loop tape.

necessary. The green of the bamboo blends in with foliage, and the stakes come in convenient lengths that can be cut to size with pruning shears. However, numerous other types are available and give you options for displaying your orchids. For example, long flexible wire stakes in natural brown or green are helpful for following the natural arch of a flower stem, especially when you need to support the entire stem.

To tie the plant to the stake, use green twist-ties or raffia. Because the wire in twist-ties can dig into the stem, take care not to twist tightly. An alternative to twist-ties is green half-inch-wide hook-and-loop tape, which is sold in rolls and has no wire to damage the plant.

Other staking and tying materials are available, some sold only to orchid growers, some with other uses. For example, curly willow, available at florists suppliers, adds a decorative touch while holding up flowers. Many people use small plastic clips to hold the stem to the stake. There are also spiral and straight wire stakes; all work fine. What matters most is that the staking enhances the flowers rather than calling attention to the stakes.

▲ Tying just below the first flower of a vanda inflorescence keeps the bloom facing out without appearing contrived.

▲ Stake paphiopedilum before flowers open to prevent them from facing straight out, which looks unnatural.

▲ Green bamboo and twist ties blend in with the foliage. Wrap the ends of the ties around the stake to keep it neat.

▲ Spanish moss attached to the top of the stake helps to disguise the twist tie.

▲ Thin-gauge wire wrapped around the stem and stake from the ground up blends in beautifully.

▲ Plastic clips in the shape of animals are popular. They come in many colors; transparent ones fade into the foliage.

▲ A long, flexible wire follows the length of the entire inflorescence of *Brassia* Edvah Lou 'Nishida'. Bending the wire into a gentle curve enhances the presentation.

Propagating orchids

Commercial growers propagate orchids by seed or with a laboratory technique called meristemming. This method rapidly reproduces exact copies of fine orchid cultivars and varieties in large numbers. Because it is speedy, reliable, and productive, most orchids on the market have been propagated by this method. For home orchid growers, however, the technique is not practical.

Fortunately, less high-tech propagation methods for orchids are available. You can divide plants using the same techniques you use to propagate houseplants and garden perennials. As with most garden perennials, division is vital to the continued health and productivity of your orchids.

You can also propagate some orchids by taking stem cuttings or harvesting offsets. These are small shoots that grow on stems or at the base of plants. Called keikis, you cut them from the plant and pot them to grow into a new plant. (Pronounced kee-kee, the term "keiki" means baby in Hawaiian.)

Orchids also can be started from seed or, for that matter, you can make crosses and compete with other orchid fanciers in judged shows.

You'll find propagating orchids to be practical, rewarding, and fun. Using a few simple gardening skills, you can quickly and easily increase your orchid collection.

The best candidates for propagation are the orchids that perform well for you. Before slicing your orchids into pieces, however, consider these criteria.

Is the orchid worth growing into a large specimen plant? If so, it would be a shame to cut it up, especially if you think you might want to show the orchid someday.

Does the orchid grow compactly and branch freely, or does it tend to march across the pot, one growth at a time? Plants that branch freely are naturals for dividing; they often split apart into appropriate-size plants when you remove them from their pots. Plants that produce only one growth at a time are more difficult to propagate, but it can be done.

Has the orchid grown too large to handle and is the next size pot going to be impossible to manage? Do you receive many requests for a start of the plant? Both instances are good reasons to propagate. You'll end up with a more manageable plant and have specimens to share.

▲ Pollination is just one of the many ways in which you can propagate orchids, and creating new hybrids is one of the most rewarding aspects of growing orchids.

Dividing orchids

Division simply means splitting an orchid into two or more actively growing pieces. It is the same technique you use to propagate any clumping garden plant.

As with any other task involving orchids, however, a thorough understanding of the plant and its growth habit is crucial to success. Nearly all sympodial orchids can be divided. They have a spreading growth habit that is not much different from those of irises or daylilies. Only a few monopodial orchids are propagated in this manner. They are ones, such as ascocentrums, that branch freely at the base and have a clumping habit.

Why divide

Dividing increases your stock as well as helps maintain orchid health and productivity. For example, if the orchid is growing in a straight line across the pot, has died in the center, or has some other defect, dividing will improve the plant's appearance and stimulate new growth.

When dividing, you have the opportunity to closely examine the plant for damage and disease, to thoroughly clean the plant and eliminate spent medium, and to treat any problems you find— either cutting them off or applying materials to control pest problems or aid healing.

As orchids grow larger, they often become less manageable and more difficult to keep healthy than small plants. As a plant's mass increases, its actively growing parts concentrate around its perimeter. In the center of the pot, the medium may never dry because few active roots exist in this section of the plant. The rhizome and foliage in the center of the plant, then, are liable to rot.

Dividing an overgrown orchid lets you remove the older portions of the plant, which are unlikely to root. This in turn facilitates vigorous new growth from the remaining divisions.

When to divide

As with garden plants, you'll have more success if you divide orchids when they are at the right size and stage of growth and are healthy.
- **Stage of growth** The right stage of growth is at the outset of a new growing season when new roots start to appear, a time that coincides with the best time to repot plants. Look for bright green root tips emerging at the base of the

▲ This orchid has nowhere left to grow in the pot. Now the question is, do you transplant it into a bigger container or do you propagate it? It is large enough and has enough new growths that it could be divided into two to three new plants.

plant. When new roots are forming, the plant is most likely to continue to thrive and bloom the following year. Timing is key to dividing and propagating orchids.

Avoid dividing an orchid when it is in bloom or in the process of sending up flower spikes or when the plant is actively growing. New shoots, whether leaves or flowers, are tender and vulnerable to the slightest bruise. It is nearly impossible not to break off flower stems or new growth.
- **Right size** To maintain a healthy flowering parent plant and ensure your orchid survives division, you need to know how big it must be in order to bloom, or in other words, what constitutes a flowering-size plant. Divided too often, orchids tend to form smaller and smaller growths because of the repeated stress of being disturbed.

These small growths may bloom, but not to their full potential. In addition,

flowering could hasten the decline of the orchid.

A genus that is famous for this lingering decline is paphiopedilum. Because this genus cannot be reliably cloned through

▲ Orchids that grow only one bulb at a time will often march across the pot, creating a thin, unappealing plant.

▲ To make cuttings of cane dendrobiums, cut the stem at its base then slice it into 2- to 3-inch-long pieces. Dip the bottom of each cutting into rooting hormone and place it in a container of moist potting media; several cuttings fit in each pot. Move the plant to a spot with a warm, humid atmosphere. The badly encrusted pot in the background indicates mineral deposits in the water that should be dealt with.

meristemming, division is the only way to propagate it. And because paphs can easily be split into single fans that bloom quickly—within a year or two—growers often divide

DIVIDING SYMPODIAL ORCHIDS

1 Soak the roots before going to work, then remove as much of the potting media as possible and loosen roots.

2 Using a sterile tool such as a razor blade, cut at the points you identified.

3 The resulting division will have five growths. This orchid could be divided into two more parts.

4 To divide a pot-bound plant, cut away the pot then slice through the roots with a knife or pruning shears.

5 If you use this technique, wash off roots before potting the divisions.

them too frequently. When divided every year, the plant has no resource reserves to draw upon to survive, and the plants become weak.

This is an extreme example, and orchid species vary in the size they must reach before flowering. Deciduous calanthes, for example, actually do best when divided into single bulbs every year. If the plants grow very large, the older bulbs often die instead of producing new growths.

● **Healthy plant** It is crucial to divide a plant before it declines. A weakened orchid—one that has lost roots and has a dead center—will be slow to recover from division and may not bloom for several years. Splitting the orchid while new roots are forming and the plant is healthy and active ensures that it will prosper.

Preparing to divide

The best way to see where to divide a sympodial orchid is to look down on the plant from above. Note how closely growths occur on the rhizome and whether the plant branches freely from a clump or grows in a straight line forming one new growth at a time. Individual growths may be close together, as in paphiopedilums, or spread out on the rhizome from 1 to 36 inches apart.

As you look down, check for the most logical dividing points or natural dividing lines in the plant. To do this, you need to identify the active developing growths, the oldest growths, and the swing growths.

Developing growths are the sections that will bloom in the coming year. They are also known as lead growths. A division containing developing growths is known as a lead or a front division.

Swing growths are pseudobulbs that join two developing growths. If you remove swing growths when you make a division, you may end up with smaller plants than you want.

Older growths are ones that are more than one year old. They have flowered and will not bloom again.

The oldest pseudobulbs with no actively growing leads are known as back bulbs, and a division consisting mainly of back bulbs is known as a back division. The back bulbs may be shriveled and leafless or plump and leafy. Though nonactive, they continue to supply food to the plant and may sprout new foliage.

To envision the parts, consider a container holding one growth of a branching-type orchid. This growth blooms during its first year in the pot and it gives rise to three new growths. It will never bloom again.

The three new growths bloom the next year, and three more new growths branch from each of them.

The first growth in the pot—the two-year-old growth—is the oldest growth or the back bulb. The one-year-old growths—the three growths that sprouted from the first—are the recently flowered growths. They too will never bloom again.

The nine newest growths are the developing or lead growths. They will bloom the next year.

● **Making front divisions** As a general rule, each front division should consist of three to five growths that include one or more recently flowered growths and two or more lead growths that will bloom in the coming season.

Clumping orchids are relatively easy to divide; often a plant that is ready for division simply breaks apart into appropriate size divisions containing front and back bulbs. Even with a little cutting, the plant habit is such that where to cut is fairly intuitive.

● **Making back divisions** Orchids that grow straight across the pot, making one growth at a time, can be hard to propagate without using back bulbs. With these types of orchids, making front

▲ Look down on a sympodial orchid to identify the best places to divide the plant. Each division should contain one or two recently flowered bulbs (1) and two or three developing growths (2).

divisions every few years ensures a good-looking plant. The older growths left in the pot after taking the front division often initiate new growth. These can grow into flowering-size plants in a couple of years.

To ensure that back bulbs sprout, orchid growers sometimes cut halfway through the rhizome one or two bulbs away from the front before taking the division while the plant is actively growing. This spurs new growth to emerge from the back bulbs before taking the front division.

Before meristemming was developed, commercial growers routinely propagated orchids by using back bulbs, ensuring that no part of the plant was wasted. Back bulbs are an excellent way to share plants without sacrificing the immediately productive front divisions. If the plant is not particularly interesting or you already have as much of it as you want, discard the back portions.

Techniques

Growers have a variety of techniques for dividing plants. Experienced orchidists often pull apart the various divisions, knowing instinctively how much pressure to exert without harming the plant. The advantage to this method is that it prevents contaminating cutting tools and spreading viral diseases between plants.

Until they become familiar with the process, most novice orchid growers usually cut divisions. You can use pruners, sharp knives, or single-edge razor blades. Sterilize the tool before cutting the plant and before moving on to another plant. More orchid viruses are spread through use of contaminated cutting tools than any other way.

To sterilize, hold the tool in the flame of a propane torch until the tool blade is smoking hot. The hot blade will cauterize cuts to prevent diseases from moving in.

When using razor blades, use a new one for each plant. If you run out of blades, you can resterilize them in a 350°F oven for 20 minutes. Cool before use.

Step by step for a symodial orchid

1. Assemble tools, pots, and potting medium. Evaluate the plant and decide where to make cuts, which will tell you the number of pots and labels as well as the amount of medium needed.
2. Remove the plant from the pot; clean as much of the old mix away from the roots as possible, trimming dead or damaged roots. Thoroughly clean the orchid, removing old sheaths and leaf bases.
3. If the plant does not break apart naturally, separate divisions by prying apart pieces at the most likely breaking points or cutting the rhizome.
4. Clean each division and discard any pseudobulbs or growths that have no roots. Rootless bulbs will not have enough energy to produce new growth. Caution: Some of the back growths may be swing bulbs.
5. Choose an appropriate size container for each division. Pot them up (page 63) then thoroughly water the plants until potting mix is moist, allowing excess water to run through. Label each division, move them into your collection, or share them.

Monopodial orchids

The challenge to propagating most monopodial orchids is that their branches come off one main stem, which makes them difficult to divide. Only monopodial orchids that branch freely at their base and grow in clumps can be divided. Instead, to propagate monopodials, you

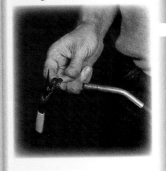

can take cuttings of the plant from the top or you can remove individual side stems.

Monopodial orchids are ready to be propagated when they have grown tall and dropped their lower leaves. Roots often emerge from the stem. Simply snap them off the mother plant or cut them off like a keiki (page 74).

Cut the stem just below these roots. Pot the cutting as you would any orchid. Leave the parent plant in its pot, and a new plant often will sprout from the old stem. When this happens, repot the orchid, or break the new plant off the old stem and pot it in a suitable size container.

Because monopodials do not have water-storage organs like sympodial orchids, divide them only when the new green root tips are emerging, or the plants may never reestablish. New roots grow from the stem; like sympodial orchids, they have bright green tips.

Although the roots of most monopodials are thicker in cross section than those of sympodials and appear to be tough, not all have thick roots and they're not all that tough. For example, angraecoids, such as jumellea, have thin, wiry roots. Also the roots of monopodials generally do

DIVIDE AND CLEAN

While dividing and repotting orchids, take time to clean them. Pull off damaged leaves and sheaths, trim brown leaf tips, and remove dead roots. Look for developing problems. With clean plants, you'll easily notice and address future problems.

DIVIDING MONOPODIAL ORCHIDS

To ensure that the division is successful, divide only when you see new green root tips.

Cut just below the roots emerging on the stem.

If you leave a monopodial orchid in its pot after taking the top, a new stem with roots often sprouts from the cut end, similar to a keiki. You can cut this off and have another new plant.

not branch as readily as those of sympodials.

Take care to not break or damage the roots. Once they're broken, nothing will grow to replace them. Soaking the parent plant and thoroughly wetting the roots makes it more pliable and easier to work with.

▲ You know a monopodial orchid is ready for dividing when it has grown tall and lower stems are leafless. Numberous roots may sprout from the stem.

Keikis

Keikis—offshoots that form on orchids—form at the base or on the lower stem of monopodial orchids, on flowering stems of certain monopodial orchids, or on canes of a few sympodial orchids. They are most common on monopodial orchids such as vandas and phalaenopsis and on cane dendrobiums, reed epidendrums, and some oncidiums.

Harvesting and planting keikis with well-developed roots is one way to propagate orchids. Because keikis form through vegetative means, they're identical to the plant that produced them. Orchids propagated from keikis often bloom within two years.

▲ Keikis may form on older, previously flowered canes on dendrobiums or from leaf nodes on the pseudobulb.

▲ Monopodial orchids, such as phalaenopsis, sometimes form keikis on flower-stem-like growths.

Keikis characteristically form in one of three ways.

● **Dormant buds** Keikis may develop when a monopodial orchid such as vanda or very old phalaenopsis has grown tall enough that the top of the plant no longer inhibits branching farther down the stem. Without the top's control, dormant buds along the lower stems sprout. Dormant buds are found at nodes—the point at which a leaf emerges from a stem—often in the axil formed by the leaf and stem; even after leaves drop, the bud remains at the node. Dormant buds may occur at the top of a pseudobulb, along a vegetative stem, and on flowering stems. Buds may grow into flowering stems, new growths, or plantlets.

In trees and shrubs, when a stem tip releases control of the buds behind it, a new branch grows from the main

▲ Keikis also form at the base and on the stems of monopodial orchids.

stem. In orchids, rather than a new stem, a new plant forms. Keikis often develop when an orchid is propagated by removing the top of the plant. Damage to plant roots also spurs the formation of a keiki from dormant buds.

● **Flower stems** When blooms are prevented from developing on flower stems, keikis may grow. Excess nitrogen fertilizer, high temperatures during the bloom period of a cool-season orchid such as

▲ Cut the stem on which the keiki grows and pot up the new plant.

phalaenopsis, or root disturbance can prevent flower growth.

Cane dendrobiums such as *Den. nobile* and *Den. thyrsiflorum* frequently form keikis on older canes that have flowered and are commonly propagated by allowing older stems to form keikis at unflowered nodes.

Phaius can be propagated by removing an old flower stem and placing it on a bed of moist sphagnum moss in a shady area; keikis will form at the nodes along the stem.

Keikis on flower stems can be a sign of poor culture or unfavorable conditions, and if your plants make them frequently, it's time to investigate the cause.

● **Keiki paste** To force flower stems to produce keikis on plants that you wish to propagate, apply a thin layer of a paste containing plant hormones to the stem. Commercial pastes contain cytokinin, which promotes cell division in plants.

Keiki growth

Keiki foliage forms first, followed by roots. Leave a keiki on the plant until emerging roots reach 1 to 3 inches long. Root growth usually begins in spring. Either twist off the keiki or cut it with a sharp sterile blade. Pot the keiki as you would any small orchid.

Avoid letting roots grow too long; long aerial roots

adapt less well to growing in pots.

When roots are slow to develop, encourage growth by bending the stem over a container filled with medium and pinning the stem to the medium with a clip to hold the keiki on the medium. When roots have grown into the medium, clip the stem with a sterile tool.

Potting

Harvested bare-root keikis make excellent gifts for orchid-growing friends, who can pot them in their choice of mix. When you keep keikis for yourself, pot them soon after harvest.

The roots of harvested keikis are generally short while foliage may be much larger. As when potting any orchid, match size of container to size of root system rather than to the size of the plant top.

Fill the container with potting medium and pot as normal. Some growers start keikis in sphagnum moss to get them going. The water-retentive and antibacterial qualities of sphagnum help plantlets root.

Label plants and move them to your growing area. Treat freshly potted keikis as you would any other newly repotted plant. As each plant becomes established and roots are actively growing, transfer it to a larger pot that more closely matches the size of the top of the plant, retaining the still-fresh potting medium.

▲ Keikis that form on stems can be harvested simply by ripping them off the stem.

Developing your own hybrids

▲ Growing orchids from seed can be challenging; however, making crosses and seeing what results can be fun and rewarding. Who knows, you could be the next big winner in an international orchid show.

As you grow in experience and knowledge, you may want to experiment with creating your own hybrids by pollinating the plants and growing out the seeds that result. This can be a highly rewarding hobby when you are patient.

Pollinating orchids is relatively easy, but growing them from seed isn't for everyone. It takes time—five to seven years on average—special equipment to sow the seed, and skill that you develop only through experience. That said, try your hand at hybridizing at least once.

Making plans

Begin by deciding what you would like from a new orchid—a new color in the species, a more compact plant, or longer life for flowers—then look for parents with characteristics that might give those traits.

Because not every orchid species or hybrid is genetically compatible with all others, select the parents from the same genus or at least ones within the same alliance. Research parentage of common hybrids in Sander's List of Orchid Hybrids or on the Royal Horticultural Society's website (www.rhs.org.uk/plants/registration_orchids.asp) to see which parents have been compatible in the past. Be sure to choose parents that bloom at the same time.

Select the best examples of plants with the traits you desire. Eliminate parents with undesirable traits, such as ones that bloom sparsely or that tend to sprawl or that have poor bloom color. These are traits you don't want to pass along.

Finally, decide which of the parents will provide the pollen and which one will play the female role. Often the more robust of the two plants will be designated the female role because seed pod development demands considerable energy.

Pollination how-to

Select the flower you wish to pollinate, making sure that it is ripe (open at least a few days). Remove the lip from the flower. Because it collapses after pollination, the lip can cause the column to rot before the seeds ripen. With the lip gone, you will have unimpeded access to the column.

Use a wooden pencil or skewer to remove a pollinium from the plant contributing the pollen. Pollinia are the golden masses under the cap at the front of the bloom, and there may be two to twelve pollinia in a flower. The sticky pollinium will likely attach to the pencil tip.

Set aside the pollinium while you remove the pollinium from the female orchid. You may want to use the female pollinium to pollinate another orchid. With this out of the way, carefully press the pollinium from the male parent onto the stigma of the female parent. The stigma is on the underside of the column and has a sticky surface that will hold onto the pollinium after the pencil is pulled away.

If pollination is successful, the ovary will swell—it looks like a pod or seed capsule—and ripen over the next three to nine months (pod ripening times vary by genus). Watch for splitting and yellowing of the capsule, which indicates it is nearly ripe. Each pod contains millions of seeds.

Sowing seeds

Orchid seeds are unlike other seeds because they do not have endosperm, the starchy nutrient material that keeps young plants alive until they begin photosynthesizing sugars. Orchid nutrients must be provided in a sterile enriched medium similar to the agar used by laboratories to culture bacteria and fungi.

To sow seeds, purchase sterile materials from orchid suppliers to create the medium and jars (or flasks). Because the medium more easily grows bacteria and fungi cultures than young orchid plants unless it is scrupulously sterilized, some orchidists prefer to send their seeds to professional labs that provide flasking services. And if you are not interested in making your own hybrids

POLLINATING ORCHIDS

The pollination process is relatively simple. All you need is a familiarity of the morphology of the flower, a skewer, and a steady hand.

Look for the pollinium hidden in the column of the flower.

The sticky pollinium will stick to your skewer as you touch it.

Removing the lip makes it easier to place the pollinium on the stigma of the female parent.

HERE'S A TIP...

When you cross two orchids of different species, you get a hybrid plant. When you self-pollinate a species orchid or cross two of the same species, you get another orchid of that same species.

but would like to try something new, labs can provide flasked orchid seedlings that have been bred by professional orchid growers from the finest plants in their collections.

When using a flasking service to grow your own seeds, harvest the seeds

Developing Your Own Hybrids *(continued)*

▲ You will find millions of seeds in an orchid seed pod. They lack the endosperm that provides nutrients to the developing seedling, which the seeds of most other types of plants have. For that reason, growing them out can be difficult.

▲ The seed-germinating process is the most difficult task in orchid breeding. For a nominal fee, laboratories will plant your seeds in sterile flasks like this one and grow them until the seedlings are ready to survive on their own, eliminating the difficulties for you.

before the ovary ripens and splits open. These are called green seeds. Most labs prefer to sow green seeds.

If the pod has split, carefully collect seeds in waxed paper, then fold the paper flat to fit a mailing envelope. Attach a label with the seeds detailing the parent genera and the date that you made the cross.

Deflasking

Plantlets will be ready for deflasking when they arrive back from the lab, which may be two to three years. Follow these steps to plant them into compots—or community

pots—until they are large enough to grow on their own. Compots are 3- to 5-inch containers filled with appropriate medium for young plants. Have plenty of pots on hand because the flask will contain hundreds of seedlings.

Wrap the flask in layers of newspaper. Carefully tap the wrapped flask with a hammer to break the glass, then discard the broken pieces.

Wash the medium from the seedlings' roots, taking care to not damage them. Separate the plants from each other if you can. If roots won't untangle, it's OK to leave them in small clumps.

Plant the seedlings in the compots using the following technique to ensure that the seedlings are planted at the proper depth. Hold the pot at an angle and fill it with medium so the top of the medium on one side is ½ inch below the rim of the pot and several inches lower on the opposite side. Line up seedlings along the high edge of the medium. With the pot still held at any angle, add a little more mix.

Make a second line of seedlings beside the first in this additional medium. Continue adding medium and lining up seedlings until the pot is filled. Tap the pot to settle the mix, then water.

Label each pot indicating the cross and the date.

Move the compots to a warm, shady, humid area. To keep humidity high around the seedlings, you can make a mini greenhouse using a coat hanger and lightweight plastic bag. Shape the hanger so that it fits over the pot rim, holds the bag above the seedlings and keeps the bag from touching them.

As plants grow, move them into individual containers. About every 12 to 18 months, they'll need to be shifted to larger pots.

Orchids will begin blooming in two to seven years after seeds germinate, depending on the species. Phalaenopsis and phragmipediums are likely to flower in two to three years; cattleyas may not bloom for seven years. On average, seedlings will take four to five years to reach flowering size. That is when you will *finally* realize how your attempts at hybridization went.

Don't be discouraged if your results are less than spectacular or when the cross fails. You'll be in fine company—most attempts fail.

The best new hybrids result from perseverance and record-keeping that prevents hybridizers from repeating their (and others') mistakes. Then when that one truly beautiful orchid appears, you'll know your efforts were worth it.

LABELING SEEDS AND SEEDLINGS

Orchid breeders follow certain conventions to ensure everyone understands the cross when they read the label of a plant. The female plant that carries the developing seed pod is always listed first, followed by a × (multiplication sign), and then the name of the pollen plant. In the case of a species or hybrid that you are self-pollinating, you simply write the plant name × self.

Crosses have a unique terminology. A selfing results when you self-pollinate a species or hybrid. A sibling results from a cross of two cultivars or hybrids of a species. Back cross means that a hybrid was crossed with one of its parent species.

Here are some examples using *Cattleya mossiae* and *Laelia purpurata*:

- **A selfing:** *C. mossiae* 'Cultivar A' × self
- **A sibling:** *C. mossiae* 'Cultivar A' × 'Cultivar B'
- **A hybrid:** *C. mossiae* 'Cultivar A' × *L. purpurata* 'Cultivar X'

Lab techniques

▲ Orchid propagation labs can grow flasks containing hundreds of mericlones so that even a small space can produce millions of plants. Each orchid in a flask is exactly the same as the other orchids, although slight variations occasionally crop up.

Even though you won't use these techniques yourself, understanding how commercial growers propagate orchids offers insight into the industry and helps you recognize why certain cultivars are on the market while others are not. Commercial growers need to have a reliable method that produces thousands of plants in the shortest amount of time. Dividing, harvesting keikis, and making cuttings are much too slow for them.

Commercial nurseries rely on two major techniques: seed culture and meristemming, both of which require sterile conditions. Seed culture is the same process you use when developing your own hybrids and sending them to a flasking service (page 76). The hybrid and species crosses made by commercial growers are much more intentional than those of home growers, however. Commercial growers make the same crosses year after year using the best plant specimens in their collections so that they always have a supply of a particular plant to sell.

Meristemming, also called mericloning, lets growers produce thousands of identical copies of a single orchid. In seed culture, there is no way to get an exact copy of the parents. Subtle variations always appear, even after making the same crosses using the same plants.

Orchids—like all plants— do not come exactly true from seed. Before growers learned the meristemming technique, the only way to create an exact copy of a plant was through division.

Meristemming

Mericloning produces the best and most uniform orchids. They are almost always made from a plant that is finer than any other of its type. The parent may have larger flowers, greater vigor, more compact growth, or better foliage.

The meristemming process begins with a plant in an antiseptically clean laboratory designed to exclude airborne fungi and bacteria. There, a technician removes the tip of a shoot.

Working with a scalpel and microscope, the technician carefully strips the tiny leaves from the shoot's tip. This reveals the meristem, a basic plant structure that is analogous to an embryo.

Meristems start out as a group of undifferentiated cells less than half a millimeter in diameter. When conditions are right, they are capable of growing into cells that form leaves, stems, roots, and flowers. (In shrubs, the meristem is deep within the bud on the tip of a stem.)

After revealing the meristem, the technician places it in a flask of sterile nutrient solution and puts the flask into a climate-controlled chamber. As equipment gently agitates it, tiny lumps of tissue swirl in the flask. The meristem cells divide and form more groups of meristem cells, which are removed and placed in other flasks. This process continues until thousands of groups have been created.

Once the target quantity of cell groups is reached, a technician moves them into flasks containing a solid sterile nutrient medium. There the cells develop into tiny plants with leaves, stems, and roots.

Eventually, these plants grow large enough to be transplanted to trays and to grow in the open air. Several years later, these orchid clones may be found blooming on windowsills and in greenhouses all over the world.

Availability

Young clones are often sold at nurseries and orchid shows in displays that include one or two flowering specimens of the orchid and dozens of small, nonflowering plants for sale. Usually, the blooming plants are for display only; the small plants are guaranteed to be exact copies of the display plants. These small, reasonably priced clones let you increase your collection inexpensively.

Among the thousands of plants propagated from a single meristem, you may find one that varies slightly, perhaps in flower color, substance, or number of flowers per inflorescence. Although rare, these variations offer a chance that your new plant may develop into a valuable orchid.

Seedlings from mass-produced culture

As tastes for orchids become more sophisticated and you search for orchid specialists and new plants, you will look for seed-raised plants. Each will vary from the original somewhat, offering the chance to happen upon a truly special cultivar.

Mericloned orchids are almost always produced from superior cultivars, but seedlings result from sexual propagation and can be anywhere on the spectrum from inferior to extraordinary. However, no hybridizer intentionally makes an inferior hybrid, so you can generally be assured that any given group of seedlings that you buy represents the best the breeder has available.

These seedling orchids may be offered at shows and nurseries in the same manner as clones. Some nurseries offer flasks of orchid seedlings growing in nutrient jelly (sterile agar).

It may take three to five years for the first blooms to appear, but depending on the cross, it is possible you may have an award winner among your flasklings.

The production of seedling orchid flasks is similar to that used for clones. Tiny orchid seeds are removed from an almost ripe pod in a process known as green pod culture (because the pod is still green and closed rather than brown and split open as it would be if it were ripe). They are spread into a flask of sterile medium that provides the necessary nutrients to enable seeds to germinate and grow.

In six to eight months, when seedlings are about ⅛ to ¼ inch high and beginning to form tiny leaves and roots, they are carefully removed and placed in a new flask with a slightly different nutrient formula where they grow for another eight to twelve months. At this point, they can be potted and moved to a greenhouse to continue to grow.

Although relatively inexpensive, these seedlings are extremely tender and a challenge for even experienced orchid growers. If you have a greenhouse or have set up a growing space under fluorescent lights, you may find it rewarding to try. Transplant the seedlings first to community pots and then to individual pots.

Troubleshooting

Orchids are generally tough disease- and insect-tolerant plants capable of enduring a considerable amount of stress. The more closely you attend to their cultural needs, the tougher and more resistant they will be.

In adverse conditions an orchid's natural defenses will weaken and problems appear. Just as humans are susceptible to illness when the body is stressed, orchids are likely to develop fungal or bacterial diseases or succumb to insect infestations when they are stressed.

Most orchid problems are related to water—too much or too little of it. Too much water in soil causes the roots to rot. The excess water drives oxygen out of the soil so the roots cannot function, and fungi and bacteria proliferate and begin infecting the roots. Water standing around roots or on leaves and petals also encourages bacterial and fungal infections.

Too little water stresses plants and invites scale insects, mealybugs, and spider mites to move in. Between the two extremes, overwatering kills plants faster than not providing enough water.

Poor sanitation also leads to many plant problems, and keeping the growing area clean eliminates the source of pest problems. For example, millions of fungal spores can grow on dead leaves, flowers, and other organic debris around the plants. And insect adults, larvae, and eggs find haven in the trash.

Crowded conditions allow pests to quickly settle into a collection and go unnoticed. Plants that are too close together are also less healthy because they have limited sunlight, air circulation, and sometimes water. In addition, when plants are crowded, it's difficult to keep a close eye on individual plants; their proximity allows pests to readily move from one plant to another.

Preventing and diagnosing problems

Each time you water, fertilize, or pot up orchids, take time to examine the plants. Make sure that their leaves are firm and lustrous, that the bulbs are plump and firm in the pot, and that the potting mix or mount is not soggy or broken down. Use a magnifying glass to help find small insects, such as mites, hiding in the foliage.

Examine the cultural conditions for your orchids to ensure that they are growing in the correct light, humidity, and warmth. Water and fertilize regularly.

Repot plants growing in spent medium or medium that holds too much water.

Clean up the orchids' area and keep it clean. Spread out the plants, removing some if necessary to make room for your favorite plants in your collection. Discard any badly infested or infected plants to prevent insects and diseases from recurring.

Cleaning and grooming

Periodically cleaning and grooming plants to clean

▲ Check plants carefully before buying them, looking for discolored flowers and foliage. You don't want to unwittingly bring home problems, such as this cymbidium mosiac virus. Isolate new plants for a week or so until you are sure they are free of insects, diseases, and other pests.

▲ Taking time to clean the foliage helps you spot problems early and removes grime that keeps plants from using all the sunlight they receive.

up leaves and remove fading flowers and dead or dying material is good for the plant and therapeutic for you, the gardener. While you're at it, be alert to the beginnings of any pest infestations so you can prevent them spreading.

If you find a few mealybugs or scale insects, dip a cotton swab in a solution of 70 percent rubbing alcohol and water and rub it on the insects. Alcohol dissolves insects' waxy coatings, and the swab reaches tight spaces. Use a 50–50 mixture of alcohol and water to spray for minor aphid infestations.

Eliminating problems

When you notice problems developing, try to figure out why. The first step is to check

▲ It's important to check plants thoroughly. With a quick glance or from a distance, an orchid may look fine with no health issues.

the growing conditions. While inspecting an ailing plant, compare what it needs with what it's getting. You can often predict a cause as well as sort out whether the problem results from an insect, disease, or poor care. You have several options for treating disease and insect problems.

● **Beneficial insects** Insect predators such as green lacewings, ladybugs, tachinid flies, braconid wasps, and others are an increasingly important method of pest control in home greenhouses and outdoor growing areas. The larvae and/or adults of these insects feed on numerous other insects including aphids, mealybugs, scale insects, spider mites, whiteflies, and certain caterpillars. Released into an enclosed growing area, they are a practical alternative to other controls.

To ensure that predators stay in an outdoor growing area, provide a source of water and other flowering plants—predators also feed on nectar from small flowers. Many garden shops and nurseries stock beneficial insects, or find them through reliable mail-order and online sources.

● **Horticultural oil** Horticultural oils are among the most convenient materials for controlling indoor plant pests. Made

▲ Getting closer though, you see that the leaves have some spotting, and the mottling that appeared to be shadows on the leaves is actually in the leaf.

from highly refined lightweight paraffin or petroleum-based materials such as superfine oils or mineral oil, they work by smothering insects.

Horticultural oils are effective against a broad range of sucking insects such as aphids, mealybugs, scale, spider mites, and thrips. They are harmless to humans and pets, as well as many beneficial insects. As a bonus they shine the plant's leaves.

Orchids that are sensitive to the oils in traditional pest controls may also be damaged by horticultural oils. Check the label for the orchid's name before buying. Also be sure to purchase horticultural, not dormant, oil. Dormant oils contain impurities that damage all actively growing plants.

● **Insecticidal soap** Some growers combine horticultural oil with insecticidal soap for a nontoxic one-two punch. Made from potassium salts of fatty acids and widely available, insecticidal soaps are effective against soft-bodied pests such as aphids, mealybugs, thrips, and spider mites. The soaps have no residual action and must be sprayed thoroughly to ensure all pests are treated. To eliminate any subsequent generations, make several applications 7 to 10 days apart. Overuse of insecticidal soap can desiccate or burn plants and flowers.

● **Pest controls** If insects do settle in, choose a control that is safe to use on orchids. It is difficult to suggest pest controls because of the size and diversity of the orchid family. Few traditional insect controls and disease controls are available for use on indoor houseplants, even fewer are labeled for use on orchids. Nothing is available to control viruses.

When buying a control, check the label to ensure you can use the product indoors and on orchids and that it controls the pest in question. If it's not for use indoors but labeled for orchids, take your plant outside to spray. Leave it outside until the spray dries.

WHICH ORCHIDS ARE WORTH KEEPING?

How do you decide which orchid to keep or to toss? Here are some criteria:

CANDIDATES FOR TOSSING:

Any orchid not "paying for its keep"
Ones that grow poorly or have few roots or shriveled foliage
Plants with streaked or deformed flowers
Orchids that never bloom

CANDIDATES FOR KEEPING:

High-performing orchids
Orchids worth propagating
Ones that do particularly well in your conditions
Orchids with sentimental value

▲ Beneficial insects, such as ladybug larva, assist in pest control in green–houses and outdoor growing areas.

The solvents in many pest controls, especially ones labeled for outdoor use, can burn orchid foliage. Applying them during the heat of the day is even more detrimental, and some soft-leaf orchids, such as lycastes, are especially susceptible to damage.

A few botanical pest controls are available. For example, neem oil, derived from tree bark, controls insects as well as it controls bacterial and fungal diseases.

Read, understand, and follow all label instructions. Select pest controls based on the label, and also check with local orchid society members and orchid professionals for advice about the products they use and recommend. Also rotate the products you use to avoid creating control-resistant pests.

Diseases

Diseases don't attack healthy plants. They go after plants that are kept too wet, in places with poor air circulation, or in areas with decaying vegetative debris. Decaying debris provides an alternate food source for pathogens, allowing them to breed and spread. When plants are so crowded that air can't circulate among them, foliage stays moist and provides the conditions in which bacteria and fungi thrive. Water splashing from infected plants to healthy ones spreads pathogens, as does water running between plants on the ground. Sucking insects such as aphids also spread disease.

The best cure for fungal and bacterial diseases is to prevent their occurrence. Provide a moderate atmosphere in which humidity is only as high as the orchids require, along with plenty of fresh moving air. Care for the orchid properly, providing water and fertilizer as needed. Remove fallen leaves and other debris as soon as you notice them.

It's difficult to control a disease once it sets in. With some diseases, cutting off and discarding any diseased portions of an orchid will help. Recognize these areas by the discolored, mushy plant tissue or sunken appearance. Make the cut below the damage, using a sharp, sterile knife, scissors, or razor blade; sterilize the tool before each cut. Reduce watering and move the plant to a location where fresh air can circulate freely around the cut. Keep recovering plants isolated from healthy ones to prevent disease spread.

If you grow orchids in a greenhouse or outdoors in high humidity, consider using a disease control once or twice a year to help prevent infection.

Orchid diseases are caused by pathogenic bacteria, fungi, and viruses and include spots, rots, and blights. Following are some common diseases.

Bacterial diseases

Bacterial diseases thrive in warm, moist areas. They enter a plant through cuts and natural openings and can move throughout the plant. Bacteria spreads in water, on nonsterile tools, and on your feet and hands. Splashing water spreads bacteria from one plant to another; so do running and standing water.

Bacterial brown spot

When soaking plants before repotting them, change the water between each plant. The only antibacterial control available to hobby growers is copper compounds; however, the compounds can damage some orchids. The best control for bacterial diseases is prevention by providing proper care.

Bacterial brown spot The most common disease of phalaenopsis orchids, brown spot can also infect other types of orchids. It is caused by the bacteria pseudomonas. The first symptom of disease is a sunken lesion that turns dark brown or black and exudes a highly infectious dark liquid.

Remove infected areas with a sharp, sterile blade or scissors. You will usually have to remove the entire leaf. Spray the plant with a bactericide containing copper and isolate it to prevent spread of the infection.

Bacterial brown spot is difficult to cure. It's often better to discard an infected plant rather than risk infecting other orchids in your collection.

Crown rot The same organism that causes bacterial brown spot also causes crown rot in phalaenopsis, particularly when the crown of the plant remains wet for any length of time. Poor air circulation and high humidity contribute.

Crown rot

A plant that gets crown rot seems to melt before your eyes; leaves drop from the top down, leaving a watery mess in the center of the plant. It usually happens so quickly that treatment is impossible. However, if you can act quickly enough, a bactericide paste applied to the infected area might stop the infection. The plant may then grow a keiki, which is not guaranteed, however, and it is often better to discard the plant to keep the disease from spreading.

Fungal diseases

The majority of plant diseases are caused by fungi. Numerous fungi cause diseases, and the same fungus can cause one disease in one plant and a different disease in another.

The moisture and temperature conditions in which fungi are active are as diverse as the number of fungi species: Some fungi prefer wet conditions; for others high humidity is enough. Some remain dormant for many years in soil and organic debris until conditions are just right.

Like bacteria, fungi enter plants through wounds and natural openings. They may also force their way into the plant through the epidermis (outer covering of the leaf). Fungi are spread via contaminated tools and in moisture. Good sanitation and proper care are key to preventing fungal diseases.

Black rot Orchids that require continuously moist potting mix can succumb to black rot. Caused by either *Phytophthora cactorum* or *Pythium ultimum,* black rot affects roots, rhizomes, foliage, and pseudobulbs. Cattleyas and phalaenopsis are particularly susceptible, especially left in standing water or decomposing growing mix.

Black rot

Symptoms include a purplish hue to the foliage followed by blackening that spreads to the bulb and rhizome. Often the fungus will show first as a discoloration in the rhizome, and the entire plant can become infected before symptoms appear on the foliage. The disease progresses rapidly, quickly kills the plant when unchecked, and can be particularly virulent in seedlings.

The best treatment is to remove damaged tissue, cutting at least half an inch into clean tissue with a sharp sterile knife or scissors. Sterilize the blade after each cut. Take the plant outside and drench it with a disease control containing copper sulfate or etridiazole. Keep the plant isolated and dry until it is healthy, then repot it in fresh growing mix.

Petal blight

Caused by the fungus *Botrytis cinerea,* petal blight is the bane of commercial and home gardeners. The disease thrives in high humidity and destroys flowers. Infected plants display small circular pink or tan spots on sepals and petals after flowers open.

Petal blight

Because antifungal sprays will ruin the flowers, the only cure is prevention. Petal blight is often seen in growing areas where dead blooms have not been not cleaned up; decaying matter is the source of reinfection. Remove and destroy any blighted flowers. Also lower the humidity in the growing area and increase air circulation around plants.

Leaf spot

Most often caused by cercospora fungi, leaf spot is often found on injured leaves. Spots begin as yellow areas on the undersides of leaves. Eventually they become visible on the top of the leaf, appearing as well-defined round or irregular-shape brown sunken areas.

Leaf spot

Remove the damaged leaf or leaves with a sharp sterile knife or scissors, sterilizing after each cut. Then spray the plant with a disease control labeled for leaf spot of orchids. Keep the plant dry and in an airy location away from other plants until it is healthy.

Root rot

Fusarium and rhizoctonia fungi are the cause of root rot in orchids. Root rot is a fungal disease encouraged by letting roots stand in water. Infected orchids appear stunted or wilted and may fail quickly or decline over many months before dying. The roots are brown and discolored; the foliage becomes yellow and twisted from the lack of nutrients. The rot may extend into the rhizome.

To control the disease, use a sharp, sterile blade to remove all damaged tissue, including infected areas of the roots and rhizomes, resterilizing the blade after each cut. Drench the plant with a disease control labeled for root rot of orchids, following instructions carefully. Let the plant dry thoroughly before repotting it in fresh potting medium.

Root rot

Viral diseases

Viruses are the most serious and most poorly understood diseases of orchids. Visual symptoms are unreliable and may be masked. Infected plants may show no symptoms beyond minor foliar discoloration, but they usually suffer from decreased vigor and productivity. Although viruses are easily transferred between plants by insect feeding, the most common cause of infection is carelessness: Growers spread the viruses on contaminated cutting tools.

Viruses are incurable. A plant with a viral disease must be discarded because of its potential as a source of infection for other plants.

To prevent viral infection, follow consistent sanitary practices. Be sure cutting tools are thoroughly sterilized before every cut.

Cymbidium mosaic virus on foliage and flower

The most common virus of orchids is cymbidium mosaic virus (CMV), related to tobacco mosaic virus. CMV-affected plants display mosaic patterns or variegations on the leaf. Eventually, leaf tissue dies, leaving brown to black elongated spots or streaks on upper and lower surfaces of the leaves.

Another strain of the disease results in the flowers developing streaks and stripes several weeks after they open. The virus prematurely ages flowers.

CMV on flowers

HERE'S A TIP...

Five ways to prevent the spread of virus
- Buy only clean, healthy plants from reliable sources.
- Use only sterilized cutting tools and sterilize after each cut.
- Wear disposable latex or vinyl gloves when working with a new plant or one that seems unhealthy. Use a fresh pair of gloves for each plant you handle.
- Water and fertilize each plant separately rather than in a communal soaking. Avoid splashing water on plants growing in a greenhouse.
- When repotting, work on an opened section of newspaper. Use a fresh sheet for each plant, folding up and discarding the top sheet before you pot the next orchid.

Insects

Insects are most likely to attack plants that are poorly tended and stressed by lack of good care. You will find them on indoor orchids as well as ones outside or in a greenhouse. They tend to favor young, fast-growing plant parts, which are succulent and full of sap. New growths formed during the orchid's normal growing period, growth pushed by excess nitrogen, and normally fast-growing species are especially susceptible. Once foliage is mature, it is relatively impervious to insect attack.

The key to insect control is spotting the pests early, before their population builds and they spread to all of your orchids. Keep your eyes open as you work among your plants; check on them every day. Pay close attention to new growth and flower stems.

Insects hide and lay eggs in organic debris, so keep the growing area clean. Good sanitation does more than keep plants and the area around them clean; it's also crucial to stopping insects from moving in. Inspect new plants and remove any weeds in the growing medium. If you see signs of spider mites, isolate the plant until you treat it and it is free of mites. Also repot mite-infested orchids to eliminate eggs that have dropped into the medium.

Watch for ants in greenhouse and outdoor growing areas. Scales, mealybugs, and aphids sometimes hitch a ride on them. In addition, ants may protect the insects because they feed on the honeydew that the pests secrete.

Fine-mesh screens on greenhouse vents and windows help to prevent insects from flying in.

Choose an insect control labeled for a specific pest on orchids and follow instructions carefully. Many orchids are harmed by the carrier in which the effective ingredient is dissolved, making it especially important to note whether the product is labeled for orchids.

You may need to make several applications at certain intervals to ensure you have stopped the pest. Applying too little insect control may lead to populations of insect control resistant pests. Using too much can be toxic to the plant.

Following are common insect pests that affect orchids.

Aphid damage to cane dendrobium

Aphids

Soft-bodied aphids are insects that are less than ⅛ inch long. They may be green, yellow, or pink. "Tailpipes" at the rear of their bodies are one identifying feature.

Aphids feed by inserting piercing mouthparts into a plant and sucking up nutrients directly from the plant's vascular system. They reproduce rapidly, forming large colonies. Aphids are particularly attracted to developing flower stems. Their feeding can stunt or deform plant growth. Honeydew,

Tiny aphids suck juices from foliage and flowers.

a sugary secretion, flows out of the tailpipes onto leaves and stems. The sticky sap attracts ants, which harvest it, and a black sooty mold may grow in it.

In the garden, spray plants with a strong jet of water to knock aphids off, break their proboscises, and prevent them from feeding. Watch your plants and spray as often as necessary; for heavy infestations, use insecticidal soap.

Caterpillars

Seldom a problem indoors, caterpillars may inch their way onto outdoor orchids in warm climates. They feed on new growths and buds.

If possible, pick off caterpillars by hand and identify them. Relocate those that will turn into desirable butterflies. Otherwise, drown them in a bucket of soapy water.

For serious caterpillar infestations, apply horticultural oil. You can also use *Bacillus thuringiensis* (Bt) to control caterpillars.

Caterpillar feeding on flower

Cockroaches

Cockroaches have carved out the edges of petals

Nibbled flowers, roots, and new growth may indicate the presence of cockroaches, which have chewing mouthparts. They are hardy and highly adaptable—and also a health hazard, carrying disease-causing bacteria that can infect humans. Cockroaches enter pots through the drainage holes, then come out at night to feed on the plants. Keep them out of your growing area by cleaning all surfaces and sealing any cracks or crevices where pests might enter. Insecticidal soap is a natural repellent, and diatomaceous earth is a contact desiccant. Baits or traps can be used in homes in which children and pets are not present.

Fungus gnats

You may notice tiny dark flying insects flitting about the surface of the potting medium. Adult fungus gnats won't harm plants, but their white larvae lying beneath the potting medium surface can be a problem; larvae feed on decaying matter in the medium. If the medium is intact and the orchid's

Fungus gnat

roots are healthy, this should not be a problem. When the medium is excessively wet or breaking down or the roots are dying, the larvae can be trouble.

Using an open or fast-draining medium that contains perlite, expanded clay pellets, volcanic rock, or other aggregate material should keep fungus gnats from being a serious threat to plants.

If their population builds, a drench containing imidacloprid may be effective. Biological controls include beneficial bacteria, parasitic nematodes, and predatory mites. Repot affected plants in a coarser mix and let it dry between watering.

Lubber grasshoppers

The bold colors, markings, and large size (2 to 3 inches at maturity) of lubber grasshoppers make these voracious pests easy to spot. The nymphs usually travel in swarms and can quickly cause widespread damage to an orchid collection, chewing large holes in the leaves. Pest controls are effective only against the immature

Lubber grasshopper

grasshoppers and are not recommended for use on orchids, so the best treatment is to prevent access. Lubbers are slow moving and harmless to humans; remove them by hand.

Mealybugs

Mealybugs are the No. 1 pest problem for most orchids. Waxy white coating and threadlike filaments around the body characterize these small oval insects. Their population can quickly build into sizeable colonies. Symptoms of their presence include yellowing leaves and stunted growth.

They can be difficult to eradicate. The best defense is to prevent colonies from developing, which requires vigilance—especially around susceptible, fast-growing plants such as phalaenopsis. Remove them with a swab dipped in 70 percent denatured or rubbing alcohol. Check every few days and repeat as necessary. Weekly spraying with insecticidal soap, horticultural oil, or acephate (Orthene) may be necessary for serious infestations. If using acephate, add a wetting agent to the sprayer to ensure the insect control penetrates the waxy coating that protects the pest.

Mealybug

Mealybug infestation

Midges

Orchid blossom midges are ½-inch-long flies with banded legs, large eyes, long antennae, and spotted wings. Their tiny white larvae hide in and feed on orchid buds and flowers, preferring dendrobium and vanda types. The larvae damage and deform floral tissues, leading to a condition called bud blast. Spray acephate mixed with a penetrant such as

Midge

LI-700 on orchid foliage and buds once a week to control adults and larvae. If the infestation is severe, remove all of the inflorescences before applying an insect control.

Scale insects

Immobile scale insects appear as ¹⁄₁₆- to ⅛-inch-long round or oval, brown, gray, or white bumps on leaves, stems, and pseudobulbs. Immature stages, called crawlers, move around on the plant until they find a satisfactory feeding location; they are smaller and much lighter in color. Scale insects exude honeydew that attracts ants and may develop sooty mold. Severe infestations can stunt the plant.

Adult insects have a hard covering, which makes chemical control difficult. Physically remove them or treat with a cotton swab dipped in 70 percent denatured or rubbing alcohol. Inspect plants often and remove pests as soon as you see them. Pest control sprays are most effective against the crawler stage before the insect develops its hard shell.

Hard scale

Boisduval scale

Boisduval scale insects are especially damaging to older cattleyas. Their dense white cottony colonies in the junctions between leaves and pseudobulbs are often hidden by the sheaths (bottom parts) of the leaves.

If you see yellow spots on the top of your cattleya leaves, look for scale insects underneath. The adults are small but do a great deal of damage. Scrub the leaves with a toothbrush dipped in horticultural oil, then spray acephate or insecticidal soap weekly until control is achieved. Discard badly infested plants. Before bringing a new orchid into your growing area, inspect it carefully to be absolutely sure it is not carrying boisduval scale insects.

Slugs and snails

Chewed leaves and petals, holes in buds, and slime trails over leaves, flowers, and other surfaces indicate that slugs and snails have moved in. Remove slugs and snails by hand and drop them into a pail of soapy water. Check plants frequently, looking under containers and pot rims for the pests; they retreat to dark corners during daylight hours. They also hide in debris. Control slugs and snails with baits containing metaldehyde or iron phosphate and labeled for the control of these pests. Prevent children's and pets' access to metaldehyde baits.

Slug damage to flower bud

Snail

Spider mites

These pests suck sap from plants. Symptoms that plants are under attack by spider mites are a general yellow to bronze speckling of foliage and fine webbing covering flowers and foliage; webbing indicates a large mite population.

Mites appear as specks on the undersides of leaves or climbing fine webbing between the leaves. They are so tiny that it's difficult to see them with the naked eye. If you suspect mites but can't see them, hold a sheet of white paper under a leaf and tap on it; if mites are present, you'll see tiny moving specks on the paper. Or run your fingers along the underside of a leaf; if it feels dusty, there may be mites; follow up with the paper test or a magnifying glass.

Spider mites are most common in hot, dry conditions. Raising humidity and hosing off the undersides of leaves while watering may help control them. Cymbidiums grown outdoors may occasionally be infested enough to require treatment with a miticide or insecticidal soap. Treat affected plants every week to control subsequent generations emerging from eggs in the soil.

Spider mite webbing and mites

Thrips

Thrips are small ¹⁄₁₆- to ⅛-inch-long yellow, brown, or black flying insects. They are difficult to see because of their size and their fast movement.

The insects have rasping mouthparts that scar any tissue they feed on. They feed on flower buds as well as on foliage. Sometimes the damage is so severe that flowers fall off.

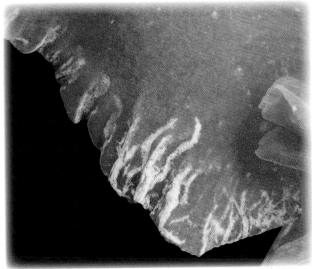
Thrip feeding creates trails of damage in petals and flower buds.

Thrip

Leaves eventually drop, and the plant may fail to grow.

Thrips thrive and reproduce rapidly in warm temperatures. Vandas and dendrobiums growing outdoors may be particularly attractive to thrips.

To control thrips on orchids in your home, use insecticidal soap. Outdoors or in greenhouses, apply acephate or other pest controls labeled for use on orchids. Some growers report success with beneficial predatory mites.

HERE'S A TIP...

Using pest controls
- Always wear protective gear as specified on the label when spraying. Wear long sleeves, long pants, and gloves. When a respirator is recommended, wear one.
- Fill the sprayer with water first, then add the pest control concentrate to avoid splashing it out of the sprayer.
- Make only as much spray solution as you think you will need. Discard any excess according to label directions.
- Triple-rinse the spray container before storing it.
- Many ready-to-use products are available, which lessens the danger of working with concentrated pest controls and eliminates the worry of what to do with excess materials. They are an economical alternative for only a few plants.

Whiteflies

If a small cloud of tiny white insects rises when you move an orchid, you are seeing whiteflies. They are about ¹⁄₁₆ inch long, congregate primarily on the undersides of leaves, and have piercing-sucking mouthparts that are used to feed on plant sap. As they feed, they secrete honeydew.

Plants weakened by whiteflies show damage and have unhealthy new growth. Leaves may become yellow and mottled then drop. Outdoors, use systemic insect controls labeled for use against whiteflies on orchids. Indoors, use similarly labeled insecticidal soaps or horticultural oils. In a greenhouse, use beneficial predatory insects to control the whitefly population.

Whiteflies fold their wings when resting so they are even harder to see until their numbers build up.

Cultural problems

Examples of cultural problems for orchidists growing plants are inadequate lighting, incorrect temperatures, and poor care. All orchid growers make mistakes occasionally; learning from those mistakes can mean growing even better orchids.

Symptoms of cultural problems often mimic those of insect and disease damage. To sort out the exact cause of a problem, you must carefully observe your plants. Along with a questioning attitude, you'll find a good 10× magnifying glass to be quite helpful.

Take a close look at an unhealthy plant in the brightest possible light. Some environmental problems are more common than others. For more unusual problems, consult an expert at an orchid nursery or orchid society meeting.

HERE'S A TIP...

Rehydrate plants
Place a small amount of sphagnum moss in the bottom of a pot to help rehydrate a dry orchid.

Insufficient light

Orchids receiving too little light (left) display dark green foliage and few blooms.

The most common cultural problem of orchids and the leading cause of failure to bloom is insufficient light. Orchids suffering from inadequate light have dark green, soft, succulent or weak growth that requires staking. Foliage may appear blanched and seem to stretch toward the light. Even when foliage appears lush, new growths may decline in size and vigor.

Too little light can result from shading by trees, shrubs, and structures outside your home or from placing the orchid too far from a window. A north window seldom has adequate light for any but jewel orchids. A lightly shaded south, east, or west window is a better choice.

Move plants exhibiting these symptoms into higher light in stages over a period of days to allow them to adjust. If moved too quickly into higher light, foliage will burn. Consider setting up a light garden containing a 50–50 mix of cool- and warm-white fluorescent tubes as a long-term solution where light will always be inadequate.

Sunburn and overheating

Sunburn occurs when foliage surface temperatures become too hot. Generally, sunburned orchids have been overexposed to high-intensity sunlight, but symptoms can occur when plants are simply too hot, as when you leave

In the second stage of sunburn, cells rupture, turn black, and die.

them in a hot car, on the sill of a closed south-facing window, or in a greenhouse with inadequate ventilation.

Symptoms of sunburn and overheating pass through several easily discernible stages that eventually result in death. In the first stage, the foliage is white or pale where chlorophyll has bleached out. Next, cells rupture and turn black. Finally, the tissue dies, leaving a brown or tan area of collapsed, dead cells. Often the plant displays a blotch in which all three stages are visible with beginning stages on the outside and dead cells on the inside. Sunburn symptoms generally occur at the broadest part of the leaf with the most surface exposed to the sun.

Finally, the overheated, sunburned tissue becomes sunken and tan or brown.

RESCUING AN ORCHID THAT'S LOST MOST OF ITS ROOTS

An orchid that has lost its roots from over- or underwatering, diseases, or other causes can sometimes be saved using these techniques:

1 Take the orchid from the pot and remove as much old potting medium as possible. Most orchids lacking roots easily come out of their pots. If it seems to be stuck, pry it out with a dull knife.

2 Cut away dead roots using a sharp sterile knife or clippers, cutting as close to the pseudobulbs as you can.

3 Spray roots with a broad-spectrum disease control to prevent fungi from moving into the cut ends and damaged areas.

4 Place a few pieces of plastic foam or similar material in the bottom of a clay pot that has been soaked an hour or so. If the plant is severely dehydrated, add a small wad of moist sphagnum. Set the orchid in the pot and water as normal. Moisture evaporating from the clay will keep the humidity high around the roots and sustain them until new roots begin to grow. When new root tips are ½ inch long, pot the orchid as normal.

Cultural problems *(continued)*

Sunburn and overheating are not usually serious problems. The damaged area dries out and remains ugly but benign. Extreme cases can lead to plant death, especially when pseudobulbs are affected. In addition, damage gives disease a chance to enter the plant.

Overheating can be a chronic problem when plants are subjected to long periods of temperatures that are just below levels that would actually burn them. Overheating stresses plants, gives them a bleached appearance, and stunts growth. Pseudobulbs grow progressively smaller; and chronically overheated plants can die.

If an area seems uncomfortably hot for you, it is likely too hot for the orchid. Touch the broad part of a leaf with your palm. If the leaf feels warm, reduce the temperature.

To lower temperatures in a greenhouse, cut light levels and increase air movement. Raise humidity by wetting down greenhouse paths and other surfaces.

Orchids grown indoors generally use all the light they can but can become bleached when they get too much too quickly. As seasons change, be aware of light levels in your home or greenhouse. The angle of the rising sun can quickly burn soft winter foliage. A filmy curtain at a south or west window is often all that's needed to moderate increasing light levels. A small fan or open window near plants also helps to moderate temperatures.

To prevent sunburn outdoors, move plants into a shady part of the yard or take them indoors.

Overwatering

Yellowing growth and shriveled foliage signal root loss caused by overwatering.

The single most common cultural problem, especially for beginning orchid growers, overwatering causes leaves and pseudobulbs to turn yellow and shrivel. Leaves have a dull texture because the plant has lost roots, which prevents the plant from taking up moisture.

Symptoms of overwatering are nearly the same as those of a plant not receiving enough water. The difference is that with an overwatered orchid, growing medium appears dark and may glisten with moisture, the pot will feel heavy, and surface roots, if present, will be dark and mushy.

The longer an orchid has been in a pot, the more broken down the medium becomes, making it easier to overwater. Frequent watering hastens decomposition. For a cure, repot the plant in fresh medium, in the smallest possible pot. Keep the plant in a shady, humid environment and water it infrequently until new root growth appears. Follow the advice beginning on page 51 for watering orchids.

Underwatering

Desiccated roots, stems, and poor growth are signs of underwatering.

Pleated leaves indicate underwatering in thin-leafed orchids.

Plants that are grown outdoors or in very dry or stressful environments may not receive enough water. The potting medium becomes light in color and the pot lightweight, the plant desiccated and shriveled. Any surface roots appear healthy and white. In severe cases, the roots may be damaged by salt buildup caused by generally poor watering practices or poor quality water, or both.

Rewet in one of two ways. Either thoroughly water the plant several times over a period of a day or so, or soak the plant in a container of water until the medium is thoroughly wet. When rehydrating more than one plant, change the water for each plant. Follow the advice beginning on page 51 for watering orchids.

Pleated leaves Another symptom of underwatering occurs on thin-leaved orchids such as ones in the oncidium alliance, especially miltoniopsis. The leaves develop accordion-like horizontal pleating. Low humidity and strong light can contribute. Pleating cannot be reversed, but you can prevent it from developing in new leaves.

Salt buildup

Salts build up on the bottom of the pot when the medium isn't thoroughly wetted at watering.

Powdery white residue on containers, saucers, and potting medium is most often salt. The high salt content can kill roots, in which case you will see symptoms on your plants as well. High-elevation orchids such as miltoniopsis and masdevallia are especially susceptible.

Salt deposits can be caused by fertilizing too much or too little, not applying enough water at a time, or by using poor-quality—hard or alkaline—water. To prevent salts from building up, water thoroughly, allowing water to run freely through the potting mix to leach existing salts through the medium and prevent buildup. Never use softened water on orchids (or other plants) because it is high in sodium chloride. If possible, use good-quality water from a local source or water filtered through a reverse osmosis system.

Days too long

When days are too long, orchids may look generally stressed, with poor growth and burned leaf tips. If they receive more than 16 hours of light a day, they may fail to bloom. Lack of rest is most common for orchids growing under lights. Put lights on an automatic timer that simulates day lengths in the orchid's native habitat.

Lack of rest

Failure to bloom and dropping of leaves may occur when orchids do not receive a rest period. Numerous orchids originated in areas with seasonal changes. For example, ones from high elevations in the subtropics are adapted to cool, dry winters and warm, moist summers. Winter is a rest period, characterized by little or no water and temperatures close to freezing. Learn your orchid's natural dormant seasons and withhold water and fertilizer for that time. Without natural seasonal changes, plants will suffer.

Poor air quality

Orchids exposed to ethylene or sulfur dioxide drop their flower buds. Sources of ethylene are ripening fruit and vegetables and gas appliances; sulfur dioxide is a component of smog. Orchids growing outdoors or by open windows in urban areas are susceptible to smog damage. Phalaenopsis, cattleyas, and dendrobiums are especially susceptible to air pollution, from either outdoor or indoor causes.

Weeds

Weeds compete for fertilizer and water and may harbor pests that can harm orchids. Pull weeds from the growing area as soon as they appear; never let them flower or set seed.

Weeds harbor pests and compete for resources.

Encyclopedia of orchids

▼ Brother Gold Wish is a hybrid phalaenopsis. Phalaenopsis is the most popular orchid on the market because of its ease of growth and tolerance of indoor growing conditions. It blooms in white, purple, pink, and yellow. Learn more on page 189.

Whether you are new to orchid growing or a more advanced enthusiast wanting to expand your collection, you will enjoy browsing this comprehensive chapter. Here you will discover almost four hundred individual species and hybrids within more than one hundred genera. Some are common, and you will recognize them when you shop in your local garden store. Others are more exotic; you may have to search for them at orchid shows, by mail order, or on the Internet. (See page 214 for sources.)

Entries are arranged alphabetically by botanical name and begin with an at-a-glance overview of the genus. This includes pronunciation, abbreviation, and growth type, along with basics, such as the amount of light and water the orchid requires, the best temperature and humidity for growing it, and whether the orchid does well in pots or on mounts.

Species descriptions follow; hybrid descriptions end each entry. Each species and hybrid listing points out who will find it easiest to grow—a beginning, intermediate, or advanced grower—and the most likely source for the orchid. You'll also find cultural advice and details on bloom time, fragrance, and other noteworthy features. If no cultural, fragrance, or bloom time information is provided for a species or hybrid, that orchid is similar to and grown like the genus.

Although orchids in this encyclopedia represent a fraction of the thousands of orchids, you are sure to find some that fit your needs as well as some to aspire to.

Encyclopedia terms

To help you understand entries, here are the key terms:

• **Growths** Orchids come in such an array of plant sizes, forms, and aspects that conventional horticultural terms are often inadequate. Orchid hobbyists have their own set of descriptive terms that may be unfamiliar to newcomers. One of the more commonly used terms is "growths." A growth is an individual component of a sympodial plant, usually comprising the pseudobulb and its leaves, although orchids without noticeable pseudobulbs are also said to have growths.

Orchids, especially paphiopedilums, are often sold by the division and priced by the growth, which, in the case of paphs, is one mature fan of leaves. Mature means the pseudobulb and leaves have reached full size and form. A flowering size cattleya will often have three to five growths: the older pseudobulbs and their leaves that have previously flowered as well as newer developing pseudobulbs and leaves from which flowers will emerge.

• **Size** Orchid sizes are classified as miniature or dwarf, small or compact, average, and large.

Miniature or dwarf Less than 6 inches tall

▲ At orchid shows you'll see numerous hybrids that may be available only at the show, if even there. For example, this unnamed hybrid is a cross between *Brassolaelia nodosa* and *Laelia tenebrosa*.

Small or compact 6 to 12 inches tall
Average 12 to 18 inches tall
Large Taller than 18 inches
• **Light** Orchids vary in their light needs. The classifications are low, medium, bright, and indirect.

Low light You can grow the orchid in a north window; to either side of an east window, or outdoors in a shady site.

Medium light Place the orchid in an east window, to the east of a south window, or in a shaded west window.

Bright light Orchids requiring bright light belong in a west window, a shaded south window, or in a greenhouse.

Indirect light Keep orchids requiring indirect light out of sunlight.
• **Temperature** The temperature ranges for orchids are as follows:
Cold
40° to 50°F nights
50° to 70°F days
Cool
50° to 55°F nights
60° to 70°F days
Mild
55° to 65°F nights
70° to 80°F days
Warm
65° to 70°F nights
80° to 90°F days
• **Humidity** The encyclopedia designates two humidity levels:
Moderate 50 to 60 percent
High Above 60 percent
• **Water**
Dry between waterings Water then wait until the medium is almost completely dry before watering again.
Keep evenly moist Let the medium become nearly dry, but not completely dry. You should feel some moisture in the medium.
Continuously moist The orchid does best in a wet but not soggy medium. Water frequently, and let the medium dry only slightly before the next watering.
• **Culture** Orchids may be easy or average in cultural needs, or they may require advanced care.
Easy The orchid requires little care beyond what you would give a typical houseplant.

▲ *Brassolaeliocattleya* Hawaiian Charm carries some of the best traits of its parents, including large frilly flowers from its cattleya parent.

Average The orchid does well with a typical or routine orchid regime.
Advanced The orchid is challenging to grow and should probably be left to experienced orchid growers.
• **Availability** Not all orchids are easy to find. In fact, some exist in only a few growers' collections. These terms help you find orchids listed in this encyclopedia.
Common The orchids are readily available and often sold at many nurseries, garden centers, and home improvement stores.
Specialty growers Look for these orchids at orchid shows, at specialty nurseries specializing in orchids, or check the Internet for them.
Rare These orchids may not be available even from specialty growers or on the Internet. Personal connections will help here.
• **Fertilizer** Unless an orchid species requires special feeding instructions, fertilizer needs are not called out in the entries. Almost all orchids should be fed regularly with a high-quality balanced fertilizer. Regularly means to supply fertilizer at one-half label strength every week or at full strength every two weeks. A balanced plant food contains nitrogen, phosphorus, and potassium (N-P-K) in equal parts, such as 10-10-10, or in nearly equal amounts, such as 8-6-3.
• **Media** Potting media are not called out for every orchid; however, a particular medium is recommended in the entry of some orchids.
Fast-draining Use coarse fir bark, coconut husk chips, osmunda, tree-fern fiber, aggregates or inert materials.
Water-retentive Use fine fir bark, soilless orchid mix, sphagnum moss, or coconut husk fiber.

Aerangis *(air-AN-gis)*

Abbreviation: *Aergs.*
Monopodial
Miniature to small, depending on species
Low to medium light, depending on species
Cool nights and days
Moderate humidity
Let dry between waterings
Pot or mount, depending on species

Aerangis orchids are compact plants suitable for growing in average home conditions or in a cool greenhouse. Their long-lasting, fragrant flowers bloom at least once a year. These orchids are related to angraecum orchids.

Aergs. articulata

Culture: Easy
Availability: Specialty growers
Considered one of the finest species in the genus, this 6-inch-tall plant with a pendulous growth habit produces an abundance of star-shape waxy white flowers every spring. Its dramatic blossoms—about 1½ inches across with a 4-inch spur—last several weeks. Their heady fragrance has been compared to jasmine. Mount this plant or pot it in fast-draining orchid mix.

Aergs. biloba

Aergs. biloba

Culture: Easy
Availability: Specialty growers
Another dwarf orchid that slowly grows to about 6 inches tall, *Aergs. biloba* produces abundant creamy white flowers that last for several weeks each spring. They come in 1-foot-long inflorescences, each blossom measuring about 1 inch across with a 4-inch spur, and exude an aroma of gardenias and lilies. Mount *Aergs. biloba* on a small slab or pot it in a well-drained orchid mix.

Aergs. citrata

Culture: Easy
Availability: Specialty growers

This species is compact yet graceful, with slender 6- to 10-inch-long flower spikes crowded with 15 or more small white flowers. The blooms have long spurs and emit a lemony aroma. *Aergs. citrata* blooms several times each year, and the flowers last for at least a few weeks. Foliage is dark green and no more than 5 inches long. Grow this orchid in a 3- or 4-inch pot on a cool windowsill or in a greenhouse where air circulates well. It's a good choice for a beginner.

Aergs. citrata

Aergs. luteo-alba rhodosticta

Culture: Easy
Availability: Specialty growers
Another good selection for low light and cool growing conditions, this highly sought-after miniature orchid has glistening cream or white flowers with contrasting red columns; they are crowded on long sprays in spring. (The species has white flowers that stay in good condition for three to five weeks.) Leaves are thin and short, no more than 3 inches long. Mount *rhodosticta* or pot it in a small container that drains quickly. It is also sold as *Aergs. rhodosticta*. A similar type, *Aergs.* Somasticta, is even more vigorous than the species.

Aergs. luteo-alba rhodosticta

Aergs. modesta

Culture: Easy
Availability: Specialty growers
Native to Madagascar, this plant looks like a bright green phalaenopsis, only smaller—its leaf span rarely reaches 10 inches. Pendent spikes bear as many as 15 white six-pointed star-shape flowers about 1 inch across. The blooms, which appear in autumn and sometimes again in spring, emit a hyacinthlike fragrance at night. Mount rather than pot this plant, but keep it continuously moist in low light and medium to warm temperatures.

Aergs. pumilio

Culture: Average
Availability: Specialty growers
This highly desirable miniature epiphyte from the lower elevations of Madagascar has a leaf span of less than 8 inches. Short sprays of 1-inch-wide cupped, crystalline-white blooms are borne in profusion in spring. The flowers are fragrant at night. Grow plants on mounts with high humidity (60 percent or higher). This species makes a good companion for phalaenopsis.

Aergs. pumilio

Angraecum *(an-GRAY-kum)*

Abbreviation: *Angcm.*
Monopodial
Miniature to large, depending on species
Medium to bright light
Mild nights and days
Moderate humidity
Let dry between waterings
Pot or mount, depending on species

These hauntingly beautiful, creamy green- to white-flowered orchids hail primarily from tropical and semitropical Africa, especially the large island of Madagascar. Carried on spikes singly or in small groups, the distinctive flowers are star-shape, have spurs, and range from as small as ½ inch across to as wide as 1 foot. Small or large, they radiate a deliciously sweet scent at night or in the early morning, when they would be pollinated by moths in their native habitat.

Angcm. sesquipedale

Strappy dark green leathery foliage contrasts well with the flower show. Some angraecoid plants are quite small, only inches tall, while others are 3 feet or taller. There are about seven hundred fifty known species, although only a fraction are in cultivation.

Not surprisingly, wild members of this large group are under threat from habitat destruction. However, because professional growers can easily raise angraecoids from seed, you can buy and grow these orchids in good conscience. Many of them are in the right size range for home gardeners.

The genus name comes from the Malaysian word *angrek,* meaning "epiphytic orchid." French botanist Louis-Marie Aubert du Petit-Thouars, who introduced some of the earliest angraecoid specimens in the early 1800s, may have given the genus its scientific name.

Orchids in this genus have fragile roots that break easily, so pick a pot or mount with permanency in mind. Mount smaller species and those with pendent inflorescences on bark; pot the larger ones. Angraecoids can be slow to mature, so if you are eager for the fragrant flowers, buy a large plant.

Angcm. didieri

Culture: Average
Availability: Specialty growers
These miniature plants, to less than 4 inches tall and 5 inches across, have upright, stiff semisucculent leaves. The creamy white blooms are as wide as 3 inches across and appear from the leaf axils in late summer to early fall, when their spicy-sweet fragrance fills the growing area at night. Pot plants in a small container of coarse, fast-draining orchid mix or mount one on a slab. Grow the orchid in bright light, mild temperatures, and humidity of about 50 percent.

Angcm. didieri

Angcm. distichum

Culture: Average
Availability: Specialty growers

Angcm. distichum

Plants are composed of overlapping leaves less than 1 inch long on freely branching, vining 6-inch-long stems. Small crystal white blooms, to about ½ inch across, are borne along the stems throughout the year and emit a daffodil-like fragrance at night. This species looks best if grown in part shade, mild temperatures, and high humidity. Because of its twining, almost vinelike growth habit, *Angcm. distichum* grows best on a slab or in a wide, shallow pan of medium-grade orchid mix.

Angcm. eburneum

Culture: Average
Availability: Specialty growers
A big plant that hails from Madagascar, Réunion, and coastal east Africa, *Angcm. eburneum* grows 4 feet wide in the wild and somewhat less large in cultivation. It does best on a slab or in a large pot in a bright, humid spot. In early winter, its thick, durable yellowish green leaves are joined by long, densely packed inflorescences of 3-inch-wide flowers. The lip of each flower is ivory; petals and sepals arrayed around them are apple green. The rich, sweet fragrance is similar to gardenia. You may find this plant labeled *Angcm. longicalcar.*

Angcm. eburneum superbum

Angcm. elephantinum

Culture: Average
Availability: Specialty growers
A miniature plant often no more than 4 or 5 inches tall and 5 inches across, this species is named for its creamy white star-shape blooms. They are often nearly 4 inches across, quite large compared with the size of the plant. The flowers bloom in winter and exude a spicy scent at night. Grow *Angcm. elephantinum* in bright light and 50 percent humidity where nights are cool and days are warm. If the leaves become succulent and the roots heavy, the plant should be allowed to dry between waterings.

Angcm. leonis

Culture: Average
Availability: Specialty growers

Angcm. leonis

If space is limited but you want an angraecoid, try this petite beauty. Plants rarely exceed 10 inches tall, yet the jasmine-scented flower display is relatively large—spikes are 3 to 5 inches long and carry three to five waxy white blooms about 1½ inches across. Flowers bloom in autumn and last for several weeks. Mount this orchid on a slab or pot it in a loose epiphytic mix. It adapts well to life on a windowsill but it will also thrive in a greenhouse or under lights.

Angcm. mauritianum

Culture: Average
Availability: Specialty growers
This dwarf species has branching pendent growth and 2½-inch leaves. It grows slowly and so is a good choice where space is limited. The sweetly jasmine-scented, pristine white flowers are about 1½ inches across, slightly curved back, and borne singly. They appear in great numbers in summer and fall and last for several weeks. Mount *Angcm. mauritianum* or pot it in a fast-draining orchid mix.

Angcm. sesquipedale

Culture: Average
Availability: Specialty growers

Angcm. sesquipedale

Also known as star of bethlehem and king of the angraecums, this big, showy species grows to 3 feet tall and wide and so must have ample display space. In mild-winter areas, attach it to a tree or grow it in a container. In all other climates, grow it in a sunroom or a greenhouse.

Angcm. sesquipedale has fans of dark green leaves. Large white flowers appear each spring, even on young plants. The blooms are 4½ inches across with a spur that can reach 15 inches long. They emit a strong, sweet scent and have a waxy texture that keeps them fresh looking for several weeks.

Charles Darwin observed the huge flowers of *Angcm. sesquipedale* in the wild and postulated that only a night-flying moth with an exceptionally long tongue—a foot long, he guessed—could pollinate them. His colleagues scoffed at the idea. Darwin had been dead 35 years before someone discovered that the true pollinator of this particular angraecoid: the hawk moth, which does indeed have a 12-inch tongue.

Angcm. **Lemforde White Beauty**
(Angcm. sesquipedale × Angcm. magdalenae)

Culture: Easy
Availability: Specialty growers
Spicy jasmine fragrance radiates every spring from the showy flowers of this outstanding hybrid. A vigorous grower, the plant eventually reaches 2 feet tall. The white flowers are between 4 and 5 inches across and last for a month or longer. The orchid's size calls attention to it by day; the scent is most powerful at night. Grow Lemforde White Beauty in bright light.

Angcm. **Veitchii**
(Angcm. eburneum × Angcm. sesquipedale)

Culture: Easy
Availability: Specialty growers
This large plant is relatively easy to grow in a greenhouse or outdoors in a mild-winter climate in medium light and mild temperatures. Heavy, strappy 4-inch-wide by 18-inch-long leaves branch off 36-inch-tall stems. Blooms appear on horizontal sprays bearing six to eight or more 6-inch greenish-white waxy blooms with long spurs in late winter to early spring. Flowers are sweetly fragrant at night and last as long as four weeks. Plant Veitchii in a 10-inch or larger pot of medium-grade mix; allow it to dry between waterings.

Angcm. Veitchii 'TC'

Angranthes **Grandalena**
(an-GRAN-thees gran-duh-LEAN-uh)
(Aeranthus grandiflora × Angcm. magdalenae)

Abbreviation: *Angth.*
Monopodial
Miniature to large, depending on species
Medium to bright light
Mild nights and days
Moderate humidity
Let dry between waterings
Pot or mount, depending on species
Culture: Easy
Availability: Specialty growers

Angranthes Grandalena

Grandalena is both attractive and a prolific bloomer. It grows 12 to 14 inches tall with a moderately compact habit. Foliage is glossy dark green; spurred white flowers are touched with pale green. The blooms reach 3 to 4 inches across and exude a jasmine fragrance. A mature plant is constantly in bloom, with flowers lasting two to three weeks.

Anguloa *(ang-yew-LOH-uh)*

Abbreviation: *Ang.*
Sympodial
Large
Low light
Cool nights and mild days
Moderate humidity
Keep evenly moist
Pot

Ang. clowesii 'Choco'

A relative of lycaste orchids (pages 158–160), this is a fairly large semi-terrestrial plant with robust 6- to 8-inch-tall pseudobulbs and broad, deciduous, palmlike leaves that are often more than 30 inches long. Anguloa's often-challenging cultural requirements are worth the effort for the unusual flowers, which do not open fully and as a result have a cupped shape. When growth matures in late fall and leaves begin to yellow, decrease water and fertilizer.

Ang. clowesii

Culture: Advanced
Availability: Specialty growers
Single yellow blooms with heavy substance are borne on multiple upright stems emerging from the base of the new growth in spring. Flowers are highly fragrant during the daytime, with medicinal and herbal overtones; they last four weeks or longer. Grow *Ang. clowesii* in a greenhouse or on a shady patio in mild climates.

Ang. clowesii

Anoectochilus *(a-neck-toh-KY-lus)*

Abbreviation: *Anct.*
Sympodial
Miniature
Medium to bright, indirect light
Mild nights and days
High humidity
Keep evenly moist
Pot
Culture: Easy
Availability: Specialty growers

One of the jewel orchids (a group of several related species), anoectochilus has erect stems of insignificant blooms, but this orchid is grown for its attractive foliage. It has pronounced rhizomes with whorls of un-orchidlike leaves in shades of rich velvety brown to nearly black, checkered in gold. Bright light helps maintain the foliage color, but keep this plant out of direct sun. Pot it in balanced houseplant mix or plant it in a terrarium. Propagate by cuttings.

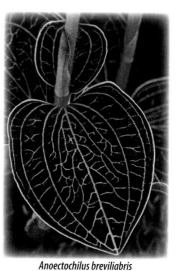

Anoectochilus breviliabris

Ansellia africana *(an-SELL-lee-uh aff-rick-ann-uh)*

Abbreviation: *Aslla.*
Monopodial
Large
Bright light
Cool to mild nights and warm days
Moderate humidity
Let dry between waterings
Mount or pot
Culture: Easy
Availability: Specialty growers

From tropical Africa and South Africa comes this impressive species, best given the extra space it needs in a greenhouse or mounted in a tree outdoors in mild climates. The striking yellow flowers of *Ansellia africana* are 1½ to 2 inches across and boldly marked with leopardlike rust-brown spots. Plants bloom in spring with a musky fragrance. As many as 100 flowers crowd the 3-foot-long branched stems that arise from the top of the large pseudobulb and from nodes along the length of

Ansellia africana Krullsmith

the canes—making for a substantial plant. Pot the plant in a wide, shallow pan in a coarse orchid mix. Reduce watering in winter to encourage spring blooms. You may find this orchid sold as *Aslla. gigantea.*

Ascocenda *(as-koh-SEN-duh)*

Abbreviation: *Ascda.*
Monopodial
Large
Bright light
Mild nights and warm days
High humidity
Let dry between waterings
Basket or pot

Beginning growers appreciate how easy these species are to grow. They are popular for an outstanding combination of traits that yields moderate size plants with relatively large blooms. Like their parents—vandas and ascocentrums—they are upright orchids with leaves branching from a main stem like a ladder and brightly colored flowers.

They do best in tropical conditions of high humidity and bright light. Best results are achieved in hanging baskets that allow robust roots to ramble freely and dry quickly after watering. Frequent water and fertilizer ensure plants that flower throughout the year on upright stems in a broad palette of colors and sizes. Plants range from 12 to 48 inches at maturity; most ascocendas are large enough to require substantial space in a greenhouse or on a frost-free patio.

Ascda. Sufun Beauty 'Orange Bell'

Ascda. Dong Tarn 'Robert' (*Ascda.* Medasand × *Ascda.* Eileen Beauty)

Culture: Easy
Availability: Specialty growers

Ascda. Dong Tarn 'Robert'

Sweetly scented brilliant red flowers on a compact plant make this AM/AOS hybrid hard to resist. Although bloom time varies, the flurry of 1¼-inch blossoms is always worth the wait. Flowers are rich, dark red with a red-and-yellow lip; as many as a dozen may line a single flower stem. This plant grows 18 or more inches tall and often branches at the base. Grow in a hanging basket that can accommodate its sprawling roots and provide the rapid drainage this hybrid requires.

Ascda. Hatos Sunshine (*Ascda.* Fuchs Star × *V. tessellata*)

Culture: Average
Availability: Specialty growers

This is a prime example of new directions in ascocenda breeding. Using the unusual *tessellata* results in distinct, charming, often fragrant blooms in a broad range of colors. Flowering peaks in spring; new stems may appear throughout the year. Plants are compact, about 24 inches tall at maturity. Give them warmth, ample humidity, and plenty of water. Feed regularly to maximize growth.

Ascda. Hatos Sunshine

Ascda. Medasand
(*V. sanderiana* × *Ascda.* Meda Arnold)

Culture: Easy
Availability: Specialty growers

Ascda. Medasand was registered in 1967. It is still popular today, but more importantly, hybridizers frequently use it as a parent. Flower colors are variable, but for the most part, flowers are salmon-orange-red with darker lips. The flowers are about 2½ inches across and borne in profusion on 8- to 10-inch spikes. Medasand is a compact plant, taking years to reach 18 inches tall. A well-established plant will bloom several times a year.

Ascda. Medasand

Ascda. Peggy Foo '#1'
(*V. Bonnie Blue* × *Asctm. curvifolium*)

Culture: Easy
Availability: Specialty growers

This cross, made more than 30 years ago, still ranks as one of the greatest because of its luminous free-flowering blossoms. The compact growth habit comes from its ascocentrum parent. Peggy Foo '#1' has been used extensively as a parent to produce larger-flowering ascocenda orchids. Bloom time varies, but plentiful 1½-inch flowers are borne in inflorescences of 15 or more blossoms in one of several color schemes depending on cultivar. Leaves spread out 10 inches while vertical growth slowly reaches 24 inches tall or more. Peggy Foo '#1' requires excellent drainage; grow it in a hanging basket. In warm, humid climates, gardeners pot this orchid in a basket with no medium.

Ascda. Peggy Foo

Ascda. Sagarik 'Rapee'
(*Ascda.* Kuhn Nok × *V. merrillii*)

Culture: Easy
Availability: Specialty growers

Rapee Sagarik is a well-known figure in the orchid world, especially in his home country of Thailand, where he was a horticulture professor and leader in the development of the orchid industry. He registered this sunny yellow first-generation ascocenda in 1967. It has masses of clear yellow flowers about 2 inches across on 12-inch spikes. The plant reaches about 18 inches tall in several years. It usually blooms in spring and summer, but a mature plant can bloom more than once a year.

Ascda. Sagarik 'Rapee'

Ascda. Suk Sumran Beauty
(*Ascda.* Yip Sum Wah × *V. Gordon Dillon*)

Culture: Easy
Availability: Specialty growers

Ascda. Suk Sumran Beauty 'Talisman Cove'

Two prizewinning parents were used to create this stunning orchid. *Ascda.* Suk Sumran Beauty is highly variable in its color range, from yellow-orange to shades of pink and cherry red and even blue. The flowers are about 2½ inches across and borne along 12-inch flower spikes, sometimes several times a year. Plants grow 1½ to 2 feet tall in several years.

Ascocentrum *(as-koh-SEN-trum)*

Abbreviation: *Asctm.*
Monopodial
Miniature to compact
Bright light
Mild nights, warm days
High humidity
Let dry between waterings
Basket

Ascocentrum curvifolium

Asctm. ampullaceum

Closely related to vandas, with which ascocentrums freely interbreed, these orchids are native to Southeast Asia. All have colorful, upright inflorescences composed of numerous blossoms. The species are generally easy to grow and make floriferous additions to just about any collection. Best results are achieved in locations with bright light and high humidity, such as outdoors in the Gulf states and southern Florida or in a greenhouse almost anywhere. Grow these orchids in slatted wooden baskets with coarse medium or none at all. Increase watering and feeding during the warmest months.

Asctm. ampullaceum

Culture: Easy
Availability: Specialty growers
This dwarf orchid, native to India, Bangladesh, and Thailand, is valued for its bountiful show of magenta, white, or orange flowers in spring to summer. Individual blooms are small, between ½ and ¾ inch across; they appear in erect inflorescences containing as many as 40 blossoms each. Leaves on the 4-inch-tall plants extend out about 6 inches.

Asctm. ampullaceum is a bushy plant with many shoots emanating from the base. It thrives in pots or baskets. The foliage develops red spots if light is too bright.

Asctm. ampullaceum aurantiacum

Culture: Easy
Availability: Specialty growers
The flower color of this knockout plant has been described as "electric mandarin red." The orange-red hue is radiant, and the dash of yellow on the flower's lip adds even more interest. Blossoms are ½ to 1 inch across, developing in 3- to 8-inch-tall inflorescences in spring and summer. Plants grow about 4 inches tall. Plant them in wooden baskets. In winter, reduce watering and lower the temperature.

Asctm. curvifolium

Culture: Easy
Availability: Specialty growers
The largest orchid of this genus, *Asctm. curvifolium* may reach 36 inches tall, branching freely from the base. Leaves are narrow and grow to 12 inches long. Upright stems hold two dozen or more 2-inch-wide brilliant orange blooms, which appear in late winter to early spring and may last four weeks or more. Mature plants bear many flowering stems and are showy.

Asctm. miniatum

Culture: Easy
Availability: Specialty growers
As the name implies, this is the miniature of the genus, growing to less than 6 inches tall and wide. It needs bright light and will do well on a windowsill or in a greenhouse. The stiff, horizontal, succulent leaves are closely ranked—arranged in rows—on the upright plants, which often branch

Asctm. miniatum

from the base. Brilliant ½-inch yellow to yellow-orange blooms appear on upright 5-inch-tall flower stems in late winter into spring. This is one of the showiest of all miniature monopodial orchids, with attractive plants and bright blooms, well worth searching for.

Asconopsis *(as-koh-NOP-sis)*

Abbreviation: *Ascps.*
Monopodial
Compact
Medium to bright, indirect light; part shade outdoors
Mild nights and warm days
High humidity
Keep evenly moist
Pot

Somewhat challenging to grow, this unusual intergeneric hybrid between ascocentrum and phalaenopsis combines the small size of ascocentrums with flowers that look like those of phalaenopsis on plants that tolerate brighter light than phalaenopsis.

Asconopsis grows slowly to 6 inches tall and 12 inches wide.

Ascps. Irene Dobkin 'York'

Its upright flower stems carry 1½-inch soft orange blooms that can last four weeks in late winter to spring.

Ascps. Irene Dobkin 'York' (Phal. Doris × Asctm. miniatum)

Culture: Advanced
Availability: Specialty growers
Irene Dobkin 'York' was one of the first monopodials to be successfully cloned. Its 1½-inch peachy-orange blooms appear in spring.

Pot this orchid in coarse bark or sphagnum moss and grow it on a windowsill or in a shady spot outdoors in frost-free zones. If the plant is healthy but fails to bloom, move it into brighter light; avoid direct light. Because some unattractive sports, or mutations, have appeared since the first introduction of *Ascps.* Irene Dobkin 'York', purchase this orchid from a reputable specialty grower or buy it when it is in bloom.

Barkeria *(bar-KAIR-ee-a)*

Abbreviation: *Bark.*
Sympodial
Compact to large, depending on species
Medium light
Mild nights and days
High humidity
Let dry between waterings; provide a dry winter dormancy
Mount

Closely related to epidendrum, this deciduous genus has canelike growth habit with elongated pseudobulbs that range from 4 to more than 18 inches long. Its leaves drop in late fall to early winter. Plants bear a few to a dozen or more 2-inch blooms in shades of lavender, rose, or white on upright terminal flower stems. Bloom time varies according to species and location; indoors they bloom in summer. Grow barkeria on cork so robust, rambling roots can easily dry. Use rainwater or distilled water. Feed plants heavily while they are growing; reduce fertilizer as dormancy approaches.

Bark. lindleyana

Culture: Average
Availability: Specialty growers
This compact Mexican native grows to about 1 foot tall.

Bark. lindleyana

Dark lavender flowers are about 2½ inches across with white markings and a contrasting royal purple lip. The roots of this species tend to escape their mounts and attach to anything in the vicinity. When the plant drops its leaves in autumn, let it dry out. Resume water and fertilizer when new growth appears in spring.

Beallara *(bee-al-LAR-a)*

Abbreviation: *Bllra.*
Sympodial
Large
Low to medium light
Mild nights and days
High humidity
Keep evenly moist
Pot

Bllra. Marfitch 'Howard's Dream'

splashed with yellow. Robust Marfitch 'Howard's Dream' grows about 18 to 24 inches tall at maturity. Pot it in a combination of medium-grade orchid mix and coconut husk chips. Warm temperatures cause lighter flower colors; bright light turns the leaves purple.

Bllra. Tahoma Glacier (*Mtssa.* Cartegena × *Odtna.* Alaskan Sunset)

Culture: Easy
Availability: Common
Flower stems up to 36 inches tall carry a dozen or more 5-inch star-shape white blooms with wine red markings. This popular orchid may bloom at any time of year, and the flowers last as long as six weeks.

Bllra. Smile Eri

Beginners find these complex intergeneric hybrids among the easiest to grow because of favorable characteristics: compact size, free-blooming habit, and ease of care. They are hybrids of crosses of brassia, cochlioda, miltonia, and odontoglossum but are oncidiumlike in their appearance. Plants may reach 18 inches tall and bear one or two upright, arching stems that each hold a dozen or more long-lasting blooms that are 4 inches wide or more. Pot beallara in a medium-grade orchid mix; keep plants evenly moist with rainwater or distilled water.

Bllra. Marfitch 'Howard's Dream' (*Mtssa.* Charles Marden Fitch × *Odm.* Fremar)

Culture: Easy
Availability: Common
Dramatic star-shape flowers always get this AM/AOS award winner lots of attention. Twice a year, 3-foot inflorescences carry as many as two dozen blooms that can last for months. Individual flowers measure 4 to 5 inches across. They are a rich wine-purple with contrasting white markings and lips

Bllra. Tahoma Glacier

Bifrenaria *(by-fren-AIR-ee-uh)*

Abbreviation: *Bif.*
Sympodial
Compact
Medium to bright light
Mild nights and days
Moderate humidity
Let dry between waterings
Pot

Closely related to lycaste and maxillaria orchids, this genus has 4-inch pseudobulbs that are nearly square in cross section and broad upright leaves that grow more than 20 inches long. Several single flowers are borne in spring and summer on short stems around the base of the newest growth. Pot bifrenaria orchids in a coarse orchid mix; repot them infrequently, as plants bloom best when pot-bound. Provide a winter dormancy with little water and no fertilizer.

Bif. harrisoniae

Culture: Advanced
Availability: Rare

Native to the damp tropical rain forests of Brazil, this fragrant orchid has a cluster of 3-inch-tall pseudobulbs and long, broad, leathery leaves. The flower stalks originate at the base of the pseudobulbs in spring. Each stalk bears one or two creamy white 2-inch-wide flowers that last as long as six weeks. This species must be kept continuously moist. It does not need a winter rest, but reduce watering in winter.

Bif. harrisoniae

Bletilla *(bleh-TIL-la)*

Abbreviation: *Ble.*
Sympodial
Average to large
Medium light or part shade
Cool to mild nights and days; tolerates cold while dormant
High humidity
Keep evenly moist
Pot or grow outdoors

This easy-to-grow hardy terrestrial orchid is often found in bulb catalogs or other general horticultural sources. Its rounded pseudobulbs usually form just below the surface of the potting medium. The broad, palmlike leaves appear in spring and reach 24 to 30 inches long. In early spring, bletilla bears up to a dozen 1½-inch rose-colored blooms on upright stems, which emerge from new growth.

Ble. striata

Culture: Easy
Availability: Common in garden centers in frost-free regions; otherwise, from specialty growers

Ble. striata

The only bletilla species commonly sold, this orchid is grown outdoors as far north as Philadelphia. Grow it in potting soil or in the garden, where it will multiply rapidly. Plants flower successively, and individual blooms may last a week, so the overall display can go on for a month or longer.

Brassavola *(bras-SAH-voh-la)*

Abbreviation: *B.*
Sympodial
Compact to large
Medium to bright light
Mild days and nights
Moderate humidity
Keep evenly moist
Pot or mount

Native to the tropical lowland forests of the Caribbean, Central America, and South America, the exotic-looking orchids in this genus are gratifyingly easy to grow. Because they are not dependent on high humidity and warm temperatures like many other orchids, brassavolas and their hybrids are a good choice for beginners and anyone who wants dependable blooms in average indoor conditions. These orchids adapt well to windowsill culture, but you can also grow them outdoors in summer. Fragrant flowers appear in summer and fall, either singly or in rows of as many as a dozen, on graceful, arching inflorescences. Individual blossoms are slender and, in some cases, almost spidery. The flowers, white, lime green, or white marked with lime green, are fragrant at night and long-lasting on the plant or in a vase.

B. grandiflora

Brassavolas have long, fleshy, cylindrical leaves that emerge from slender round or club-shape pseudobulbs. Plants grow vigorously into impressive specimens. They tolerate low humidity but may bloom better in increased humidity during times of active growth. Pot brassavolas in fast-draining orchid mix or mount them on bark for outdoors in mild climates. Some growers coax two or more bloom cycles a year by alternating periods of regular water and fertilizer with periods of dormancy to encourage new growth.

The genus name honors Antonio Musa Brassavola, a 16th-century Venetian botanist. Fewer than 20 brassavola orchids have been identified, and experts have transferred a few to a closely related genus, *Rhyncholaelia* (page 202); look under both names when you search for any species.

B. acaulis

Culture: Easy
Availability: Specialty growers
Native to Guatemala, Panama, and Belize, this species grows best on a mount because of its pendulous habit. Its leaves grow 12 to 24 inches long. Flowers, which appear in summer, are 2½ inches across and up to 4 inches long. Blossoms are greenish (sometimes with purple blush) with white lip. They have a rich lemony fragrance most intense after dark. Individual flowers last a few weeks; because they are borne sequentially and frequently, the display goes on for more than a month. Give *B. acaulis* bright but not direct light. You may find it sold as *B. lineata* or *B. mathieuana*.

B. acaulis 'Talisman Cove'

B. flagellaris

Culture: Easy
Availability: Rare
The fragrance of this Brazilian native will win you over—it smells like cocoa. The flowers are about 3 inches across; they are composed of slender, creamy white petals and sepals are accented by a white heart-shape lip, which has a chartreuse throat. Flowers appear in late summer or fall, last for several weeks, and are carried on 3- to 5-inch stems, three to five flowers per stem. The slender leaves are up to 18 inches long. Grow *B. flagellaris* on a windowsill or in a greenhouse, either in a clay pot or a basket filled with a fast-draining orchid medium. As people discover its delicious scent, growers respond to the increased demand, so this species is becoming easier to find.

B. nodosa

Culture: Easy
Availability: Specialty growers
This gratifyingly easy beginner's orchid has the added virtue of blooming year-round. Its spidery flowers are fairly large for a brassavola, between 3 and 6 inches across. They are either white, soft greenish-white, or cream; the lip may be speckled with tiny purple dots. Flowers exude a powerful perfume after dark—hence the common name "lady of the night." Leaves are 4 to 12 inches long.

This relatively small plant has an upright habit that looks good mounted on a slab (or, in mild climates, outdoors on a

B. nodosa

tree branch). *B. nodosa* also can be grown in pots containing a coarse-grade, fast-draining orchid mix. Native to Mexico (primarily), Central America, and the West Indies, it does best in warm, humid conditions year-round, and it doesn't require a dry rest period.

B. David Sander
(B. cucullata × B. digbyana)

Culture: Easy
Availability: Specialty growers

B. David Sander 'Talisman Cove'

This exceedingly fine primary hybrid has the vigor and charm of its parents. Compact plants grow to 12 inches tall, with a form that is more like *B. cucullata* than *B. digbyana*. In summer one or two large 6-inch-wide pale green blooms offset by a heavily fringed lip appear. The flowers are often fragrant at night. David Sander is best grown in a basket or on a mount.

B. Little Stars
(B. nodosa × B. subulifolia)

Culture: Easy
Availability: Specialty growers

This vigorous hybrid is an ideal beginner's orchid. Often in the fall but also throughout the year, it generates scads of enchanting 2-inch-wide star-shape blooms, each lasting a few weeks. They are a soft greenish-white that seems to glow in the evening hours, which is also when their sweet perfume is strongest. The plant is only about 12 inches tall, and when in full bloom, it is impressive.

B. Little Stars 'Hensbests Passion'

Brassia (BRAS-see-a)

Abbreviation: *Brs.*
Sympodial
Compact to large, depending on species
Medium light
Mild nights and days
Moderate humidity
Keep continuously moist
Pot or mount

Brs. Rex 'Sakata'

These showy plants, popularly known as spider orchids, are closely related to oncidiums and share the growth habits of that genus. The 6-inch-tall pseudobulbs and 18-inch or longer, broad, bright green leaves combine into 24- to 30-inch-tall growths. These bear one or two upright 24-inch-long arching flower stems from the lower leaf axils, each stem holding 12 to 18 elongated blooms. Most species flower in late summer, and some hybrids may flower twice a year; the blooms last as long as three weeks. Some emit a musky fragrance in the warmth of the day. Flowers are not brightly colored but usually come in shades of green with mahogany barring. Their large size and unusual shapes, however, make them among the showiest of all orchids.

Brassias are native to damp tropical forests of the West Indies, Mexico, and South America. Flowers resemble spiders, with long pointy petals and sepals that radiate from the center like long legs. In the wild, this arrangement attracts spider-hunting wasps, which pollinate the flowers. Each plant consists of a smooth flattened green pseudobulb up to 6 inches long and 1 to 2 inches wide. The bulb generates two or three thick leaves between 2 and 3 feet long.

Outdoors in frost-free climates, mount plants on a tree where they will be in the shade during the hottest part of the day. Indoors, pot plants in a fast-draining orchid mix or in a basket of bark to show off the arching inflorescences. The roots may climb out of the potting mix, which is normal.

After brassias flower, reduce fertilizer and increase light to give plants a rest period that will help them bloom again. Repot annually, especially when plants are young, moving them into a slightly bigger container each time.

Brs. gireoudiana

Culture: Easy
Availability: Specialty growers

Brs. gireoudiana

One of the best of the genus, *Brs. gireoudiana* has flowers that may exceed 15 inches long from top to bottom. Pale yellow-green blooms spotted with mahogany appear in late spring to summer. They are fragrant during daylight hours. Blooms may last for several weeks.

Brs. longissima

Culture: Easy
Availability: Specialty growers

Brs. longissima

The 7- to 8-inch-long flowers of *Brs. longissima* start out greenish but change to orange over several days. Petals, sepals, and lips all are speckled with maroon markings. Each arching stem, up to 18 inches long, bears six to eight blooms along its length, from which a delicate candylike fragrance wafts. These "spiders" appear mainly in summer and fall and can last as long as six weeks. Pot *Brs. longissima* in a fast-draining orchid mix and grow it on a windowsill or in a warm greenhouse.

Brs. verrucosa

Culture: Easy
Availability: Specialty growers

The inflorescences of this species, approaching 12 inches long, are not as large as some others, but the plant is easier to find than many other brassias. Its green-blotched-with-brown blooms appear in late spring to early summer and are lightly fragrant.

Brs. verrucosa

Brs. Datacosa 'Coos Bay'
(Brs. verrucosa × Brs. caudata)

Culture: Easy
Availability: Specialty growers

This wonderful primary hybrid is prized for its free-blooming habit. Plants (pseudobulbs and leaves) may reach 18 inches tall and often bear two arching flower stems holding 12 or more large light green spiders marked with brown splotches. The late summer flowers are borne in two rows along the stem and may be as long as 15 inches. The plants are large and do well in pots and slat baskets in sunrooms and greenhouses or outdoors in frost-free regions. They respond well to copious amounts of fertilizer and water.

Brs. Datacosa 'Coos Bay'

Brs. Edvah Loo 'Nishida' HCC/AOS
(*Brs. longissima* × *Brs. gireoudiana*)

Culture: Easy
Availability: Specialty growers

Brs. Edvah Loo 'Nishida'

Edvah Loo 'Nishida' is one of the largest of the widely distributed primary hybrid brassias. Typical of the brassias, it has upright growth from which arching stems emanate. Each stem holds 12 to 15 spidery blooms. The 20-inch-long flowers appear in late spring and are yellow to chartreuse with chocolate markings and often a musky scent.

Brs. Rex
(*Brs. verrucosa* × *Brs. gireoudiana*)

Culture: Easy
Availability: Specialty growers; often at spring orchid shows
This vigorous orchid is probably the most commonly seen brassia hybrid because it is propagated by mericloning. Some cultivars, the ones most commonly sold, are easier to bring to bloom than others. Rex's flowers, up to 18 inches long, are among the largest of the genus. Their fragrance is slight. Plants may bloom several times a year. Provide the same growing conditions as cattleya and laelias.

Brs. Rex 'Sakata'

Brassidium (bras-SID-ee-um)

Abbreviation: *Brsdm.*
Sympodial
Average
Medium light
Mild nights and days
Moderate humidity
Keep evenly moist
Pot

Exotic flower shapes and color combinations on moderately sized plants, to about 18 inches tall, make this a popular genus for home culture. It results from a cross between brassia and oncidium. The flowers are spidery like those of brassia, but they are also a bit more rounded, like those of oncidium. Plants are often as floriferous as their oncidium parent. Flower stems usually grow straight up but occasionally branch. Keep these orchids moist but not soggy.

Brsdm. Fly Away 'Miami' HCC/AOS
(*Brsdm.* Gilded Urchin × *Onc. maculatum*)

Culture: Easy
Availability: Common
Bright yellow flowers of heavy substance that last for several weeks line the 3-foot-long stems of this hybrid. Blooms are speckled with chocolate or maroon markings. Each blossom measures 3 to 3½ inches across, and a typical stem bears 12 to 15 of them. A healthy plant will produce flowers in profusion every summer and into fall. For best results, grow Fly Away 'Miami' in moderate to bright light on a windowsill or under lights.

Brsdm. Fly Away 'Miami'

Brsdm. Kenneth Bivin
(*Onc. cariniferum* × *Brs. longissima*)

Culture: Easy
Availability: Fairly common in the trade, though specialty nurseries would be the best source
Sometimes sold as *Odbrs.* Kenneth Biven, this showy orchid has spidery mahogany-and-yellow blooms to 6 inches long

Brsdm. Kenneth Bivin

on upright spikes. Plants most often bloom in fall, but they can bloom anytime throughout the year. The flowers last three to four weeks.

Brsdm. White Knight
(*Brs. Rex × Onc. leucochilum*)

Culture: Easy
Availability: Specialty growers

White Knight is a fine example of the type, illustrating the very dark coloration that can result from the use of *Onc. leucochilum* in a cross, as well as the exotic spidery flower shape from the brassia parent. Plants are robust with 6-inch or taller pseudobulbs. These give rise to upright flower stems bearing 12 to 18 blooms, 5 inches wide, in spring and often again in fall. Grow White Knight in a medium-grade mix; keep plants evenly moist.

Brsdm. White Knight

Brassocattleya *(bras-soh-KAT-lee-a)*

Abbreviation: *Bc.*
Sympodial
Average
Medium to bright light
Mild nights and warm days
Moderate humidity
Let dry between waterings
Pot

This intergeneric combination between brassavola and cattleya most often has *Brassavola nodosa* as one parent, but hybrids with *Rhyncholaelia digbyana*, a close brassavola relative, are also included in this genus. Beginners enjoy these sturdy plants for the heady perfume that often accompanies the flowers. Growth habit is generally upright, from about 12 to 18 inches, depending on parentage. Flowers are large, to 6 inches or more, and often distinctly frilled if rhyncholaelia is a parent. Pot brassocattleyas in a medium-grade orchid mix and keep them in slightly brighter light than you would other cattleyas, to encourage flowering.

Bc. Binosa 'Kirk'
(*C. bicolor × B. nodosa*)

Culture: Easy
Availability: Specialty growers and at spring orchid shows

Bc. Binosa 'Kirk'

Exhibiting the best of both parents, Binosa 'Kirk' is showy and colorful (green sepals flank a bright pink lip) like a cattleya, but a bit smaller and more generous with its flowers, like a brassavola. Its rich, almost spicy fragrance comes from both parents. Flowers are about 3 inches across and appear singly or in pairs on 4-inch flower stems throughout the year and last up to several weeks. Plants grow about 15 inches tall.

Bc. Cynthia 'Whimsey'
(*Rhynch. digbyana × C. walkeriana*)

Culture: Easy
Availability: Specialty growers and at spring orchid shows

This popular hybrid is easy to grow and compact enough to fit on a windowsill. Plants grow only 8 to 10 inches tall and wide, producing loads of substantial, fragrant flowers from summer to fall that stay fresh for weeks. The 3-inch-wide

Bc. Cynthia 'Whimsey'

flowers of the cultivar 'Whimsey' are soft pink with a dash of yellow in the throat and exude a sweet scent that can permeate an entire room.

Bc. Maikai
(B. nodosa × C. bowringiana)

Culture: Easy
Availability: Specialty growers and at spring orchid shows
One of the showiest and easiest brassocattleyas for use as a potted plant, this hybrid produces four to six 4-inch rose-colored blooms around Christmastime, although mature plants may bloom again in summer. Plants and flowers resemble a fully formed *B. nodosa*. Plants grow 8 inches tall, while flower stems reach 12 inches tall. The flowers are lightly fragrant during daytime and last three to four weeks or occasionally longer under cooler conditions. For the best floral display, grow Maikai in a basket in a location where it can be undisturbed for several years. It makes a good patio plant in frost-free areas.

Bc. Mt. Hood 'Orchidglade'
(Bc. Deesse × C. Claris)

Culture: Easy
Availability: Specialty growers
While many cultivars of this famous hybrid have been developed, even ones that have won awards, 'Orchidglade' has endured and remained in cultivation. Typical of large, standard brassos, this plant may reach 20 inches in total height. It bears one to three 8-inch or wider heavy-

Bc. Mt. Hood 'Orchidglade'

substanced pink blooms with a fringed lip. Easy to grow with other cattleyas, Mt. Hood 'Orchidglade' needs extra space to grow well.

Brassolaelia *(bras-soh-LAY-lee-a)*

Abbreviation: *Bl.*
Sympodial
Compact
Bright light
Mild nights and days
Moderate humidity
Let dry between waterings
Pot or mount

Brassolaelias—a combination of brassavola and laelia—are easy and rewarding to grow, with abundant, fragrant flowers. Like brassidiums, they are often bred with *B. nodosa* as one parent. Plants are usually upright, to about 12 inches tall, and have pseudobulbs and quill-like leaves like those of the brassavola parent. *B. nodosa* and its hybrids are more tolerant of both high and low temperatures than cattleyas. If you have trouble growing brassias, try one of these. Basket culture encourages large size and heavy flowering.

Major Hawaiian nurseries have made *B. nodosa* and its hybrids, such as *Bl.* Morning Glory and *Bl.* Richard Mueller, mainstays of their breeding programs in the past decade. The results have been an array of wonderful cattleya alliance hybrids in a range of colors and forms, all of which are very easy to grow and bloom readily, often more than once per year. It may be hard to find every named cultivar or hybrid you hear about or see in photos, but it's likely you'll come across something similar from specialty growers.

Bl. Morning Glory
(B. nodosa × L. purpurata)

Culture: Easy
Availability: Specialty growers and at spring orchid shows

You can't miss this plant's glorious flower. It's large—up to 4 inches across—and intensely fragrant in the evening because of its *B. nodosa* parentage. Its distinct coloration, a gift from its laelia parent, also stands out. Soft white flowers have a hint of lavender, while the prominent lip is marked with vivid hot pink. For an abundant display, especially during winter, grow Morning Glory in bright light. Mount it on a slab where it may spread 12 inches or more.

Bl. Morning Glory 'Talisman Cove'

Bl. Richard Mueller
(B. nodosa × L. milleri)

Culture: Easy
Availability: Specialty growers and at spring orchid shows
First bred 40 years ago, this hybrid has been "remade" many times recently, with several growers crossing plants of the original species. As a result, it's usually easy to find Richard Mueller. Compact, upright plants are generally less than

Bl. Richard Mueller

12 inches tall and wide, with flower stems rising nicely above the foliage and bearing four to six 4-inch-wide blooms in shades of orange, often with darker red spotting. Compact size and temperature tolerance make this plant a good choice for locations such as a windowsill or outdoors on a frost-free patio. Flowers may bloom throughout the year but most often appear in spring. They last as long as four weeks.

Brassolaeliocattleya (bras-soh-LAY-lee-oh-KAT-lee-a)

Abbreviation: *Blc.*
Sympodial
Compact to large, depending on species
Medium to bright light
Mild nights and days
Moderate humidity
Let dry between waterings
Pot

Frilly brassos are a combination of brassavola, laelia, and cattleya and show off the best characteristics of each parent. Their fully formed petals and sepals, set off by a highly fringed lip, are often the picture that comes to mind when orchids are mentioned. Colors range from purest white to deepest red to brilliant chrome yellow. Many have a characteristic citrus fragrance during daytime. A common intergeneric combination in the cattleya alliance (all cattleyas and their relatives), brassolaeliocattleyas offer

Blc. Yen Corona 'Green Genius'

a great opportunity for beginners to learn orchid culture. Choose compact species for home growing, and pot them in a medium-grade orchid mix.

Blc. Apache Sunrise
(Blc. Apache Gold × B. nodosa)

Culture: Easy
Availability: Specialty growers

Blc. Apache Sunrise 'Von Scholl'

Grow this winter-blooming orchid for its amazing flowers, which never fail to get lots of attention. About 3 to 4 inches across and headily fragrant, they are a striking combination of colors. The petals and sepals are warm tropical hues of orange to yellow, while the contrasting lip is brilliantly marked with hot pink, plum-purple, or ruby red, all edged in white to stand out even more. The plant reaches about 12 inches tall and grows well in a spot with bright light and good air circulation.

Blc. Formosan Gold
(Lc. Lorraine Shirai × Blc. Spun Gold)

Culture: Easy
Availability: Specialty growers

This is one of the most dazzling bicolor orchids, with rich golden petals and sepals that contrast dramatically with a dark red ruffled lip. The flowers measure about 6 inches across and have an intense fragrance, strongest during the day, that is reminiscent of vanilla. Expect Formosan Gold to bloom for several weeks during the winter months, just when you are longing for a good flower show. Grow it in a pot of medium-textured shredded bark and display it on a windowsill or in a greenhouse.

Blc. Formosan Gold

Blc. Goldenzelle 'Lemon Chiffon' AM/AOS
(*Blc.* Fortune × *C.* Horace)

Culture: Easy
Availability: Specialty growers

Blc. Goldenzelle 'Lemon Chiffon'

The lemon yellow blossoms of this striking hybrid have
a splash of ruby red on the lips. Flowers measure about
6 inches across and are borne singly or in pairs on 6-inch
inflorescences in winter. Their sweet fragrance is strongest
during daytime. Pot the plant in medium-textured bark.

Blc. Hawaiian Charm
(*Blc.* Fred Stewart × *Lc.* Prophesy)

Blc. Hawaiian Charm

Culture: Easy
Availability: Specialty growers
Hawaiian Charm represents the pinnacle of more than
120 years of breeding brassolaeliocattleyas. It grows at least
18 inches tall and in fall has rich color blooms that can be
more than 7 inches wide. During the day plants may also
have a heavenly sweet fragrance.

Blc. Pamela Hetherington 'Coronation' FCC/AOS
(*Lc.* Paradisio × *Bc.* Mount Anderson)

Culture: Easy
Availability: Specialty growers
The American Orchid Society awarded this orchid its
prestigious First Class Certificate. Its 6-inch flowers are
flawless in form, and their color—lavender-pink with pink

Blc. Pamela Hetherington 'Coronation'

ruffled lips and a yellow throat—makes the blooms look as if
they're lit from within. Sturdy 6-inch flower stems in winter
bear one to three sweetly fragrant blooms, each lasting for at
least a few weeks. An average-size plant will thrive in a pot of
medium-textured bark on a windowsill or in a greenhouse.

Blc. Yellow Imp
(*Bc.* Daffodil × *Lc.* Neon)

Culture: Easy
Availability: Specialty growers
Clear yellow blossoms abound on this dependable dwarf
plant. The flowers measure 3 inches across and appear in
winter to early spring, brightening the indoors on short,
gloomy days. Because of plant size, about 10 inches tall,
it can be displayed on a sunny windowsill.

Broughtonia *(bro-TOH-nee-a)*

Abbreviation: *Bro.*
Sympodial
Miniature
Bright light
Mild nights, warm days
High humidity
Let dry between waterings
Mount

Hailing from Jamaica, this genus consists of just three species, only one of which is readily available. The nearly dwarf plants, no more than 6 inches tall, have round, flattened pseudobulbs topped by two stiff 1-inch-wide by 4-inch-long upright leaves. Wiry flower stems may occasionally branch; more often they are topped by a cluster of circular flat 2-inch-wide blooms that are exceptionally full. Color is typically rose; modern breeding has introduced white, yellow, cream, and splash petal types. Mount broughtonias to facilitate rapid drying after frequent watering. These orchids are closely related to cattleyas.

Bro. sanguinea

Culture: Intermediate
Availability: Specialty growers
Bro. sanguinea grows only about 3 to 4 inches tall and bears clusters of 1-inch-wide flowers for several weeks during summer on arching 8- to 16-inch stems. The flowers vary in

Bro. sanguinea

color from red to pink and are usually veined in dark purple. Plants do well on mounts. Provide bright light. You can grow them as a landscape plant in South Florida.

Bulbophyllum *(bulb-oh-FILL-um)*

Abbreviation: *Bulb.*
Sympodial
Miniature to large, depending on species
Low to medium light
Mild nights, warm to hot days
High humidity
Keep continuously moist
Pot or mount

The orchids in this varied genus have complicated flowers unlike any others in the world. Some give off a pleasant, fruity scent, while others smell like rotting meat, all in an effort to attract pollinating flies. Color and markings vary widely. So does flower form: some are chubby, some are elongated, and some look like undersea creatures. They all share a common, curious feature—a hinged lip that wiggles or bobs as you brush past the plant or a breeze stirs it.

A large pseudobulb is common to the genus and gives it its name. The bulb grows from a substantial rhizome (creeping stem); it can be nearly round or egg-shape, and it generates just one thick leaf. However, individual plants tend to produce chains of these along the rhizome. The flower spikes arise from the rhizome between pseudobulbs and carry anywhere from a few to dozens of blooms. Flowers can be quite tiny (only 1/16 inch across), while others grow to 6 inches across. Small or large, their unusual and complex forms are always worth contemplating, even if you need a magnifying glass.

Bulb. deari

Orchids were still a new plant to Western civilization in the 1800s when members of this genus were brought into cultivation. The French botanist Louis-Marie Petit-Thouars bestowed the name—literally "bulb" and "leaf" in Greek. The moniker seems too general now; so many other orchids have prominent pseudobulbs.

Bulbophyllums come from the rain forests and cloud forests of tropical Asia and Africa. There are at least 2,000 species in this genus, although not all are in cultivation. Some botanists separate some of the species into a different, closely related genus, *Cirrhopetalum,* and you may find the genus names used interchangeably by some orchid nurseries.

Because the rhizome tends to form chains of pseudobulbs over time, mount these orchids or pot them in a shallow hanging basket, and then avoid repotting. Water generously when the plant is growing actively, and provide high humidity and consistent warmth. Because of their forest origins, these orchids do not require bright light.

Prevent rot by making sure the plants get adequate air circulation. The scent of a few, notably *Bulb. beccarii* and *Bulb. phalaenopsis,* has been likened to "100 dead elephants rotting in the sun." They are not common in cultivation, but if you grow them you will want to isolate them or keep them on a protected porch or patio—away from the neighbors, too—while they are in bloom.

Bulb. echinolabium

Culture: Advanced
Availability: Rare

Bulb. echinolabium

This one is one of the stinkers and is at its most pungent during daytime. Native to Borneo and the Indonesian island of Sulawesi, its flowers are dark cream decorated with mahogany stripes, and each elongated sepal trails up to 1 foot long. Twelve-inch flower stems display one flower at a time for several weeks in summer. By comparison, the plant is rather plain, staying compact in habit and reaching no more than 6 to 8 inches tall.

Bulb. graveolens

Culture: Average
Availability: Specialty growers

Sometimes sold as *Cirrhopetalum graveolens* or *Cirr. robustum,* this handsome native of the forests of Papua New Guinea has broad, flat leaves and 8-inch-long inflorescences that bloom spectacularly for several weeks in spring to fall. Flowers appear in umbrella-shape clusters called umbels; they have yellow-and-green stripes with a dashing maroon lip. The putrid scent can be intense. Plants reach 30 inches tall. Provide warm temperatures, medium light, high humidity, and copious water when it is growing actively.

Bulb. graveolens being pollinated by flies

Bulb. lobbii

Culture: Average
Availability: Specialty growers

Bold straw-yellow blooms are borne singly on upright stems arising from the base of newest growths of this species. Flowers may be as large as 4 inches wide and tall with a "rocking" lip, sometimes marked with fine red dots. Flowers are often fragrant during the day and last about three weeks. Average-size plants, with 2½-inch pseudobulbs and leaves to 8 inches, have rhizomes of an inch or so. Pot this orchid in fine-grade, fast-draining mix and keep it in part shade.

Bulb. lobbii 'Kathy's Gold'

Bulb. medusae

Culture: Average
Availability: Specialty growers

Bulb. medusae

A rambling species with fairly long rhizomes between individual 6-inch-tall growths, *Bulb. medusae* does best when grown as a large specimen in a basket or on a mount. Healthy, mature plants will be covered with flower umbels that resemble Medusa's head of snakes, hence the name. The blooms are the color of straw and individually insignificant but as a display have few equals. They last about three weeks. Grow this orchid in part shade and keep it evenly moist.

Bulb. phalaenopsis

Culture: Advanced
Availability: Specialty growers

Bulb. phalaenopsis 'Suzanne'

This gargantuan plant requires a greenhouse environment. Pseudobulbs may be the size and shape of an apple, each with a single broad, flat, pendent leaf to more than 6 inches wide and 36 inches long. Mature plants require a large basket or pot. Clusters of 6 to 10 waxy, hairy blood red blooms emerge from the base of most recent matured growth, each subtended by a prominent light green bract. Flowers resemble wax candy lips, or, as other call it, maggot-infested meat. The repulsive fragrance sets this species apart. Fortunately, flowers last two weeks at most.

Bulb. polystictum

Culture: Average
Availability: Rare
From the forests of Malaysia and Thailand comes this unusually beautiful species, sometimes labeled *Bulb. polystichum* or *Cirrhopetalum polystictum*. A plant of variable height but averaging 12 inches, it generates long stems in the fall, each bearing a single 3-inch-wide by 4-inch-long unscented flower. The petals and sepals are a warm orangey-pink striped with dark pink, and the lip is pink. Move the plant into brighter light if it's slow to bloom.

Bulb. polystictum

Bulb. rothschildianum

Culture: Advanced
Availability: Rare
Native to India, this species has the sweet scent of ripe peaches. The unusual inflorescence is a 12-inch flower spike that supports a cluster of five or six flowers for several weeks from spring to fall. Blooms are about 1 inch wide and may be 7 inches long, wine red with a glowing yellow base. Sometimes sold as *Cirrhopetalum rothschildianum*, it's does well on a windowsill, under lights, or in a warm greenhouse. Pot it in a shallow container or mount it on a tree-fern slab.

Bulb. rothschildianum 'Red Chimney'

Bulb. Daisy Chain
(*Cirrhopetalum makoyanum* × *Cirr. amesianum*)

Culture: Average
Availability: Specialty growers
Umbels of unscented pale yellow and rose-red blooms with "rocking" lips are borne well above the foliage on wiry, upright 6-inch-tall stems. They last about three weeks. Flowers may bloom almost any time of the year, but summer is most common. The plants are dwarf, to about 6 inches, with only an inch or so of rhizome between pseudobulbs. Grow this orchid in part shade in a fine-grade, fast-draining mix kept evenly moist; repot it infrequently. Cirrhopetalum orchids are often separated from bulbophyllum based on their umbellate inflorescence—that is, cirrhopetalum flowers are arranged in a whorl from a central point. Thus you may see this plant labeled *Cirr.* Daisy Chain.

Bulb. Elizabeth Ann
(*Bulb. longissimum* × *Bulb. rothschildianum*)

Culture: Average
Availability: Specialty growers

Bulb. Elizabeth Ann

Winner of many awards, this dazzling hybrid is valued for its especially large (up to 7 inches), downward-sweeping, richly colored unscented flowers. They are cream-color and generously marked with deep pinkish red stripes. The plant is a vigorous grower, frequently reaching 12 inches tall. You may find it sold as *Cirrhopetalum* Elizabeth Ann.

Burrageara (BUHR-aj-ar-uh)

Abbreviation: *Burr.*
Sympodial
Average size
Medium light
Mild temperatures nights and days
Moderate humidity
Keep evenly moist
Pot

Burrageara is a complex hybrid genus resulting from crosses between odontoglossum, cochlioda, miltonia, and oncidium. It was named for Albert C. Burrage, first president of the American Orchid Society. The hybrids are among the easiest and showiest of the oncidium-type orchids and generally worth a try.

It is difficult to make generalizations about this group because of the number and variety of parents involved. For example, some prefer warm conditions, others cool or intermediate. However, plants most likely found at orchid shows, in local garden centers, or at an orchid nursery are liable to fit the profile above. Consult a local orchid grower to find the best one for your conditions.

Burr. Living Fire
(*Vuylstekeara Edna* × *Onc. maculatum*)

Culture: Easy
Availability: Specialty growers

Burr. Living Fire 'Glowing Embers'

Living Fire is a floriferous orchid with long branched arching flower spikes that sport long-lasting 2-inch-wide fiery red flowers. An established plant grows about 18 inches tall and will bloom several times a year.

Burr. Nancy Carpenter
(*Vuyls.* Monica × *Onc.* Elegance)

Culture: Average
Availability: Specialty growers
This burrageara is particularly notable for its ease of culture under a variety of conditions. It tolerates warmer conditions than its vuylstekeara parent and will grow well under intermediate conditions or as a patio plant where frost does not threaten. Grow it in a mix suitable for oncidiums in moderate light; keep plants evenly moist. Mature plants have impressive inflorescences in spring, often two per pseudobulb, branching, with more than fifteen 3-inch blooms. Pseudobulbs are 6 inches tall with 12-inch-long leaves.

Burr. Nancy Carpenter

Burr. Nelly Isler 'Swiss Beauty'
(*Burr.* Stefan Isler × *Milt.* Kensington)

Culture: Average
Availability: Specialty growers
Dutch orchid growers have cloned this variety widely, so it is often available in garden centers or from florists as a flowering potted plant. Plants are 15 inches tall and have multiple flowering stems on each pseudobulb with six

3-inch red blooms per stem. They bloom throughout the year, with a peak in late winter and early spring. Grow like oncidiums, keeping them evenly moist and regularly fed. With its floriferous nature and bright blooms, Nelly Isler 'Swiss Beauty' is worth searching out.

Burr. Nelly Isler 'Swiss Beauty'

Burr. Stefan Isler 'Lava Flow' (*Vuyls.* Edna × *Onc. leucochilum*)

Culture: Easy
Availability: Specialty growers

This hybrid earns its picturesque name with blood red flowers that have a glowing yellow lip. Each pseudobulb bears two flower spikes in winter. Plants grow vigorously 14 to 16 inches tall. It is an easy orchid to grow; provide a medium-grade bark mix and moderate humidity.

Cadetia (kuh-DEE-sha)

Abbreviation: None
Sympodial
Miniature
Low light
Mild to warm nights and days
High humidity
Keep evenly moist
Pot

While closely related to dendrobium, the sixty or so species of this genus more generally resemble pleurothallis in their dwarf growth. They are popular for their prolific habit and attractive overall appearance. The crystal white blooms, to about ½ inch wide, are borne singly at the junction of leaf and pseudobulb in summer to fall; plants may rebloom several times in warm conditions. A fine specimen plant can be grown indoors in a shallow 4-inch pot of fine-grade, fast-draining orchid mix.

Cadetia taylori

Culture: Average
Availability: Specialty growers

Cadetia taylori 'Mem. Rodney Wilcox Jones'

The blooms of this species may have contrasting lips in any color. Plant habit is upright to about 4 inches, and profuse branching from the base quickly results in a full pot.

Calanthe (ka-LANTH-ee)

Abbreviation: *Cal.*
Sympodial
Average to large
Bright, indirect light
Cool nights and mild days
Moderate humidity
Keep continuously moist
Pot

This genus consists of two main groups, evergreen and deciduous. Evergreen types are not often seen in Western collections. They are best represented by *Cal. discolor,* with almost inconspicuous pseudobulbs and large, broad, thin leaves resembling palm fronds.

Cal. rosea

Deciduous types, such as *Cal. vestita* and related hybrids, are more popular. They have robust, conical pseudobulbs that are often square in cross section. The broad leaves drop in late fall as the newest growth matures. One or two hairy, upright flower stems emerge from the base of the most recent growths in late winter, developing rapidly to produce small flowers in white, pink, or rose. The flowers open a few at a time over three weeks or longer, giving a long-lasting display. Reduce water and fertilizer as the plant matures.

Cal. vestita

Culture: Average
Availability: Specialty growers

The large broad leaves of *Cal. vestita* may reach more than 30 inches long on mature plants. They top silvery pseudobulbs that can be 8 inches or taller. Upright inflorescences grow rapidly with arching form as the first white to pink flowers start to bloom.

Cal. vestita

Many growers propagate plants by dividing them into single bulbs and placing several bulbs in one pot. Provide bright light, frequent watering, and regular fertilizer. A fine-grade, fast-draining orchid mix allows for frequent watering while plants are actively growing. It is deciduous, losing its leaves in fall. Water sparingly until new sprouts appear in spring.

This species and its many hybrids derived from it, is similar to the related species *Cal. rosea* and *Cal. rubens* in growth and flowering characteristics.

Catasetum (kat-uh-SEE-tum)

Abbreviation: *Ctsm.*
Sympodial
Small to large
Bright, indirect light or part shade
Mild nights and days
Moderate humidity
Keep continuously moist during growing season; let dry during dormancy
Pot

These robust plants have tall, cigar-shape pseudobulbs and broad, palmlike deciduous leaves along the length of the upright pseudobulbs. Erect, often arching, flower stems develop at the base of the newest growths, occasionally more than once a year, and flowers last one or two weeks. The blooms are unisex, which is the characteristic that sets this group apart from all other orchids.

Grow catasetums in small pots of fine-grade orchid mix that drains quickly. Keeping the plants pot-bound will encourage blooms. Direct sunlight could burn developing

Ctsm. Rebecca Northen

foliage. Humidity higher than 50 percent helps discourage spider mites, which are attracted to the young leaves. Reduce water and fertilizer when leaves begin to turn yellow, then stop almost entirely after the leaves drop. Resume when new growths begin to grow roots.

Ctsm. fimbriatum

Culture: Average
Availability: Specialty growers

Flower stems of this species grow to 18 inches and carry 7 to 15 or more 1½-inch-wide yellowish blooms heavily spotted with red. The flowers are exotic looking but last no more than one or two weeks in late spring or early summer. Enjoy their spicy fragrance during daytime.

Ctsm. fimbriatum

Ctsm. pileatum

Culture: Average
Availability: Specialty growers

Ctsm. pileatum aurantiacum

This is probably the most frequently seen catasetum. Its pseudobulbs are robust and large. Gently arching flower spikes grow to 12 inches and carry 4 to 10 blooms apiece in fall. Ivory to pale yellow flowers open flat to about 4 inches across and exude a powerful fragrance during daytime.

Ctsm. tenebrosum

Culture: Average
Availability: Specialty growers

Ctsm. tenebrosum

One of the most distinctive and desirable of the catasetums, this species is slightly smaller than others. Its 1½-inch-wide flowers are rich chocolate brown with a bright chartreuse lip. Arching flower stems grow to 12 inches or more and bear 6 to 10 or more blooms in the fall.

Ctsm. Orchidglade
(*Ctsm. pileatum* × *Ctsm. expansum*)

Culture: Average
Availability: Specialty growers

Ctsm. Orchidglade

Waxy-texture 2-inch-wide flowers of this hybrid appear from summer into fall. They are creamy white, liberally sprinkled with red dots, and give off a spicy scent (stronger in the male flowers). They're crowded onto 6- to 8-inch inflorescences, with as many as 15 flowers on a spray. Grow this orchid in a basket to provide the fast drainage it needs. Withhold water until new growths have begun to produce roots.

Ctsm. Susan Fuchs
(*Ctsm. expansum* × *Ctsm.* Orchidglade)

Culture: Average
Availability: Specialty growers

Ctsm. Susan Fuchs

A hybridization technique, line breeding, in which a hybrid is crossed with one of its parents, is a common way to develop new orchids, except for catasetums. Susan Fuchs came about through this method and the results were highly satisfactory. Robust plants have 15-inch-tall pseudobulbs. Flowers bloom on strong pendent stems bearing 12 or more 4- to 5-inch light green blooms that are often splotched with maroon. Grow Susan Fuchs in a basket.

Cattleya *(KAT-lee-uh)*

Abbreviation: *C.*
Sympodial
Miniature to large, depending on species
Medium to bright light
Cool nights and warm to hot days
Moderate humidity
Let dry between waterings
Pot or mount, depending on species

Cattleya is probably the most recognized of all orchids due to its widespread use by florists. Native to the moist forests of South America, its species were not named or brought into cultivation until the early 1800s. Since then, numerous worthwhile species and countless cultivars have entered commerce. Technically, they are divided into two main groups: Unifoliates, such as *C. labiata* and *C. mossiae*, have a single leaf and large but few blossoms; bifoliates are two-leaved and tend to be taller and more floriferous. They also have a more elongated pseudobulb.

Flower colors vary widely among the cattleya species. Unifoliate cattleyas are particularly varied, and breeders have made good use of the range of color types to produce the palette of colors on the market. Among the colors you'll find in unifoliate cattleyas are lavender with a darker lip (the typical color), pure white with a yellow throat, pure white with a magenta lip (semialba), caerulescens (blue), and other, rarer combinations of these colors.

Many unifoliate cattleyas display "sparkling" or "diamond dust" texture. Texture refers to appearance of flower surface, much as pansy blossoms have a matte or velvety finish. Where texture is sparkling, light reflects from the surface, giving the flower a gemlike appearance.

Most cattleya flowers are long-lasting, and many are fragrant. They are unrivaled for vivid colors, including hot pink, gold, lavender, shades of blue, and chartreuse—often in striking bicolors, tricolors, and patterns. Petal and lip margins may be ruffled or undulating, which makes flowers look even fancier. Blossoms are displayed on spikes singly or in multiples up to two dozen. A fragrant flower is at its best for three to five days after opening. Cutting a flower for a vase or corsage causes the scent to dissipate.

This genus was named for William Cattley, a British horticulturist, after some were shipped to him inadvertently as a wrapping for moss and lichen specimens. Cattley rescued the plants and succeeded in getting them to bloom. He showed his exotic-looking plants to a renowned young botanist, John Lindley, who researched the genus and named it. A period of "orchidmania" followed the discovery, as 19th-century Europeans hurried to find and propagate more orchids in this group.

Cattleyas are extremely easy to grow in average home conditions. Pot them in a loose, medium-grade orchid mix, such as fir bark or coconut chunks. Adding charcoal and coarse perlite to the mix will help it drain faster and last longer but it is not necessary to add these materials. Use a clay container for stability. Water and fertilize regularly only when your plant is actively growing; reduce care at all other times (the thick pseudobulb helps the plant survive dry periods). Stake a top-heavy plant or nest it in a larger, sturdier pot. Repot before the mixture has decayed—about once a year, when new growth and roots are evident.

A catt growing in a quick-draining mix may need more frequent watering during active growth. During shorter days and cooler temperatures of winter you may be able to water less often. Overwatering leads to lush spindly growth, rotted roots, and poor flowering. Repot only when new roots are developing, preferably in spring or summer. Short winter days may cause a freshly potted plant's growth to stall.

Cattleya violacea

C. aclandiae

Culture: Advanced
Availability: Specialty growers
This dwarf species, growing to 6 inches, is bifoliate and grows best on a mount so robust roots can ramble. Water frequently and keep humidity about 50 percent to encourage healthy growth. Single (occasionally two) flowers are borne during warm months and may last four weeks. Blooms may reach 4 inches across and have heavy substance and distinctive olive green coloration with heavy barring and magenta lip. Flowers exude a rich perfume during daytime.

C. aclandiae KG's Pink Tiger

C. aurantiaca

Culture: Easy
Availability: Specialty growers; garden centers in
  frost-free zones

Mature plants of this species can grow fairly large, 24 to
30 inches tall, requiring 10-inch or larger pots. However, the
floral display of these specimen-size plants is worth the extra
effort. Heads of 1-inch-wide starry orange blooms appear in
late winter and early spring above bifoliate growths and may
last up to four weeks. This is a good plant for patio culture
in warm-winter climates.

C. aurantiaca

C. bicolor

Culture: Average
Availability: Specialty growers

C. bicolor

This species offers dramatic 3-inch-wide two-tone flowers
that contrast chocolate-brown petals and sepals with a vivid
pink lip. It has 8- to 10-inch-long flower stems with as many
as 10 flowers each in fall and lasting a few weeks. They have
a delicate spicy-rose scent. Grow *C. bicolor* in a pot of fast-
draining, medium-grade mix and display it on a sunny
windowsill or in a bright greenhouse. Repot only when it
shows new roots.

C. forbesii

Culture: Easy
Availability: Specialty growers

C. forbesii

This dwarf bifoliate comes from Brazil and is prized for its especially long-lasting blooms—individual blossoms can last four to six weeks. Flowering begins in early summer and continues well into fall. The waxy flowers are usually tan or green edged in bronze, with a creamy white lip, and have the fragrance of bubble gum. The 6-inch-tall plants bear flowers singly or in pairs on arching stems. *C. forbesii* is an ideal orchid for beginners.

C. guttata

Culture: Average
Availability: Specialty growers and international orchid shows

C. guttata

One of the tallest of the bifoliate species, *C. guttata* can reach 5 feet tall or more. A greenhouse or frost-free patio is necessary to provide the space it requires. Its 4-inch-wide waxy blooms are borne in showy clusters of up to 30 flowers that last three to four weeks in autumn. Repotting at the proper stage is crucial to success. To ensure you're repotting at the right time, watch the developing growth for emerging root tips, which indicate when the plant is most likely to reestablish itself quickly.

C. intermedia

Culture: Easy
Availability: Specialty growers

C. intermedia tipo

Starting in summer, this classic beauty's 4-inch-wide blossoms are displayed for several weeks. The flowers are usually pastel pink with a contrasting dark purple lip but can be found in various shades of pink and white; they radiate a sweet aroma. Plants are sturdy and grow about 15 inches tall; leaves are typically 6 inches long. Grow *C. intermedia* in a medium-grade orchid mix.

C. labiata

Culture: Average
Availability: Specialty growers
This species is the archetype for the genus—a desirable choice for almost any orchid collection. Vigorous unifoliate plants reach 18 inches tall. The flowers are 7 inches or more across and come in a variety of colors from the typical lavender form to blue (caerulescens) to white. The trumpet-shape lip is often a darker contrasting color. Three to five blooms are borne on upright stems in fall and last as long as four weeks, emitting a rich perfume during daytime.

C. labiata

C. lueddemanniana

Culture: Average
Availability: Specialty growers

C. lueddemanniana Dark × Tina

One of the most beautiful in the genus, this unifoliate species has slightly thinner pseudobulbs than those of many other cattleyas. Shorter than some, the plants grow to about 12 inches. They bear three to five rose-lavender flowers on upright stems in late winter from growths that matured the previous summer. The lips of the flowers have darker veins, similar to those of the better-known *C. mossiae*, a close relative. Blooms are up to 7 inches across and have a sparkling texture. As with other unifoliate catts, many color forms are also available. Flowers are sweetly fragrant during daytime and may last as long as four weeks.

C. luteola

Culture: Average
Availability: Specialty growers

C. luteola

This unifoliate orchid typically grows about 8 inches tall, but it can begin blooming when it is only 2 inches tall. It displays an abundance of appealing 2-inch-wide lemon yellow flowers for several weeks during winter. A splash of red in the tubular lip helps them stand out. The light fragrance that wafts from *C. luteola* in early morning is timed to attract its pollinator in the wild, a type of bee. Hybridizers frequently use this species to add a diminutive growth habit to new hybrids. Grow *C. luteola* in a basket or on a mount.

C. maxima

Culture: Easy
Availability: Specialty growers

C. maxima

This species has large lilac flowers about 7 inches across that bloom in fall or winter with as many as six flowers on a stem, each one lasting a few weeks. Plants are easy to grow. They can reach 24 inches tall but more commonly are 12 to 15 inches tall. For best flower production, grow *C. maxima* in fast-draining mix in bright light. It is Peru's national flower.

C. mossiae

Culture: Average
Availability: Specialty growers

This is the species from which all modern spring-blooming lavender cattleyas arise. A unifoliate type that grows to 15 inches tall, it has pseudobulbs that are often rounded and robust. After a cool winter rest, the flowers appear on growth that matured the previous year. Rose-lavender blooms as wide as 8 inches across have contrasting darkly veined lips and are borne three to six or more on each stem in spring. They are sweetly fragrant during daytime and may last as long as four weeks.

C. mossiae

C. skinneri

soft sweet scent and appear in great numbers for several weeks from winter to spring. The 2-foot-tall bifoliate plant generates abundant new growth every year. It is an excellent orchid for beginners because it is adaptable to various growing conditions.

C. violacea

Culture: Advanced
Availability: Specialty growers

This species comes from lower elevations than most other cattleya species and can be difficult to grow except in very warm climates. Even then, many growers simply cannot succeed with this species. However, this species' late-winter reddish pink flowers are among the most lovely of any cattleya species, making the effort to try growing it at least once worth the effort. Some growers find the plants do best on cork mounts where high humidity can be maintained.

C. skinneri

Culture: Easy
Availability: Specialty growers

The national flower of Costa Rica, this elegant orchid's 3-inch-wide flowers bloom in shades of rose and occasionally all white; all variations have a glittery sheen and give off a

C. walkeriana

Culture: Average
Availability: Specialty growers

This bifoliate from Brazil is frequently used as a parent to impart dwarf size and vanilla-and-citrus fragrance to hybrids. Its flowers bloom in late winter or spring and have durable, pristine white petals with just a splash of hot pink

Chocolate Drop, a bifoliate, has 3-inch intense color flowers of heavy texture that frequently last more than a month. Blooms may be mahogany red, glossy wine red, or even sultry orange. Their heady lily-of-the-valley scent will permeate a room. A healthy plant produces flowers in great numbers in winter and spring.

C. Chocolate Drop 'Kodama'

C. Henrietta Japhet
(*C. loddigesii* × *C. eucharis*)

Culture: Easy
Availability: Specialty growers
This is an older hybrid but still revered, particularly for corsage use. The long-lasting blooms are 6 inches or more across and considered the standard by growers and florists alike because of their flawless form and pure white color. Bloom time is generally spring and summer. This excellent plant is named in honor of the hostess of a 1945 gathering of the Houston Orchid Society. It is the parent of many other fine cattleyas.

C. walkeriana semi-alba 'Kenny'

on the lower lip. Cultivars of the species offer many different color forms of this miniature gem. Individual flowers are about 4 inches across; there are as many as three on a stem. Mount the plant on a tree-fern slab or keep it in a shallow basket or pot to accommodate its rambling growth habit.

C. warscewiczii

Culture: Average to advanced
Availability: Specialty growers
Also sold as *C. gigas,* this species is appropriately named, as both the plants and the flowers are the largest in the unifoliate group. The robust, upright plants may reach 30 inches tall, and the sweetly scented flowers can be more than 9 inches across. Blooms are light lavender with a dark magenta lip and two bright yellow "eyes" in the throat. Four to six or more blooms are not uncommon on the tall stems that emerge from the newest growth as it develops. The flowers bloom in summer and last only three weeks. Repot as new roots emerge right after flowering.

C. Chocolate Drop
(*C. guttata* × *C. aurantiaca*)

Culture: Easy
Availability: Specialty growers

C. Henrietta Japhet

C. Irene Holguin
(*C. Astral Beauty* × *C. J. A. Carbone*)

Culture: Easy
Availability: Specialty growers

C. Irene Holguin 'Grand Lady'

From the late 1960s until today, Irene Holguin has been the standard by which other spring-blooming lavender cattleyas are judged. With many awarded cultivars in cultivation and fairly readily available, *C.* Irene Holguin is easy to grow and a vigorous hybrid. Lasting several weeks, the strong flower stems bear four to seven 8-inch sparkling rose blooms highlighted by a dark lip. Plants can be a bit large, 24 inches tall or more. But their long-lasting, fragrant blooms are worth the space.

C. Peckhaviensis
(*C. aclandiae* × *C. schilleriana*)

Culture: Average
Availability: Specialty growers
This hybrid combines the best of its parents' characteristics to create a dwarf fragrant catt with crisp dark markings on its flowers. Peckhaviensis is easier to grow than either parent. Its 3-inch-wide flowers of heavy substance last for several weeks and feature shiny, purple-speckled golden petals splayed in a star shape and centered by a bright magenta lip. Their sweet fragrance is most potent on warm, sunny afternoons. Pot this dwarf in a medium-grade epiphytic mix.

Cattleytonia (*kat-lee-TOH-nee-a*)
(*Cattleya* × *Broughtonia*)

Abbreviation: *Ctna.*
Sympodial
Miniature to large, depending on the hybrid
Bright light
Mild nights and days
High humidity
Let dry between waterings
Pot or mount

Cattleytonias result from crosses between cattleya and broughtonia. One of the best and generally easiest of the modern miniature catts, they are dwarf, often to no more than 6 inches tall, although some may grow to 12 inches depending on the exact species or hybrids used in the cross.

Their many-flowered upright inflorescences often branch, extending the floral display. Many types will bloom more than once a year, and the blooms last four to six weeks. The flower shape is round and the bright colors run the gamut; blooms are rarely fragrant. Keep cattleytonias pot-bound in clay containers; grow them in a long-lasting, fast-draining mix. You can also grow them in baskets or on mounts.

Ctna. Why Not
(*C. aurantiaca* × *Bro. sanguinea*)

Culture: Easy to average
Availability: Common
It's easy to see why this modern dwarf hybrid is so widely grown: The flowers have intense color, they bloom repeatedly, and they last for a month or longer. Abundant ruby-red flowers have a rich golden throat. Only an inch and a half across, they're carried in branching inflorescences for a breathtaking effect. Plants reach about 8 inches tall. Why Not is a great choice for beginners. An unusual cross, Why Not 'Orglade's Gold Strike' has brilliant golden-yellow flowers. It is only occasionally available from growers.

Ctna. Why Not 'Orchidglades Gold Strike'

Chondrorhyncha (*kon-droh-RIN-ka*)
Abbreviation: *Chdrh.*
Sympodial
Small
Low to medium light
Mild nights and days
Moderate humidity
Keep evenly moist
Pot

Closely related to zygopetalum and lycaste orchids, this genus is an important component of the "soft-leaf" group of orchids. Soft leaf refers to the orchids' unusual growth habit. Plants lack pseudobulbs and have fans of alternating medium-size green leaves. This trait makes the plants attractive even when they're not in bloom. Flowers are borne singly from the leaf axils, and any growth may bear many flowers over its lifespan. The blooms last three to four weeks.

Chdrh. discolor

Chdrh. aromatica

Culture: Easy
Availability: Specialty growers

Also sold as *Cochleanthes aromatica*, this native of Panama can be grown outdoors with cymbidiums or indoors on the windowsill or under lights. The plants are attractive, with fans of pale green leaves to 6 inches long. Creamy ivory flowers are borne singly from the leaf axils at the base of the fans and are offset by a prominent tubular blue lip. They have a medicinal fragrance not unlike menthol. Plants bloom in summer, although it is not uncommon for them to bloom throughout the year. Grow *Chdrh. aromatica* outdoors in frost-free zones.

Cochleanthes *(coke-lee-AN-theez)*

Abbreviation: *Cnths.*
Sympodial
Miniature to large, depending on species
Low to medium light or shade
Mild nights and days
High humidity
Keep evenly moist
Pot or mount

This genus is often confused with chondrorhyncha (page 124) and others in the soft-leaf group because it looks similar and requires similar culture. *Cnths. amazonica* is the best-known species; it has been highly inbred by crossing superior forms of the species over a period of several generations. As a result it has large white blooms offset by grape purple lining in the throat of the prominent lip. Flowers last three to four weeks. Grow cochleanthes outdoors in frost-free zones.

Cnths. Amazing
(*Cnths. amazonica* × *Cnths. flabelliformis*)

Culture: Average
Availability: Rare

Among white hybrid orchids, this is one of the most elegant. Petals and sepals are pure, sugary white. The proportionately large lip is gracefully striped with purple—overall, the flower is about 3 inches across. The plant grows to about 8 inches tall and has shiny green leaves that serve as a contrasting backdrop when the flowers bloom in spring or summer.

Cnths. Amazing

Cnths. Moliere
(*Cnths. amazonica* × *Cnths. discolor*)

Culture: Average
Availability: Rare

From its *amazonica* parent this sensational hybrid gets a 2-inch-wide flower with large lip marked with rich purple; from its *discolor* parent, it gets some pink coloration, mainly at the petal tips. From both parents, it gets its sweet scent. The plant has a fanlike habit and matures to about 8 inches tall. Flowers bloom in spring or summer. Constant moisture is required; if you grow this orchid in a pot, add some sphagnum moss to the mix. To provide the best air circulation, mount it on tree-fern bark or cork.

Cnths. Moliere

Cochlioda (coke-lee-OH-da)

Abbreviation: *Cda.*
Sympodial
Average
Bright, indirect light
Cool nights and days
High humidity
Keep evenly moist
Pot or mount

This epiphytic genus has been an important source of red color in the breeding of oncidiums, odontoglossoms, and related orchids, resulting in many colorful hybrids. In its native Peru, Ecuador, and Colombia, hummingbirds pollinate the flowers. Each olive-size, slightly flattened pseudobulb produces one 10-inch-long terminal leaf. Wiry, arching stems grow from the base to 18 inches tall, carrying six or eight 2-inch scarlet blooms. Use only filtered water. Pot or mount the plant with permanency in mind. If you grow it outdoors, locate it where it will not be disturbed.

Cda. vulcanica

Culture: Advanced
Availability: Specialty growers

Cda. vulcanica

Challenging to grow but worth the effort, this species is sought after for its bright pink flowers with pristine white lips. Six to ten flowers, each just less than 2 inches across, are carried on 10-inch inflorescences in summer to fall. The plant reaches about 12 inches tall. Pot it in a fine-grade, long-lasting mix that retains moisture.

Coelogyne (see-LAHJ-in-ee)

Abbreviation: *Coel.*
Sympodial
Miniature to large, depending on species
Medium light
Cool or warm nights and days, depending on species
High humidity
Keep evenly moist
Pot

The different species that make up this large and widespread genus appear to have little in common. Ranging in size from less than 6 to more than 36 inches tall, most have plicate leaves (arranged in folds or pleats like a fan) topping angular pseudobulbs. Flowers are often fragrant and range from 1 to 6 inches across, in colors from purest crystal white to yellow, deep green, brown, and tan. Flower stems may be strictly upright or cascading, although all emerge from the center of the developing growth. Perhaps the only horticultural feature that unifies the genus is an intolerance of repotting. Even when carefully potted at precisely the correct time, plants will stall for a year or more before resuming active growth and flowering, a trait that detracts from their popularity. Grow them in a fine-grade, fast-draining mix.

Coel. cristata

Culture: Average
Availability: Specialty growers

Often used in Victorian days as a houseplant, this species does best grown in a basket outdoors in frost-free regions where days and nights are cool and where the plant will not be disturbed. Pseudobulbs may reach the size and shape of a golf ball and are topped with two green leaves. Cascading flower stems emerge from the developing growths in late winter and early spring. Three to eight 4-inch crystal-white blooms are offset by a rich yellow throat in the lip. Flowers last as long as four weeks.

Coel. cristata

Coel. flaccida

Culture: Average
Availability: Specialty growers
This Himalayan species does best in intermediate temperatures and constant moisture. Grow it in a basket to allow the pendulous flower stems display to best advantage. The inflorescences emerge from developing growths in late spring, elongating rapidly to 24 inches or longer and carrying up to a dozen light tan blooms offset by a dark yellow lip. It may succeed as a patio plant in frost-free areas where cymbidiums can be grown outdoors year-round.

Coel. pandurata

Coel. flaccida

Coel. mooreana

Culture: Average
Availability: Specialty growers
This is one of the finest species in the genus, with spectacular pure white blooms to 5 inches or more and golden hairs in the throat of the showy lip. Flower stems emerge straight up from developing growths in late winter and last as long as four weeks. The plant grows to 18 inches tall. Keep it pot-bound where it will not be disturbed.

Coel. pandurata

Culture: Average
Availability: Specialty growers
In a greenhouse or in a frost-free permanent outdoor location, try this plant with pseudobulbs to 5 inches tall and broad leaves more than 30 inches tall. The distance between pseudobulbs can be 4 inches or more. *Coel. pandurata* is called the black orchid for the almost black markings in the lip on 4-inch deep apple-green blooms. Gracefully arching stems of six to eight or more evenly spaced blooms are borne in autumn and last only three to four weeks. Grow this species in mild temperatures in a basket or on a mount to accommodate its size and to keep the plant undisturbed.

Colmanara *(kol-ma-NAR-a)*

Abbreviation: *Colm.*
Sympodial
Compact to large, depending on species
Medium light
Mild nights and days
Moderate humidity
Let dry between waterings
Pot

Because of the diversity of its parents—miltonia, oncidium, and odontoglossum—it's challenging to generalize about colmanara. However, the most commonly grown hybrids are among the easiest and most satisfying orchids for beginners. Plants resemble an archetypal oncidium, with oval, flattened pseudobulbs to 6 inches tall, topped with two leaves that grow an inch and a half wide and 15 inches long. With many colmanaras, two branching flower stems emerge from each leaf axil at the base of the newest pseudobulbs. Stems have an attractive, upright habit that may gently arch at the top.

Flowers appear throughout the year, most heavily in late summer and early autumn, in bright yellows, reds, and browns and as much as 2 inches across. Flowers have good carriage, held on strong stems that support and show them off. Combined with its spiky habit and flowers that last as long as six weeks, colmanaras make popular houseplants. Pot them in fine-grade, fast-draining mix in relatively small pots to allow for frequent watering and quick drying. In frost-free zones, grow them outdoors on the deck or patio.

Colm. Wildcat
(*Odtna.* Rustic Ridge × *Odcdm.* Crowborough)

Culture: Easy
Availability: Specialty growers; common in retail outlets in frost-free regions
As many as 50 flowers, each about 3 inches across, are carried on branched spikes in late spring to early summer. Sepals and petals are bright yellow and heavily marked with

Colm. Wildcat

maroon; the lip is darker red with yellow accenting. Their waxy texture makes the flowers especially long-lasting. The plant grows to 3 feet or taller. Grow Wildcat in mild temperatures night and day, keeping it below 80°F. 'Bobcat' is one of many available cultivars.

Cycnoches chlorochilon (SICK-no-keez klor-OH-ky-lon)

Abbreviation: *Cyc.*
Sympodial
Average to large
Medium to bright, indirect light
Mild nights and warm days
High humidity
Let dry between waterings
Basket
Culture: Average
Availability: Specialty grower

Cynoches chlorochilon

An easy and handsome plant, this species is notable for its large, fragrant flowers, up to 6 inches across, in shades of cream and lime green. These appear in great numbers starting in late summer and continue well into fall. The columns are long and arched, resulting in the common name swan orchid. Male flowers have a more pronounced swanlike neck and bolder color. The spicy fragrance is strongest in the morning. The plant is attractive even when not in bloom and may reach 2 feet tall.

Cymbidium (sim-BID-ee-um)

Abbreviation: *Cym.*
Sympodial
Average to large, depending on species
Bright, indirect light or part shade
Cool nights and days
Moderate to high humidity
Keep evenly moist
Pot or mount for basket culture

Cymbidium

Cymbidium orchids must have been an exotic and exciting sight to Western eyes when they were introduced from Asia around 1800. Their flower shape is the most distinguishing characteristic—petals and sepals are about equal in size and, for the most part, free and erect, while the lip hass three lobe and is attached to the base of the column. Waxy in texture, flowers vary from ½ inch to 5 inches across and are carried in elegant spikes. The spikes of some cascade from the base of the plant. Color varies among the species, and some species are highly fragrant. Cymbidium flowers can last for 10 weeks or more. They are excellent cut flowers; those with large flowers are a popular choice for corsages.

Cym. **Crescent Tears**

Swedish botanist Olof Peter Swartz gave the genus its name, derived from the Greek word *cymbid,* which means "hull of a boat," no doubt an acknowledgment of the shape of the lip in some species.

The durable lance-shape green leaves are as long as 2 feet and vary from thin to thick and succulent, depending on the species. A yellowish green hue is a sign of good health; plants with dark green leaves are not getting enough light. Stems arise from short, plump pseudobulbs, frequently clasped by the base of the leaves.

As a rule cymbidiums do best in strong but indirect light, so reserve a spot in a bright sunroom or greenhouse. You can display plants outdoors in a sheltered spot out of direct sunlight that's protected from damaging or drying winds. For the most spectacular flower display, fertilize monthly from spring into summer.

To encourage flower bud development, keep your plant cooler than usual for six weeks or longer in fall and winter. In frost-free areas, you can leave the plant outdoors when nights are cool.

Flower spikes may need to be staked. Because stems are brittle and can snap, set the plant in a warm spot for a day to make them pliable before staking.

During the spring season when they are in flower, find cymbidiums widely offered as blooming pot plants. They are commonly sold in 6- to 8-inch pots with one or more flowering stems. The market in cymbidium potted plants consists mainly of surplus cut-flower types that have been recycled into potted plants and of seedlings that have not proven worthy of commercial propagation. In the last few years, some cultivars have appeared that have been specifically bred for the potted plant market, but they are the exception. Beginners who want to grow cymbidiums should work with a nursery to find the best specimen in the desired color and size rather than buying a plant off the shelf or trying to find a specific hybrid.

Cym. devonianum

Culture: Average
Availability: Specialty growers
This unusual dwarf cymbidium has tiny pseudobulbs topped with several long, broad leaves to 4 inches wide and 12 inches long. It flourishes in low light—lower than many of its relatives require—and its leaves burn or bleach easily when the light is too bright. Cascading flower stems bear as many as a dozen or more 2½-inch olive green blooms offset by a boldly magenta-banded lip. Flowers appear in late spring from the base of the most recent growth and can last

four weeks. Basket culture is recommended because of the cascading habit of flowering stems. Keep plants evenly moist in fine-grade medium and fertilize heavily May through September. Stop feeding in September. For best flower production, grow *Cym. devonianum* where summer nights stay below 60°F.

Cym. ensifolium

Culture: Average
Availability: Specialty growers

Cym. ensifolium

Cym. ensifolium has an elegant appearance, with grassy leaves to 18 inches long arising from small, insignificant pseudobulbs. It tolerates warmer conditions than many of its relatives and will bloom where summer night temperatures stay above 60°F. Upright flower spikes of four to seven 2-inch starry cream-colored blooms appear in late spring and give off a sweet perfume during the heat of the day. Flowers may last three weeks.

Cym. lowianum

Culture: Average
Availability: Specialty growers

Cym. lowianum

Clustered, prominent pseudobulbs give rise to narrow, grassy leaves that are 36 inches or longer. Bright light and cool nighttime temperatures combine to trigger the formation of long, arching flower stems bearing 20 or more 5-inch deep green blooms offset with a red-banded lip. The arching, almost pendulous inflorescences are best displayed in a basket. *Cym. lowianum* blooms from winter into spring, each blossom lasting four to six weeks.

Cym. madidum

Culture: Average
Availability: Specialty growers

An important parent in many hybrids, this species hails from tropical Australia. Its stiff, leathery, upright leaves are 2 inches wide and 30 inches long; they arise from large, robust pseudobulbs. Pendulous flower stems bear dozens of widely spaced 2-inch blooms in shades of buff to deep green, many offset by a red mark in the throat of the lip. Flowers bloom late in May and last three to four weeks. Because this species does not tolerate being wet or cold, growing it under traditional cymbidium conditions often results in failure. *Cym. madidum* does best in bright light and warm temperatures. Plant it in a basket to display the cascading flower stems to best advantage. The orchid can be quite heavy at maturity, so hang the basket carefully and securely.

Cym. parishii

Culture: Average
Availability: Specialty growers

The variety *sanderae* (*Cym. parishii sanderae*) is the one seen most often. It grows to about 24 inches. When used in breeding, the resulting hybrids have increased tolerance to

Cym. parishii

warmth than other cymbidiums. The upright 30-inch-tall flower stems carry 3½-inch pure white blooms offset by a red-spotted lip. Flowers bloom in midwinter and may last four weeks.

Cym. pumilum

Culture: Average
Availability: Specialty growers

Native to Japan, this orchid grows less than 12 inches tall. It is the parent of many of today's most popular small cymbidiums. Flower stems emerge straight out from the base of the newest growth and remain horizontal unless carefully staked. The 1½-inch mahogany to pale green blooms have a red-banded or spotted lip. Flowers bloom in winter and last as long as four weeks. Display *Cym. pumilum* for its nearly cascading flower stems in a basket.

Cym. Golden Elf 'Sundust' (*Cym. ensifolium* × *Cym.* Enid Haupt)

Culture: Average
Availability: Specialty growers

Cym. Golden Elf 'Sundust'

This award-winning orchid is a miniature within the world of cymbidiums, where the standard size is 2 to 3 feet tall. At about 18 inches tall, Golden Elf 'Sundust' commands attention, blooming from summer to fall. Golden yellow flowers are about 2½ inches across and carried four to six to a spike. They last just two weeks with a sweet rose-scented perfume. Grow Golden Elf 'Sundust' in bright light on a windowsill or in a greenhouse. Fairly heat-tolerant, it doesn't need as much cooling as some other cymbidiums in order to form buds—a good choice for mild climates.

Cym. Maureen Carter 'Sweet Fragrance' (*Cym. sinense* × *Cym.* Sleeping Beauty)

Culture: Average
Availability: Specialty growers

'Sweet Fragrance' is a prime example of the type of modern cymbidium hybrids beginning to enter the general horticultural trade. Growing to about 18 inches tall, these cultivars are more compact than traditional cymbidiums, and they also have a much better chance of reblooming than their more-demanding cousins.

Keep plants evenly moist in medium-grade mix and provide plenty of light. Where possible, plants should summer outdoors to allow for maximum light. Flowers

Thick robust flower stems appear with the emergence of new growth in spring. The 3-inch-wide flowers come in shades of rich gold and mahogany. Some species also have prominent and showy subtending bracts that add to the overall display. Flowers typically bloom in spring and last for four to six weeks. Plant cyrtopodiums in large pots and medium-grade orchid mix. They make good patio or deck plants in frost-free areas; an outdoor location easily accommodates their size.

Cyrtopodium andersonii

Cym. Maureen Carter 'Sweet Fragrance'

appear in late winter and again in fall under ideal conditions; they are sweetly fragrant. Bright yellow blooms reach 3 inches across and last two to three weeks.

Cym. Via Nogales 'Pink Pearl' (*Cym.* Solana Beach × *Cym.* Sussex Dawn)

Culture: Average
Availability: Specialty growers
The famous cymbidium breeders Gallup & Stribling produced this highly regarded hybrid that grows 24 to 36 inches tall and requires plenty of growing space. In winter and spring, tall flower spikes of 4-inch-wide soft pink flowers with darker markings appear. Via Nogales 'Pink Pearl' does best in a bright greenhouse or outdoors in direct sun in a cool but frost-free environment.

Cyrtopodium *(sir-toh-POH-dee-um)*

Abbreviation: *Cyrt.*
Sympodial
Large
Bright light
Mild nights and warm days
Moderate humidity
Keep evenly moist; allow dry dormancy in winter
Pot

This genus of large upright plants has cigar-shape 36-inch-long pseudobulbs along which 2-inch-wide by 12-inch-long leaves arise. Leaves are often deciduous. Typically, orchids in this genus form "nests" around the base—stiff, upright-growing roots that catch nutrient-laden debris.

Darwinara *(dar-win-ARE-uh)* (*Ascocentrum* × *Neofinetia* × *Rhynchostylis* × *Vanda*)

Abbreviation: *Dar.*
Monopodial
Compact to large, depending on cross
Medium light
Mild nights and days
Moderate humidity
Keep evenly moist
Pot

This complex intergeneric hybrid was created expressly for easy-to-grow potted plants that would adapt to home growing conditions. Flowers of many members of the group offer the sweetly spicy morning and evening fragrance of the neofinetia parent and last four weeks or longer. Grow darwinaras along with paphs or oncidiums on a windowsill. Provide more light if flowering seems slow.

Dar. Charm 'Blue Star' HCC/AOS (*Neof. falcata* × *Vasco.* Tham Yuen Hae)

Culture: Easy
Availability: Specialty growers
The charm of this cultivar lies in its compact growth habit—it reaches a mere 6 inches in spread—and in its correspondingly miniature flowers, which are 1 inch across. The narrow leaves grow in a fan; upright flower stems emerge from the leaf axils throughout the year. Flower color is purple-blue. Good drainage is a must for *Dar.* Charm 'Blue Star'; grow it in a wooden basket or shallow pot of medium-grade, fast-draining mix.

Dar. Charm 'Blue Star'

Degarmoara (dee-gar-moh-ARE-uh)

Abbreviation: *Dgmra.*
Sympodial
Compact to large, depending on cross
Medium light
Mild nights and days
Moderate humidity
Keep evenly moist
Pot

Most of the plant varieties available in this genus have been bred to be easy to grow and to flower for beginners. They result from crosses between brassia, miltonia, and oncidium. Their plant habit is similar to that of oncidium, with compressed oval pseudobulbs often narrowing toward the top and narrow 15-inch-long leaves. One or two upright arching, unbranching flower stems emerge from the base of mature growth. The flowering season varies among the group, but many types bloom as the pseudobulbs mature throughout the year; blooms last four weeks or longer.

Dgmra. Winter Wonderland 'White Fairy' (Mltssa. Cartagena × Odm. Gledhow)

Culture: Easy
Availability: Specialty growers

Dgmra. Winter Wonderland 'White Fairy'

The scent of ripe bananas is the most distinguishing characteristic of this selection. The pretty flowers are large and white, with slightly reflexed sepals and a lip dusted with red. They measure more than 3 inches across. Established plants grow vigorously to about 24 inches tall and produce several flushes of bloom a year. Medium light and intermediate temperatures are preferred. This hybrid will grow well in pots with any well-drained medium-textured orchid mix; warm and damp growing conditions are needed.

Dendrobium (den-DROH-bee-um)

Abbreviation: *Den.*
Sympodial
Miniature to large, depending on species
Medium to bright light, depending on species
Cool to warm days and nights, depending on species
Moderate to high humidity
Keep evenly moist; provide dry winter dormancy for some species
Pot or mount, depending on species

Den. All Jensens Blue

About 1,500 dendrobium species have been named, and literally thousands of hybrids exist. Although it is hard to generalize, most produce attractive long-lasting flowers, have either pseudobulbs or canes, and are epiphytic.

Among the species and hybrids, flowers vary widely in color and form. In general, they have three equal-size sepals. The petals may be the same size as the sepals or broader. Petals can be flat, twisted, or elongated, or they may have undulating margins. Their lips may be fringed or smooth; all have a hard, waxy projection called a callus. Dendrobiums carry their flowers either at the end of the flower stem or along its length; heavy-flowering plants can be top-heavy. Some species have scented flowers.

Plants are deciduous or evergreen. Individual leaves can be as petite as 1 inch or as strapping as 15 inches long. The leaves may be thick or thin and flat or tapering, depending on the species. Some species have little rounded pseudobulbs, while the pseudobulbs of others are massive and canelike, growing as long as 5 feet.

Swedish botanist Olof Peter Swartz named this genus. Dendrobium translates as "life in a tree," which refers to the epiphytic nature of the vast majority of the species.

Knowing your plant's origins will help you provide the best care. Most dendrobiums are native to the Asian and Pacific tropics, from jungles to snowy mountainsides. Papua New Guinea is home to about a third of all dendrobium species. They require a winter rest, as they have in their native habitat. Most species require good air circulation and high humidity. Other than that, dendrobiums vary widely in their cultural needs. Many are heavy feeders while they are actively growing, but need few nutrients during their dormant period. Watering needs vary according to species. Some dendrobiums need brighter light or longer days. If yours seems slow to bloom or has spindly growth, move it to a spot with more light. Because dendrobiums vary so much in their needs, you'll want to get as much information as you can from the supplier before taking a new plant home.

Dendrobiums are among the most widely distributed orchids as flowering potted plants; they are available in an array of sizes, colors and forms. Many have been bred from *Den. phalaenopsis;* many other species have been mixed in over time. Because so many hybrids and cultivars have been bred, it is difficult to find specific hybrids or cultivars based on what you may see in photos. Cymbidiums and phalaenopsis are difficult as well. However, you can often find something similar. Consult a local orchid nursery or grower about the colors and size of the plant you have your eye on; the grower should be able to point out suitable substitutions. Also check out specialty growers on the Internet or attend orchid shows, where many new hybrids are offered.

Den. aggregatum

Culture: Average
Availability: Specialty growers

Den. aggregatum

Golden yellow honey-scented flowers adorn this small plant in spring. Although only about 1 inch across, blooms appear in showy branched clusters of three or more inflorescences. Lips of the flowers are broad and almost heart-shape. As the plant matures, flowering becomes abundant. For best results, mount this species on a slab with permanency in mind; it does not tolerate moving and division. This species has been renamed *Den. lindleyi.*

Den. cruentum

Culture: Average
Availability: Specialty growers

Den. cruentum

This compact orchid makes a big impression with its delicately scented 1½- to 2½-inch-wide, long-lasting flowers. Lime-green sepals contrast dramatically with a scarlet lip, which is edged in cream. The species name cruentum means "blood red" and refers to that vivid lip color.

Give the plant a week or two off from water and food in winter to encourage bud development, then enjoy the show from spring to fall. *Den. cruentum* grows to about 10 inches tall in warm and moderately humid conditions. It is considered endangered in its native Thailand; buy from reputable orchid growers who raise plants from seed.

Den. cuthbertsonii

Culture: Advanced
Availability: Rare

This dwarf evergreen species is never dormant and its 1-inch wide fiery orange to hot pink flowers last on the plant about nine months. Its abundant blooms overwhelm the 2-inch-long attractively speckled foliage. Because *Den. cuthbertsonii* is native to the warm, humid, high cloud forests of New

Den. cuthbertsonii

Guinea, it requires similar growing conditions at home: high humidity, no exposure to drafts, low to medium light, and constant moisture. Mount *Den. cuthbertsonii* or grow it in a fast-draining orchid mix in a shallow pot to prevent it from becoming soggy.

Den. griffithianum

Culture: Average
Availability: Rare
This magnificent bloomer comes from Myanmar. In spring and summer, it produces numerous pendulous inflorescences displaying many dainty bright golden yellow

Den. griffithianum

and rich orange blossoms. Heavy texture blooms last long on the plant or in a vase. Grow *Den. griffithianum* in a fast-draining mix in a location where air circulates freely. During winter, give it a break from food and water.

Den. kingianum

Culture: Easy
Availability: Specialty growers
Den. kingianum is a durable, floriferous, and easy-to-grow orchid. Its fragrant flowers, which appear in early spring,

Den. kingianum

are 1 to 1½ inches across and bright pink, purple, or white with darker markings on the lip. With as many as 15 flowers on an inflorescence, the fragrance can be strong.

Australian growers continue to produce hybrids of this native plant. They vary greatly in flower color, but are usually some combination of pink and purple or cream, or all white. They also vary in growth habit and size, from less than 6 to more than 18 inches tall.

Den. kingianum is evergreen and a vigorous grower. Pot it in a fast-draining orchid mix. Water every day, reducing food and water slightly during the winter months. It can tolerate cooler temperatures better than most other dendrobiums and must receive several weeks of cool (50°F or slightly below), dry conditions to bloom.

Den. lawesii

Culture: Average
Availability: Specialty growers
This colorful orchid comes from the jungles of Papua New Guinea. Although only 1 inch across, the flowers are so bright—a fiery, tropical orange-red tipped in yellow—that they can't be missed. They appear in late winter and early

spring and exude a rich honey fragrance. Plants carry many inflorescences of eight flowers on leafless spikes; because they are waxy, blooms last for many weeks. To promote blooming, provide a dry winter rest period for the plant.

Den. lawesii

Den. loddigesii

Culture: Average
Availability: Specialty growers
Each bare, arching cane of this species bears one 2-inch flower, which lasts about three weeks. Petals and sepals are

Den. loddigesii

pink, while the highly fringed lip is edged in pink, then white, with glowing yellow interior. Blooms have a soft, sweet scent.

Den. loddigesii is a rambler, so it does best on a mount. If grown in a pot, allow space for its generous aerial roots. When leaves drop in autumn, give the plant a dry winter rest period and reduce night temperatures to 50°F.

Den. nobile

Culture: Average
Availability: Common
As a group, these hybrids are among the loveliest orchids a hobbyist can grow. They are justly popular. Flowering begins in late winter or early spring, and individual flowers can last four weeks or longer. They bloom in a variety of colors and bicolors (mostly in the pink, purple, and white range), usually measure about 3 inches across, and are carried two to four to an inflorescence. They also have a soft scent similar to honey and musk.

Den. nobile

An upright 1- to 2-foot-tall plant, *Den. nobile* and its hybrids needs a cool rest period in late fall. Stop feeding, reduce water, and let the leaves fall off. Resume watering and fertilizing when new leaves and buds appear.

Den. parishii

Culture: Average
Availability: Specialty growers

Den. parishii

Native to Asia, this charming species has springtime blooms that smell like sun-ripened raspberries. The flowers are a rich pink with a dab of darker maroon inside the lip. They're about 2 inches across and borne on short spikes; the plant itself grows 1 to 2 feet tall. Mount it on a slab or grow it in a porous mix. After the leaves drop, withhold water and fertilizer until new growth appears.

Den. petiolatum

Culture: Advanced
Availability: Rare
A tiny but eye-catching native of New Guinea, this semideciduous plant grows only 5 to 6 inches tall. The equally small flowers are clustered in short inflorescences from spring to summer. Somewhat cupped and only ¾ inch across, they stand out because they're bright purple with contrasting orange lips. Grow this orchid in a small pot of fast-draining orchid medium.

Den. rhodosticum

Culture: Average
Availability: Specialty growers
The flowers of this species are often compared to a bird in flight because of their upswept petals and sepals. The blossoms are white and sometimes rimmed in dark pink around the lips. Measuring 2½ to 3½ inches across, they are displayed in short inflorescences of two to six in winter to spring. The plant grows to about 10 inches tall. Whether you

Den. rhodosticum

mount this species or grow it in a pot of fast-draining mix, it is important to keep roots continuously damp. You may find *Den. rhodosticum* also sold as *Den. madonnae*.

Den. sulawesii

Culture: Advanced
Availability: Rare

Den. sulawesii

Sometimes labeled *Den. crepidiferum* and sometimes as *Den. glomeratum,* this species is popular for its brilliant color. The plants bloom in late spring to summer. Its hot pink or magenta petals and sepals contrast with a rich orange lip. As the species name indicates, this orchid comes from Sulawesi (in Indonesia), and thus it requires moderate light, warm temperatures, and high humidity to thrive and bloom.

Den. superbum

Culture: Average
Availability: Specialty growers
This particularly large-flowered and fine form of a widespread species is native to Malaysia and the Philippines,

grows about 3 feet tall, and has deciduous 3-inch leaves that drop in fall. In spring 3-inch dark pink flowers with dark red-purple throats cover leafless stems.

Grow *Den. superbum* on a mount or hang in a basket to show off slender cascading flower stems. Keep the plant continuously moist during the growing season and in a location with bright light, high humidity, and good air circulation. Provide a dry dormant period during winter to trigger late winter or early spring flowering. Pot aerial growths as new plants after they show roots.

Den. superbum giganteum

Den. unicum

Culture: Easy
Availability: Specialty growers
Native to Thailand, Laos, and Vietnam, this easy-to-grow orchid has odd-looking flowers that emit a sweet tangerine scent. They're a mere 2 inches across and highly reflexed. The petals and sepals are hot orange-red, and the distinctive tubular lip is cream with orange-red accents. Give *Den. unicum* a one- to two-week dry period in winter to encourage blooming in late winter or spring. Mount it on a slab or pot it in a fine-grade, fast-draining mix.

Den. unicum

Den. violaceum

Culture: Average
Availability: Specialty growers
A somewhat variable species from New Guinea, this small 6-inch-tall plant offers a winter-to-spring show of small flowers in pink, some shade of purple, or almost blue. Measuring just 1½ inches across, they grow in tight clusters. There are two subspecies in cultivation: *Den. violaceum violaceum* and *Den. violaceum cyperifolium*. Violaceum has an upright habit; cyperifolium is pendulous. Mount *Den. violaceum* on a slab or pot it in a fine-grade, fast-draining mix. Keep it damp at all times.

Den. Nalene Bui
(Den. Iki × Den. Princess)

Culture: Easy
Availability: Specialty growers
This outstanding hybrid has inherited a compact growing habit from its parent Iki. The comparatively large 2½-inch-wide bluish-pink flowers bloom from winter into spring. The plant reaches only 6 to 8 inches tall, so it fits well in small spaces or on a windowsill. Best of all, it's easy to grow—a great choice for beginners.

Dendrochilum (den-dro-KY-lum)

Abbreviation: *Ddc.*
Sympodial
Miniature to large, depending on species
Medium light
Mild nights and days
Moderate humidity
Keep evenly moist
Pot

Although dendrochilum is a large genus, many species comprising it are similar in habit. Their pseudobulbs are rounded and cylindrical and produce one or two terminal leaves much longer than they are broad. Plants range from less than 4 inches to more than 30 inches tall. Strongly upright flower stems emerge from developing growth, arch at the tip, and cascade from just below the point of the first flower. The ½-inch-wide blossoms are closely set and alternate on the stem. Showy bracts below the flowers add to the overall display and give rise to the common name chain orchid. Flowers last about three weeks.

Plants tend to branch freely and have multiple flower stems, resulting in a full pot in a short time. Only a few of the many species are readily available, but new ones are discovered every year.

Ddc. cobbianum

Culture: Easy to average
Availability: Specialty growers

Ddc. cobbianum

Ddc. cobbianum is one of the most popular and widely grown of the genus. Its unusual flower spikes of straw yellow blooms are borne on twisting stems in autumn. The flowers emit a musky fragrance during daytime. Plants have short pseudobulbs and 15-inch-long leaves.

Ddc. magnum

Culture: Average
Availability: Specialty growers

Ddc. magnum

Ddc. magnum is the best of the genus, with showy floral display on plants 24 to 30 inches tall. Long dangling inflorescences carry burnt-orange flowers framed below by light green bracts in mid- to late summer. Flowers are less than ½ inch across and line up so densely along the stems that they've inspired common names for this plant that include golden chain orchid and necklace orchid. They last for three weeks or more and release a musky scent that some gardeners do not like. Grow *Ddc. magnum* in a container of moss and tree fern that allows air to circulate freely.

Diacrium (die-AK-ree-um)

Abbreviation: *Diacm.*
Sympodial
Large
Bright light
Mild to warm nights and days
High humidity
Let dry between waterings
Pot

These robust plants have large hollow pseudobulbs, each bearing a pair of leaves. In native habitats of South America and the Caribbean, the hollow pseudobulbs are often home to ants that fiercely defend their territory. Upright flower stems bear lightly citrus-scented 3-inch-wide white blooms over a period of several weeks in spring. Grow diacrium outdoors where winters are frost-free. Clarkarea and iwanagara are closely related.

Diacm. bicornutum

Culture: Average
Availability: Specialty growers

Diacm. bicornutum

Also called *Caularthron bicornutum,* this species is a fine addition to the subtropical patio garden. Its citrus-scented white flowers with purple spotted lip appear in spring. In areas where frost is not a threat it can be naturalized onto a tree in the garden; otherwise, grow it indoors in a pot or plant it in a basket of medium-grade orchid mix that you can take indoors.

Clarkeara Memoria Polly Bates (*Sl.* Gratrixiae × *Iwan.* Appleblossom)

Culture: Average
Availability: Specialty growers
Clarkeara hybrids are an example of modern complex cattleya alliance breeding. This newly named genus contains five genera: diacrium, cattleya, brassavola, laelia, and sophronitis. Flowers have good color for the type of breeding, with yellow base often suffused with red along edges of flower parts. Bloom season varies because of the

Clarkeara Memoria Polly Bates

variety of species in the hybrid; most bloom in late winter into early spring. Some examples may have the brasso citrus fragrance. Plants are compact to 10 inches tall. Grow like other members of the cattleya alliance.

Iwanagaara Appleblossom 'Fantastic' (*Caulaelia* Snowflake × *Blc.* Orange Nugget) *ee-wan-ah-GAH-ara*

Culture: Average
Availability: Common
This orchid, named for a Hawaiian family famous for orchid hybridizing, represents the successful crossing of four genera in the cattleya alliance, a group that covers all cattleyas and their relatives. Appleblossom 'Fantastic' grows about 18 inches tall and blooms in winter or spring with 3½-inch-wide delicately scented flowers that can last a month. Blooms are soft pink with dark coloring along the edges and a matching lip with buttery yellow throat. Grow Appleblossom 'Fantastic' in medium to coarse mix.

Iwanagara Appleblossom 'Fantastic'

Dialaelia (die-uh-LAY-lee-a)

Abbreviation: *Dial.*
Sympodial
Compact
Bright light
Mild nights and days
Moderate humidity
Let dry between waterings
Pot

One of the nicest and most adaptable of cattleya-related intergeneric crosses, dialaelia is especially tough and adaptable. Most of the commonly available hybrids have 2-inch-wide white blooms successively borne several at a time on upright 12-inch flower stems in late summer. Grow dialaelia in pots of coarse bark for best drainage. Dialaelia results from crosses between diacrium and laelia.

Dial. Mizoguchi 'Sunset Valley Orchids' AM/AOS (Dial. Snowflake × L. anceps)

Culture: Easy
Availability: Specialty growers

Dial. Mizoguchi 'Sunset Valley'

These bifoliate hybrids may reach 18 inches, with 36-inch stems of four to six 5-inch-wide white blooms. Flowers last six weeks or longer and appear in winter. In California cymbidium fanciers like to grow other orchids alongside their cymbidiums. Mizoguchi 'Sunset Valley Orchids' is a natural cymbidium companion because of its *L. anceps* parent and the parent of *Dial.* Snowflake, *L. albida.*

Dial. Snowflake (Diacm. bicornutum × L. albida)

Culture: Easy
Availability: Specialty growers, spring orchid shows, and warm-climate garden centers

Sought for its long-lasting floral display of a dozen or more flowers that open successively over a period of weeks in winter, this plant grows less than 12 inches tall and is a good choice for beginners. Grow Snowflake on a sunny windowsill or outdoors on a patio or deck in frost-free regions.

Disa (DEE-sa)

Abbreviation: None
Sympodial
Miniature to large, depending on species
Medium light
Cool nights and mild days
Moderate to high humidity
Continuously moist
Pot

While several hundred species make up this largely South African genus, only a few are in general cultivation. Plants are terrestrial and have no pseudobulbs. Instead, they have subterranean tubers from which stems emerge bearing whorls of soft green leaves in spring. Experts disagree on whether sharp sand or living sphagnum moss is the medium for disa, although all agree that using rainwater or other purified water is an absolute necessity to mimic the plant's natural habitat, which is in and around running water.

Disa uniflora

Culture: Advanced
Availability: Rare

"The Pride of Table Mountain," *Disa uniflora* is the best known of the *Disa* genus. Despite its name, which means "one-flowered," plants can bear as many as five 4-inch vivid scarlet-red blooms in late spring. The flowers, which last several weeks, are remarkably complex and unlike any other orchid. They are triangular in shape; their reproductive parts are hard to distinguish.

Disa uniflora

Doritaenopsis *(doh-RYE-ton-op-sis)*
(*Doritis* × *Phalaenopsis*)

Abbreviation: *Dtps.*
Monopodial
Average size
Medium to bright light, depending on hybrid
Mild nights and days
Moderate humidity
Keep evenly moist
Pot

Dtps. Brother Vanessa Hannay 'De Leon #1'

Doritaenopsis, along with phalaenopsis, are by far the most popular and common flowering orchids in today's retail market. Many experts argue that most doritaenopsis hybrids are really phalaenopsis (they result from crosses between doritis and phalaenopsis). The reasons for this are highly esoteric and affect neither the culture nor plant availability. However, you may look for a hybrid under one name and find it under the other.

Doritaenopsis plants are attractive, with large broad 12-inch-long, 6-inch-wide, flat leaves arranged like those of a phalaenopsis. If well grown, very old plants may reach 12 inches tall and nearly 36 inches across. Flowering stems emerge from the leaf axils in spring and grow more or less upright, arching at or near their tops about where the first flower appears. These stems often branch, depending on both the breeding background and the health of the plant. The doritaenopsis flowering season starts a little later in winter than that of phalaenopsis.

Like phalaenopsis, doritaenopsis are excellent houseplants with similar cultural needs. A shaded west window is an ideal location, but they'll grow fine in a lightly shaded south window. Keep plants evenly moist and feed regularly.

Because most doritaenopsis are raised from seed, and most hybrids are made only once, the availability of any given hybrid is ephemeral. Cloning, which allows the distribution of exact cultivars, is becoming more common for doritaenopsis but is still the exception. Check with a nursery to find the color, size, or shape rather than search for exact cultivars.

Dtps. Chain Xen Diamond
(*Phal.* Golden Peoker × *Dtps.* Judy Valentine)

Culture: Easy
Availability: Rare

Chain Xen Diamond is one of the few plants to receive the American Orchid Society's highest award, the First Class Certificate. It is a type of hybrid referred to as harlequin. Bred from a harlequin-flowered clone of *Phal.* Golden Peoker, its flowers are splotched beet red.

Chain Xen Diamond has broad, well-shaped pale amethyst flowers with prominent darker purple markings. They are borne several at a time in branched inflorescences and, because of their heavy substance, are long-lasting. Plants usually bloom in spring and stay in bloom for several months. Attractive glossy green leaves are about 12 to 14 inches long, and the plant grows 6 to 8 inches tall. Thanks to modern cloning techniques, it is affordable.

Dtps. Leopard Prince
(*Dtps.* Sun Prince × *Phal.* French Fantasia)

Culture: Easy
Availability: Rare

Exotic vivid color distinguishes this worthy hybrid. Its 3- to 4-inch-wide blossoms are creamy white, liberally and prominently spotted with purple-pink; the lip contrasts in wine red. Leopard Prince has dark green leaves that approach 12 inches long, and the plant grows about 6 inches tall. Easy and rewarding to grow, it usually blooms in spring, with the flowers lasting at least a couple of months.

Some cultivars of this hybrid have French spots: a fine, even spotting on the blossoms. French-spotted orchids tend to have large flowers of average substance. (Similarly, orchid flowers with Taiwanese spots sport irregular blotches and bars. Those with Taiwanese spots are smaller but have brighter markings and better substance.)

Dtps. Leopard Prince

Dtps. Memoria Clarence Schubert
(*Dor. buyssoniana* × *Phal.* Zada)

Culture: Easy
Availability: Specialty growers
This hybrid, registered in 1965, is still a winner. Its brilliant reddish pink flowers, about ½ inch across, glisten in light. They form on erect flower spikes that grow about 18 inches tall. Plants are about 6 inches tall, with 12-inch leaf spread. This eyecatching variety needs bright light but is otherwise undemanding in its cultural requirements.

Dtps. Minho Princess
(*Dtps.* Sun Prince × *Phal.* Ta Lin)

Culture: Easy
Availability: Rare
Breathtakingly beautiful blossoms adorn this justly popular hybrid. About 4 inches across, they look as though dark pink candy stripes were painted on the edges of the flowers. The lips of the flowers are the same dark pink. Coloration makes Minho Princess immediately special and identifiable.

Minho Princess grows about 6 inches tall and 12 inches wide and has dark green leaves. It blooms at any time of year

Dtps. Minho Princess

but most commonly in late winter to early spring, producing several flowers on an 18-inch-tall spike. The plant will stay in bloom for a couple of months or longer.

Dtps. Musick Lipstick
(*Phal.* Kuntrarti Rarashati × *Dor.* Abed-nego)

Culture: Easy
Availability: Rare
This is an unusual hybrid with small, round, bright red flowers. They're only 1½ inches across but are produced in abundance every spring and summer. The plant is nicely compact, with slow-growing leaves that eventually reach no more than 10 inches tall. These qualities make it a good choice for a windowsill. Musick Lipstick is easy to care for. Pot it in a fine- to medium-grade, fast-draining orchid mix or in sphagnum moss.

Dtps. Purple Gem
(*Dor. pulcherrima* × *Phal. equestris*)

Culture: Easy
Availability: Specialty growers
Purple Gem is the perfect windowsill plant. It's easy,

compact, and blooms eagerly in spring and summer. The 1-inch-wide flowers range from light to dark purple. The plant grows slowly and remains dwarf, eventually reaching about 6 inches. Grow it in a pot of fine-textured mix or moss in a location where temperatures are consistently warm.

Dtps. Sogo Manager
(*Dtps.* Brother Lawrence × *Dtps.* Autumn Sun)

Culture: Easy
Availability: Rare

Dtps. Sogo Manager 'Crown Fox'

Bred by Sogo, a highly respected phalaenopsis breeder in Taiwan, Sogo Manager sets a high standard with its fragrant 2-inch-wide colorfast canary yellow flowers. Until the 1940s, no yellow doritaenopsis or phalaenopsis orchids existed. The earliest ones faded after a short time in bloom; Sogo Manager's color does not fade. The plant grows about 12 inches tall and 12 inches wide and has glossy green leaves. It blooms mostly in late winter to spring; the flowers last for months.

Dtps. Taida Salu
(*Phal.* Salu Spot × *Dtps.* Happy Beauty)

Culture: Easy
Availability: Rare
You will get at least two flower shows a year from this dramatic hybrid from Taiwan. The blooms—wine red with golden veins—have a rich, jewellike quality; they can get as big as 4 inches across. If the plant is healthy, it will retain the flowers for two or three months. Grow Taida Salu in a pot of

Dtps. Taida Salu

sphagnum moss or bark mix in a warm, humid spot with bright, indirect light.

Doritis *(doh-RYE-tis)*

Abbreviation: *Dor.*
Monopodial
Average
Medium to bright light, depending on species
Mild nights and days
Moderate humidity
Let dry between waterings
Pot

When not in bloom, doritis orchids look like phalaenopsis. When brought into cultivation, they were classified as phals. They have a stemless monopodial plant form like that of phalaenopsis, as well as characteristic oblong thick leaves that are stiff-texture, dark green on top and sometimes purplish on the underside. Some experts classify doritis as phalaenopsis; flowers are so distinctively different, however, that most experts give it its own genus.

Doritis orchids are natives of Myanmar, Thailand, Malaysia, Vietnam, Laos, Cambodia, and the Indonesian island of Sumatra. Unlike pastel hues of phalaenopsis, flowers are light to dark purple and carried on otherwise bare stiff spikes that rise straight up from the clump of leaves in summer. Blooms are comparatively small, no more than 1½ inches across.

Dor. pulcherrima

The three-lobed lip also sets doritis apart. The middle lobe tends to be larger and have a slightly wavy margin. Also, two "antennae" rise from the lip base, looking a little like ears. In 1833, the botanist John Lindley gave the species its name, which means "spear" in Greek, reflecting the flowers' appearance. It is also an alternative name for Aphrodite, goddess of love and beauty. Although there are doritis species, they are frequently bred with various phalaenopsis species and hybrids.

Warmth and consistent humidity are the most important requirements for growing doritis. The plants also need brighter light than phalaenopsis. Grow them in fine-textured bark. Sometimes you can get a second flush of bloom by removing the spike after flowers fade. Cut it off just above the second jointed node from the bottom.

Over time, roots tend to lift the plant in the pot. It can be lowered when repotting, but roots will likely lift it again.

Dor. pulcherrima

Culture: Easy
Availability: Specialty growers; also sold at retail garden centers in warm climates in late spring

These plants have shorter, stiffer leaves and will take slightly more light than phalaenopsis. Otherwise, culture is the same as for phals (pages 189–193). You may find this plant labeled *Phal. pulcherrima*. Straight, upright flowering stems grow 24 inches or taller and bear 1½-inch blooms in shades of rose and lilac in late spring. Flowers open sequentially, extending the floral display for four to six weeks or longer.

Beardara Henry Wallbrunn (*Ascps.* Irene Dobkin × *Dor. pulcherrima*)

Culture: Advanced
Availability: Rare

Beardara is the result of intergeneric crosses involving doritis, phalaenopsis, and ascocentrum. *Bdra.* Henry Wallbrunn is an unusual and charming hybrid that grows only 6 inches tall after several years. It blooms in early to late spring and has 1-inch round, warm apricot-orange flowers—a rare color for doritis hybrids and much treasured. The leaves have a red tint and a spread of about 6 inches.

Dracula *(DRUH-kew-luh)*

Abbreviation: *Drac.*
Sympodial
Miniature to large, depending on species
Low light
Cool nights and mild days
High humidity
Keep evenly moist
Basket

Draculas are challenging to grow. They need cloud forest conditions—that is, high humidity and constant, moderate temperatures, along with heavy shade. All species bloom from the base of the plant, with the flowering stems of most draculas growing straight down. The kite-shape blooms offer some of the most unusual and subtle color combinations found in the orchid family. Many have cup-shape white lips that mimic the fungus that their pollinator, a gnat, searches out for egg-laying. Plants have upright, fleshy leaves, varying from 4 to nearly 10 inches long. Grow them in baskets so you can view the downward-facing blooms. Closely related to masdevallias (pages 161 to 164), these orchids were recently classified as this separate genus.

Drac. marsupialis

Drac. marsupialis

Culture: Advanced
Availability: Rare

A native of Ecuador, this species has white petals and sepals marked heavily with dark maroon. The pouch-shape lip that gives the plant its species name is white outside with a glowing touch of yellow within. Flowers are about 3 inches across and have a fuzzy texture.

Dyakia *(dye-AHK-ee-a)*

Abbreviation: None
Monopodial
Miniature
Bright light
Warm nights and
  hot days
Moderate to high humidity
Keep evenly moist
Pot or mount

Closely related to the ascocentrums, dyakia differs from their relatives in leaf shape and flower structure. They are small plants, to only 4 inches tall and 6 inches across, with distinctive soft, broad light green leaves. In spring, upright flower stems bear 30 brilliant magenta-rose blooms, each 1 inch across. Blooms last as long as four weeks. Dyakias are easy to grow with needs similar to phalaenopsis. Plant them in small pots containing fast-draining, fine-textured medium, or mount them on cork.

Dyakia hendersoniana

Dyakia hendersoniana

Culture: Average
Availability: Specialty growers
Also sold as *Asctm. hendersonianum,* this petite species from Borneo is described as small yet mighty. Growing no more than 3 or 4 inches tall, from spring to summer it puts on an outstanding show of 1-inch-wide flowers in clusters of as many as 30 on a stem. Flower color is brilliant pink, magenta, or hot pink, with a white spur. Blooms are softly scented and last two months. Grow *Dyakia hendersoniana* in a small pot or basket of fast-draining orchid mix.

Encyclia *(en-SY-klee-a)*

Abbreviation: *E.*
Sympodial
Dwarf to large, depending on species
Bright to medium light
Mild nights and days
Moderate humidity
Let dry between waterings
Pot or mount

Related to cattleya and similar in growth requirements, many of the most commonly cultivated encyclia species and hybrids grow seasonally during warm months. Some can reach considerable size, with pseudobulbs the size of a baseball topped by two stiff leaves that are 1 inch wide and 15 inches long. Plants fit into many collections, especially, in warm climates, as valuable summer-flowering subjects.

Their stout, upright, branching stems bear a multitude of waxy 2-inch-wide blooms in shades of yellow, mahogany, red, and almost orange. Some also tolerate cool weather.

A large genus, encyclias were once classified with epidendrum. The separation from epidendrum and the shift of some related orchids to the genus *Prosthechea* has created confusion when it comes to hybrid names. New combinations are replacing old ones, such as *Catyclia* instead of *Epicattleya* and *Encylaelia* instead of *Epilaelia.* Find these orchids labeled various ways.

E. adenocaula

Culture: Average
Availability: Specialty growers
Also sold as *Epidendrum nemorale,* this plant has medium-size round or conical pseudobulbs from which spring 12-inch leaves. The 24-inch-tall flower stems branch near their tip and hold a dozen or more spidery 4-inch pink blooms. The flowers appear in early summer and last three to four weeks. One of the most prized of the genus, this species makes a good patio plant in frost-free regions.

E. boothiana

Culture: Easy
Availability: Specialty growers

E. boothiana

Round but flattened pseudobulbs give this intriguing species its common name, the silver dollar orchid. Grow it on a mount, which is the best way to display the flowers. They're a mere ¾ inch across; petals and sepals are green with purple speckles, while the contrasting lip is white with gold. Blooms appear in great numbers in spring and summer. Native from Florida to Central America, it thrives in humid growing conditions. You may find *E. boothiana* labeled as *Prosthechea boothiana.*

E. bractescens

Culture: Average
Availability: Specialty growers
This Central American native has small conical pseudobulbs and narrow grassy leaves that reach about 12 inches long. Graceful, arching inflorescences, also about 12 inches long,

E. bractescens

emerge in spring (and sometimes again in the fall) and are loosely decorated with 1-inch-wide blooms. These have bronze petals and a white lip liberally marked with wine red veins. *E. bractescens* relishes warmth and bright light and is best grown on a mount or in a basket.

E. cochleata

Culture: Easy
Availability: Common
Native from Florida to Venezuela, this novelty orchid is popular because it is so easy to grow and because it

E. cochleata

continuously generates blooms from fall through winter and well into spring. The 3-inch-wide flowers have slender, twisty chartreuse sepals and petals. The ornately striped purple upside-down lip inspired the common name cockleshell or clamshell orchid. Inflorescences typically bear four blossoms at a time, with more always coming on.

The plant grows 12 to 20 inches tall. Mount it or grow it in a pot of medium to coarse orchid mix in a spot with warm temperatures and bright light. This species is highly recommended for beginners; you may find it labeled as *Prosthechea cochleata.*

E. cordigera

Culture: Easy
Availability:
 Specialty
 growers
Easy to grow and prolific, this plant is big—eventually reaching 2 feet tall. Put it where it will have ample space in medium to bright light. Its onion-shape pseudobulbs generate big, straplike leaves. The rosy pink flowers bloom in spring and

E. cordigera

summer and release a sweet vanilla scent. The species is native to Mexico and south into Central America and is sometimes sold as *Epidendrum atropurpureum.*

E. fragrans

Culture: Easy
Availability: Specialty growers
The deliciously spicy, gardenia-like aroma earns this species its name. Flowers bloom in late spring and are green-white except for the lip, which has red stripes. The sturdy plants

E. fragrans

grow 10 to 15 inches tall. *E. fragrans* is easy to grow and it blooms readily—a perfect choice for beginners. You may find it labeled as *Prosthechea fragrans*.

E. mariae

Culture: Average
Availability: Specialty growers
This dwarf has 2-inch rounded silvery pseudobulbs topped by two glaucous 1-inch-wide by 6-inch-long leaves that are

E. mariae

often deciduous. Heavy-substanced apple-green blooms with a trumpet-shape white lip appear in early summer and last three to four weeks. This species is native to a habitat that has a pronounced dry season and does best grown on a mount to provide adequate air circulation.

E. tampensis

Culture: Easy
Availability: Specialty growers, or garden centers in the southeast United States
One of the few tropical epiphytes native to the continental United States, this small plant has 1-inch rounded pseudobulbs topped by two ½-inch-wide, 8-inch-long leaves. Wiry, branching flower stems to 24 inches long bear 2-inch-wide olive green blooms that last as long as four weeks in late spring. You may detect a delicate honey fragrance during the daytime, and bees are attracted to

E. tampensis

flowering plants kept outdoors. This orchid does best mounted or in a slatted wood basket to allow frequent watering and quick drying. You can also grow it outdoors on a deck or patio in frost-free zones.

E. Orchid Jungle (*E. alata* × *E. phoenicea*)

Culture: Easy
Availability: Specialty growers
This popular hybrid is often remade. The large plants have pseudobulbs nearly the size of baseballs, which in summer give rise to 4-foot branching stems of 2½-inch rich mahogany blooms offset by rose red lips. The blooms give off a piercing sweet fragrance during the warmest time of day. Plants do well indoors or outside on a frost-free patio.

Epicattleya (eh-pea-KAT-lee-uh)
(*Epidendrum* × *Cattleya*)

Abbreviation: *Epc.*
Sympodial
Compact to large
Medium light
Mild nights and days
Moderate humidity
Let dry between waterings
Pot or mount

Epicattleyas—hybrids between epidendrum and cattleya— are among the most varied in the cattleya alliance because of the variety of parents and combination of parents used to breed them. For this reason, it is difficult to generalize about flowers or colors.

Many epicatts make outstanding garden subjects in the Gulf States—Florida and Texas—because they tolerate high temperatures and humidity. In general, epicatts have similar cultural needs to cattleyas.

This hybrid genus may disappear. Lately, most breeding to gain characteristics similar to epicattleyas have used encyclias rather than epidendrums. Resulting hybrids are known as *Catcyclia (Encyclia* × *Cattleya).*

Catcyclia Calandria

Culture: Easy
Availability: Specialty growers
This primary hybrid between two widely divergent species *Enc. adenocaula* and *C. aurantiaca* has charm. The plants share traits of both species, with 8-inch-tall pseudobulbs topped with two 6- to 8-inch-long leaves. In winter, upright flower stems bear clusters of a dozen or more 4-inch-wide starlike blooms in pastel sunset shades of peach, orange, and yellow. Plants tolerate a wide array of conditions. They are good patio plants in frost-free regions.

Catcyclia Calandria

Epc. El Hatillo (*C. mossiae* × *Enc. tampensis*)

Culture: Easy
Availability: Specialty growers

Epc. El Hatillo

El Hatillo's superb bicolored blooms appear in force during the summer months and offer a sharp contrast between greenish white sepals and a deep hot-pink lip. Each flower measures about 2½ inches across. This is an easy-to-grow, vigorous orchid, adapting easily to a clay pot or slatted basket or a driftwood slab—whatever suits your home or garden. Eventually it will reach a mature size of about 14 inches tall. Plants resemble small cattleyas, with compact pseudobulbs to 4 inches tall. Also sold as *Cattcyclia* El Hatillo, it is the parent of some other worthy bicolors.

Epc. Rene Marques (*Epi. pseudepidendrum* × *C.* Claesiana)

Culture: Easy
Availability: Specialty growers

An example of the diversity within this hybrid genus, Rene Marques has a growth habit more like a reed-stem epidendrum, with tall, spindly 36-inch-long growths 6-inch-long and 2-inch-wide leaves alternating along the length of the stem. In winter, each canelike growth will form a 6- to 8-inch-tall flower stem with eight to twelve 2½-inch green blooms offset by an orange lip. The substance of the

Epc. Rene Marques 'Tyler'

flowers is very heavy, so they are long-lasting. Old flower stems may branch, similar to phalaenopsis, giving a second floral display. It likes the same conditions as cattleyas.

Epidendrum (eh-pea-DEN-drum)

Abbreviation: *Epi.*
Sympodial
Dwarf to large
Medium to bright light
Cool nights and mild days
Moderate to high humidity
Let dry between waterings
Pot

All epidendrums are native to the subtropical and tropical areas of the New World—southern Mexico, Central America, much of South America, southern Florida, and some of the Caribbean islands. Many are prized cultivated plants, and excellent hybrids have been developed.

The plants exhibit a lot of variation, but those most commonly in cultivation have either reedlike growth or a pseudobulb with leaves emerging from its end. Colorful flowers unite the group. Blooms are generally on the small side, between 1 and 3 inches across. The sepals are all the same size, although they can be either reflexed (pointing back) or spreading. Petals are all the same length, but they are narrower than the sepals. The distinctive lips are three-lobed, and the terminal one varies in form, sometimes sporting a fringed or toothed edge. Inflorescences carry one to many blooms.

The Swedish physician and botanist Carl von Linné (Linnaeus) named the genus in the early 1700s. In Greek, *epi* means "upon" and dendrum means "tree," a reflection of the epiphytic nature of these orchids. Over time, many plants have been moved out of this genus and into their own, but there are still plenty of genuine epidendrums.

Epidendrums do best in bright light and moderately warm temperatures, which can be provided in a variety of settings, including windowsills. Good drainage is important, so pot this orchid in medium-textured bark. The reed-stem types do not require a rest period, but plants with pseudobulbs should be given a few weeks of dormancy after they mature in the fall, when the pseudobulbs are full size and have stopped growing. If a plant becomes top-heavy with age, nest its pot inside a larger, sturdy pot to give the bottom extra weight. If a reed-stem plant outgrows its pot, divide it, cut it back, or both.

Epi. carpophorum

Culture: Easy
Availability: Specialty growers

Epi. carpophorum

Native to tropical Central America, this exquisite species features large, elegant flowers with a heady fragrance that is intense in the evening hours (because of that, it is sometimes called *Epi. nocturnum*). Star-shape blooms 3 to 5 inches across have distinctive apple-green sepals, white petals, and a white lip with a dash of gold in the center. Flowers are carried singly or in pairs from summer into fall. Plants can get large, up to 3 feet tall, with 5-inch-long leaves. Grow *Epi. carpophorum* in an epiphytic potting mix and high humidity.

Epi. stamfordianum

Culture: Average
Availability: Specialty growers

Epi. stamfordianum roseum

What sets this species apart is its habit of producing flower stems from the base of the plant, rather than from the tops of the pseudobulbs as all other epidendrums. Four to six leaves grow from the top of the 18-inch-tall spindle-shape pseudobulb, each about 6 inches long and 2 inches wide. Plants bloom in late spring. The 30-inch-long inflorescences are upright to arching with 1½-inch-wide starlike blooms. These are generally yellow with red markings; the variety *roseum* has pink flowers. Grow *Epi. stamfordianum* in baskets to get the full effect of the floral display.

Gongora (gone-GOH-ruh)

Abbreviation: *Gga.*
Symodial
Large
Medium light
Mild nights and days
Moderate humidity
Keep evenly moist
Basket or mount
Culture: Average
Availability: Specialty growers

Closely related to stanhopea and coryanthes, gongoras offer unusual flowers, often with bizarre medicinal fragrances, for adventurous gardeners. Their pseudobulbs are generally

Gga. galeata Brooklyn Botanic Garden

about 3 inches long, rounded or conical, heavily ridged, and topped with a broad, palmlike 24-inch-long leaf. The unbranched, pendulous flower stems grow nearly straight down from the base of the newest growth; growing them in a basket or on a mount helps to show them off. Flowers face downward and are 2 to 4 inches tall, with odd lip structures framed by outstretched sepals that resemble the wings of a bird. Flowers last two to four weeks and drop, rather than wilt, when they are spent. *Gga. quiquenervis* has bright yellow blooms that are dotted with red in fall.

Grammatophyllum (gra-ma-toh-FILL-um)

Abbreviation: *Gram.*
Symodial
Average to large
Bright light
Warm nights and days
High humidity
Keep evenly moist
Pot or basket

Related to cymbidium, this genus is a large and rapid grower with dramatic flowers. Pseudobulbs can reach 10 to 12 feet or more, with long leaves along the length of the growth. Mature plants have been known to weigh tons. Stout, upright, branching flower stems arise from the base of the enormous growths, with 6-inch-wide or larger tiger-barred yellow-and-brown blooms that last for many weeks. When a *Gram. speciosum*, one of the largest types, flowers outside of its native South Pacific environs, it is usually a newsworthy item. Tropical conditions, warm temperatures, high light, and lots of water and fertilizer are necessary for these showy, demanding plants.

Gram. scriptum

Culture: Average
Availability: Specialty growers and garden centers in the southern United States
While not as large as some of its relatives, this orchid is big, with 5- or 6-inch-long pseudobulbs and 2- to 3-inch-wide leaves that may be more than 18 inches long. Stout, unbranched flower stems emerge from the base of the

growths in summer and reach 48 inches tall. Up to a hundred 3-inch-wide blooms appear and stay fresh for weeks. The common form of the species is leopard-spotted yellow-and-brown. 'Hihimanu', which has greenish yellow flowers, is frequently available as well. *Gram. scriptum* can be susceptible to spider mites, so wash the undersides of the leaves when watering.

Gram. scriptum

Hawkinsara *(haw-kin-SAR-uh)*

Abbreviation: *Hknsa.*
Symodial
Compact
Medium to bright light
Mild nights and days
Moderate humidity
Let dry between waterings
Pot or basket

A complex intergeneric cross between broughtonia, cattleya, laelia, and sophronitis, these generally compact plants grow to about 8 inches tall and have brilliant, long-lasting blooms. Grow hawkinsara in a pot of coarse bark or in a wooden basket so it can dry quickly between waterings.

Hknsa. Kat Golden Eye
(*Ctna.* Jamaica Red × *Slc.* Mahalo Jack)

Hknsa. Kat Golden Eye

Culture: Easy
Availability: Rare
Compact but floriferous, this hybrid bears stunning clusters of 2½-inch-wide rich wine-purple flowers with a radiant yellow throat. They appear multiple times a year and last at least a few weeks. The cultivar 'Carmela' has bright red flowers and may be easier to find.

Howeara *(how-ARE-uh)*

Abbreviation: *Hwra.*
Sympodial
Compact
Medium to bright light
Mild nights and days
High humidity
Let dry between waterings
Pot

This intergeneric hybrid offers small, 4-inch plants with stiff leaves that overlap at the base to form a fan, similar to those of closely related oncidium and tolumnia orchids. Howeara results from crosses between leochilus, oncidium, and rodriguezia. Small blooms as wide as 1½ inches are closely arranged along 6- to 8-inch arching stems, similar to the rodriguezia parent. Flowers appear throughout the year and last for three to four weeks. Mount howearas to allow frequent watering and fast drying. They are sometimes sold as zelenkoara.

Hwra. Lava Burst
(*Hwra.* Mini-Primi × *Rdza. lanceolata*)

Culture: Easy
Availability: Specialty growers

Hwra. Lava Burst 'Puanani'

One of the easiest, most rewarding dwarf orchids, Lava Burst requires little effort and delivers a dramatic show every spring to summer. The brilliantly colored, long-lasting flowers are borne in well-branched sprays. Individual blooms measure about 1 inch across and are usually fiery red with bright orange markings on the lip. Lava Burst grows about 8 inches tall. Pot it in a fine-textured mix and grow it in medium light. 'Puanani' is one of the most common cultivars.

Huntleya melaegris (HUNT-lee-uh)

Abbreviation: *Hya.*
Sympodial
Compact
Low to medium light
Mild nights and days
High humidity
Keep evenly moist
Pot
Culture: Average
Availability: Specialty growers

Huntleyas are attractive even when not in bloom. Their single flowers arise from leaf axils on short 3-inch-long stems. The star-shape blooms may be 4 inches across and are rich mahogany-brown with a white center. They are framed by a fan of foliage. They appear in late summer and early autumn and may last four or more weeks.

This epiphytic soft-leaf orchid is related to zygopetalum and bollea. It has 18-inch-tall fans of soft green leaves that are 2 to 3 inches wide and overlap at the bases. The rhizomes between the fans can be 3 inches or longer, often rendering plants too large to grow in containers.

Mount huntleyas with moss or grow them in a medium-grade bark mix in proportionately small pots to allow for frequent watering and fast drainage. *Hya. meleagris* is the best known of the genus. It has appealing tricolored flowers spring through fall.

Hya. melaegris

Jumellea (joo-MEL-lee-uh)

Abbreviation: *Jum.*
Monopodial
Miniature to large, depending on species
Bright light
Mild nights and warm days
Moderate humidity
Let dry between waterings
Pot, mount, or basket, depending on species

Jum. peyrottii 'Sea Breeze'

Related to angraecums, jumelleas are somewhat smaller and distinguished by flat, fanlike growth habit. Leaves are 1 to 2 inches wide, and they overlap at their bases to form a characteristic fan shape. Plants may grow to 24 inches wide or more. They bear multitudes of 2-inch birdlike white flowers on individual upright stems arising from the leaf axils. Blooms exude a powerful spicy scent at night and last up to four weeks. Grow jumellea in a shallow pot of coarse bark in a location where air circulates freely.

Jum. fragrans

Culture: Average
Availability: Specialty growers
This is one of the most common jumelleas because its multitudes of charming white fragrant flowers appear during December holidays, which makes it popular with nurseries that propagate it and consumers who use it for seasonal decorations. Its habit and flowers are typical of other jumelleas but both are slightly larger and showier.

Laelia *(LAY-lee-uh)*

Abbreviation: *L.*
Sympodial
Miniature to large, depending on species
Medium to bright
Mild nights and warm days; some species need cool winter nights
Moderate humidity
Let dry between waterings
Pot or mount

From the forests of Brazil, Central America, and Mexico comes a group of epiphytic orchids closely related to cattleya. For most, the flowers are a shade of purple or lavender with a contrasting darker lip. Sepals and petals tend to be the same color, though the petals may be broad and the sepals slender. Flowers are 2 to 8 inches across and held singly or in clustered inflorescences of up to twenty blossoms; some are scented. Flower stems may extend as long as 6 feet. Flowering times vary by species.

The lip of the flower may be laelia's most distinguishing trait—it is almost always three-lobed and pronounced (although likely to be smaller than that of a cattleya). Another distinctive characteristic is the number of pollinia (clumps of pollen grains) in each flower. Laelia has eight; cattleya has four.

The English botanist John Lindley, who did much work with orchids in the early 1800s, is credited with naming laelia, but nobody is certain of the inspiration for the name. One theory is that he was thinking of the historic Roman family Laelius; Laelia would refer to the ladies of that house—thus the name would be a tribute to female beauty and grace.

Laelia pseudobulbs vary in size and shape from flat and round to egg-shape to nearly reedlike. All sizes and shapes produce thick, substantial leaves—in some species, one to a pseudobulb, in others two or more. These orchids need slightly brighter light than cattleyas—a few even tolerate full sun. They also need warm, humid growing conditions. Because they are epiphytes, they are good candidates for growing on tree-fern or cork slabs or in a quick-draining orchid mixture that will allow them to dry out between waterings. Reduce water and fertilizer in winter to give the plant a short rest period, which encourages blooming.

L. anceps

Culture: Average
Availability: Specialty growers

L. anceps

A remarkably tough plant, this orchid is also beautiful. Native to Mexico, it has been shown to survive heat as high as 100°F as well as subfreezing temperatures. In winter, 3-inch-tall stems carry two to six vividly colored 2½- to 4-inch-wide flowers. They are lavender-pink with a darker lip and a golden throat striped with red. Flowers can last a month or more on the plant but will fade in a vase.

This orchid has a single leaf up to 8 inches long that emerges from a 4- to 6-inch-long pseudobulb. Pot or mount this plant or hang it in a basket. *L. anceps* has been used to create many excellent cultivars and intergeneric hybrids.

L. briegeri

Culture: Advanced
Availability: Specialty growers or international orchid shows

L. briegeri

A dwarf plant that grows no more than 6 inches tall, this rupicolous (rock-dwelling) species is native to Brazil. An important parent in hybrids, it can be difficult to grow, requiring bright light and close attention to watering. Overwatering leads to root loss and rapid plant decline. Upright 12- to 15-inch-tall flower stems bear four to six 2-inch-wide starlike chrome yellow flowers that last three to four weeks in early summer. To allow rapid drying, grow *L. briegeri* in a proportionately small pot of coarse medium.

L. lundii

Culture: Average
Availability: Specialty growers
A sweet scent wafts from the 1-inch blossoms of this attractive species. Blooming from winter to spring, the flowers have glistening white petals and sepals and a bright

L. lundii

magenta lip. Each inflorescence is composed of one to three flowers. The plant consists of a stout, creeping rhizome with two narrow leaves. Native to the Brazilian prairie, *L. lundii* tolerates cooler temperatures. You may also find it sold as *Bletia lundii, L. regnelli,* or *L. reichenbachiana.*

L. milleri

Culture: Average to advanced
Availability: Specialty growers

L. milleri

This small (to only 8 inches at most) rock-dwelling species from Brazil is famous for being the only truly red-flowered laelia. As with other species, healthy growth depends on good watering practices. Upright 12-inch-tall flower stems bear four or five 2½-inch red blooms that last as long as four weeks. Look for this species as divisions from seed-raised populations only.

L. perrinii

Culture: Easy
Availability: Specialty growers

L. perrinii

Spicy fragrance and large, pretty flowers create the appeal for this Brazilian species. Blossoms can be as large as 6 inches across; the color is lavender with a darker purple, trumpet-shape lip and a white throat. Bloom time is usually in the fall. *L. perrinii* is a fairly tall plant, attaining about 16 inches over time, so give it ample space. Robust and easygoing, it is a good choice for a beginner.

L. pumila

Culture: Easy to average
Availability: Specialty growers
This dwarf laelia grows less than 6 inches tall, but flowers, which emerge from developing growths in spring, are proportionately large. The 4-inch-across or larger blooms are lavender with dark purple lip. They last three to four weeks. Grow *L. pumila* in a small pot of fast-draining, fine-textured mix on a windowsill or outdoors on a frost-free patio.

L. pumila

L. reginae

L. purpurata

Culture: Easy to average
Availability: Specialty growers

L. purpurata

This native of Brazil, which is said to be the country's national flower, is a large, upright plant to 24 inches or more, closely resembling related cattleya species. Pseudobulbs are strictly upright in good light conditions, with upright leaves to 12 inches or more. Strong, upright flower stems rise above the foliage with four to seven 6-inch blooms in shades of white through lavender and rose, many with contrasting darker lips. This plant flowers reliably for Mother's Day and may be found in garden centers and retail stores in warm climates in May. The flowers last up to three weeks and emit a licorice scent in the warmth of the day. Plants can be grown on a deck or patio in frost-free zones.

L. reginae

Culture: Average
Availability: Specialty growers
This is a desirable miniature species with flowers in soft white, cream, or cream touched with lavender. A mere ¾ to 1 inch across, the blooms appear in small groups of two to six on short inflorescences in late spring. The plant consists of a cluster of conical pseudobulbs that generate single, succulent leaves. Only a few inches tall, the plant is a good choice for a windowsill. Native to Brazil, it has been used as a parent to pass on its diminutive size.

L. tenebrosa

Culture: Average
Availability: Specialty growers
Dramatic contrast is what the flowers of this species have to offer. The petals and sepals are yellow, orange-red, coppery brown, or a shade in between, while the lips are pink-purple rimmed in white with a yellow throat. Typically there are three or four flowers on a head, each one 7 inches across, carried on a 12-inch inflorescence, and borne summer to fall. A mature plant reaches 18 inches tall, and its leaves may have an attractive purplish blush. Grow it in a pot of a coarse, fast-draining orchid mix in medium light.

L. tenebrosa

Laeliocattleya *(LAY-lee-oh-KAT-lay-uh)*

Abbreviation: *Lc.*
Sympodial
Miniature to large, depending on species
Medium to bright, depending on species
Mild nights and warm days
Moderate
Let dry between waterings
Pot

Lc. Butterfly Wings 'Orchidglade'

Laeliocattleya, which results from crosses between cattleya and laelia, closely resembles cattleya (pages 118–124) in growth habit and form. The flowers range from miniature to 7 inches across, depending on parentage. Most hybrids are easy to grow in greenhouses or in warm rooms with bright light. Some will thrive outdoors in frost-free gardens, especially when one of the parents in the cross is *L. anceps*.

Lc. Angel's Treasure (*C.* Tropical Angel × *Lc.* Tiny Treasure)

Culture: Easy
Availability: Specialty growers
Pastel hues on this robust hybrid are especially appealing. The 3-inch-wide flowers, which appear from winter to spring, are lavender-pink with a touch of yellow in the throat. Angel's Treasure is a compact grower, gradually reaching 10 inches tall. Pot it in medium-grade epiphytic orchid mix.

Lc. Canhamiana (*C. mossiae* × *L. purpurata*)

Culture: Easy
Availability: Specialty growers

Lc. Canhamiana

This antique hybrid is a classic and one of the easiest and most prolific of all laeliocattleyas. It has been remade several times recently, with several growers crossing plants of the original species, ensuring its availability. The upright plants grow 18 inches tall. Flowers, which may be lavender, white, or blue depending on the parentage, can be up to 6 inches across; they are borne three to six on an upright 8-inch flower stem in spring. Flowers last four or more weeks and are fragrant during daytime.

Lc. Dr. Robert Bannister (*Lc.* McCormick Phoenix × *Lc.* George E. Baldwin)

Culture: Easy
Availability: Specialty growers
This orchid is typical of large-flowered lavender cattleya-type orchids grown for cut flowers or corsages. Plants can be

Lc. Dr. Robert Bannister

Lc. Fire Dance 'Patricia'

large, 24 inches tall including pseudobulb and leaf. The 10-inch-tall flower stems hold three or four 7- to 8-inch-wide fragrant blooms in sparkling rose-lavender offset by a striking lip that is darker. Grow Robert Bannister in medium-grade orchid mix; let plants dry between waterings.

Lc. Fire Dance 'Patricia'
(*C. aurantiaca* × *Lc.* Fire Island)

Culture: Easy
Availability: Specialty growers

Abundant 3-inch flowers, which appear from winter to spring, are fiery reddish orange with a somewhat darker lip—a welcome sight at that time of year. They are carried in clusters, which only increases their impact. The plant has a compact habit and grows 10 to 12 inches tall. Pot it in a medium-grade epiphytic orchid mix.

Lc. Gold Digger 'Fuchs Mandarin'
(*Lc.* Red Gold × *C.* Warpaint)

Culture: Easy
Availability: Specialty growers

This orchid was registered more than 35 years ago and has taken its place in the pantheon of "all-time" orchids for its ease of culture and freedom of bloom. Its bright golden yellow blooms are borne in profusion on 15-inch-tall plants in late winter and early spring. Flower stems carry six to eight of the 4-inch-wide blooms. Gold Digger 'Fuchs Mandarin' makes a wonderful patio plant in frost-free areas.

Lc. Gold Digger 'Fuchs Mandarin'

It is a standard at South Florida orchid shows where huge plants bearing hundreds of blooms are common. Grow them in slatted wood baskets, which allow maximum time between pottings and allows large specimen plants.

Lc. Green Veil 'Dressy' (*Lc.* Cuiseag × *C.* Landate)

Culture: Easy
Availability: Rare
Elegant green flowers make quite an impression, not only for their rarity but also for their delicate beauty. Blooms are about 2½ inches across and appear in great numbers in winter and spring. Compact plants remain less than 12 inches tall and are easy to grow in a pot of medium-grade orchid mix. Green Veil 'Dressy' is the product of the famous Japanese orchid breeder Hanajima, who is noted for developing fine, compact cattleya alliance hybrids.

Lc. Hsinying Excell (*Lc.* Excellescombe × *L.* briegeri)

Culture: Easy
Availability: Specialty growers
This enchanting hybrid blooms twice a year. Its 3-inch-wide flowers, carried in clusters of two to four, are a soft, sweet

pink with darker pink flares and a dark red lip; a yellow throat adds a soft glow. The plant has stiff, upright-growing leaves and reaches only about 7 inches tall. This miniature hybrid thrives on a windowsill in bright light.

Lc. Hsinying Excell

Lc. Irene's Song (*Lc.* Mari's Song × *Lc.* Irene Finney)

Culture: Easy
Availability: Specialty growers
Glorious color, large blooms, and sweet scent make this orchid especially appealing. Flowers are almost 4 inches across. The sepals are a warm pink, the petals are splashed pink with purple, and the golden yellow fringed lip is touched with red—a dazzling combination. The plant remains compact at 8 to 10 inches tall and is easy to grow—a great choice for beginners.

Lc. Love Knot (*C.* *walkeriana* × *L.* *sincorana*)

Culture: Average
Availability: Specialty growers
For fragrance and small size, this lovely 6- to 8-inch-tall plant may be what you're looking for. It blooms in late

Lc. Love Knot 'Kahon'

spring, producing two or three 5-inch rose-lavender flowers on a 4-inch stem. Flower stems arise from developing new growth. The flower is as large as the entire plant, a conversation piece. Scent is delightfully sweet, thanks to the *C. walkeriana* parentage. *C. walkeriana* is the premier parent for this type of orchid, and Love Knot is one of the best-known of its progeny. There is also a blue-flowered form, *Lc.* Love Knot coerulea, which has a contrasting white lip edged in dark blue-purple. Grow Love Knot in a greenhouse or on a sunny windowsill.

Lc. Mini Purple (*C. walkeriana* × *L. pumila*)

Culture: Easy
Availability: Specialty growers

Lc. Mini Purple 'Blue Hawaii'

One of the highly scented miniatures, Mini Purple abounds in fragrant 3-inch blooms, pink with a contrasting dark pink lip. The compact plant grows only 5 inches tall but bloom two or three times a year. Pot it in a medium-grade orchid bark or coconut husk chip mix. Many clones of this popular hybrid are easy to grow.

Lc. Puppy Love (*C.* Dubiosa × *L. anceps*)

Culture: Easy
Availability: Specialty growers

Lc. Puppy Love 'True Beauty'

Another classic hybrid, Puppy Love is important not only for its intrinsic beauty and ease of culture but also as a parent of a line of hybrids that share its many good traits. Plants are upright to 24 inches tall, with strong, upright flower stems bearing four to six 6-inch-wide soft pink blooms. Flowering occurs in winter and also may reoccur throughout the year. The strongly scented blooms last six weeks or longer.

The best-known cultivar—and one of the best of all cattleya-alliance members—is 'True Beauty', HCC/AOS, AM/RHS. One of the first orchids to be patented, it is outstanding in all aspects. It is easy to grow, free-flowering often more than once a year and has long-lasting, highly perfumed blooms.

Lc. Trick or Treat (*L.* Icarus × *Lc.* Chit Chat)

Culture: Easy
Availability: Specialty growers

Lc. Trick or Treat

Winter and spring bring a riot of color from Trick or Treat just when you need it most. The 2-inch-wide flowers are rich yellow with bright orange markings and overlays; they appear in clusters. Plants grow to about 12 inches tall.

Lc. Tsiku Hibiscus (*Lc.* Mini Purple × *Lc.* Aloha Case)

Culture: Easy
Availability: Specialty growers
A fragrant bloomer, this hybrid orchid bears 3-inch-wide lavender-pink flowers with darker lips. The plant grows no more than 6 to 8 inches tall but produces abundant flowers in winter and spring. Pot it in medium-grade bark or coconut husk mix.

Leptotes *(lep-TOH-teez)*

Abbreviation: *Lpt.*
Sympodial
Dwarf
Medium to bright
Warm nights and days
High
Let dry between waterings
Mount

Lpt. bicolor

Leptotes is a dwarf relative of cattleya, growing at the most 4 inches tall and resembling a miniature brassavola (pages 102–104). Short flower stems form at the base of quill-like leaves, ending in sparkling pale lavender flowers to 2 inches wide; blooms may last two to three weeks. Mount leptotes and place it where it will have good air circulation and the leaves can show to best advantage.

Lpt. bicolor

Culture: Average
Availability: Specialty growers

Lpt. bicolor 'Karem'

This late-winter or early-spring bloomer is the most commonly available of the several species in the genus. Magenta-lipped white blooms are up to 2 inches across and often do not open fully, remaining cupped. The flowers last two to three weeks and are fragrant during daytime.

Ludisia discolor *(loo-DEE-see-uh DISS-col-or)*

Abbreviation: *Lus.*
Sympodial
Miniature
Low
Mild to warm nights and warm days
Moderate to high
Keep evenly moist
**Terrarium or pot outdoors where winters
   are warm and humid**
Culture: Easy
Availability: Specialty growers

Ludisia discolor

Another of the jewel orchids, this species is sometimes sold as *Haemaria.* Erect stems of insignificant white blooms appear from winter to spring. The major attraction is showy foliage. The 2- to 3-inch deep maroon leaves have contrasting veins that grow in whorls from spreading pronounced rhizomes. *Lus. discolor* is easy to grow outdoors in warm, shady conditions. It is one of few orchids that do well in terrariums. Plant it in humus or houseplant potting mix and keep it evenly moist. New plants are easily propagated from cuttings of the fleshy stems.

Lycaste *(lye-KAS-tee)*

Abbreviation: *Lyc.*
Sympodial
Compact to large, depending on species
Medium
Cool to mild nights and mild days
Moderate to high
Keep evenly moist while in active growth
Pot

Lycaste has prominent oval pseudobulbs and thin, broad pleated leaves that can be as long as 36 inches, depending on the species. Most are deciduous, losing leaves sporadically, like *Lyc. skinneri,* or all at once, as in the Mexican species. Flowers are borne singly, but each plant has multiple flower stems, from as few as three to dozens. The upright stems originate at the base of the most recently matured pseudobulb. Flowers are generally triangular in shape and range from 2 to 6 inches or more across. Blooms often last four or more weeks, and those of some species are fragrant. Pot lycaste in a fast-draining orchid mix for best results. To encourage flowering in deciduous species such as *Lyc.*

Lyc. tricolor

aromatica, withhold water when the pseudobulbs reach their full size in late summer and early fall.

Lyc. aromatica

Culture: Easy
Availability: Specialty growers

Lyc. aromatica, a deciduous Mexican orchid, produces multitudes of cinnamon-scented 3-inch-wide yellow-orange blooms from late winter into early spring; flowers last three to four weeks. When it drops its leaves in late fall, withhold water until new growth begins. Grow it outdoors with cymbidiums in frost-free regions.

Lyc. aromatica

Lyc. cochleata

Culture: Average
Availability: Specialty growers

These orchids are slightly larger than *Lyc. aromatica* but otherwise similar in appearance. In late spring, 20 or more flower stems emerge from the base of the most recently maturing growths. Each bears a single 3½-inch-wide clear yellow bloom. The plants have large palmlike leaves and can take up a good deal of space during the growing season. As houseplants, their size is difficult to accommodate. However, the leaves are often deciduous, and

Lyc. cochleata

many people find they can grow *Lyc. cochleata* outdoors during summer then have room for plants in the house in winter. When plants drop leaves in late fall, withhold water until new growth begins. In frost-free regions, you can grow *Lyc. cochleata* outdoors year-round.

Lyc. deppei

Culture: Easy
Availability: Specialty growers

Lyc. deppei

Another of the deciduous Mexican species, this orchid bears 4-inch pale green blooms flecked with mahogany in spring. Expect as many as eight blooms on upright stems for each pseudobulb; they last four weeks or longer. Grow *Lyc. deppei* outdoors in frost-free gardens.

Lyc. macrobulbon

Culture: Average
Availability: Specialty growers
This is one of the largest orchids in the genus, with 6-inch or taller pseudobulbs and leaves to 12 inches wide and 36 inches long. Many 3- to 4-inch brilliant yellow blooms are borne on upright individual stems from the base of the new growth in late spring. Flowers last four weeks or longer.

Lyc. skinneri

Culture: Average
Availability: Specialty growers

Lyc. skinneri

One of the loveliest of all orchids, its pastel pink, white, dark pink, or red blooms can be more than 6 inches across. The white form, *Lyc. skinneri alba,* is the national flower of Guatemala, often known as La Reina (The Queen). Flowers appear in spring and may last up to six weeks under good conditions. The best varieties are highly sought after, rarely available, and quite expensive.

Lyc. Auburn (*Lyc.* Balliae × *Lyc.* Sunrise)

Culture: Average
Availability: Specialty growers
Lyc. Auburn is a large plant—leaves can be 24 inches long and 10 inches wide—and needs plenty of space to spread. It bears four or more 6-inch yellow-pink blooms in spring, each one lasting to four weeks or longer. This orchid is the most famous and widely known of the lycaste hybrids.

Expect to pay high prices for choice varieties. Several cultivars have been formed from Auburn, including 'Santa Barbara', which has white flowers dusted rose-red.

Lyc. Lucianii (*Lyc. skinneri* × *Lyc. lasioglossa*)

Culture: Easy
Availability: Specialty growers
A strong, spicy fragrance radiates from the elegant flowers of this easy-to-grow orchid. The sepals are rosy pink; the much smaller petals are white and clasped around the fuzzy red lip; throats glow yellow. Individual flowers are about 6 inches across, carried singly on 6- to 8-inch stems. Bloom time varies but is usually in spring or summer. Beginners should have good luck with this hybrid because of its natural toughness and ease of bloom. Water and feed plants regularly during active growth. Once growth stops water to prevent shriveling. Allow it to go dormant if leaves drop.

Maclellanara (*mac-lel-LAN-ar-uh*)

Abbreviation: *Mclna.*
Sympodial
Large
Medium
Mild nights and days
Moderate
Keep evenly moist
Pot

Mclna. Pagan Lovesong 'Willow Pond' FCC/AOS

This strong orchid results from crosses between brassia, odontoglossum, and oncidium. It has pseudobulbs like those of oncidium (pages 177–181), but it is more robust, growing 6 to 8 inches tall with leaves to 24 inches long. Its sturdy, occasionally branching flower stems may reach 36 or more inches tall. Plants bear 6-inch-wide blooms that last four or more weeks in fall. Colors will vary according to parentage but are typically green with brown bars. Grow maclellanara outdoors in a frost-free garden year round where winters are warm and humid.

Mclna. Pagan Lovesong
(*Odcdm.* Tiger Butter × *Brs. verrucosa*)

Culture: Easy
Availability: Specialty growers

This is the first hybrid of this complex genus to be registered; it is a popular and widely cultivated orchid. Plants can grow quite large, with pseudobulbs as massive as 10 inches tall and 6 inches wide, leaves to 18 inches long, and inflorescences to 5 feet or taller. The star-shape flowers are green with brown bars and may reach more than 6 inches across. Flowers typically appear in autumn, but the plant may bloom at almost any time of year. This spectacular orchid is adaptable to a variety of growing situations. It does best in moderate temperatures. Pot it in a fast-draining orchid mix and keep it evenly moist.

Macodes petola (ma-KOH-deez pet-OH-luh)

Abbreviation: *Mac.*
Sympodial
Compact
Low
Mild to warm nights and days
High
Keep evenly moist
Terrarium or pot in houseplant mix
Culture: Easy
Availability: Specialty growers

Macodes petola

Another of the jewel orchids occasionally offered by specialty growers, macodes is easy to grow in warm, shady conditions; it also does well in terrariums. As is the case with anoectochilus and ludisia, the erect stems of white blooms are not the major attraction of these showy foliage plants. Instead it's the whorls of dark green leaves with glittering golden veins that attract people. Pot macodes in a terrestrial

orchid medium or even in houseplant potting mix. Keep it evenly moist, watering from below if possible. New plants are easily propagated from cuttings. Macodes is a pretty tough orchid and will do as well as any houseplant under less than ideal conditions.

Masdevallia (maz-deh-VAL-lee-uh)

Abbreviation: *Masd.*
Sympodial
Miniature to large, depending on species
Medium
Cold, cool, or mild nights and days, depending on species
High
Keep continuously moist
Pot or mount, depending on species

Masd. caudata Pul

Masdevallia, with its exotic flowers, looks like no other orchid. The blooms can be as small as 1 inch across or as large as 12 inches across, although most are in the 4- to 6-inch range. Colors may be scarlet, orange, purple, or white, or a combination of these colors. Some species have green and brownish black flowers.

Flower form is striking. The sepals are most distinctive, each flaring into broad segments and tapering to a long tail, which are actually rolled ends of the sepals. The petals and lip are much smaller and hidden by sepal tubes. Blooms are carried aloft on leafless stalks—usually alone—but occasionally in twos or threes. Some species have fragrant flowers.

The small plants lack pseudobulbs and send up single lance-shape leaves no longer than 12 inches. Some species are epiphytic while others are terrestrial. Most are native to Central and South America, especially the Andean cloud forests of Colombia.

More than 380 species have been identified. Two Spanish explorers, Hipólito Ruiz López and José Antonio Pavón y Jiménez, discovered masdevallia in Peru in 1777 and named it for a colleague, José Masdeval.

Orchids in this genus can be tricky to grow, although newer hybrids are somewhat easier. In general, masdevallias require high humidity and cool to moderate temperatures. The plants need constant moisture because they lack pseudobulbs, but take care to provide adequate air circulation to prevent leaf rot from fungal infection. Many beginning orchid growers find masdevallia hybrids easier to grow than the species because hybrid plants are vigorous.

Epiphytic species may be mounted on tree fern or osmunda. Terrestrial species do best potted in a mixture of equal parts peat moss, perlite, and sand. Water with rain or distilled water to prevent buildup of damaging mineral salts. Fertilize at half-strength no more than once a month.

Most masdevallias do poorly when temperatures exceed 80°F, especially when humidity is low. Watering more frequently during hot weather usually does more harm than good and often results in root rot.

Masd. ampullacea

Culture: Average
Availability: Rare
The sepals on this unusual species from Ecuador curl or roll inward, creating a "flask." Ampullacea in Latin means flask or tube shape, hence the name. The 2-inch-wide yellow flowers form a ruff around the base of the miniature plant

Masd. ampullacea

in early spring. Each bloom faces outward as though to capture water in its flask. This species does best in moderate temperatures. Grow it in a pot to ensure that roots remain evenly moist.

Masd. caloptera

Culture: Average
Availability: Specialty growers
Masd. caloptera is a dwarf plant, growing about 5 inches tall, with attractive purple-tipped dark green leaves. Its name means "beautiful wings," and the little flowers look like birds poised for flight. Only ¾ inch across, they are so numerous that a plant in bloom makes an impressive display. The 6-inch-tall spikes of burgundy-splattered white flowers with sunny yellow tails bloom from spring to summer. *Masd. caloptera* does best in cool to moderate temperatures. Pot it in a fast-draining orchid mix.

Masd. coccinea

Culture: Advanced
Availability: Specialty growers

Masd. coccinea

The vivid blooms of *Masd. coccinea* appear from spring to summer. They're typically lavender-purple but can be red, white, or yellow. The inflorescences are long and graceful, up to 18 inches, and carry just one 3-inch flower apiece. Plants grow 7 to 10 inches tall—among the tallest of masdevallias—and do best in cool temperatures. Pot *Masd. coccinea* in a fine-grade, fast-draining orchid mix.

Masd. erinacea

Culture: Advanced
Availability: Specialty growers

Masd. erinacea

This curious miniature native to Costa Rica and Panama has a name that means "hedgehog," referring to the prickly round ½-inch flowers. They're dark red topped in yellow, and the sepals have long yellow tails; they bloom spring to summer. A compact, tuft-forming plant also sold as *Masd. horrida,* it remains less than 2 inches tall. Low to medium light, moderate temperatures, and a pot of fast-draining, fine-grade orchid mix provide best results.

Masd. pinocchio

Culture: Advanced
Availability: Rare

Masd. pinocchio

The back sepal of this species does looks a bit like a long nose. The tiny 2-inch-wide flowers are borne singly on 6-inch-long stems in spring to summer. Their color is soft yellow with crimson overlay. The plant is native to Ecuador and does best in cool to moderate temperatures. *Masd. pinocchio* is a 6-inch-tall dwarf type, suitable for mounting on a slab or growing in a small container of fine-grade orchid mix.

Masd. pozoi

Culture: Advanced
Availability: Rare

Masd. pozoi

Although the flowers on this plant are only ½ inch across, they are bright colored. A typical inflorescence carries up to 15 of them, so they readily stand out. Enjoy their perky color, white speckled with maroon and vivid yellow tails, from spring to summer. A dwarf from Peru, this orchid grows only about 5 inches tall. Pot it in fine-grade orchid mix or sphagnum moss in cool to moderate temperatures and keep it constantly damp.

Masd. tridens

Culture: Average
Availability: Specialty growers

Masd. tridens looks like a gathering of small sunbursts when it is in bloom. The 1½-inch-wide individual flowers are soft pink with small burgundy markings and spots, red lips, and long yellow tails. They combine in 10-inch-long inflorescences with as many as 12 flowers apiece—

Masd. tridens

quite a splashy show. A dwarf, *Masd. tridens* grows to about 8 inches tall. It is native to Peru and likes cool temperatures and moist growing conditions. Pot it in sphagnum moss or a fine-grade orchid mix.

Masd. venezuelana

Culture: Advanced
Availability: Rare
This enchanting orchid grows only 3 inches tall at maturity, and its tiny trident-shape brilliant yellow flowers, borne singly, are no more than ½ inch across. A native of Venezuela, this species blooms winter to spring. Grow *Masd. venezuelana* in moderate temperatures in the way that best allows you to enjoy it: mounted on a small slab, potted in a fine-grade orchid mix, or tucked into a moist terrarium.

Masd. Elven Magic (*Masd. davisii* × *Masd. infracta*)

Culture: Average
Availability: Specialty growers
With a name like Elven Magic, you'd expect a dwarf plant, and that's what you get—a compact grower that remains between 4 and 5 inches tall. The flowers bloom on erect

Masd. Elven Magic

stems in late winter and early spring. Tropical orange-red hues brighten the scene; at 2½ inches across, the flowers are big compared with the size of the plant. For best results, grow Elven Magic in low to medium light, cool to moderate temperatures, and a fine-grade orchid mix.

Masd. Golden Monarch (*Masd.* Golden Angel × *Masd.* Monarch)

Culture: Average
Availability: Specialty growers
Blazing yellow flowers make this vigorous hybrid impossible to ignore. The single flowers bloom on erect stems from winter into spring. At 3 inches long and 2 inches wide, their size and lively color stand out on a relatively small plant, around 4 to 5 inches tall. Grow this orchid in moderate temperatures in a fast-draining orchid mix.

Masd. Pat Akehurst (*Masd.* Heathii × *Masd. yungasensis*)

Culture: Average
Availability: Specialty growers

Masd. Pat Akehurst

The shimmering color and dependable, plentiful blooms on this dwarf are the reasons for its popularity. You can look forward to a grand show of bright 3-inch flowers with vibrant red stripes and orange tails every winter to spring. Grow Pat Akehurst in moderate temperatures in a fast-draining orchid mix.

Dracuvallia Blue Boy (dra-kew-VAL-lee-uh) (*Masd. uniflora* × *Drac. chimeara*)

Culture: Advanced
Availability: Specialty growers
This brilliantly colored intergeneric dwarf hybrid is reportedly more vigorous and easier to grow than either

Dracuvallia **Blue Boy**

of its parents. From spring into summer, you'll get 4-inch cherry red blooms with 1½-inch-wide petals. Grow this 6-inch plant in medium light and cool to moderate temperatures in a container of fast-draining orchid mix.

Maxillaria *(max-il-LAIR-ee-uh)*

Abbreviation: *Max.*
Sympodial
Dwarf to large, depending on species
Medium to bright light
Mild to warm nights and days
Moderate humidity
Let dry between waterings; allow winter dormancy
Mount or pot

Native to the tropics of Central and South America, maxillarias are epiphytes with unusual-looking, sometimes richly scented flowers. Spanish botanists Hipólito Ruiz López and José Antonio Pavón y Jiménez wrote the earliest descriptions of this species in 1777. The distinctive flower lips and columns reminded them of insect jaws, and *maxillae* means "jawbone."

Maxillaria is one of the largest genera with nearly six hundred identified species. It is also one of the most diverse in flower and plant appearance and size. Sizes range from less than 1 inch to many feet in height. Larger species have an almost vining habit; others resemble vandas in growth habit, appearing to be monopodial even though sympodial.

Plants often dwarf the flowers, but because blooms are colorful and displayed one to a stem, they stand out. Bloom size varies from ½ inch to 6 inches across. Sepals are all the same size, arranged in a triangle around the petals, which are smaller, less prominent, and sometimes stand upright from the sepals. The small lip curves inward, almost coming into contact with the column. Flowers arise from the base of pseudobulbs (sometimes more than one bloom per bulb) in winter to spring and are generally white, yellow, or red with dark red, purple, or brown spots. Some are headily fragrant, with scents of chocolate, coconut, or watermelon.

Long dark green leaves usually emerge from clustered

Max. picta

pseudobulbs. One major group has short internodes on the rhizomes, while the other has longer internodes and pseudobulbs that are arrayed in a chain. Pseudobulbs may be smooth, fluted, or flattened. Leafy bracts sheath the bulb.

Maxillarias vary widely in their cultural needs. In general, mount them on tree fern or bark, or pot them in a container of fast-draining orchid mix or sphagnum moss. Most species respond poorly to repotting, so choose your medium with permanance in mind. Mimic the conditions of the orchid's mountain rain forest origins—that is, offer high humidity and regular water and food when the plant is actively growing. Good air circulation is key; you may need to use a fan around the plants.

Although the genus includes many desirable orchids, many species are not very showy. Do some basic research before buying a maxillaria to ensure it is one that is worth your time and effort.

Max. densa

Culture: Average
Availability: Rare

Max. densa

This orchid's name means "crowded"—and its clusters of flowers do look as if they are tumbling out from the sheathed pseudobulb in late winter or early spring. Individual blossoms are ½ to ¾ inch long with a pleasantly sweet fragrance; the clusters can be 6 inches in diameter. Flower color varies; it's often purple but may be reddish purple or deep maroon or even white. Plants grow about 18 inches tall. This orchid does best in cool to moderate temperatures, mounted or grown in a basket.

Max. sanderiana

Culture: Challenging
Availability: From specialty growers
Max. sanderiana is a compact plant for a maxillaria, with 3-inch-tall pseudobulbs, 12-inch-long leaves, and short rhizomes. The large ivory flowers, as wide as 6 inches across, emerge from the base of the plant. They appear singly on 6-inch flower stems and may last four weeks or longer. Flower shape is generally triangular, and the sepals and petals are splashed with blood-red, especially around the center of the flower. This species must have the cool, moist conditions of its native cloud forest habitat to thrive. Called the best of the genus, *Max. sanderiana* is well worth seeking if you can accommodate its specialized needs.

Max. sanguinea

Culture: Average
Availability: Specialty growers
The dramatic flowers on this plant, native from Panama to Nicaragua, have a fruity fragrance. The blooms arise from the base of the plant from winter into spring. They are only

Max. sanguinea

about ⅝ inch across and have a brilliant blood-red hue. *Max. sanguinea* does best mounted on a slab, but some growers have had success raising it in a container of fast-draining mix, such as shredded tree fern fiber. At only 4 to 5 inches tall, it is easy to manage.

Max. tenuifolia

Culture: Easy
Availability: Specialty growers

Max. tenuifolia

A tantalizing aroma of coconut wafts from the strikingly beautiful summer flowers of this sought-after species. Although only 2 inches across, blooms are complex in form and color. Petals and sepals are dark ruby red, and the bold yellow lip is spotted with red. Native to Mexico, Nicaragua, and Costa Rica, *Max. tenuifolia* is otherwise ordinary looking, with slim 8-inch dark green leaves emerging from an upright-growing rhizome. This orchid grows well mounted on cork or wood but also can be potted in a fast-draining orchid mix—just keep it moist.

Mexicoa *(mex-IH-koh-uh)*

Abbreviation: *Mxc.*
Sympodial
Dwarf
Medium light
Mild nights and days
Moderate humidity
Keep evenly moist
Pot

Mexicoa is a dwarf genus, about 8 inches tall. It is closely related to oncidium, and the plants making up the genus have only recently been reclassified as mexicoa. Plants have ½-inch-tall compressed pseudobulbs topped by one or two ½-inch-wide by 6-inch-long grassy leaves. Plants bloom in spring and summer, sending up four to six flowers. The flowers, which are 1½ inches wide, brownish yellow highlighted with a broad light yellow lip, last as long as four weeks. Flower stems are so short—8 to 10 inches—they sometimes do not clear the foliage. Pot mexicoa in a fast-draining orchid mix.

Mxc. ghiesbreghtiana

Culture: Average
Availability: Specialty growers

Mxc. ghiesbreghtiana

This orchid offers a bountiful display of flowers carried on 10-inch spikes, each about 1 inch across. Sepals and petals are burgundy-brown or occasionally yellow, and the lips are always yellow. The plant's habit is neat and dwarf, between 6 and 8 inches tall.

Miltassia *(mil-TAS-see-uh)*

Abbreviation: *Mtssa.*
Sympodial
Average
Medium light
Mild nights and days
Moderate humidity
Keep evenly moist
Pot

Miltassias are intergeneric hybrids between brassias and miltonias, resulting in plants with lots of flowers in bright colors and exotic shapes. They have upright, compressed pseudobulbs that taper toward the top. Two 1-inch-wide, 12-inch-long leaves develop from the top of the bulb. Arching flower spikes, to 24 inches long, arise from the base of the most recent growth, one or two per pseudobulb. They can carry a dozen or more exotic, spidery blooms 6 inches across or wider. Flower colors vary according to parentage; blooms last three to four weeks or more. Grow miltassias in medium light and moderate temperatures. Pot them in a medium-grade orchid potting mix.

Mtssa. Royal Robe
(*Mtssa.* Erachne × *Milt.* Seminole Blood)

Culture: Easy
Availability: Specialty growers

Mtssa. Royal Robe 'Jerry's Pick'

Aptly named for its burgundy blossoms, this majestic hybrid has the bonus of being easy to grow. Its star-shape flowers, 3 inches or more across, bloom in spring and fall and emit delicate, sweet perfume. Plants are vigorous, eventually reaching 14 to 16 inches tall and have a tidy growth habit. Royal Robe was developed in Florida and is more heat tolerant than others in its genus. 'Jerry's Pick' HCC/AOS is one of the most common of this variable grex.

Mtssa. Memoria Donald Christian (*Brs. Rex × Milt.* Honolulu 'Warne's Best')

Culture: Easy
Availability: Specialty growers
A pastel beauty that blooms winter to spring, Memoria Donald Christian has 4-inch lavender flowers with contrasting pink lip. There are some darker pink markings and a bit of white, but the overall effect is simple, soft, and elegant. The plant is vigorous and grows about 14 to 16 inches tall. Pot it in a fine-grade, fast-draining orchid mix, and keep it moist.

Miltonia *(mil-TOH-nee-uh)*

Abbreviation: *Milt.*
Sympodial
Compact
Low to medium light
Mild nights and days
Moderate to high humidity
Keep continuously moist
Pot

Milt. San Paulo

The plants in this genus must be in bloom for any but the most sophisticated botanist to be assured of their identity. Their habit and leaves are similar to those of other orchids, particularly brassias, odontoglossums, and oncidiums. Miltonias have low, flattened pseudobulbs, up to 4 inches across, that tend to crowd together in a clump. Grassy leaves as long as 12 inches arise from the pseudobulbs. Inflorescences carrying as many as nine flowers each arise from the base of the youngest pseudobulbs.

Individual flowers can be relatively large, about 4 inches across. The sepals and two lateral petals are nearly the same size and shape, often coming to a point. The showy lip is bigger, broader, flattened, and attached to the base of the column. Flower color is generally yellow, pink, or white, although some plants have brown or maroon blooms.

Named in the early 1800s for the English Earl FitzWilliam, Viscount Milton, miltonias are native to Brazil, and they grow best in warm, humid conditions. Pot them in a medium-grade orchid mix and protect them from bright light. Healthy leaves develop a slightly pinkish cast.

Even though they have pseudobulbs, miltonias will falter if they become too dry. If new leaves appear to be pleated, gradually increase watering until smooth leaves unfurl. You may also add some moisture-retentive sphagnum moss to the potting mix.

Milt. clowesii

Culture: Average
Availability: Specialty growers
One of the nicest of the miltonias, *Milt. clowesii* has 5-inch-tall, laterally compressed pseudobulbs topped with two narrow 1-inch-wide, 10-inch-long medium green leaves. Upright flower stems emerge from the leaf axils at the base of the plant in fall. Each stem bears about ten 3-inch-wide starry tan blooms with mahogany barring and a pink lip.

Milt. clowesii

Milt. spectabilis

Culture: Easy
Availability: Specialty growers

The biggest flowers in the genus occur on this species. Each upright 8-inch-tall flower stem carries a
4-inch-wide vanilla-white blossom splashed with pink in the center, with a broad pink lip and purple column. The variety *moreliana* is the most commonly offered variety. It has rich concord-grape purple flowers with a lighter lip striped in dark purple. Flowers appear in spring and summer and emit a spicy rose-scented perfume. *Milt. spectabilis* is

Milt. spectabilis

10 inches tall and is suitable for growing on a windowsill in bright but not direct light and moderate temperatures.

Milt. Goodale Moir 'Golden Wonder' (*Milt. flavescens* × *Milt. clowesii*)

Culture: Easy
Availability: Specialty growers

Renowned Hawaiian orchid breeder Goodale Moir created this easy-to-grow hybrid. The compact 10-inch plant blooms from winter to spring. Flowers are 3 inches across and primarily yellow, with some burgundy spots and a white lip decorated with a purple splash. Grow this orchid in a fast-draining, fine-grade orchid mix. It adapts well to most home temperatures.

Miltonidium *(mil-toh-NIH-dee-um)*

Abbreviation: *Mtdm.*
Sympodial
Average
Medium light
Mild nights and days
Moderate humidity
Keep evenly moist
Pot

This cross between a miltonia and an oncidium usually results in a plant that looks like an oncidium. Yet miltonidiums can vary widely, depending on which species were used in the cross. Flower stems may be upright, arching, or occasionally branching, and many carry exotic colors and patterns of long-lasting blooms.

Mtdm. Bartley Schwarz (*Milt.* Red Pali × *Onc.* Honolulu)

Culture: Easy
Availability: Specialty growers

A good orchid for beginners because of its dependable flowering, Bartley Schwarz also has a sweet fragrance.

Mtdm. Bartley Schwarz

Abundant 3-inch-wide flowers are bright red with white lips marked with red that appear in spikes of as many as a dozen. They waft a wild-rose scent and last up to 10 weeks. Grow this 12-inch-tall plant in moderate temperatures in a container of fine-grade orchid mix.

Mtdm. Issaku Nagata (*Onc. leucochilum* × *Milt. warscewiczii*)

Culture: Easy
Availability: Specialty growers

Mtdm. Issaku Nagata

Also sold as *Onc.* Issaku Nagata, this orchid is a wonderful example of the spray-type of oncidiums that are produced from *Onc. leucochilum*. Pseudobulbs can be more than 8 inches tall and 4 inches wide and give rise to large branching inflorescences, often two per lead bulb. The 2-inch-wide flowers are borne in profusion, often with more than 50 per spike. Blooms are in shades of brown offset by a white lip marked in red. Grow these large showy orchids in a greenhouse or outdoors in frost-free gardens.

Miltoniopsis (mil-toh-nee-OP-sis)

Abbreviation: *Mltnps.*
Sympodial
Small to average, depending on species
Medium light
Mild nights and days
Moderate to high humidity, depending on species
Keep evenly moist
Pot

These are the popular pansy orchids, which at one time were classified as miltonias. That genus is now restricted to Brazilian orchids related to *Milt. spectabilis,* while miltoniopsis consists of Colombian types and their hybrids.

Miltoniopsis Falcon

The two groups diverge in several ways. Pseudobulbs of true—or Brazilian—miltonias are generally taller than they are wide and two to three narrow leaves grow from the top of the pseudobulb. The pseudobulbs of miltoniopsis are about as tall as they are wide with only one leaf growing from their tips. The pseudobulbs may also have several leaves growing from their base.

Each miltoniopsis pseudobulb generates up to four flower spikes—thinner than those of their Brazilian cousins and almost always arching. Miltonia flower spikes are usually upright. Cultural needs are also different. Miltoniopsis, native to high-elevation rain forests from Costa Rica to Peru, thrive in cooler temperatures than do miltonias.

Miltoniopsis plants range from compact species *phalaenopsis* no more than 6 inches tall to the robust *vexillaria* at 18 inches. Two or three (occasionally four) arching, slender flower stems form at the leaf axils of the lead growth in spring. Flowers are generally 5 inches across.

Repot plants annually after they bloom. Grow them in small pots to allow the roots to go through frequent wet and dry cycles. Use only good-quality water and keep temperatures consistently moderate. Growers who can provide these conditions or who live where they occur naturally will be rewarded with some of the most beautiful flowers in the orchid family.

Mltnps. phalaenopsis

Culture: Advanced
Availability: Specialty growers
A lily-of-the-valley scent radiates from this species. The dainty flowers are soft white and pansy-shape, and the lip has a distinctive rosy purple waterfall pattern. (This species is the source for similar patterns on the lips of a number of hybrids.) The 10-inch-tall inflorescences consist of three to five flowers, each 1½ to 2 inches across. Plants grow 6 to 12 inches tall and do best in a fine-grade orchid mix. Keep them warm during the

Mltnps. phalaenopsis

summer months when they bloom, then provide a cooler, drier winter rest period.

Mltnps. roezlii

Culture: Easy
Availability: Specialty growers
This beautifully marked species, discovered by Benedict Roezl in 1873 in Colombia, is closely related to *Mltnps. santanaei.* It has a similar pansylike flower shape but with conspicuous burgundy red markings on the upper petals.

Mltnps. roezlii

Mltnps. santanaei

Culture: Easy
Availability: Specialty growers
Easy to grow, warmth tolerant, and fragrant: The combination of these excellent qualities has made *Mltnps. santanaei* popular as a breeding parent. Its abundant pristine white flowers with a splotch of bright yellow on the lips bloom at least twice a year. As is typical of this genus, their form is pansy-shape and flat. Their soft scent is reminiscent of tea roses. This compact beauty fits on a windowsill.

Mltnps. vexillaria

Culture: Advanced
Availability: Specialty growers

Mltnps. vexillaria

Spring and summer bring a fabulous flower show with this popular, pastel-hued species. Blooms are large, up to 4 inches across, with creamy white and rose pink sepals and petals. The big white lip splits into two plump lobes and features red-and-yellow markings. *Mltnps. vexillaria* is native to Ecuador, Peru, and Colombia.

Mltnps. Hamburg 'Red Velvet' (*Milt.* Robert Paterson × *Milt.* Lingwood)

Culture: Easy
Availability: Specialty growers
Rose-scented flowers abound on this award-winning beauty in late winter to spring. The velvety flowers resemble pansies, rich red with yellow centers and white rims. The plant grows 12 to 14 inches tall. This orchid is coveted by collectors, but beginners can grow it successfully too. Pot it in a fine-grade, fast-draining orchid mix and keep it continuously moist.

Mltnps. Venus (*Milt. phalaenopsis* × *Milt. vexillaria*)

Culture: Advanced
Availability: Specialty growers
From summer to fall expect a sparkling display of flowers from this venerable hybrid. The compact plant grows 8 to 10 inches tall with tiny 1-inch-long leaves. Blooms are only 1 inch wide and 2 inches long, and so attractive and plentiful that size doesn't matter. Petals are pink, and the pink lip has a darker pink blotch, dazzling waterfall pattern, and a touch of yellow deep in the throat. Pot Venus in a fine-grade, fast-draining orchid mix and keep it continuously moist.

Neofinetia *(nee-oh-fih-NAY-tee-uh)*

Abbreviation: *Neof.*
Monopodial
Miniature
Medium light
Cool to mild nights and days, depending on species
High humidity
Keep continuously moist
Mount or pot

This unusual genus consists of only one species. It has been cultivated for centuries in Japan and Korea, where it is native. In Japan, it is known as the wind orchid *fu-ran*, associated with samurai culture and celebrated in woodblock prints. Neofinetia has been used extensively and successfully in breeding. It's been called a collector's joy— or obsession, some might say; collectors are always seeking plants with subtle variations in the color and fragrance of the delicate blossoms or variegation in the foliage.

The orchid was originally named *Orchid falcata* in 1784 by Carl Thunberg and published in *Flora Japonica*. H. H. Hu renamed it *Neofinetia falcata* in 1925, after the French botanist and orchid expert Achille Finet.

Neof. falcata

Culture: Average
Availability: Specialty growers
The lone species in this genus, *Neof. falcata* blooms in

Neof. falcata

summer. Its dainty white flowers exude a sweet fragrance similar to jasmine. Blooms are about 1 inch wide and feature a 2-inch-long spur that curves backward. Collectors value cultivars with pink or yellow blush. The clump-forming plant grows only 3 to 6 inches tall and has correspondingly small, alternately arranged leaves. *Falcata* means "sickle-shape," referring to leaf form or curved flower spurs.

Neof. falcata may be grown on a windowsill and is especially appealing displayed in a hanging basket. Successful growth requires high humidity, cool to moderate temperatures, and careful watering. The roots should be wet but not soggy. Mount this epiphytic orchid or pot it in a porous, fast-draining mix or sphagnum moss. Use good-quality water to avoid buildup of mineral salts. Reduce watering in winter to allow a dormant period.

Yonezawaara *(yone-zah-WAH-rah)*
(*Vandofinetia* Virgil × *Rhy. coelestis*)

Culture: Average
Availability: Specialty growers

This intergeneric hybrid, whose parent includes another intergeneric hybrid between vanda and neofinetia (vandofinetia), is a compact grower with an 8-inch spread. Its sweetly scented flowers appear in spring, about six to a spike. They're only 1½ inches across, with vanilla white petals and sepals and a purple-blue lip, which comes from the rhynchostylis parent. The plant will thrive in a pot or basket of medium-grade orchid mix. It spreads slowly.

Yonezawaara hybrid

Neostylis *(nee-oh-STY-lis)*

Abbreviation: *Neost.*
Monopodial
Dwarf
Medium light
Cool to mild nights and days
Moderate humidity
Keep evenly moist
Pot

This intergeneric hybrid is a simple cross between neofinetia and rhynchostylis. The resulting miniature orchids resemble the neofinetia parent in scent and growth habit, often freely branching from the base to form clumps 8 inches across and 6 inches tall. Upright flower stems bear a dozen or more birdlike light blue blooms to 1½ inches wide. Plants bloom in spring, although they may rebloom throughout the year. Fragrant flowers last as long as four weeks. Pot neostylis in a fast-draining mix or grow it in a basket, which it will rapidly fill for a dramatic display.

Neost. Lou Sneary
(*Neof. falcata* × *Rhy. coelestis*)

Culture: Easy
Availability: Specialty growers

Neost. Lou Sneary

Fuller and more prolific than its *Neof. falcata* parent, this hybrid appears to burst with tiny white blossoms. Their vanilla fragrance is noticeable from many feet away, especially in the evening. If the plant gets plentiful light and humidity, it will continue blooming through much of the summer. It will not tolerate wet roots, so pot it in a fast-draining orchid mix.

Odontioda (oh-don-tee-OH-da)

Abbreviation: *Oda.*
Sympodial
Compact to large, depending on species
Low to bright light, depending on species
Cool nights and days
Moderate to high humidity
Keep evenly moist
Pot

These orchids result from a cross between cochlioda and odontoglossum. Most odontiodas closely resemble the form of their odontoglossum parent, which is most often *Odm. crispum.* However, the plants are slightly smaller, as are the flowers, which come mainly in shades of red. Take special care to protect the leaves from hot sun and temperatures. Use only purified water when watering.

Oda. Margarete Holm 'Alpine' (*Odm.* Bic-ross × *Oda.* Adolf Rohl)

Culture: Easy
Availability: Specialty growers

Oda. Margarete Holm 'Alpine'

The striking bright-color flowers of this terrific hybrid are white overlaid with bold red blotches. They are about 3 inches across and open profusely on mature plants. Plants are compact, 8 to 10 inches tall, and bloom in spring. They do best in bright light and cool temperatures. Although Margarete Holm 'Alpine' looks like an odontoglossum, it is much less demanding to grow. Pot it in a medium-grade orchid mix.

Odontobrassia (oh-don-toh-BRASS-ee-uh)

Abbreviation: *Odbrs.*
Sympodial
Dwarf to large, depending on species
Medium light
Mild nights and days
Moderate humidity
Keep evenly moist
Pot

A cross between brassia and odontoglossum, odontobrassias have patterned, spidery flowers, similar to those of their brassia parent. Plants are generally of average size with laterally compressed pseudobulbs that taper toward the top and sprout two upright 15-inch-long leaves. Flower stems are upright or arching depending on parentage. Flowers last three or four weeks. Pot odontobrassia in a fast-draining orchid mix.

Odbrs. Gordon Dillon 'Rainbow Falls' (*Brs. maculata* × *Odm. bictoniense*)

Culture: Average
Availability: Specialty growers

Odbrs. Gordon Dillon 'Mary K'

The 2-inch-wide by 3-inch-long flowers of this complexly beautiful hybrid orchid display an outstanding combination of colors. They have a wide russet-red lip. Slender sepals and petals are chartreuse and barred and spotted in brown. Blooms appear in summer and fall and last several weeks.

Odontocidium *(oh-don-toh-SID-ee-um)*

Abbreviation: *Odcdm.*
Sympodial
Compact to large, depending on species
Medium light
Mild nights and days
Moderate humidity
Keep evenly moist
Pot

These intergeneric crosses between odontoglossum and oncidium result in robust specimens. They have large compressed oval pseudobulbs, each with two long, narrow leaves to 2 inches wide and 24 inches long. Flower stems, one or more per growth, are generally tall and branched, carrying numerous 2-inch flowers. Because the floral display may last up to six weeks, species in this genus make decorative houseplants. Grow plants outdoors in frost-free regions.

Odcdm. Black Beauty
(*Odm. bictoniense* × *Onc. leucochilum*)

Culture: Easy
Availability: Specialty growers

This is an example of the extraordinarily fine showy progeny of *Onc. leucochilum.* The robust plants may reach 24 to 30 inches, with strong upright branching inflorescences to 48 inches tall. The name comes from its 2½-inch burgundy blooms that are nearly black. Black Beauty is easy to care for under moderate conditions or outdoors in the same setting as cymbidiums require.

Odcdm. Tiger Crow 'Golden Girl' HCC/AOS
(*Odcdm.* Tiger Hambuhren × *Odcdm.* Crowborough)

Culture: Average
Availability: Specialty growers

Bright, fragrant flowers abound on this excellent hybrid that merits the coveted HCC/AOS award. They're golden yellow throughout, and the sepals and petals are speckled with maroon. Each bloom is about 2½ inches across. Expect them to appear in spring and last for several weeks or longer. A mature plant is about 18 inches tall and will bloom more than one time each year.

Odontoglossum *(oh-don-toh-GLOSS-um)*

Abbreviation: *Odm.*
Sympodial
Miniature to large, depending on species
Medium light
Cool nights and days
High humidity
Keep continuously moist
Pot

A close relative of oncidium, this genus is distinct in its own right. The name means "tooth tongue," which aptly describes the toothlike crest on the lips of the flowers of most orchids in the genus. Bloom time varies among the species. All carry their flowers in great arching sprays that remain good-looking on the plant for as long as a month. There are many color variations—everything from pink to red to yellow to white, plus green, purple, and brown. Bars, splashes, stripes, and speckles in contrasting colors are common. The plants have pseudobulbs and thin, tall foliage.

Most species in this genus come from the high-altitude cloud forests of the Andes, so they do best in medium light with good air circulation. Pot them in medium-grade orchid mix and fertilize them year-round.

Heat causes odontoglossums to stop growing and blooming. Keep temperatures below 75°F during the day and around 50°F at night. Gardeners who live where the weather is mild and humid can grow odontoglossums outdoors spring through fall.

Odm. bictoniense

Odcdm. Black Beauty 'Ken'

Odm. bictoniense Album 'Orchid Man'

Culture: Average
Availability: Specialty growers

These robust specimens have large compressed oval pseudobulbs, each topped by two narrow leaves, 15 inches long or longer. The upright flower stems bear sequentially opening 2½-inch reddish brown blooms with a pink, heart-shape lip in early spring. Flowers may last four to six weeks. Also sold as *Lemboglossum bictoniense,* this orchid does well on a frost-free patio.

Odm. crispum

Culture: Challenging
Availability: Specialty growers

Odm. crispum

This is one of the most significant orchids among collectors and also one of the most beautiful. One or two upright, arching, sometimes branched flower stems bear 20 or more 4-inch crisp white blooms, often marked with red blotches. The flowers bloom in fall and winter and last for four weeks. This species needs cloud-forest conditions: high humidity, temperatures below 70°F, and purified water.

Odm. grande

Culture: Average
Availability: Specialty growers

Odm. grande

Odontoglossum grande, the tiger orchid has large round, slightly compressed pseudobulbs. Two broad leaves grow from the top of the bulbs and are held at a 45-degree angle. Flower stems emerge from developing pseudobulbs in late spring and can reach 24 inches tall, carrying 6-inch yellow blooms heavily barred with reddish brown. Flowers last three to four weeks and are famous for a tiny shape in the center of the lip near the column that resembles a Santa Claus figure. Although it needs occasional water during winter months, *Odm. grande* must have a dry rest period. This species has been reclassified as *Rossioglossum grande*

Odm. wyattianum

Culture: Average
Availability: Specialty growers

Odm. wyattianum

An unusual species native to Peru and Ecuador, *Odm. wyattianum* blooms from winter to spring. The 2-inch-wide by 3-inch-long flowers are chocolate brown marked with burgundy, and sport a white lip with wine-red markings. Compact and tidy, the plant grows 10 to 12 inches tall. Do not let this species become dry.

Odm. Hallio-Crispum (*Odm. crispum* × *Odm. hallii*)

Culture: Challenging
Availability: Specialty growers

Odm. Hallio-Crispum

A venerable hybrid in production since 1896, Hallio-Crispum turns heads when it is in full bloom. Its white-and-yellow flowers, more than 3 inches across, have dark yellow markings. Plants reach about 16 inches tall and usually bloom in spring. Hallio-Crispum needs cool growing conditions with plenty of light. It suffers damage when temperatures are above 80°F.

Odontonia (oh-don-TOH-nee-uh)

Abbreviation: *Odtna.*
Sympodial
Large
Medium light
Mild nights and days
Moderate to high humidity
Keep evenly moist
Pot

Hybrids in this group result from crosses between miltonia and odontoglossum, and sometimes with miltoniopsis. Because miltoniopsis is sometimes used, growth habits can be variable Most have narrow, upright, 12- to 15-inch-long leaves and oval pseudobulbs. Flowers range from white to coral to shades of red, some with patterns on the petals and sepals. Best results are achieved by growing odontonia as you would miltoniopsis, in evenly moist soil, mild temperatures, and moderate humidity. Protect plants from mineral salts by using filtered water.

Odtna. Vesta 'Charm' (*Odtna.* Dora × *Milt.* William Pitt)

Culture: Easy
Availability: Specialty growers
This intergeneric hybrid made its appearance in 1928 and is still popular. A compact grower, it reaches 10 inches tall, a perfect size for growing on a windowsill or under lights. Vesta 'Charm' is a prolific bloomer. In spring and fall, it bears multiple spikes of 3-inch-wide white flowers marked with fuchsia and yellow. Pot it in a fine-grade mix.

Odtna. Yellow Parade 'Alpine' (*Odnta.* Yellow Bird × *Odm.* Parade)

Odtna. Yellow Parade 'Alpine'

Culture: Advanced
Availability: Specialty growers
Six butter yellow 4-inch blooms top the upright flower stems of Yellow Parade in spring and, occasionally, again in fall. A result of two generations of odontonias bred with yellow *Odm. crispum* types, Yellow Parade closely resembles its odontoglossum parent and requires the same mild temperatures. The plants are compact, to about 12 inches. Grow Yellow Parade in mild to cool conditions.

Oncidium (on-SID-ee-um)

Abbreviation: *Onc.*
Sympodial
Miniature to large, depending on species
Medium to bright light
Mild to warm nights and days, depending on species
High humidity
Keep evenly moist
Pot or mount, depending on species

Onc. Macmex 'Woodlands Bounty'

Most oncidium orchids are easy to recognize. Dubbed dancing ladies, they feature long, arching sprays adorned with numerous flowers with broad lips—the ladies' skirts—and spreading petals—their arms.

This genus is large—three hundred or more species and hybrids. Flower sizes range from less than 1 inch across to as large as 5 inches across. Some have single flowers; others have large sprays of yellow, pink, red, reddish purple, white, or green blooms. All have common flower form. The three sepals tend to be the same size and shape; the two petals match or are somewhat larger; and the flared lip is attached to the column's base and often features wartlike calluses.

Oncidiums vary in size and leaf color and most are epiphytic. Pseudobulbs are usually large and round and generate only one leaf. Leaves can be as short as 2 inches or as long as 2 feet. They may be slender and floppy or thick and leathery. Some oncidium relatives, such as tolumnias (page 208), are commonly called equitants because their leaves overlap at the base like a fan. Their leaves are usually smaller than those of oncidiums; they lack a pseudobulb; and they require warmer temperatures and more air circulation than oncidiums.

All oncidiums hail from southern Mexico through tropical South America and the Caribbean islands. They were introduced to England in the 1790s and were initially grouped with the genus *Epidendrum*. As more plants arrived and were scrutinized, botanist Olof Peter Swartz decided they merited their own genus. Observing bumpy growths on the lips of many oncidiums, he derived the name from Greek *onkos*, meaning "warty" or "swelling."

Most orchids in this genus are fairly easy to grow. Give them ample light, high humidity, and warm temperatures. Mount or pot them in a fast-draining orchid mix. Allow the roots to dry somewhat between waterings. Thick-leaved species are more tolerant of drying; thin-leaved ones have to be watched and watered often. Fertilize regularly when the plant is actively growing.

Onc. ampliatum

Culture: Average
Availability: Specialty growers
This classic and appealing species is native to Venezuela, Bolivia, and Guatemala. Sprays of 1-inch yellow flowers appear in spring through summer. These large plants need adequate space. Big round pseudobulbs generate substantial leaves, growing to 15 inches long and 5 inches wide; mature plant flower spikes can be as long as 4 feet. For best results, grow this oncidium in warm temperatures.

Onc. ampliatum

Onc. cheirophorum

Culture: Average
Availability: Specialty growers
Onc. cheirophorum is a dwarf plant with tiny pseudobulbs topped with one or two ½-inch-wide, 4-inch-long leaves. Plants quickly grow into clusters of foliage. They bloom in spring, forming one or two wiry, branching 8-inch arching flower stems with bright yellow blooms less than 1 inch across. Flowers have a musky fragrance during the day. They last four or more weeks. This orchid is a good choice for windowsills or under lights.

Onc. cheirophorum

Onc. crispum

Culture: Average
Availability: Specialty growers

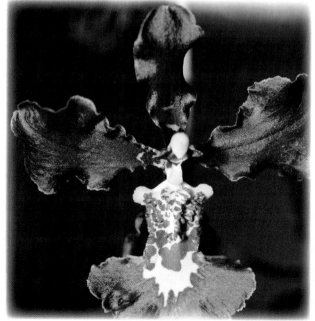

Onc. crispum

Deep red, almost chocolate color flowers (sometimes tending toward greenish brown) decorate this Brazilian orchid. Appearing from spring to summer, the blossoms are large, as wide as 3 inches across. They have an accenting splash of yellow or bright orange on the lip and signature warty bumps on the crest. The top sepal is almost as large as the lip. Inflorescences consist of as many as eighty musky-scented flowers along the length of the slender flower stem, which on a mature plant may reach 3 feet. Overall, this is a modest-size plant with plump pseudobulbs; its leaves are between 6 and 9 inches long.

Onc. forbesii

Culture: Average
Availability: Specialty growers
Also called gold-laced or Forbes' oncidium, this is a superb Brazilian species with handsome flowers from summer into fall. Flowers are 2½ inches across and mostly chocolate brown with yellow edging marbled in brown. They are borne in long, often branched, inflorescences 24 to 30 inches long. Plants are medium size, about 12 inches tall. Pot or mount *Onc. forbesii*, keeping it continuously moist when it is actively growing. During the winter, allow it to dry somewhat between waterings.

Onc. forbesii

Onc. maculatum

Culture: Easy
Availability: Specialty growers
This Mexican species is one of the easiest oncidiums to grow. It tolerates a wide range of conditions, from warm to mild, and even does well outdoors with cymbidiums in coastal California. Plants are compact, with laterally compressed 5-inch-tall pseudobulbs topped with two 12- to 15-inch-long leaves. Erect, arching flower stems sometimes branch; they can reach 24 inches long. The 2-inch-wide chartreuse-yellow flowers are barred with mahogany. Plants bloom in summer

and fall. *Onc. maculatum* is a popular parent and gives rise to hybrids such as *Onc.* Macmex, from a cross with the primary hybrid *Onc.* Mexico *(Onc. tigrinum × Onc. leucochilum).*

Onc. maculatum

Onc. ornithorhynchum

Culture: Easy to average
Availability: Specialty growers
An odd fragrance distinguishes this orchid: Some people find it candy-sweet while to others it is unpleasantly musky. *Onc. ornithorhynchum* has small compressed oval pseudobulbs and upright arching leaves to more than

Onc. ornithorhynchum

18 inches long. In summer growths bear up to four wiry arching, branching flower stems holding many 1-inch-wide lavender blooms with a yellow spot in the center of the lip. Flowers last four weeks or longer. Grow this species outdoors in frost-free areas.

Onc. sarcodes

Culture: Average
Availability: Specialty growers

Onc. sarcodes

This colorful species is another native of Brazil. Its long-lasting flower show occurs in spring. Long inflorescences reach about 2 feet and are abundantly adorned with 1½- to 2-inch-wide blooms that are yellow with red accents. Grow *Onc. sarcodes* in a basket or pot or on a mount. For best results, keep plants continuously moist while they are actively growing; let them dry somewhat between waterings during the winter.

Onc. sphacelatum

Culture: Easy
Availability: Specialty growers

Onc. sphacelatum

This strong-growing, upright orchid has large compressed oval pseudobulbs and thin leaves more than 18 inches long. It produces large clumps rapidly, and each growth bears one to three upright branching flower stems that are 6 feet or longer. Each carries hundreds of 2-inch-wide golden-yellow blooms barred with light mahogany. The fountain of flowers lasts four weeks or longer in fall. This orchid makes an appealing patio plant in frost-free regions.

Onc. varicosum

Culture: Average
Availability: Specialty growers

Onc. varicosum

The large oval pseudobulbs of this species taper toward the top and are often ribbed. They sport two long, narrow terminal leaves, 2 inches wide and up to 12 inches long. Flower stems grow upright and branch near the top, carrying 30 or more 3-inch-wide brilliant yellow blooms in fall that last up to four weeks. The flower's prominent feature is its broad skirt-shaped lip that bobs in the slightest breeze. Water and fertilize often during active growth, then withhold both water and nutrients almost entirely after growth matures in late fall.

Onc. Kukoo
(*Onc. onustum* × *Onc. cheirophorum*)

Culture: Average
Availability: Specialty growers

Onc. Kukoo

Lots of sweet-scented flowers make this dwarf hybrid a winner. The 4- to 5-inch plant blooms from spring into summer with plentiful 1-inch-wide brilliant yellow flowers. The *cheirophorum* parent adds the fragrance and contributes a shorter inflorescence, about 12 inches long. Pot or mount *Onc.* Kukoo. You may find it sold as Zelenkocidium Kukoo.

Onc. Sharry Baby
(*Onc.* Jamie Sutton × *Onc.* Honolulu)

Culture: Easy
Availability: Common

Onc. Sharry Baby

This hybrid is reputed to be one of the most popular in the world, possibly because of its blooms with the delicious strong fragrance of chocolate. It tends to bloom twice a year and one of those times is around Christmas. The ½-inch-wide flowers are wine red rimmed in yellow; the large flared lip is white with a splash of purple in the middle. Blossoms are carried abundantly on short flower stems. Plants may grow as tall as 30 inches.

Onc. Twinkle 'Fragrance Fantasy'
(*Onc. cheirophorum* × *Onc. ornithorhynchum*)

Culture: Average
Availability: Specialty growers

Onc. Twinkle

A small plant with great charm, this orchid is only 6 to 8 inches tall. When it blooms—which can occur any time of year and sometimes more than once—it delivers a profuse display of sweetly scented 1-inch light yellow or pink blossoms that last as long as four weeks. Grow Twinkle 'Fragrance Fantasy' in a pot of fine- or medium-grade mix in medium light and mild to warm temperatures.

Rodricidium
(*Oncidium* × *Rodriguezia*)

Culture: Easy
Availability: Specialty growers
Rodricidium is an intergeneric hybrid resulting from crosses between oncidium and rodriguezia. Plants are compact, with clumps of 3-inch-long leaves, and floriferous. They are good choices for beginners. Abundant 1¾-inch-wide blooms appear in spring and summer in various shades and markings of red, pink, orange, and white. Pot rodricidium in a fine-textured, fast-draining orchid mix and grow it on a windowsill in medium to bright light.

Paphiopedilum *(paf-ee-oh-PED-il-um)*

Abbreviation: *Paph.*
Sympodial
Miniature to large, depending on species
Medium to bright, indirect light
Cool nights and mild days; mild nights in winter
High humidity
Keep continuously moist
Pot

Unusual, dramatic flowers set these popular orchids apart. Paphiopedilums are nicknamed slipper orchids because the lips are shaped in a pouch that looks like a slipper toe. The pouches can be substantial, and the edges may roll in or out. More dramatically, the upper, or dorsal, sepal tends to be large and vividly marked. It may be broad and rounded or taper to a point. The two lateral sepals are fused and often hidden behind the lip. Petals spread out from the flower, standing straight out or drooping like a mustache. They may be long and narrow or broad and rounded, smooth or warty, or tufted with dark hairs.

Usually, the flowers are carried one to a sturdy flower stem, but some species or hybrids may have six or more blooms on a stem. Flower colors vary and can be purple, brown, green, pink, or white, often with mottling or striping. Because of their substantial, waxy texture, flowers last an amazingly long time, remaining fresh for several months.

Orchids in this genus lack pseudobulbs. Instead, three to seven thick, tough leaves emerge in a fan from a tightly clasped base. Individual leaves may reach 15 inches long and 2 inches wide. Leaves are generally solid green, but in some species they are attractively mottled.

Paphs make good houseplants. Warm temperatures and bright but indirect light are the main requirements. Regular watering and fertilizing during periods of active growth ensure good health and maximum flower production.

Many paphs are forest-floor natives rather than epiphytic. Grow them in fine-grade medium, such as fine bark or shredded and chopped sphagnum moss, to retain moisture. Choose a deeper than average pot because their furry root systems tend to grow downward. Keep medium continuously moist. Repot plants when the medium seems spent—this orchid responds well to repotting.

Paphiopedilums are native to tropical Asia (southern India, China, Vietnam, the Philippines, and New Guinea). Many are in commerce, and splendid new hybrids are constantly being introduced. The genus name, bestowed by botanist Ernst Pfitzer, refers to the Mediterranean island of Paphos, known for its temple to Venus, the goddess of love and beauty. Pedilon means "sandal."

Paph. bellatulum

Culture: Advanced
Availability: Specialty growers
This mottled-leaved orchid comes from the humid forests of Thailand and Myanmar. Its standout blossoms have an unusual form: Petals are rounded and bigger than the dorsal sepal. Flower color varies from creamy white to soft yellow, liberally sprinkled with maroon-purple freckles. The 3-inch-wide flowers appear in spring on short stems that barely clear the foliage. Plants grow about 6 inches tall, a good choice for growing on a windowsill or under lights. Let *Paph. bellatulum* dry between waterings. It does not tolerate poor-quality water that is high in salts or chlorides.

Paph. bellatulum

Paph. callosum

Culture: Easy
Availability: Specialty growers
One of the choicest and easiest paphiopedilums for home growing, *Paph. callosum* bears one or two 4-inch-wide pink, green, and brown blooms throughout the year. Each flower lasts six weeks or longer. Beautiful fans of heavily marbled foliage grow to 12 inches long. Fertilize *Paph. callosum* lightly and grow the plant in low light or shade in evenly moist potting medium.

Paph. callosum

Paph. concolor

Culture: Average
Availability: Specialty growers
Similar in size and flowers to *Paph. bellatulum* but easier to grow, this compact native of China and Myanmar grows a mere 3 inches tall. Its 2- to 2½-inch-wide pale yellow blossoms have a dusting of purplish freckles. Plants bloom in spring and summer with two or three blossom on each

Paph. concolor

flower stem. *Paph. ×conco-bellatulum* is a natural hybrid between *Paph. concolor* and *Paph. bellatulum;* orchid growers also produce this hybrid. The hybrids tend to be easier to grow than either parent. It has large round flowers, about 4 inches wide, in shades ranging from creamy white to soft yellow. Many sport fine dots all over the flower. Plants bloom throughout the year but most often in spring. Keep them in a relatively small pot of fine orchid mix. Fertilize lightly and use good-quality water.

Paph. lowii

Culture: Average
Availability: Specialty growers
Paph. lowii has 5-inch-wide flowers consisting of a pronounced mahogany pouch, a greenish yellow dorsal sepal, and brown-spotted yellow-green petals with pink tips. These tips are broader than the rest of the petal, creating a spoon shape. These are carried along 24- to

Paph. lowii

30-inch-tall stems. The plant itself, which has plain green leaves, grows about 14 inches tall. Medium light and warm temperatures (no lower than 55°F on winter nights) are ideal.

Paph. malipoense

Culture: Average
Availability: Specialty growers
Every winter to spring, large 4-inch-wide apple-green flowers with an inflated pouch grace this relatively new introduction from southern China and Vietnam. Blooms are elegantly marked with dark netting, particularly on the petals, and have a soft, fruity fragrance reminiscent of raspberries or apples. Color may be more greenish white than creamy. Flower stems are 1 to 2 feet long and usually bear one flower each. Handsome dark green leaves also have some dark mottling.

Paph. malipoense

Paph. glaucophyllum moquettianum

Culture: Easy
Availability: Specialty growers
This orchid is prized for its ability to remain in bloom for a year or more. It can bloom at any time of year with as many as 20 flowers on a spike produced sequentially, resulting in an extraordinarily long bloom period. The lime-green and peppermint pink flowers are about 2½ inches across. Keep plants

Paph. glaucophyllum moquettianum

moist but not soggy and grow them in a spot with bright light. *Paph. moquettianum* is native to Indonesia.

Paph. parishii

Culture: Average
Availability: Specialty growers

Paph. parishii

Paph. parishii has long, slender, dark burgundy petals that twist and hang like an old-fashioned mustache. Lips are a greenish cream with a burgundy blush; sepals are cream striped in green. Blooms are about 3 inches across and 6 inches tall or more. As many as 10 may decorate the flower stem in early spring. Leaves are stiff and plain green.

   Paph. parishii is a robust plant when given ample water, fertilizer, and bright light during active growth periods. Grow it in a fast-draining mix to prevent rot. Thailand, Myanmar, and Laos are home to this dramatic species.

Paph. rothschildianum

Culture: Average
Availability: Specialty growers

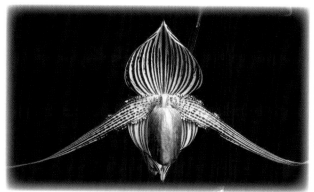

Paph. rothschildianum 'Matt Brown'

This native of Borneo is a parent in a number of worthy hybrids, but the pure species is spectacular. Sturdy upright spikes carry two to six distinctive 12-inch-wide flowers. Sepals and the wavy-edged petals are rich mahogany-purple with cream stripes, while the pouch is yellow. Green leaves, as long as 20 inches, serve as a handsome backdrop for the blooms. Plants can take several years to reach blooming size, but the wait is worth it. Mature plants grow 2 feet tall. For best results, provide ample water and fertilizer during active growth. Modern growing methods have made this once wildly expensive and rare orchid affordable.

Paph. spicerianum

Culture: Easy
Availability: Specialty growers

Paph. spicerianum

Probably the most notable feature of this dwarf species is its pristine white dorsal sepal, accented with a line of violet-purple down the center. Breeders value this dramatic feature. The rest of the 2-inch-wide flower is worth admiring too. Petals and pouch harmonize in shades of green, brown, and violet-purple. Leaves are dark green and semiglossy. Plants bloom from winter to spring and reach about 3 inches tall when mature.

Paph. Delrosi
(*Paph. delenatii* × *Paph. rothschildianum*)

Culture: Advanced
Availability: Specialty growers

Paph. Delrosi

This impressive hybrid has large white flowers with red veins and a dark pink pouch. The 6-inch-wide flowers rise above the mottled foliage in winter and spring. Leaves are 1 inch wide and 4 to 8 inches long. Grow Delrosi in a fine-grade, fast-draining orchid mix.

Paph. Gloria Naugle
(*Paph. rothschildianum* × *Paph. micranthum*)

Paph. Gloria Naugle

Culture: Average
Availability: Specialty growers

Proportionately large 6-inch-wide flowers and dramatic markings distinguish this elegant hybrid. Pouches are bright purple-pink; sepals and petals are burgundy striped with cream. The bold striping comes from the *rothschildianum* parent, while the hot pink coloration is from the *micranthum* parent. Flowering occurs from winter to spring. The plant sports attractively patterned foliage and grows to about 6 inches tall with 6-inch flowers.

Paph. Hsinying Fairbre
(*Paph. Macabre* × *Paph. farrieanum*)

Culture: Easy
Availability: Specialty growers

Paph. Hsinying Fairbre 'Macabre'

The glossy springtime blossoms on this orchid are so shiny they look almost varnished. Their downswept petals are chartreuse-striped and blushed with red, a strong influence from the *farrieanum* parent. The pouch is dark red with darker veining, and the dorsal sepal is white with red stripes. Individual flowers are about 2¼ inches wide and 3 inches long, yet the compact plant grows only to 5 inches tall.

Paph. Langley Pride 'Burlingame' HCC/AOS
(*Paph.* Euryostom × *Paph.* Maginot)

Culture: Easy
Availability: Specialty growers

Paph. Langley Pride 'Burlingame'

This hybrid is an example of the old-fashioned standard paphs, now more popularly known as "toads" because of their coloration and warty texture. They were first produced in the middle of the 20th century and have retained their value as highly decorative orchids with long-lasting, stylish blooms. Langley Pride typically blooms from late fall into spring. The creamy white flowers can reach 6 inches wide and are heavily spotted. West Coast growers often find that Langley Pride hybrids do well in frost-free gardens. Combine them in the garden with other shade-loving slipper orchids. Keep plants evenly moist; fertilize lightly.

Paph. Magic Lantern
(*Paph.* micranthum × *Paph.* delenatii)

Culture: Easy
Availability: Specialty growers

This dwarf hybrid is about 4 inches tall with rounded blooms up to 3 inches across. Flowers appear from spring to summer and have pink with darker pink markings; the inflated lip is solid pink. Blooms show up well against the attractively mottled foliage.

Paph. Magic Lantern

Paph. Maudiae
(*Paph.* lawrenceanum × *Paph.* callosum)

Culture: Easy
Availability: Common

A gorgeous orchid recommended for beginning growers, this hybrid is one of the most popular and least demanding slipper orchids. Its white-and-green blooms measure about 3 inches across and are borne on 14-inch-long stems.

Paph. Maudiae

Flowering begins in late winter and continues into spring; individual blooms last as long as three months. The plant grows 6 inches tall and has mottled light and dark green leaves. It tolerates normal household temperatures and low light. Also available are hybrids in shades of red, called *coloratum* types, and ones with nearly black or wine color flowers, called *vinicolor* types.

Paph. Milmoore
(*Paph.* Mildred Hunter × *Paph.* Farnmoore)

Culture: Easy
Availability: Specialty growers

Milmoore is a classic spotted complex hybrid registered in 1953 by the British orchid firm Sanders. In late winter, it displays 4-inch-wide or larger flowers with a beautiful white dorsal sepal, spotted dark brown-red.

Paph. Milmoore

The petals are burgundy-red, and the red pouch is edged in chartreuse. The glossy flowers have heavy substance. The 10-inch-tall hybrid has been used as a parent but by itself is a treasure. Like most of the other complex hybrids, Milmoore is vigorous and easy to grow. Use a fine or medium mix that drains quickly.

Paph. St. Swithin
(*Paph. philippinense* × *Paph. rothschildianum*)

Culture: Average
Availability: Specialty growers
Considered by many experts to be the finest paphiopedilum hybrid, St. Swithin blooms readily and exhibits the best characteristics of its parents in an outstanding show. The 8-inch-wide flowers consist of creamy yellow sepals striped in dark brown, a yellow pouch with darker veining, and slender, dangling yellow-and-brown-striped petals displayed four or more on 18- to 24-inch flower stems in spring or summer. Plentiful, bright light is key to growing St. Swithin.

Paph. St. Swithin

Pescatorea (pes-kuh-TOH-ree-uh)

Abbreviation: *Pes.*
Sympodial
Small to average, depending on species
Low to medium light
Mild nights and warm days
High humidity
Keep continuously moist
Pot

One of the soft-leaf orchids, characterized by the soft texture of its leaves, this genus has upright fans of broad 3-inch-wide by 10-inch-long leaves that overlap at the base. The 3½-inch-wide blooms are borne from leaf axils on 4-inch stems. Plants lack pseudobulbs but form attractive clumps that are handsome even without bloom. Provide good air circulation for best results. Pescatoreas are related to zygopetalums, bolleas, and huntleyas.

Pes. lehmannii

Culture: Average
Availability: Specialty growers

Pes. lehmannii

Certainly the finest of the genus, *Pes. lehmannii* has fragrant ivory flowers striped with rich grape-purple and a short fuzzy purple lip. Plants bloom in spring to summer. Flower shape is rectangular or triangular, and the waxy flowers last as long as six weeks. Grow this orchid in a fast-draining potting medium to prevent rot.

Phaius *(FAY-ee-us)*

Abbreviation: none
Sympodial
Large
Medium light
Mild nights and warm days
High humidity
Keep evenly moist
Pot or in ground in frost-free areas

In spring spectacular 36- to 48-inch flower spikes rise from the foliage of these large terrestrial orchids that have conical tapering pseudobulbs to 3 inches tall and large ridged leaves that may be 8 inches or wider and 36 inches long. Plants grow into large mounds of arching to upright leaves.

Nurseries have discovered how to grow these plants rapidly from seed—often in less than two years—making it easier to sell them as potted flowering plants.

Grow phaius in a terrestrial orchid mix, choosing a proportionately large pot. Plants can stay outdoors in warm-winter climates.

Phaius tankervilleae

Phaiocalanthe Krytonite 'Chariot of Fire' (a phaius hybrid)

Phaius tankervilleae

Culture: Easy
Availability: Specialty growers; garden centers in spring
With their fat buds of unopened flowers, the tall flower spikes—up to 3 feet—of this orchid resemble asparagus spears or hosta flower stalks. Each spike holds a dozen or more fragrant 3-inch-wide reddish brown flowers with pink lips. Blossoms open from the bottom of the spike upward and are borne on short stalks. Plants bloom in spring, and flowers last up to four weeks.

Phaius Dan Rosenberg
(*Phaius tankervilleae* × *Phaius tuberculosa*)

Culture: Easy
Availability: Specialty growers; garden centers in spring
This is an example of the new types of orchids coming on the market as flowering plants. Thanks to advances in cultural techniques, plants can be grown from seed to flowering in a year or two rather than several years as in the past. Dan Rosenberg has 3-inch-wide golden yellow flowers with a rounded pink lip that has a white center. It produces

Phaius Dan Rosenberg

20 or more flowers per stem in spring. Pot this fast-growing orchid in terrestrial mix. Keep plants evenly moist and fertilize regularly. Grow Dan Rosenberg on a patio in frost-free climates. You may find it sold as a *Gastrophaius*.

Phaius Micro Burst
(*Phaius pulcher* × *Phaius tankervilleae*)

Culture: Easy
Availability: Specialty growers
Flower stalks of this relatively new hybrid bear pretty flowers in sunset shades of yellow and caramel with a rich purple to burgundy lip. Spikes are only 2 feet tall. For best results grow Micro Burst in pots of terrestrial mix and keep plants evenly moist. Feed them regularly.

Phalaenopsis *(fal-en-OP-sis)*

Abbreviation: *Phal.*
Monopodial
Miniature to large, depending on species
Low to medium light
Warm nights and days; mild in the winter
Medium to high humidity, depending on species
Let dry slightly between waterings
Pot or mount

Phalaenopsis hybrids are the most popular orchid in the world. They comprise the majority—perhaps more than 90 percent—of orchids sold in flower in the United States. A classic phalaenopsis flower resembles a winged insect in flight, hence the common name moth orchid. Blooms consist of three sepals and two petals, usually about the same size and color (some have wider petals). There aren't many species—perhaps fewer than fifty. There are, however, hundreds of hybrids and intergeneric hybrids, and all are easy to grow and bring into bloom.

Among the species and hybrids, shape and color of lips are highly variable. All have three lobes, two of which stand upright on some varieties or are fused on others. The third lobe may end with two antennae or have appendages that resemble a handlebar mustache. Appendages may extend like a tray, be pinched in places, or split at the tips.

Phalaenopsis flower colors span the rainbow—typically pink, red, yellow, or green, often with spots, splotches, bars, or stripes. Blooming is profuse, and flowers last a long time, sometimes six months. Cut flowers can remain fresh for as long as two weeks.

Phalaenopsis orchids are epiphytic and lack pseudobulbs. Their leathery, glossy green leaves, as long as 2 feet and as wide as 8 inches, are sometimes mottled purple underneath. Flower spikes emerge from the leaf axils, varying in height from a few inches to several feet.

Vigorous hybrids make especially fine houseplants on a sunny windowsill or under lights. Many of these lovely orchids originated on remote Philippine islands and do best in moderate warmth and humidity. Water and fertilize regularly when plants are growing actively. Epiphytic phalaenopsis often do well mounted on slabs or tree-fern bark. In pots, use a fast-draining medium, perhaps including charcoal chunks to help keep the mix open as the bark breaks down.

Maintain consistent humidity and protect the plants from drafts to prevent bud drop (flowers drying up and falling off before opening). Stake long inflorescences as they are forming to help support the flowers as they develop. Once in bloom, flowers will last longer if you provide slightly cooler temperatures and medium light.

Thousands of hybrids are made each year for commercial use, and millions of seedlings are grown and sold as potted flowering plants, sometimes labeled with hybrid name, sometimes not. Hybrids profiled in this section are just a few and illustrate the range of colors and forms available. Few may be readily available as named; but numerous phalaenopsis hybrids are available at garden centers. Ask orchid growers to help you find a color combination.

Phal. amabilis

Culture: Easy
Availability: Specialty growers
This is the species from which almost all modern white phalaenopsis orchids originate. Rarely branching, upright flower spikes bear 5 to 20 or more 4-inch-wide white blooms from mid fall through winter. Flowers last six weeks or longer and make an excellent display. Plants have three to five flat broad leaves to 12 inches long and 5 inches wide.

Phal. amabilis

Phal. aphrodite

Culture: Easy
Availability: Specialty growers

Bred in Taiwan to exceptionally high quality, these compact orchids closely resemble *Phal. amabilis,* differing only in being slightly smaller and having red markings inside their lips. The 3-inch-wide brilliant white blooms are held on upright flower stems that arch at the tips. They last six weeks or longer. Plants have bright green leaves.

Phal. aphrodite

Phal. bellina

Culture: Average
Availability: Specialty growers

Sometimes sold as *Phal. violacea* 'Borneo', or *Phal. violacea bellina,* this Malaysian beauty has 2-inch flowers in cream, apple green, and pink. They're borne sequentially, three or four at a time, on 4- to 6-inch inflorescences. Bloom time varies but can be spurred by warm temperatures and low light. Like other phalaenopsis, *Phal. bellina* has thick, waxy flowers that last a long time. Plants have shiny green leaves as

Phal. bellina Krull's Pretty Girl

long as 10 inches. Because of its relatively compact habit, *Phal. bellina* can be grown on a windowsill. *Phal. bellina* is susceptible to crown rot, which you can prevent by ensuring the plant's growing point is dry by late in the day.

Phal. cornu-cervi

Culture: Average
Availability: Specialty growers

An exotic-looking species native to India and the Indonesian islands of Java and Sumatra, *Phal. cornu-cervi* is prized for its ability to flower prolifically most of the year. The 2-inch-wide flower is greenish yellow with reddish brown spotting. They form along the flower stem, usually beginning in early summer. As spikes elongate, more buds develop along the lengths while new inflorescences continue to emerge from the plant's base. Pinch off lower blooms as they fade, leaving new buds and flowering stems to continue the show for weeks and months.

For this species and its cultivars, keep the fleshy roots well hydrated—water plants daily during hot weather. Some gardeners find it easiest to monitor moisture by allowing the root system to hang freely, either by mounting the plant or allowing it to grow beyond the bounds of a shallow pot.

Phal. equestris

Culture: Easy
Availability: Specialty growers

Phal. equestris

An outstanding winter- to spring-blooming dwarf, *Phal. equestris* comes in three color forms. The ½-inch-wide flowers may be white with a lavender blush, pink with a white picotee edging, or pure white. The types with pure white flowers may have yellow markings on the lips (the variety *aurea*) or not (the variety *alba*). Leave spikes on the plant because plants will rebloom. When blooming has finally finished, keikis will develop at the tips of the spent flower stalk. Let the keikis grow three 3-inch-long roots, then clip them off and pot them up as new plants. *Phal. equestris* grows 3 inches tall with leaves to 6 inches long.

Phal. mannii

Culture: Average
Availability: Specialty growers

Abundant flower production is a hallmark of this dwarf species, which is native to China, India, Nepal, and Vietnam. Inflorescences begin to appear and branch in midspring;

soon they are cloaked with 1- to 2-inch-wide yellow flowers accented with brown and a white-and-purple lip. A typical inflorescence produces many blossoms; flowering can last as long as three months. Flowers emit the sweet scent of fresh-cut oranges. The plant is only a few inches tall and has glossy green 6- to 18-inch-long leaves that spread outward. You can mount it or grow it in a fast-draining orchid mix.

Phal. mannii

Phal. schilleriana

Culture: Easy
Availability: Specialty growers

Phal. schilleriana

From winter to spring, fragrant pastel flowers cascade from the long, dangling, branched flower stems of this popular orchid. Measuring 2½ to 3½ inches across, they may be soft rosy pink, creamy white, or something in between. Their scent is reminiscent of roses.

Phal. schilleriana is a substantial plant, to about 18 inches tall. It is notable for its dark green leaves marbled with silver and brushed with magenta below. Leaves grow as long as 1 foot and as wide as 5 inches. This native of the Philippines thrives in high humidity; make sure it does not dry out.

Phal. stuartiana

Culture: Easy
Availability:
  Specialty growers
The broad pendulous leaves of this species are heavily pigmented with red underneath and patterned with silvery markings on top. In spring, upright, branching flower stems bear two dozen or more 2½-inch-wide white blooms finely spotted with red.

Phal. stuartiana

Phal. Ambo Buddha 'SW' (*Phal.* Brother Buddha × *Phal. amboinensis*)

Culture: Easy
Availability: Specialty growers

Phal. Ambo Buddha 'SW'

This knockout hybrid comes from Taiwan. Its sweetly scented 2½-inch-wide flowers deliver hot tropical color—yellow background and bright red spots plus a rich blend of yellow and pink in the lip—during winter and spring. Plants are 4 inches tall and have large leaves that grow to about 12 inches long.

Phal. Baldan's Kaleidoscope (*Phal.* Hausermann's Candy × *Phal.* Daryl Lockhart)

Culture: Easy
Availability:
  Common
Intense color makes this hybrid stand out. About 4 inches across, flowers are luminous bright yellow, marked and striped with cranberry red. They decorate long, branching 3-foot inflorescences in spring and may last four months or longer before fading. Plants are about 12 inches tall.

Phal. Baldan's Kaleidoscope 'Golden Treasure'

Phal. Ember 'Blumen Insel' AM/AOS
(*Phal.* Mahalo × *Phal.* George Vasquez)

Culture: Easy
Availability: Specialty growers
Sweetly scented 2½-inch-wide glossy red flowers appear twice a year on this AM/AOS award-winning hybrid. Their waxy texture allows them to last for many weeks. A compact plant, Ember 'Blumen Insel' is perfect for growing under lights or on a windowsill.

Phal. Ember 'Blumen Insel'

Phal. Formosa San Fan 'CR' (*Phal.* Misty Green × *Phal.* Mok Choi Yew)

Culture: Easy
Availability:
    Specialty growers
Cream-yellow flowers with striking dark red barring make Formosa San Fan 'CR' a real standout. Flowers are delicately scented, about 2½ inches across, and borne on 6-inch flower spikes; well-suited to small spaces.

Phal. Formosa San Fan 'CR'

Phal. Golden Peoker 'BL'
(*Phal.* Misty Green × *Phal.* Liu Tuen-Shen)

Culture: Easy
Availability: Specialty growers
Despite the "golden" in its name, this hybrid cultivar has bright white flowers with raspberry pink markings; patterns vary from flower to flower on the same plant. Originally, the flowers were white with fuchsia spots, but as Taiwanese breeders were propagating the orchid, a mutant appeared. Aficionados refer to the mutation as the harlequin look, and this hybrid is the ancestor of all harlequin phalaenopsis.

Plants bloom mainly in late winter and early spring, slightly later than other phals. Because of their waxy texture, flowers are exceptionally long-lasting—on the plant or in a vase. Golden Peoker 'BL' has 14- to 18-inch-tall flower spikes and 12-inch-long glossy green leaves. Plant height is about 6 inches.

Phal. Golden Peoker 'BL'

Phal. Jackie Debonis 'Fangtasic'
(*Phal.* Rucy Lih Stripes × *Phal.* Chih Shang's Stripes)

Culture: Easy
Availability:
    Specialty
    growers
With two striped parents, this superb hybrid couldn't help but have a striped flower. It's bright white with bold peppermint-pink stripes and measures about 3 inches across. Blooms appear in spring and summer. The plant is 6 inches tall. Keep it warm and moist year-round.

Phal. Jackie Debonis 'Fangtasic'

Phal. Nobby's Amy
(*Phal.* Be Glad × *Phal. rothschildianum*)

Culture: Easy
Availability: Specialty growers
Dwarf Nobby's Amy is a perfect choice for small warm locations. Expect an outstanding display of 2½-inch-wide creamy white flowers suffused with yellow and pink from winter to spring. They are borne on 24-inch or longer, upright to arching, branching flower stems. Leaves grow outward to about 10 inches long, and mature plant height is a mere 4 inches.

Phal. Nobby's Amy

Phal. Orchid World 'Roman Holiday' AM/AOS
(*Phal.* Malibu Imp × *Phal. deventeriana*)

Culture: Easy
Availability: Specialty growers

Phal. Orchid World 'Roman Holiday'

A strong, spicy fragrance is the hallmark of this superb AM/AOS award-winning hybrid. Its 2½-inch-wide flowers are bright yellow with vivid red bars, carried in 12-inch inflorescences with as many as six flowers each in spring. Blooms remain intact and fresh looking for many weeks. A mature plant fits well on a windowsill or can be grown in a greenhouse or under lights. Leaves are about 12 inches long. Although easy to grow, Orchid World 'Roman Holiday' must have warm temperatures to thrive and bloom well.

Phal. Penang Girl
(*Phal. violacea* × *Phal. venosa*)

Culture: Easy
Availability: Specialty growers

Popular for its sweet fragrance, this hybrid is often recommended for beginners. It blooms from winter to spring, producing lots of long-lasting 2½-inch-wide orange-yellow flowers overlaid with red. The compact plant is about 4 inches tall, with leaves that spread to about 10 inches. Grow this orchid in warm temperatures.

Phal. Penang Girl

Phal. Perfect Sara 'Orange Delight'
(*Phal.* Sara Gold × *Phal.* Perfection Is)

Culture: Easy
Availability: Specialty growers

Phal. Perfect Sara 'Orange Delight'

A newer hybrid, this orchid has long-lasting fragrant orange flowers accented with purple bars in spring to summer. The compact plant has a 10-inch leaf spread and grows to about 6 inches tall. Its flower spike is relatively short, about 12 to 14 inches, so it doesn't need to be staked. Keep the plant warm and moist year-round.

Phragmipedium (frag-mih-PEE-dee-um)

Abbreviation: *Phrag.*
Sympodial
Large
Medium light
Mild nights and warm days
Moderate humidity
Keep continuously moist
Pot

Although not a large group—only about a dozen species—this genus includes orchids unique and beautiful enough to enjoy enduring popularity. Most phragmipediums are native to Peru, Ecuador, Colombia, and Brazil; a few may be found as far north as southern Mexico. The species have contributed to a number of excellent hybrids.

There are epiphytic and terrestrial species; all have the same form. Their long, flat, leathery dark green leaves join in clusters of eight to form a fan. Leaves may be 3 feet long and 2 inches wide. Many species and hybrids are vigorous growers, quickly forming so many fans that it is difficult for the untrained eye to discern one fan from another.

The genus name phragmipedium is a reference to the plants' distinctive flower form. In Greek, phragma means "fence," a reference to the flower's divided ovary, while pedilon, or "slipper," describes the shape of the lip. The unscented flowers have a large, distinctive dorsal sepal and a lip resembling a pouch or the toe of a slipper. Petals may be narrow, long, and may be twisted. Fine hairs cover the column, so the center of the flower looks furry. Flower colors tend toward green and brown, often accented with yellow or purple. Plants bloom in winter and spring on 3-foot stems.

Phragmipediums do best in mild to warm temperatures, medium to bright light (a windowsill out of direct light is fine, as is a spot under lights), and continuously moist potting mix, such as sphagnum moss, bark, and charcoal. You'll gain the best results from repotting infrequently and letting your plants grow into multiple fan specimens. Phrags are light feeders; overfertilization inhibits flowering.

In their native settings, phragmipediums grow by streams where their roots are always damp. An easy way to make sure the plants have all the water they need when actively growing indoors is to set the pots in a shallow tray of water. Use purified or good-quality water that is free of accumulated mineral salts or other contaminants.

Phrag. besseae

Culture: Average
Availability: Specialty growers

Phrag. besseae

The flowers of this species are ruby red or rich orange-red, a rare color for phragmipediums. Tall, branched flower stems develop in late winter and early spring and soon are covered with dozens of 2-inch-wide blossoms. Plants are medium in size, with handsome dark green strappy leaves that reach about 10 inches long. Grow *Phrag. besseae* in cool temperatures (it can tolerate winter nighttime temperatures as low as 48°F) and always keep its roots damp. This species was discovered and brought into cultivation in the 1980s and is native to Peru, Ecuador, and Colombia.

Phrag. caricinum

Culture: Average
Availability: Rare

Sometimes sold as *Phrag. pearcei*, this orchid has been in cultivation for more than 100 years. Its compact clumps of slender foliage look like reed grass; at maturity leaves reach 12 inches tall. In spring *Phrag. caricinum* sends up 18-inch-tall spikes of 3-inch-wide flowers in shades of green and dark red with some striping and long twisty petals. Because this species is compact and tolerant of home temperature variations, it's a good choice for windowsills. Pot it in long-fibered sphagnum moss, preferably of Chilean or New Zealand origin, and keep humidity high—around 80 percent.

Phrag. caudatum

Culture: Average
Availability: Specialty growers

Phrag. caudatum warscewiczianum

This species has strongly folded leaves held at a 45-degree angle to one another. From mid-winter to spring, upright flower stems grow 12 to 15 inches tall and bear flowers with exceptionally long—24 inches or longer—petals, among the longest of all orchids. Petals stop growing when they touch a surface, so elevating the plant helps to encourage extra-long growth. Flowers last three to four weeks and then drop while still in perfect condition. Grow *Phrag. caudatum* in mild temperatures in a water-retentive orchid mix; keep it constantly wet with purified water. Repot infrequently.

Phrag. pearcei

Culture: Average
Availability: Specialty growers

Phrag. pearcei

This diminutive plant is similar to and often confused with *Phrag. caricinum.* It has grassy, narrow leaves that may reach 6 inches long. The slender flower stem barely clears the foliage. Up to six 2-inch green-and-brown blooms outlined in red are borne sequentially up the stem, starting any time of year, but generally in spring to summer. Keep it constantly moist to mimic its native streamside habitat—it is hard to overwater this species. Fertilize lightly.

Phrag. schlimii

Culture: Average
Availability: Specialty growers
Unlike most phragmipediums, this one is fragrant. The 2-inch-wide rose-scented flowers are creamy white with pink pouches. They occur two or three to an arching, 12-inch stem. Plants can bloom almost any time of year, although spring is most common. A mature plant spreads 18 inches wide, and you may need a greenhouse or a wide windowsill to accommodate it.

Phrag. schlimii

Phrag. Grande
(*Phrag. caudatum* × *Phrag. longifolium*)

Culture: Easy
Availability: Specialty growers
This hybrid of *Phrag. caudatum* is slightly easier to find and grow than others. It has broader bright green leaves, more arching and less formal than *Phrag. caudatum.* The upright flower stem bears as many as four large brown blooms with long, narrow petals hanging down like a mustache. Keep Grande evenly moist in a shady location in cool to mild temperatures. Grow it outdoors in frost-free regions.

Phrag. Grande

Phrag. Hot Lips
(*Phrag.* Hanne Popow × *Phrag.* Living Fire)

Culture: Average
Availability: Specialty growers

Phrag. **Hot Lips**

This hybrid provides shapely, richly colored dark pink flowers with a touch of yellow in the center. The flowers are about 4 inches across. An orchid that represents the new breeding directions of this genus, it has larger, brighter color flowers than the species on slightly shorter plants—18 to 24 inches tall.

Phrag. Jason Fischer
(*Phrag.* Memoria Dick Clements × *Phrag. besseae*)

Phrag. Jason Fischer

Culture: Average
Availability: Specialty growers
A typical flower of this hybrid is 4 inches across and vivid red, with full, rounded, flat petals and a velvety texture. Bloom time is spring or autumn, although the inflorescences may appear at other times of the year. Sometimes a single inflorescence will bloom for an entire year. Grow Jason Fischer in cool temperatures with constant moisture.

Phrag. Noirmont
(*Phrag. longifolium* × *Phrag.* Memoria Dick Clements)

Phrag. Noirmont

Culture: Average
Availability: Specialty growers
Large flowers and deeper, silkier color are the highlights of this outstanding newer hybrid. It blooms sequentially, usually beginning in spring or fall. Individual flowers are 3 to 4 inches across and last for a few weeks, but a spike can continue to produce blooms for three to six months. Flowers are red and yellow; the slippers are dusted with red-orange. Overall color may have an underlying hint of green. Noirmont is a large plant and tolerates warm temperatures.

Phrag. Sorcerer's Apprentice
(*Phrag. sargentianum* × *Phrag. longifolium*)

Culture: Average
Availability: Specialty growers
Sorcerer's Apprentice has been used extensively as a parent. Large, dramatically colored flowers with twisted petals grace this impressive hybrid from winter into spring. They can be as big as 10 inches across and come in hues of burgundy, green, and brown. Flower spikes grow to 3 to 4 feet. Provide ample water while plants are in bloom. Foliage grows about 18 inches long and 1 inch wide.

Phrag. Sorcerer's Apprentice

Pleione (plee-OH-nee)

Abbreviation: *Pln.*
Sympodial
Average
Low to medium light
Cool nights and mild days
High humidity
Keep evenly moist
Pot

Native to the mountainous elevations of India and China, these little-known terrestrials have flattened, round to slightly conical pseudobulbs that may be less than 1 inch tall and across, and 12-inch-long deeply folded deciduous leaves. Flowers appear singly from emerging growths in shades of purple, pink, yellow, or white, sometimes with contrasting, frilly lips marked in red. The species are largely Himalayan and do well in cool home conditions or in a protected frost-free spot in a garden. Pot them in a rich, fast-draining potting soil; keep plants moist during the growing season. Allow a period of dry dormancy in winter.

Pln. formosana

Culture: Easy
Availability: Specialty growers

Pln. formosana

Pln. formosana is a small deciduous terrestrial orchid. An easy-to-grow species, it may be challenging to find but is worth the search. The fragrant 3-inch-wide white or pink flowers have a frilly white lip. Plants bloom in late winter. Grow *Pln. formosana* in a pot that is wider than deep filled with terrestrial orchid mix or regular potting soil.

Pleurothallis (ploor-oh-THAL-lis)

Abbreviation: *Pths.*
Sympodial
Miniature to large, depending on species
Low light
Mild nights and warm days
High humidity
Keep continuously moist
Pot or mount, depending on species

Pths. nossax

Pleurothallis tends to have small flowers that are pollinated by gnats and other tiny insects. This widespread New World genus has more than a thousand members, and as plant explorers range farther into unexplored areas, they discover more new species. Among them are the smallest orchids, less than $1/32$ inch tall, as well as some that grow more than 36 inches tall. Pleurothallis' native range varies from sea level to 10,000 feet above sea level in the Andes. All species require high humidity and must be kept out of direct sunlight. They are closely related to masdevallias.

Pths. grobyi

Culture: Easy
Availability: Specialty growers
One of the best known of the genus, this species is a 2-inch-tall, densely clustering plant that forms attractive mats. Mounted and given adequate humidity, it will form a ball of foliage in little time. Short flower stems barely clear the foliage, and each carries three or four nodding, tubular yellow blooms less than $1/2$ inch across. The plant blooms several times a year, but flowers last only a couple of weeks. Grow *Pths. grobyi* in low light and mild temperatures.

Pths. grobyi

Pths. pterophora

Culture: Easy
Availability: Rare
Deliciously scented, long-lasting flowers help this orchid stand out. Only $1/2$ inch across, the soft white blooms are abundant in spring and summer. They emit a sweet rose fragrance. The plant may bloom twice a year with flowers emerging even from older pseudobulbs. Mount this 4-inch dwarf plant, or display it in a small container of very fine-grade mix in mild temperatures.

Pths. strupifolia

Culture: Average
Availability: Specialty growers
This small but prolific, pendulous plant from Brazil is best suited to growing on mounts. Its 12-inch leathery pendulous leaves are dark green with purple undertones. Several times a year, the flower spikes cascade from the bottom of the leaves, the chains of handsome little flowers hanging with the leaf as a background. Individual blossoms are royal purple and bright white. Keep plants in cool to mild temperatures out of direct light, and provide high humidity.

Pths. truncata

Pths. strupifolia

Pths. tribuloides

Culture: Easy
Availability: Rare
This warmth-tolerant species is relatively easy to grow. The miniature plants are 2 to 3 inches tall and form a tight clump of foliage. In winter and spring, short spikes bear lots of ⅜-inch-wide scarlet flowers. These have a fleshy texture that helps them stay fresh longer. Blue-green seedpods follow the blooms. Mount *Pths. tribuloides* or grow it in fine-textured mix in low to medium light and mild temperatures.

Pths. truncata

Culture: Easy
Availability: Rare
A novelty within the genus, this small plant is only 4 inches tall. Its winter or spring flowers are a mere 1/16 inch wide and lie across the leaf's midrib like tiny golden jewels on display. To grow this plant, just give it a spot in medium or low light in mild temperatures.

Potinara (poh-tih-NAR-uh)

Abbreviation: *Pot.*
Sympodial
Compact
Medium to bright, indirect light
Mild nights and warm days
Moderate humidity
Let dry between waterings
Pot

Potinaras result from a cross between brassavola, cattleya, laelia, and sophronitis. Flowers are similar to those of cattleya hybrids such as laeliocattleyas. Their brightly colored flowers come in shades of red, orange, or yellow. Lips, sepals, or petals may be ruffled on the edge; sometimes the entire flower is ruffled. Many of the species are fragrant.

The growth habit and growing needs of the plant are similar to those of other cattleya hybrids (pages 118–124), but their sophronitis background makes them slightly smaller. Cylindrical pseudobulbs are topped with one or two succulent leaves.

Pot. Burana Beauty 'Burana' (Pot. Netrasiri Starbright × C. Netrasiri Beauty)

Culture: Easy
Availability: Specialty growers
This compact plant has proved itself a popular cattleya alliance member with its easy culture under a variety of conditions, free-flowering habit, and bright color blossoms. In spring, clusters of large 4-inch-wide bright yellow fragrant flowers striped in red cover the plant, each lasting four weeks or longer. Plants are 12 inches tall or less at maturity. Grow Burana Beauty 'Burana' in a coarse-grade, fast-draining bark. It is widely propagated in Thailand and sold worldwide.

Pot. Burana Beauty 'Burana'

Pot. Twenty-Four Carat

Pot. Little Magician
(*Lc.* Tokyo Magic × *Pot.* Little Toshie)

Culture: Average
Availability: Specialty growers
Little Magician is one of many new hybrids in this group
that will tempt beginning growers with compact, often less
than 8-inch-tall, growth habit and ease of flowering. Round
blooms to 3 inches wide are produced through the year in
shades of yellow, often with contrasting red lip and
occasionally with bold red flares in the petals. Little
Magician is good for growing on windowsills or under lights.
Allow plants to dry between waterings; fertilize regularly. Pot
Little Magician in medium-grade mix and grow it on a
windowsill in medium light.

Pot. Twenty-four Carat 'Lea' AM/AOS
(*Pot.* Lemon Tree × *Blc.* Yellow Imp)

Culture: Easy
Availability: Specialty growers
Brilliant golden yellow flowers with a rich citrus fragrance
are the highlight of this beautiful orchid. Exaggerated
(flared) lips contribute to the impact. Compact, 15-inch-tall
plants bloom in spring, with each 6-inch inflorescence
consisting of one or two 4-inch-wide flowers. Twenty-four
Carat 'Lea' has earned its AM/AOS designation.

Promenaea stapelioides
(prom-en-AY-uh stuh-pea-LEE-oy-dez)

Abbreviation:
Prom.
Sympodial
Dwarf
Medium light
Mild nights and
warm days
Moderate
Humidity
Keep evenly moist
Pot
Ease of care:
Average
Availability:
Specialty growers

Promenaea stapelioides

This group of
dwarf orchids
deserves to be better
known. Plants have
waxy yellow
unscented flowers
heavily marked
with red-brown.
In late summer
2-inch-wide flowers
ring the plants,
borne on short
stems at the base of the newest pseudobulbs, one to three at
a time. Each bloom lasts as long as four weeks. Plants grow
6 inches tall. Their compressed round pseudobulbs, often
no larger than ½ inch, are topped with a single 4-inch-long
single gray-green leaf. Grow *Promenaea stapelioides* under
lights or on a windowsill in small pots of fine-grade orchid
medium. The plant needs cool to mild temperatures.
Promenaeas are related to zygopetalum, with which breeders
often make crosses.

Psychopsis papilio (sy-KOP-sis puhp-ILL-ee-oh)

Abbreviation: *Pyp.*
Sympodial
Average
Medium light
Mild nights and warm days
High humidity
Let dry between waterings
Pot or mount
Culture: Advanced
Availability: Specialty growers

This unusual plant is often called the butterfly orchid because its yellow-and-brown flowers resemble an insect, from the broad lip to the prominent dorsal sepal and slender upright petals that look like antennae. Beginning in spring, 10- to 15-inch-tall inflorescences emerge from the base of the newest pseudobulb. Each is topped with a single flower. As the oldest fades, a new one takes its place, and the plant is in bloom for several months. Individual flowers measure about 6 inches across and have no scent.

Plants have flattened oval, strongly furrowed pseudobulbs. A single broad 15-inch-long dark green leaf with red markings sprouts from each bulb. Plants grow 12 inches tall at most. The thick reddish leaves have green patches.

Grow psychopsis in a fast-draining orchid mix. Provide consistently warm temperatures and high humidity. In its native habitat (Brazil, Colombia, and the West Indies), temperatures are fairly even year-round, with daytime highs in the 80s and nighttime lows in the 60s. Water and fertilize generously when the plant is actively growing, spring through fall, but allow plants to dry between waterings.

Sometimes sold as *Oncidium papilio*, psychopsis captivated "The Bachelor Duke," William George Spencer Cavendish (1790–1888), 6th Duke of Devonshire.

Psychopsis papilio

Psygmorchis pusilla (sig-MORE-kiss pew-SILL-uh)

Abbreviation: *Psgmrc.*
Sympodial
Miniature
Medium light
Warm nights and days
High humidity
Keep evenly moist
Mount
Culture: Advanced
Availability: Specialty growers

These enchanting orchids sport relatively large, 1- to 1½-inch-wide sunny yellow-skirted unscented flowers in spring and summer. Plants bloom over a long period, although each flower may last only a week. The

Psygmorchis pusilla

inflorescences emerge from the axils of the flattened leaves. These overlap at their bases to form the orchid's characteristic fan shape. Plants grow no more than 3 inches tall.

Psygmorchis strongly resembles a small oncidium, to which it is related. It is one of the fastest-growing orchids, often flowering from seed in less than a year.

This species is native to Mexico, Trinidad, and Brazil, and can be tricky to grow. It needs high humidity as well as good air circulation. In nature, these plants occupy the outermost fringes of the forest canopy and are called twig epiphytes. Airy, rapidly drying conditions are a must for their successful cultivation indoors; growing them on a mount can help provide those conditions.

Renanthera (ren-AN-thair-uh)

Abbreviation: *Ren.*
Monopodial
Large
Bright light
Warm nights and hot days
High humidity
Keep continuously moist
Mount or baskets

Most renantheras have arching, branched flower stems with a dozen to several dozen unscented brilliant red or orange blooms, giving rise to their common name of fire orchid. Flowers range from 1½ inches to wider than 3 inches and last for weeks. Summer is the main bloom season, but plants may flower throughout the year.

Renantheras are tall plants, ranging from 2 to 6 feet tall. The more tropical species can grow to virtually unlimited heights, vining against and through any support present. Renantheras are closely related to vandas, but generally have broader and stiffer leaves. All are epiphytic.

Grow these rambling plants in a slatted basket with little or no medium, or mount them on slabs or trees outdoors.

Ren. monachica

Culture: Easy
Availability: Specialty growers

Ren. monachica

With its 1½-inch-wide, brilliant-hue flowers lighting up the plant, *Ren. monachica* creates quite a display. Its branched inflorescences can reach 18 inches tall and support as many as 30 flaming reddish orange flowers at a time for at least a month. Even out of bloom the plant is dazzling, with purple-tinged leaves and a rambling, climbing growth habit. Plants are easy to grow, ideally on a south-facing windowsill in a warm home or greenhouse, in a small pot of coarse-textured mix. This species is native to the Philippines.

Ren. Mauricette Brin 'Kiaora' (Ren. Bangkok Flame × Ren. storei)

Culture: Average
Availability: Specialty growers

One of the newest hybrids in this fascinating group, *Ren.* Mauricette Brin offers spectacular, arching, branched inflorescences of 3-inch-wide flame red blooms. Plants may reach 6 feet or more, which may be too tall for some home growers. It also requires tropical conditions, which can be a problem for fanciers in temperate regions. Plants do not tolerate temperatures below 60°F and do best with constantly warm temperatures in the 70s to 90s. High humidity, in the 70 percent range, is also required. Grow them in slatted wood baskets with little or no medium.

Ren. Mauricette Brin 'Kiaora'

Restrepia (res-TREP-ee-uh)

Abbreviation: *Rstp.*
Monopodial
Compact
Bright, indirect light
Cool nights and mild days
High humidity
Keep continuously moist
Pot or mount

This group of orchids has some of the most unusual-looking flowers among all orchids. The lateral or lower sepals are fused into one large tongue. Narrow petals extend out from the flower, while the slender dorsal sepal is spoon-shape at the base, narrows in the center, then broadens at the tip, like a little knob. Flowers are brightly hued and may be purple, rose, orange, or yellow; stripes, spots, and gradations of color through the flower are common. Restrepias are especially appreciated as indoor plants. Many species bloom from the base of older leaves over a period of several years, providing a worthwhile display in limited space.

Restrepias are native to Central and South America. They do well in cool temperatures, although they are somewhat tolerant of temperature variations. Grow them in shade in a moist orchid medium, and provide high humidity and good air circulation. Many restrepias produce keikis at the base of older leaves.

Rstp. antennifera

Rstp. contorta

Culture: Average
Availability: Rare

Flowers of *Rstp. contorta* are bright orange with undertones of purple, yellow, or red, and they are heavily spotted with red. Plants bloom in great numbers in spring through summer, with each flower about 2 inches across. Grow *Rstp. contorta* on a mount or in a fast-draining, very fine-grade mix. It is native to Colombia and Venezuela.

Rhyncholaelia *(rin-koh-LAY-lee-uh)*

Abbreviation: *Rhynch.*
Sympodial
Compact
Bright light
Mild nights and warm days
Moderate humidity
Let dry between waterings
Pot or mount

This genus is made up of two epiphytic species, *Rhynch. digbyana* and *Rhynch. glauca.* Each has upright growths of large, flattened, cylindrical pseudobulbs topped with a single stiff, upright 1-inch-wide by 6-inch-long leaf.

The single flowers originate at the base of the leaf on 6-inch stems. White, sometimes with a greenish cast, they last four weeks. Flowers of both species have a sweet, intense citrus fragrance at night.

Pot rhyncholaelia in a cattleya orchid mix and grow it in bright light. Because it does not like soggy roots, this orchid does well on a mount. Rhyncholaelias were once classified with brassavola; sometimes they are sold under that name.

Rhynch. digbyana

Culture: Average
Availability: Specialty growers

This plant's slender succulent leaves, up to 10 inches long, have a silvery cast. Large apple green flowers (each as wide as 6 inches across) with highly fringed lips last for several weeks in summer to fall and radiate an enticing citrusy fragrance in the evening. The frilly lip gives this distinctive species a delicate, lacy look. *Rhynch. digbyana* is often crossed with laelias and cattleyas to create larger flowers with a similar lip.

Give this epiphyte warmth and bright light for best flowering—then let it rest as you reduce water and stop fertilizing. Because its roots can rot when kept too moist, some growers mount it on bark.

Rhynch. digbyana

Rhynch. glauca

Culture: Average
Availability: Specialty growers

Rhynch. glauca 'Woltman'

Rhynch. glauca is similar to *Rhynch. digbyana* to which it is closely related. Plants are slightly smaller, to only about 8 inches tall. They have single 5-inch-wide ghostly pale green blooms with broad lips that are smooth rather than fringed as in *digbyana*. Plants bloom in fall to winter; flowers are fragrant at night with the "brasso" citrus scent.

Rhynchostylis *(rin-koh-STY-lis)*

Abbreviation: *Rhy.*
Monopodial
Average to large, depending on species
Bright light
Warm nights and hot days
High humidity
Keep continuously moist
Mount or basket

This genus, closely related to vanda, has similar cultural needs. Like vandas, most members have closely held leaves with bases overlapping to cover short stems. Some species branch from the base more freely than others. All rhynchostylis are moderate size, to 24 inches tall and wide.

Flowers emerge from the axils of the most recently developed leaves near the base of the plant. The spikes are tightly packed, giving rise to the common name foxtail orchid. Flowers are often pendulous, hanging over the side of the basket; they also may be upright or horizontally arching. All species are decorative, with blooms that last four to five weeks—most are lightly fragrant during daylight.

Grow rhynchostylis like vandas, in slatted baskets with little or no medium so roots can dry rapidly between waterings. Use a very coarse grade of medium.

Rhy. coelestis

Culture: Average
Availability: Specialty growers

This is the smallest of the three best-known rhynchostylis species, growing to 12 inches tall and 18 inches across. Its upright spikes bear 1½-inch-wide light blue blooms, looking somewhat like a hyacinth. The fragrant flowers last three to four weeks in late spring. The plant branches freely at the base, quickly forming an attractive, floriferous clump. Leaves fold laterally and curve slightly downward, framing the spikes of flowers. Well-grown plants look similar to lupines or foxgloves with upright, densely flowered stems.

Rhy. gigantea

Culture: Average
Availability: Specialty growers

Rhy. gigantea 'Alba'

These 10-inch-tall plants can become quite substantial, sprawling out as new stems emerge from the base of the plant, hence the "gigantea" in the species name. *Rhy. gigantea* is commonly mounted or grown in a hanging basket. Either way, it will generate pendulous clusters of long-lasting flowers in late winter. Citrus-scented flowers are only about an inch across and borne thickly on 15-inch inflorescences. They are typically white with fuchsia spots; other color forms, such as those of the cultivar 'Sagarik Strain,' with its wine-red flowers, occur. This species, native to Thailand, Vietnam, and Myanmar, thrives in humidity.

Rodriguezia *(rod-rih-GEZ-ee-uh)*

Abbreviation: *Rdza.*
Sympodial
Miniature to large
Bright light
Cool nights and warm days
High humidity
Let dry between waterings
Pot or mount
Culture: Average to advanced
Availability: Specialty growers

This group of ephemeral twig epiphytes hails from the cloud forests of Mexico and Central and South America. They're called twig orchids because plants grow on the slenderest twigs of trees growing in the outermost fringes of the tropical forest. Plants have inconspicuous, flattened pseudobulbs from which grow several 8-inch-long leaves. Arching flower spikes hold 6 to 12 or more 1-inch-wide blooms in shades of rose, pink, and white. Flowers bloom in fall and winter and last two to three weeks.

Ensure high humidity and good air movement around these plants to help the roots dry quickly. Grow rodriguezia in a pot of fine-grade mix or mount it. Sprays of *Rdza. lanceolata* are coral-red; plants grow 24 inches tall. This orchid is sometimes sold as *Rdza. secunda*. *Rdza. venusta* grows just 8 inches tall. Its white flowers marked in yellow have a strong citrus scent. *Rdza. bahiensis* offers dwarf size and lots of dazzling flowers from spring to summer. Its blooms are bright white with yellow markings at the top of the lip, and it will eventually grow to about 6 inches tall. This orchid is harder to find than *lanceolata* or *secunda*.

Rdza. batemanii

Sarcochilus hartmannii
(sar-KOH-kih-lus heart-MAN-ee-i)

Abbreviation: *Sarco.*
Monopodial
Dwarf
Medium light
Cool nights and mild to warm days
Moderate to low humidity
Keep evenly moist
Pot
Culture: Easy
Availability: Specialty growers

This is the best-known and most common sarcochilus species. These lithophytic spring bloomers produce erect to arching inflorescences holding as many as twenty-five 1-inch-wide white blooms with red-spotted throats. The 6-inch tall plants can grow into huge clumps. In Australia, where the orchid is native, plants grow enormous; they can be 4 feet or more across, with dozens of flower stems and hundreds of blooms.

Sarco. hartmannii originated at moderate elevations, which means it grows best in intermediate temperatures, with excellent drainage and good air movement. Pot it in a mix suitable for phals or oncidiums; keep plants evenly moist. Plants can be grown outdoors in frost-free regions.

Sarco. hartmannii 'Lindisfarne'

Schomburgkia *(shom-BERG-kee-uh)*

Abbreviation: *Schom.*
Sympodial
Large
Bright light
Mild nights and warm days
High humidity
Let dry between waterings
Pot or mount

Schomburgkias are easy to recognize by their 10- to 16-inch-tall, slender, sometimes hollow pseudobulbs. In their native habitat in the West Indies and Central and South America, the hollow bulbs often harbor stinging ants. Two or three stiff leaves held at a 45-degree angle top the pseudobulbs.

Plants can be huge, from 2 to 6 feet tall depending on the species, and their stiff, upright flower stems may reach more than 10 feet tall. The large blooms are borne at the tips in a whorl and sometimes have showy bracts. Plants bloom in winter, spring, summer, or fall depending on the species.

Grow schomburgkias in a coarse-grade orchid mix and give them plenty of bright light for best results. Pot them in 18-inch-wide or larger containers, or mount them on large cork or tree-fern slabs. Gardeners in warm-winter zones can grow them as a landscape plant in a shady part of the yard.

Schom. superbiens

Culture: Average
Availability: Specialty growers

Schom. superbiens

Formerly known as *Laelia superbiens,* this large, 30-inch-tall orchid is a favorite of West Coast cymbidium fanciers. Its flower stems reach 6 feet tall and are topped with six or more 6-inch-wide rose-lavender blooms. The sepals and petals have a characteristic wavy or curly shape. Plants grow best in coarse orchid medium or on mounts. The pseudobulbs are widely spaced and mounts accommodate them more easily. Grow *Schom. superbiens* outdoors in frost-free areas.

Schom. tibicinis

Culture: Easy to average
Availability: Specialty growers

This winter-flowering tropical species bears wavy 4-inch-wide chocolate-scented rose-pink flowers. Pseudobulbs can be more than 30 inches tall; they give rise to 8-foot-tall inflorescences. Plants are not easy to contain in a pot. They do better on a mount or attached to a tree in frost-free regions.

Sedirea japonica *(sed-ih-REE-uh juh-PON-ih-cuh)*

Abbreviation: *Sdr.*
Monopodial
Dwarf
Low and medium light
Mild to warm nights and warm days
High humidity
Keep evenly moist; slightly drier in winter
Pot
Culture: Easy to average
Availability: Specialty growers

Only one species makes up this genus. It's unusual and may be hard to find, but it is well worth the search.

Sedirea japonica has horizontally arching flower stems that bear short racemes of up to a dozen delicately scented greenish white flowers marked with pinkish purple spots on the lips and bars on the lower sepals. Blooms last for several weeks in winter. Their sweet fragrance is most noticeable during the day.

These dwarf plants grow to 8 inches tall, with strappy, 1- to 2-inch-wide leaves. Pot them in a rich medium-grade mix.

Sedirea japonica

Sobralia *(so-BRAL-ee-uh)*

Abbreviation: *Sob.*
Sympodial
Miniature to large, depending on species
Bright light
Mild nights and warm days
High humidity
Keep evenly moist
Pot

Sobralias are terrestrial orchids that grow into large clumps. They're known as bamboo orchids, a reference to their tall, canelike stems. Flowers are borne successively from the tip of the newest growths over a period of weeks; each bloom lasts for just a day. Plant size varies enormously among the species. A few species are small, 8 inches to a foot tall; some grow as tall as 40 feet. Most are in the 2- to 4-foot range.

Grow them in a terrestrial orchid mix, taking care to minimize root damage when potting. Plants do best in greenhouses but can be grown outside as landscape plants in frost-free regions. Most sobralias are started from seed, and plants can take seven years or more to start flowering. For that reason, they are often expensive.

Sob. callosa

Culture: Average
Availability: Specialty growers

Sob. callosa

Said to be rare in cultivation, this sobralia is unusual in that it is a dwarf plant, less than 8 inches tall. Relatively large, 3-inch or larger, fuchsia-colored flowers are borne successively from the tips of the short cane growths in summer and fall. You can easily accommodate this plant in a 4-inch pot of terrestrial mix. Keep plants evenly moist.

Sophrolaelia *(soh-froh-LAY-lee-uh)*

Abbreviation: *Sl.*
Sympodial
Miniature
Medium light
Warm nights and days
Moderate humidity
Let dry between waterings
Pot

Sophrolaelias are intergeneric hybrids between laelia and sophronitis. They have the compact habit and vivid flower colors of sophronitis with attractive flower shapes and free-blooming habit of laelias. They thrive under fluorescent lights. Numerous hybrids and cultivars are available.

Sl. Psyche 'Prolific' AM/AOS (*L. cinnabarina* × *Soph. coccinea*)

Culture: Average
Availability: Specialty growers
This excellent hybrid combines the eager-blooming habit of laelia with the bright flower colors and compact growth of sophronitis. It was one of the first mini cattleyas to be bred and was first seen more than 100 years ago. Its influence still shows in today's

Sl. Psyche 'Talisman Cove'

newer hybrids. (Mini cattleyas or minicatts is a generic term for all miniature members of the cattleya alliance.)

Psyche 'Prolific' grows only about 6 inches tall yet bears abundant 2-inch-wide flowers the color of a ripe mango with an accenting yellow lip in spring and summer. Pot it in a medium-grade, fast-draining mix.

Sophrolaeliocattleya *(soh-froh-LAY-lee-oh-KAT-lay-uh)*

Abbreviation: *Slc.*
Sympodial
Bright light
Mild nights and warm days
Moderate humidity
Let dry between waterings
Pot

Another intergeneric hybrid, this genus combines cattleya, laelia, and sophronitis. These orchids are on the small side, growing 6 to 8 inches tall, and because they tolerate slightly cooler temperatures than many other orchids, they make good houseplants. The flowers are brilliant reds, oranges, and yellows. Grow them in a fast-draining medium such as bark or outdoors in frost-free zones, and provide a period of cool, dry dormancy in winter.

Slc. Crystelle Smith 'Aileen' (*Sc.* Beaufort × *C. loddigesii*)

Culture: Easy
Availability: Specialty growers
An outstanding AM/AOS miniature, this hybrid is gratifyingly easy to grow and bloom. It grows no taller than 5 inches and blooms in winter and spring. The fragrant 2½-inch-wide flowers have unusual coloration—salmon pink with a soft yellow lip rimmed in red. Pot this plant in a medium-grade, fast-draining mix.

Slc. Crystelle Smith 'Aileen'

Slc. Jewel Box 'Scheherazade' AM/AOS (*C. aurantiaca* × *Slc.* Anzac)

Culture: Easy
Availability: Common
This older cross is an AM/AOS award winner that continues to be popular 40 years after its introduction because it is easy to grow and bloom. The orchid bears 3-inch-wide clear red flowers in winter and spring on a compact plant that grows 10 to 12 inches tall.

Slc. Jewel Box 'Dark Waters'

Slc. Leopard Lou
(*Slc.* Precious Stones × *C.* Penny Kuroda)

Culture: Average
Availability: Specialty growers

This orchid has bursts of two to four 3-inch blooms throughout the year. Flowers are brilliant yellow to orange and often heavily spotted with red. The small plants, about 8 inches tall, do well under lights or on a windowsill.

Slc. Leopard Lou

Slc. Paprika 'Black Magic' (*Lc.* Orange Gown × *Slc.* Anzac)

Culture: Easy
Availability: Specialty growers

This cultivar's rose-scented flowers are up to 5 inches across and a vivid shade of rose-red with a glimmer of yellow in the throat. Bloom time is winter to spring. The plant is compact, reaching 10 to 12 inches tall.

Slc. Smile Again 'Hawaii' AM/AOS
(*Lc.* Pink Favorite × *Slc.* Jeweler's Art)

Culture: Average
Availability: Specialty growers

Slc. Smile Again 'Hawaii'

Combining the best of modern breeding lines, these compact plants are no more than 10 inches tall at maturity. Prolific growers, they may produce blooms at almost any season, although most flowering occurs in late winter and early spring. Colors are reminiscent of a tropical sunrise and highlighted by a beautiful diamond-dust texture.

Sophronitis *(soh-froh-NY-tis)*

Abbreviation: *Soph.*
Sympodial
Miniature
Medium to bright, indirect light
Mild nights and days
High humidity
Keep continuously moist; allow a brief dry rest after blooming
Pot or mount

Botanists assign only a handful of species to this genus, which is native to Brazil and Paraguay. All are miniature epiphytes with small blooms that seem large for the plant. The shimmering cherry-red or warm sparkling orange-red flowers on such compact plants are highly desirable traits and sophronitis have made major contributions to intergeneric breeding with cattleya and laelia.

The plants sprawl rather than grow upward, so plant height is a few inches at most. They have a dense cluster of pseudobulbs; a single, 1- to 3-inch-wide, shiny dark to grey-green leathery leaf grows from each bulb.

Sophron means "modest" in Greek, which probably refers to the plant's small size. In late autumn and winter, short flower stalks, each carrying one to five richly colored flowers, arise from the pseudobulbs. Blooms measure 1 to 3 inches across. The lateral petals tend to be broader than the sepals; the lip is three-lobed. The column is short, wide, and hook-shape. Some species have fragrant blooms.

Species sophronitis are challenging to grow; the hybrids tend to be easier. They like medium to bright light, warm days and cooler nights, high humidity, good air circulation, and plenty of water. During periods of active growth, you may need to water and fertilize more frequently. Fast-draining sphagnum moss or fine-grade fir bark, or both, will produce good results. When the potting material gets old and stale, discard it and repot.

This orchid's moisture requirements are crucial to its health. Keep the humidity high and the pot or mount continuously moist but not soggy.

Soph. cernua

Culture: Average
Availability: Specialty growers

These are dwarf plants, with pseudobulbs rising to no more than ½ inch, and small, stiff 1-inch rounded leaves. When exposed to bright light, leaves and pseudobulbs display reddish pigmentation. Short stems to 2 inches bear ½-inch cinnabar-red blooms in fall. The flowers last three to four weeks. Mount this plant for best results. *Soph. cernua* tolerates warmer temperatures than *Soph. coccinea.*

Soph. cernua

Soph. coccinea

Culture: Challenging
Availability: Specialty growers

This highly variable species is always charming. It blooms from fall into winter, and the mature plant—no more than 4 inches high—is covered with blooms, each one carried singly. Flower size is usually only 1 inch but can be as big as 3 inches across. Blooms are typically in the orange-red range, although occasionally yellow or rosy purple, and all colors sparkle in bright light. Stiff, slender dark green leaves fill in around the flowers. Grow this plant in mild temperatures year-round.

Spathoglottis *(spath-oh-GLOT-tis)*

Abbreviation: *Spa.*
Sympodial
Compact to large, depending on species
Bright light
Warm nights and days
High humidity
Keep continuously moist
Pot

This genus of Asian terrestrial orchids is the source of new species and hybrids that may become garden staples in warm-winter climates. Commonly called ground orchids, spathoglottis can be grown as an attractive groundcover in frost-free regions.

The plants have prominent egg-shape pseudobulbs that give rise to narrow, pleated leaves. Upright flower stems rise from a basal leaf axil and bear a succession of flowers all summer and sometimes all year. Flowers may be showy and brilliant in color, or they may be self-pollinating and thus never open. Plants do best in light shade but will grow in brighter light. Water and fertilize heavily during spring and summer. In early fall, reduce watering and fertilizing to allow plants to rest. Overwatering can lead to fungal problems. Grow spathoglottis in a rich, fast-draining potting mix. Plant them in deep pots that can accommodate their large root systems.

If you grow spathoglottis as a groundcover, space plants about 18 inches apart. Avoid planting them too deep; the orchid crown should be at the same depth as it was in the nursery container.

Spa. kimballiana

Culture: Average
Availability: Specialty growers
One of the smaller species in the genus, this orchid grows to 15 inches tall and has small compressed pseudobulbs to 1 inch tall. The 2-inch-wide bright chrome yellow blooms are borne sequentially at the top of a 24-inch flower stem. Grow it in a terrestrial mix or in well-drained potting soil. This species can be challenging to find.

Spa. plicata

Culture: Easy
Availability: Specialty growers
Rose-lavender blooms are borne sequentially at the top of a 30-inch stem and provide a show over an extended period. A white-flowering variety, *Spa. plicata alba*, is also available. This species is often self-pollinating. Some retail nurseries sell *Spa. plicata* as dormant bulbs, which makes it difficult to tell whether the flowers will open fully. Purchase plants in flower or get bulbs from orchid specialists to ensure flowering.

Spa. plicata

Stanhopea *(stan-HOH-pea-uh)*

Abbreviation: *Stan.*
Sympodial
Compact to large, depending on species
Medium light
Mild nights and warm days
High humidity
Keep evenly moist
Pot

Stanhopeas are pollinated by a type of tropical bee known as euglossine or orchid bees. The males of these unusual bees "collect" scents and are drawn to stanhopeas' heavily fragrant flowers. In some species the scent is like vanilla; in others it is medicinal.

The exotic-shape flowers hang straight down from the plant base. Colors may be pure white or yellow and flowers may be speckled in maroon. Plants usually produce several rounds of blooms that last only two days to a week.

Plants have fat egg-shape pseudobulbs topped with a single upright 8-inch-wide by 18-inch-long leaf. They can grow 8 to 20 inches tall and wide.

Plant stanhopeas in hanging baskets to allow the flowers to develop. They do well in wire baskets lined with long-fiber sphagnum moss. Use a porous medium, such as cymbidium mix or sphagnum moss. Ensure good air movement and abundant water and fertilizer during the growing season. In a greenhouse, provide shade during summer to avoid burning the leaves.

Stan. grandiflora

Culture: Average
Availability: Specialty growers
A rarity among stanhopeas, *Stan. grandiflora* has white flowers. The large blooms, 6 inches across or more, are borne on flower stems that emerge from the base of the plant, often through the bottom of the basket. Blooms face down and are strongly fragrant during the day.

Stan. grandiflora

The plants are typical of the genus, with conical 2-inch-tall pseudobulbs crowned with broad, stiff leaves, which are up to 8 inches wide and 16 inches long. Grow plants in baskets; keep them evenly moist.

Stan. tigrina

Culture: Easy
Availability: Specialty growers
One of the easiest to grow of the genus, this orchid is forgiving of adverse conditions and neglect. It does best in mild temperatures and can be grown outdoors in frost-free areas. Large, heavy, highly perfumed blooms are borne from the base of the plant in summer but last only three days or so. They are creamy yellow with heavy red-mahogany blotching and a white column.

Tolumnia *(toh-LUM-nee-uh)*

Abbreviation: *Tolu.*
Sympodial
Miniature
Bright light
Mild nights and warm days
High humidity
Let dry between waterings
Mount

Mixed tolumnia

These Caribbean natives have small, showy wine-red, yellow, or red flowers, which look like dancers in flowing skirts. The flowers so closely resemble those of oncidiums, in fact, that the plants were once classified as oncidiums.

Plants are small, as short as 4 inches or as tall as 8 inches in some of the newer hybrids, and fan-shaped. Even the larger varieties are suited to small spaces.

Sprays of 2-inch-wide unscented flowers grow 8 to 18 inches tall, often branching and reblooming later, much like phalaenopsis. The main bloom season is late winter into spring, but many plants often bloom again in fall. Flowers last four weeks or more.

Pseudobulbs are either inconspicuous or the plant may have no pseudobulbs. In the later case, the folded leaves overlap at the bases.

Best results are achieved by growing plants on mounts or in small clay pots with little or no medium. Plants must be able to dry rapidly after watering.

Tolu. Margie Crawford (*Tolu. triquetra* × *Tolu.* Stanley Smith)

Culture: Average
Availability: Specialty growers
This diminutive hybrid, only 4 to 5 inches tall, was bred by miniature-orchid enthusiasts Don and Margie Crawford of Pittsburgh in their backyard greenhouse. It is noted for its ample 1-inch-wide, rose-red flowers with a touch of yellow in the center that are borne on a 12-inch flower spike. Bloom time is spring and summer.

Tolu. Savanna La Mar 'Golden Galaxy' (*Tolu.* Red Belt × *Tolu.* Catherine Wilson)

Culture: Average
Availability: Specialty growers
Another miniature of high quality, this hybrid packs many flowers on a 3-inch-tall plant. Blooms, about 1½ inches long and bright sunny yellow with dark red markings, are carried aloft on an upright inflorescence in spring or early summer.

Trichocentrum *(trik-oh-SEN-trum)*

Abbreviation: *Trctm.*
Sympodial
Miniature to large, depending on species
Medium to bright light
Mild nights and days
Moderate humidity
Let dry between waterings
Pot or mount

Orchids in this group are epiphytes that grow 4 to 24 inches tall or more. Their open inflorescences consist of several showy flowers that look so much like those of oncidiums that orchids in this genus were once considered oncidiums. Plants have stiff erect leaves and no pseudobulbs.

Trctm. splendidum

Trctm. lanceanum

Culture: Easy
Availability: Specialty growers
This species used to be called *Onc. lanceanum* because the thick leaves have the typical oncidium shape. The long-lasting summer blossoms, as wide as 2½ inches across, waft a honey fragrance. They are somewhat flat, and the colors are yellow and brown with a lip of white and purple. Maturing to about 1 foot tall, this orchid is a good choice for beginners. Water plants regularly throughout the year.

Trctm. splendidum

Culture: Average
Availability: Specialty growers
Formerly called *Onc. splendidum,* this is a large orchid with short oval compressed pseudobulbs topped with a single broad, heavy mule-ear leaf to 24 inches long. The upright flower stem grows 48 inches tall and branches near its top. Yellow flowers with brown bars appear in late spring and last as long as four weeks. Grow this species as you would cattleya, in bright light in a clay pot with medium-grade orchid mix. Allow roots to dry between waterings.

Trctm. Nathakhun
(*Onc.* Maui Gold × *Trctm. lanceanum*)

Culture: Easy
Availability: Specialty growers

Sometimes sold as *Onc.* Nathakhun, this hybrid gets its size (12 inches or so) and mule-ear foliage from its *lanceanum* parent. The long-lasting, flat 2- to 3-inch-wide flowers, borne on a 12-inch or longer flower spike in summer, are yellow and covered with brown markings on the petals and sepals. The lips are brilliant white topped with lavender-pink, and the fragrance is rich and honeylike. Easy to grow in bright light, this orchid can tolerate drier conditions and grows well in medium-grade bark or mounted on a slab.

Trichoglottis *(trick-oh-GLOT-tis)*

Abbreviation: *Trgl.*
Monopodial
Large
Medium to bright light
Warm nights and days
High humidity
Keep evenly moist
Basket or mount

Trgl. philippinensis

Plants in this genus grow 3 feet tall, often branching profusely from the base to form clumps. The leaves are small and as wide as they are long, about 1 inch wide and 3 inches long. Flowers occur singly at the leaf axils. Some species have an upright habit; others are pendulous.

Trichoglottis is related to vanda, and intergeneric hybrids are occasionally available. As with most vanda types, this orchid seems to grow best in an open basket of coarse medium or without medium. You can also mount pendulous species.

Fertilize weekly during the growing season and every other week in the off-season. Keep plants moist and maintain high humidity and good air circulation.

Trgl. brachiata

Culture: Average
Availability: Specialty growers, particularly in warm climates

This is the most commonly available species. Its rich wine-colored flowers have a rose lip. Rapidly elongating stems bear abundant single 2-inch-wide blooms in summer.

Trichopilia *(trick-oh-PEA-lee-uh)*

Abbreviation: *Trpla.*
Sympodial
Average
Medium light
Mild nights and days
Moderate humidity
Let dry slightly between waterings
Pot or mount
Culture: Average
Availability: Rare

Trichopilia suavis 'Cape Fair'

Orchids in this uncommon genus of epiphytes are worth searching for—especially the fragrant ones. Plants grow 12 to 15 inches tall and have laterally compressed pseudobulbs, often with sharply creased sides and a single broad leaf. The pendulous flowers are borne from emerging new growths on short stems that grow straight out from the base of the plant. Mount plants on tree-fern or pot them in a container, setting them slightly high in it to allow flower stems to emerge. *Trpla. suavis* is the prettiest species in the genus. Light pink flowers with a showy darker pink-spotted lip bloom in spring and are highly fragrant during the day.

Vanda (VAN-duh)

Abbreviation: *V.*
Monopodial
Compact to large, depending on species
Bright, indirect light
Warm but not hot nights and days
Low to high humidity
Keep continuously moist but not wet
Pot

Vandas and their relatives are a popular group of orchids, and it's easy to see why. They're relatively simple to grow well—in mild climates, you can grow them outdoors in your garden. And all have huge, colorful blooms.

V. Robert's Delight 'Torblue'

Because of diversity in the wild species, of which there are around fifty, and the ease of cross-breeding them, vandas offer a rainbow of high-quality flower hues, including lavender-blue. Florists often use them in bouquets and corsages. Some species are fragrant too. Plants are distinctly upright, with their leaves arranged in tight rows up the stem. Tangled aerial roots branch off the stems and catch nutrients to nourish the plants. New growth takes place at the top of the plant; some species can grow up to 6 feet tall, but most are more compact.

There are two distinct types of leaf forms in this group. The majority of vandas have strappy green leaves that may be as short as 2 inches or as long as 12 inches. In this group, the base of each leaf clasps the plant's main stem, giving the effect of a V-shape ladder. Inflorescences emerge from the leaf axils along the stem.

The other group—terete-leaved vandas—have pencil-thin cylindrical green leaves that also come off the main stem with their bases encircling the stem. They are shorter, generally no more than 6 inches long, and have either sharp or blunt tips. In these vandas, inflorescences originate opposite a leaf.

All vanda flowers are recognizable for bright color as well as distinctive form. The spectrum of colors includes purple, brown, yellow, white, red, and blue, and combinations of these hues. Flowers are produced on tall spikes. Blooms measure 1 to 6 inches across, and the sepals and petals are similar in shape and color, although the petals may be a bit smaller. The dorsal—or upper—sepal is wider than the others.

These tropical orchids are native to Thailand, Myanmar, India, Malaysia, Laos, Vietnam, the Indonesian island of Sumatra, and the Philippines. Many of the species are in cultivation, but vandas have also been used extensively in breeding, leading to a wealth of excellent hybrids.

The genus name, a Sanskrit word used to describe the growth habit of plants in this group, was assigned by William Roxburgh, the director of the Royal Botanic Garden in Calcutta in the early 1800s when many of the plants were discovered, described, and brought into cultivation.

Grow vandas in hanging, slatted baskets or pots of coarse, fast-draining mix in a location where they will have room to spread their aerial roots and get plenty of light year-round. (They do not do well under lights.) Because the plants lack pseudobulbs, they must be kept continuously moist. Some may require daily watering. Monthly fertilizing is not mandatory but encourages healthier growth and more abundant flowering.

The heavy tangled roots can be brittle; handle them gently if you must repot. Healthy vandas quickly grow into large plants, so you may need to cut back the tops to keep them a manageable size. Repot pruned-off tops to grow new plants.

V. coerulea

Culture: Average
Availability: Specialty growers

A rare blue flower color makes this species highly sought-after. At maturity, the plant is 2 to 4 feet tall. In fall and winter, it produces 18-inch-long inflorescences, each one bearing five to fifteen 4-inch flowers that last for four to six weeks. Humidity above 60 percent and cool to mild temperatures (as low as 48° F on winter nights) are best for this unusual species.

V. coerulea

Unfortunately, wild plants of this species have been plundered, and populations are endangered. Tissue culture and seed propagation, however, have made it possible to create more plants and meet demand in ethical ways.

V. denisoniana

Culture: Advanced
Availability: Specialty growers

A heady, sweet scent emanates from the spring blooms of this species. Flowers, yellow with white center and some light red spotting, measure about 2 inches across and line short, erect inflorescences—four to six on each 6-inch spike. The plant is a slow grower, reaching about 1 foot tall after several years. It is a fine choice for a warm patio or greenhouse.

V. sanderiana

Culture: Average
Availability: Specialty growers

This is one of the finest vandas and indeed one of the best of the entire orchid family. The large plant has closely overlapping leaves that may reach 36 inches or longer; plants may form keikis at their base. Upright stems carry 6 to

V. sanderiana

10 round, flat 4-inch-wide or larger flowers in shades of pink and brown in fall. Flowers may last as long as six weeks. This orchid does not tolerate cold; provide high heat and humidity and fertilize heavily. This species is sometimes labeled as *Euanthe sanderiana*.

V. tricolor suavis

Culture: Average
Availability: Specialty growers

Native to Borneo and Java, this exotic-looking species has a rich, sweet fragrance similar to vanilla. The plant grows 2 to 3 feet tall and blooms in winter. The inflorescences sport as many as a dozen flowers. Each bloom is about 2 inches across and creamy white with brown or dark red spots and a purple-pink lip.

V. tricolor suavis

V. Arjuna 'Wink' HCC/AOS (*V. tessellata* × *V. Mimi Palmer*)

Culture: Average
Availability: Specialty growers

A powerful fragrance is the most striking feature of this HCC/AOS award-winning hybrid. The 2-inch-wide flowers have complex coloration—pale green with olive green highlights and a lavender blush—and the lip is violet and white. Because the flowers are hard and waxy, they are especially durable and long-lasting. The plant is a strap-leaf type and grows about 2 feet tall.

V. Kasem's Delight (*V. Sun Tan* × *V. Thospol*)

Culture: Average
Availability: Specialty growers

Vivid royal purple to rich maroon 4-inch round flowers abound on this strap-leaf hybrid. Bloom time is spring to summer. The plant grows to around 2 feet tall and has 16-inch-long leaves. It needs bright but indirect light and continuous moisture, but water it a bit less in winter. Kasem's Delight is widely used in hybridizing.

V. Kasem's Delight 'Mollie Zweig'

V. Keeree's Delight (*V. Keeree* × *V. Kasem's Delight*)

Culture: Average
Availability: Specialty growers

V. Keeree's Delight 'Mary Eleanor Graham'

Another striking purple-blue vanda, this hybrid has 3-inch-wide flowers lightly dusted in a darker blue. The plant grows 2 or 3 feet tall over time with a leaf spread of about 18 inches. For best results, grow Keeree's Delight in bright light and warm temperatures where the air circulates well.

V. Nellie Morley (*V. Emma van Deventer* × *V. sanderiana*)

Culture: Average
Availability: Specialty growers

If you've been greeted in Hawaii with a lei—an orchid necklace—it may have been this hybrid or one of its grandparents. Registered in 1952, it is still one of the most popular orchids on the islands because of its reputation as a constant bloomer. It requires bright light year-round and grows to 2 or 3 feet tall before it blooms. Grow it outdoors in tropical climates. The bluish-pink flowers are about 2½ inches across and covered with pinpoints of darker red.

V. Sansai Blue (*V. Crimson Glory* × *V. coerulea*)

Culture: Average
Availability: Specialty growers

This blue-flowered, navy blue-lipped, strap-leaf hybrid tends to bloom from winter to spring with possible encore performances other times of the year. Some growers report that it blooms four times a year. Flowers are almost 4 inches across on 10- to 12-inch flower stems. Plants grow 3 feet tall. Give Sansai Blue medium to bright light, mild to warm temperatures, and moderate to high humidity.

V. Sansai Blue 'Acker's Pride'

Vanilla *(va-NIL-la)*

Abbreviation: *Vl.*
Vining
Large
Bright light
Mild to warm nights and days
High humidity
Keep evenly moist
Pot

One of the few vining orchids, vanilla can reach truly prodigious size in its native habitat, up to hundreds of feet long. Some species are leafless while others have thick, succulent stems with alternating fleshy leaves at intervals of a foot or more. Fragrant 2½-inch tubular pristine white to light yellow-green flowers are borne in clusters at the leaf axils in spring and normally last only a day.

Vl. planifolia

Care: Advanced

Vl. planifolia

Availability: Specialty growers
It is neither the plant nor the flower that earns vanilla its fame; it is the ripened and cured seedpod of the species *planifolia,* the vanilla of the food trade, that gets the attention. This plant is challenging to grow indoors except in a greenhouse large enough to support the weight of the vines. Also, vanilla flowers must be pollinated by hand in the morning. If pollination is successful, ripening takes months, and then the pods must be cured. If you're ready for the challenge, search for cuttings on the Internet or at orchid nurseries and shows.

Vascostylis *(vas-ko-STY-lis)*

Abbreviation: *Vasco.*
Monopodial
Compact to large, depending on species
Bright light
Warm nights and days
High humidity
Keep evenly moist
Pot

Originally bred in Hawaii to create a vanda-type orchid with compact size and flowers like those of rhyncostylis, modern vascostylis is deservedly popular for its ease of culture and free-flowering habit. Plants generally grow no bigger than 18 inches tall and 12 inches wide. Because they branch from the base, however, plants may be larger. Mature plants produce multiple flowering stems, each bearing dozens of 2-inch-wide bright blooms. Plants may bloom at almost any time of year, although spring seems to be when many plants are at their peak bloom. As with most vandaceous hybrids, best results are obtained by growing vascostylis in warm and humid conditions and bright light. Pot them in slatted wood baskets with little or no medium.

Vasco. Crownfox Red Gem (*Ascda.* Red Gem × *Rhy. gigantea*)

Culture: Average
Availability:
    Specialty growers
A superior hybrid registered in 1998, this orchid offers about a dozen citrus-scented ruby red flowers almost 2 inches across on a 12-inch inflorescence in late winter or early spring. The compact plant grows a foot or so tall after several years. It does best in bark in a wooden basket in mild to warm temperatures.

Vasco. Crownfox Red Gem

Wilsonara *(WILL-son-are-uh)*

Abbreviation: *Wils.*
Sympodial
Small to large
Medium to bright light
Cool to mild nights and days
Moderate humidity
Keep evenly moist
Pot

This complex intergeneric hybrid results from crosses with cochlioda, odontoglossum, and oncidium. As with burrageara and many other complex intergeneric hybrids in the odontoglossum group, it is not wise to generalize about the care of this genus. The parents have a broad range of temperature preferences and so do the offspring. Indeed, some wilsonaras may require cooler temperatures than odonts, if oncidium species from high elevation are in the background. Generally, wilsonaras are bred to introduce the temperature tolerance and higher flower count of oncidiums into the more traditional *Odm. crispum* types.

Plants resemble many oncidiums, with laterally compressed 6- to 12-inch-tall pseudobulbs topped with two long, narrow leaves. Flower stems are typically upright, sometimes arching at the tip, and branching. They carry brightly patterned 2- to 4-inch-wide blooms with a white or yellow base color overlaid with red to maroon markings. However, colors vary wildly, so you're often best off buying plants in bloom or from reliable growers who provide a picture of the flower. Pot wilsonaras in a medium-grade, well-drained orchid mix, and feed them regularly. Some grow year-round on patios in frost-free regions; most others are good for growing on windowsills.

Wils. Kolibri (*Wils.* Intermezzo × *Odm. nobile*)

Culture: Average
Availability: Specialty growers

Wils. Kolibri 'Woodlands Marvel'

The 4-inch-tall or shorter pseudobulbs of these moderately sized plants give rise to 36-inch-tall branching flower stems bearing 2-inch-wide brightly patterned white blooms. The bloom season varies, but late winter is most common. Although it is not as tolerant of warm conditions as some other wilsonaras, Kolibri is particularly sought because it resembles *Odm. crispum* type hybrids. Keep temperatures mild, below 90°F, and water freely.

Wils. Mountain Island Nugget (*Wils.* Bonne Nuit × *Odcdm.* Annegret Gralher)

Culture: Average
Availability: Specialty growers

Wils. Mountain Island Nugget

The *Onc. sphacelatum* grandparent of this hybrid imparts massive, branching inflorescences, often longer than 4 feet, with dozens of 3½-inch-wide yellow blooms. Plants can be large, with 8-inch-tall pseudobulbs and 24-inch-long leaves. With their height and number of flowers, plants are showy when in full bloom, making them an impressive indoor decoration. Keep plants evenly moist.

Zygopetalum (zy-goh-peh-TUH-lum)

Abbreviation: *Z.*
Sympodial
Compact to large, depending on species
Medium light
Cool to mild nights and warm days
Moderate humidity
Keep evenly moist
Pot

Although the flowers last only three weeks or so, many zygopetalum species are powerfully fragrant and easy to grow. The nearly round pseudobulbs range from 1 inch tall in the smallest species to 4 inches or taller in the most robust; pseudobulbs are sometimes tapered toward the apex. Two or three broad, flat 3-inch-wide and 18-inch-long leaves grow from the bulbs.

The upright, unbranched flower stem emerges from newly developing pseudobulbs, extending rapidly to display four to eight 3-inch blooms. The fragrant flowers are green with mahogany bars and a distinctive blue-veined lip. Flowering season is mainly fall, although some hybrids may rebloom in summer. The sweet scent is most noticeable during daytime. Look for hybrids with *Z. maxillare* as one parent if you want a compact plant.

Most orchids in this genus are easy to grow. They do well in anything from a mix used for paphiopedilums or cymbidiums to a commercial peat moss-based medium. Keep plants evenly moist, but allow them to dry partially before watering again.

Provide strong, bright light in fall to encourage maximum flower production and robust growth, and prevents diseases. Leaves should be erect and light green rather than droopy and dark green. Plants respond well to regular fertilization.

Some zygopetalums are difficult to bring into bloom. Avoid buying large plants that have many pseudobulbs. Also avoid ones that show no signs of having bloomed previously or have few flower spikes.

Z. James Strauss

Z. Artur Elle

Culture: Average
Availability: Specialty growers

This cultivar offers rich color and full shape. Bloom time is fall, although often again in winter, but not all cultivars are reliably fragrant. This orchid can be challenging to find but is beginning to become more common at retail locations during its flowering season.

Glossary

AD/AOS Award of Distinction from the American Orchid Society for a cross that represents a worthy new direction in orchid breeding

AM/AOS Award of Merit awarded by the American Orchid Society for an orchid species or hybrid given 80 to 89 points out of 100 at a judging

AQ Award of Quality for a cross exhibiting improvement over the type

Alliance A shorthand way in which to refer to orchids that are related, ones that are in the same subtribe of the Orchid Family. For example, as members of the laelinae subtribe, cattleya, laelia, encyclia, and brassavola are in the cattleya alliance.

Angraecoid Orchids from Africa that look like Angraceum orchids; any large monopodial orchid from Africa

Anther The male reproductive structure in a flower which bears pollen

Aphid An insect that feeds on numerous plants, including orchids, by sucking sap

Axil The space within the angle formed where a leaf and a stem join

Back bulb An old pseudobulb or growth that is no longer actively growing; may no longer bear leaves but is still alive

Back cross A cross between a hybrid orchid and one of its original parents

Bigeneric Having two different genera as parents, for example, a hybrid created by crossing a cattleya and a laelia orchid

Bifoliate Bearing two leaves

Bilabiate Having two lips

Binomial A name composed of two parts; a botanical name

Botanical name The scientific name of a plant consisting of the genus and specific epithet. Together the two parts are the name of a species. Because botanical names bring uniformity to plant names, people across all cultures and communities throughout the world recognize which plant the name refers.

Break When vegetative buds—those of stems and leaves—begin to open

Bud An unopened flower; an embryonic leaf that has not yet started growing and is protected by an outer covering

CBRA/AOS Certificate of Botanical Recognition, an American Orchid Society award given to a cultivar of a species or natural hybrid deemed worthy of recognition for rarity, novelty, or educational value

CCE/AOS Certificate of Cultural Excellence, an American Orchid Society award given to an exhibitor of a robust orchid scoring at least 90 points and bearing an unusually large number of flowers

CCM/AOS Certificate of Cultural Merit, an American Orchid Society award given to the exhibitor of a robust orchid scoring between 80 and 89 points bearing an unusually large number of flowers

CHM/AOS Certificate of Horticultural Merit, an American Orchid Society award given to a beautiful cultivar of a well-grown, well-flowered species or natural hybrid that contributes to orchidology

Caeruleus Sky blue

Calyx The sepals of a flower

Chlorotic Yellowed foliage resulting the breakdown of chlorophyll

Coeruleus Dark blue

Coerulea Having a blue color

Column A floral structure in which the male and female parts of a flower are fused together; often quite showy in orchids

Column wings Appendages that protrude from the column of some orchid species

Common name The popular name of a plant, such as slipper orchid

Community pot A container holding dozens of small seedlings or mericlones recently transplanted from flasks

Complex hybrid A hybrid resulting from crossing a hybrid orchid with another hybrid or species

Compot A nickname for community pot

Concolor Having the same color throughout

Crest A toothed, fringed, or hairy thickened portion of the disc of a lip

Cross The hybrid resulting from pollinating a flower with pollen from a different plant, usually not the same species

Cross-pollination The act of pollinating a flower with pollen from a different plant

Cultivar Short for cultivated variety; a variation in a species or hybrid that is distinctly different from the species or hybrid, not found in nature, and is capable of being reproduced

Deciduous A plant that loses its leaves as it goes through a dormant period

Desiccate To dry up or become dehydrated

Desiccation The process of drying or becoming dehydrated

Division The act of cutting a plant into pieces as a means of propagating it; also, the portions resulting from dividing a plant

Disc The upper surface of the center of a lip

Dormant Not actively growing

Dormancy The rest period during which plants are not actively growing; many orchids require a dormant period

Epiphyte A plant that gains sustenance—moisture and nutrients—from the air

Equitant Leaves that overlap each other in two ranks

Eye A bud on a vegetative portion of a plant, such as a rhizome

Flask Any container used to grow mericlones or to germinate orchid seed

Flasking The process of sowing seed or mericlones in a flask

FCC/AOS First Class Certificate, an award from the American Orchid Society for a species or hybrid scoring 90 points out of a possible 100

Gregarious Orchids that grow together in clusters or colonies; orchids that bloom at the same time

Genus A group of plants or animals that are so similar that they are hard to distinguish. For plants, the classifications are usually based on similarities in the anatomy of the flowers, however, some related groups are alike in their growth habits and foliage as well. The plural of genus is genera.

Germination The sprouting of a seed

Grex A hybrid

Growing season The time period during which a plant is actively growing

Growth An individual component of a sympodial orchid consisting of the pseudobulb and its leaves; growths on orchids without leaves consist of a developing daughter plant arising from a rhizome

Growth habit The shape, outline, or form of a plant

HCC/AOS Highly Commendable Certificate, an award given by the American Orchid Society for an orchid species or hybrids that scores 75 to 79 points out of a hundred

Habitat The natural environment in which an orchid originates; rainfall, temperatures, amount of sunlight, other plants, and animals contribute

Hapuu The Hawaiian term for tree-fern fiber

Hemi-epiphyte A terrestrial orchid whose roots do not grow into the soil, but instead grow in the organic matter on top of the soil

Hybrid The result of a cross between two species, which may be in the same genus or in different genera

Inflexed Bent inward, as with petals

Inflorescence The entire flower structure of a plant consisting of one or many individual blossoms and the stems holding them; the arrangement of the flowers and stems

Insecticide Any material that kills or controls insects

Internode The portion of a stem between two nodes or joints on a stem

Intergeneric hybrid A hybrid resulting from the cross of two species in different genera

Interspecific hybrid A hybrid in which the parents are in the same genus; also called an interspecific grex

Introduction A plant brought from its native region or country to a new area

JC/AOS Judges Commendation, an award from the American Orchid Society given to single or groups of flowers or plants that have a distinctive characteristic or historical importance that the judges deem worthy of recognition

Keiki An offshoot that develops from an orchids stem or inflorescence

Labellum The lower petal of an orchid flower that is modified into the shape of a lip

Labiatus Having a large lip

Lasioglossus Having a rough or hairy lip

Lath house A shade structure build from lath strips or other lightweight wood

Latilabrus Having a broad lip

Lithophyte A group of epiphytic orchids that grow on rocks

Lucid Having a shiny surface

Macule The spot of color at the base of the lip of a miltonia flower

Medium Any substance in which a plant grows, including soil, potting soil, bark, gravel, tree-fern fiber, agar, and many more

Mericlone Another name for a micropropagated plant

Meristem The tissue at the tips of stems in which new cells are created so that plants can grow; the plants that result from micropropagation

Meristemming A laboratory technique that uses meristems to propagate plants; also called micropropagation or tissue culture

Microchilus A small lip on an orchid

Microclimate The immediate growing conditions around a plant; the growing conditions in a small, distinct area of a yard, a house, a greenhouse, or other area

Mini-cattleyas or minicatts A generic term for miniature members of the cattleya alliance

Monodelphous Stamen filaments that are fused into a column or tube

Monopodial A type of orchid that has a single stem of growth with one growing tip on the end of the stem

Natural hybrid A hybrid that occurs naturally in the wild

Necrotic Dead tissue

Node The point at which buds form on a stem; the point from which new leaves and stems originate from the stem; the joints on a stem

Odontochilus Having a toothed lip

Orchidist A grower who is interested in orchids as a hobby or for the plants' horticultural uses

Orchidologist One who studies orchids' evolution and relationships

Orchidology The branch of botany that deals with orchids and their study

Osmundine The roots of osmunda ferns cut for use as a growing medium for epiphytic orchids; also called osmunda

Overpot Planting an orchid in a pot that is too large or larger than necessary; may be done to lengthen the time between repotting, to allow more room for root growth, or to increase plant growth Overwater To provide too much water too often; to keep the growing medium to wet

Originator The owner of the seed-bearing plant at pollination

Peloric An orchid whose lip looks the same as the petals or the petals look like the lip

Pendulous Hanging or drooping

Pest Any organism that is detrimental to an orchid; a weed, insect, fungus, virus or other microorganism

Pesticide Any material that kills or controls a pest

Petalloid Shaped like a petal

Photosynthesis The process by which plants use sunlight and chlorophyll to convert the water and nutrients taken in by the roots into the starches and sugars they use in their life process

Plaited Folded like a fan

Pod The generic term for the seed capsule of an orchid

Pollen The particles carrying the male chromosomes of a plant

Pollinia A waxy mass of pollen found in the anther (male structure) of an orchid flower

Pollination The process of transferring pollen from the anther of a plant to the female structure, known as a stigma

Primary The first

Propagation The process of reproducing a plant, which may occur naturally or by artificial means

Pseudobulb A thickened portion of an epiphytic orchid's stem that the plant uses to store water and from which foliage and new growths arise

Reflasking Transferring seedlings from one flask to another larger flask containing fresh medium

Remade A hybrid that is recreated by crossing the original parent species; if different cultivars of the respective parents are used, the seedlings may have different characteristics from the original hybrid

Rhizome A modified stem that bears roots, grows horizontally—often just below or on top of the ground—and from which new leaves, stems, and growths arise

Rupicolous Growing in cliffs or ledges

Selfing Pollinating an orchid with its own pollen; self pollination; the resulting seedlings

Soft leaf group Epiphytic orchids that have thinner leaves than is typical

Sparkling The texture of certain flowers that makes the flower appear to sparkle or shine

Species The individual member groups of a genus; a population of plants that is isolated from other members of the genus and that diverges enough to become a distinct group different from the other members of the genus

Stamen The male structure holding the anthers from which pollen originate

Stigma The female structure of a plant containing the ovary, in which seeds develop

Substance Firmness and durability qualities of a flower

Sympodial An orchid that grows from rhizomes

Taxonomy The science of classifying and naming plants and animals

Terrestrial An orchid that grows on or in soil

Terminal The end; in plants, the bud at the tip of a stem from which new growth develops

Tessellated Text

Type The original representative of a species or genus displaying the distinguishing characteristics on which all species or genera are compared against

Unifoliate Having one leaf

Vandaceous Any large monopodial orchid from Asia

Variety A natural population of plants that vary slightly from the species, for example in plant or flower size, leaf or flower color, or other characteristic

Variegated Marked with several colors, as in a leaf

Vegetative propagation Propagating plants through means other than pollination; using cutting, divisions, or meristems to reproduce plants

Velamen A thick corky layer around the outside of epiphytic orchid roots, which prevents excess water loss from the roots, absorbs moisture from the air, protects the center of the root, and helps the root adhere to the tree or rock

World Orchid Conference An international orchid conference held every three years

Resources

Organizations

The American Orchid Society
16700 AOS Lane
Delray Beach, FL 33446-4351
www.aos.org
Telephone: 561-404-2000
Fax: 561-404-2100
Email: The AOS@aos.org

Membership costs $60 per year for individuals and $75 for couples. Discounted rates apply for two-year memberships. Students can join for $35. International rates are higher.

The American Orchid Society (AOS) is an 87-year-old nonprofit organization dedicated to extending the knowledge, production, use, preservation, and appreciation of orchids. Over the years, the Society has funded more than $1 million in grants and fellowships for projects furthering the advancement of orchid knowledge, and its members play a lead role in formulating world orchid conservation policies.

Benefits of membership include the opportunity to meet and communicate with other orchid fanciers in your community and around the world. You also are invited to the Society's semi-annual meetings where you can hear lectures, see displays of beautiful orchids, and check out the sales area while expanding your collection.

Membership includes a subscription to the magazine Orchids, which presents articles on orchid growing, profiles of orchid genera, and a calendar of shows and other events. You also receive a copy of the Orchid Source Directory, updated yearly, access to the member-only area of the AOS website, discounts on purchases from the Orchid Emporium gift shop, and free admission to the AOS Visitors Center and Botanical Garden as well as discounted admission to reciprocating botanical gardens across North America.

AQPlus 3.0

This new software replaces the publication Awards Quality. It inclues 42,000 images and serves as a pictorial encyclopedia of award-winning orchids. It is the official record of American Orchid Society awards, serving as a reference for judges and helping readers enhance their orchid collections. An enhanced search function helps you to quickly find specific plants and awards.

The software runs on PCs with Windows 95SE through Vista, and on Macs with Virtual PC or Parallels Desktop for Intel/Mac. Your computer should have 3GB of space and up to 6GB.

Quarterly updates on CDs are sent at no additional cost.

Plants

Cal-Orchid, Inc.
1251 Orchid Dr.
Santa Barbara, CA 93111
805-967-1312
805-967-6882 (fax)
calorchid@cox.net
www.calorchid.com

Carter and Holmes Orchids
629 Mendenhall Rd.
Newberry, SC 29108
803-276-0579
803-276-0588 (fax)
orchids@carterandholmes.
   com
www.carterandholmes.com

Carib Plants
26505 SW 203 Ave.
Homestead, FL 33031-2109
305-245-5565
305-245-5113 (fax)
caribplants@att.net
www.caribplants.com

Fantasy Orchids
830 W. Cherry St.
Louisville, CO 80027
303-666-5432
303-666-7730
orchidsite06@yahoo.com
www.fantasyorchids.com

H&R Nurseries, Inc.
41-240 Hihimanu Street
Waimanalo, HI 96795

808-259-9626
808-259-5422 (fax)
Web: www.hrnurseries.com

Hoosier Orchid Company
8440 W. 82nd St.
Indianapolis, IN 46278
317-291-6269
orchids@hoosierorchid.com
www.hoosierorchid.com

Krull-Smith
2815 Ponkan Rd.
Apopka, FL 32712
407-886-4134
407-886-0438 (fax)
sales@krullsmith.com
www.krullsmith.com

Norman's Orchids
11039 Monte Vista
Montclair, CA 91763
909-627-9515
909-627-3889 (fax)
sales@orchids.com
www.orchids.com

Oak Hill Gardens
37W550 Binnie Rd.
Dundee, IL 60118
847-428-8500
847-428-8527 (fax)
oakhillgardens@sprintmail.
   com
www.oakhillgardens.com

Orchids by Hausermann, Inc.
2N 134 Addison Rd.
Villa Park, IL 60181-1191
630-543-6855
630-543-9842 (fax)
info@orchidsbyhausermann.
   com
www.orchidsbyhausermann.
   com

Plantío La Orquídea
3480 Tallevast Rd.
Sarasota, FL 34243
By appointment only
Telephone: 941-504-7737
Fax: 941-360-9162
Email: info@
   plantiolaorquidea.com
Web: www.plantiolaorquidea.
   com

R.F. Orchids
28100 SW 182 Avenue
Homestead Florida 33030-
   1804
305-245-4570
305-247-6568 (fax)
info@rforchids.com (email)

sales@rforchids.com (orders)
tours@rforchids.com (tours)
www.rforchids.com

SLO Orchids
955 Branch Mill Rd.
Arroyo Grande, CA 93420
805-489-3319
orchids@sloorchids.com
www.sloorchids.com

Santa Barbara Orchid Estate
1250 Orchid Dr.
Santa Barbara, CA 93111
805-967-1284
805-683-3405 (fax)
sboe@sborchid.com
www.sborchid.com

Woodland Orchids
1816 Hart Road.
Charlotte, NC 28214
704-393-1740
orchid_frau@
   woodlandorchids.com
www.woodlandorchids.com

Supplies

Calwest Tropical
11614 Sterling Ave.
Riverside, CA 92503
951-351-1880
951-351-1872 (fax)
800-301-9009 (orders)
cwtropical@1stconnect.com
www.calwesttropical.com

Charley's Greenhouse & Garden
17979 State Rt. 536
Mt. Vernon, WA 98273
800-322-4707
800-233-3078 (fax)
customerservice@
   charleysgreenhouse.com
www.charleysgreenhouse.com

Kelly's Korner Orchid Supplies
P.O. Box 6
Kittery, ME 03904-0006
207-439-0922
207-439-8202 (fax)
info@kkorchid.com
www.kkorchid.com

OFE International Inc.
12100 SW 129th Ct.
Miami, FL 33186
888-633-4685
877-251-8245 (fax)
sales@ofe-intl.com
www.ofe-intl.com

Index

METRIC CONVERSIONS

U.S. UNITS TO METRIC EQUIVALENTS			METRIC EQUIVALENTS TO U.S. UNITS		
To convert from	Multiply by	To get	To convert from	Multiply by	To get
Inches	25.4	Millimeters	Millimeters	0.0394	Inches
Inches	2.54	Centimeters	Centimeters	0.3937	Inches
Feet	30.48	Centimeters	Centimeters	0.0328	Feet
Feet	0.3048	Meters	Meters	3.2808	Feet
Yards	0.9144	Meters	Meters	1.0936	Yards
Square inches	6.4516	Square centimeters	Square centimeters	0.1550	Square inches
Square feet	0.0929	Square meters	Square meters	10.764	Square feet
Square yards	0.8361	Square meters	Square meters	1.1960	Square yards
Acres	0.4047	Hectares	Hectares	2.4711	Acres
Cubic inches	16.387	Cubic centimeters	Cubic centimeters	0.0610	Cubic inches
Cubic feet	0.0283	Cubic meters	Cubic meters	35.315	Cubic feet
Cubic feet	28.316	Liters	Liters	0.0353	Cubic feet
Cubic yards	0.7646	Cubic meters	Cubic meters	1.308	Cubic yards
Cubic yards	764.55	Liters	Liters	0.0013	Cubic yards

To convert from degrees Fahrenheit (F) to degrees Celsius (C), first subtract 32, then multiply by ⁵⁄₉.

To convert from degrees Celsius (C) to degrees Fahrenheit (F), multiply by ⁹⁄₅, then add 32.

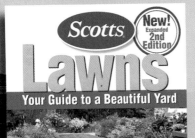